Mastering Elastic Stack

Get the most out of the Elastic Stack for various complex analytics using this comprehensive and practical guide

Ravi Kumar Gupta
Yuvraj Gupta

BIRMINGHAM - MUMBAI

Mastering Elastic Stack

First published: February 2017

Production reference: 2280317

Published by Packt Publishing Ltd.
Livery Place
35 Livery Street
Birmingham
B3 2PB, UK.
ISBN 978-1-78646-001-1

www.packtpub.com

Credits

About the Authors

Ravi Kumar Gupta is an author, reviewer, and open source software evangelist. He pursued an MS degree in software system at BITS Pilani and a B.Tech at LNMIIT, Jaipur. His technological forte is portal management and development.

He is currently working with Azilen Technologies, where he acts as a Technical Architect and Project Manager. His previous assignment was as a lead consultant with CIGNEX Datamatics. He was a core member of the open source group at TCS, where he started working on Liferay and other UI technologies. During his career, he has been involved in building enterprise solutions using the latest technologies with rich user interfaces and open source tools.

He loves to spend time writing, learning, and discussing new technologies. His interest in search engines and that small project on crawler during college time made him a technology lover. He is one of the authors of Test-Driven JavaScript Development, Packt Publishing. He is an active member of the Liferay forum. He also writes technical articles for his blog at TechD of Computer World (`http://techdc.blogspot.in`).

He has been a Liferay trainer at TCS and CIGNEX, where he has provided training on Liferay 5.x and 6.x versions. He was also a reviewer for Learning Bootstrap, Packt Publishing.

He can be reached on Skype at kravigupta, on Twitter at `@kravigupta`, and on LinkedIn at `https://in.linkedin.com/in/kravigupta`.

Seven blessing and my gratitude to my wife, Kriti. Despite tough times, she motivated me throughout the writing period. Support from my wife and my family, specially my father and mother-in-law helped me a lot. I can't forget my co-author, Yuvraj, for his excellent support and understanding. He has been a great friend and help. Without him, it was not possible to finish. I would also like to thanks PACKT team, reviewers and editorial team for their cooperation. I truly appreciate you guys. Thank you.

Yuvraj Gupta is an author and a keen technologist with interest towards Big Data, Data Analytics, Data Visualization, and Cloud Computing. He has been working as a Big Data Consultant primarily in domain of Big Data Testing. He loves to spend time writing on various social platforms. He is an avid gadget lover, a foodie, a sports enthusiast and love to watch tv-series or movies. He always keep himself updated with the latest happenings in technology. He has authored a book titled *Kibana Essentials* with Packt Publishers. He can be reached at gupta.yuvraj@gmail.com or at LinkedIn www.linkedin.com/in/guptayuvraj.

I would like to thank my family and friends for encouraging and motivating me to write the book. I would like to thank the reviewers and the whole team of PacktPub who were involved in producing this book without their support it would never have been possible. I would like to thank everyone else who helped me directly or indirectly in writing this book. Also I would like to thank my teachers, professors, Gurus, schools and university for playing an important part in providing me with the education which has helped me to gain knowledge. Lastly but not the least I would like to thanks my co-author Ravi without whose help, guidance and support, the book would never have been completed.

About the Reviewer

Marcelo Ochoa works at the system laboratory of Facultad de Ciencias Exactas of the Universidad Nacional del Centro de la Provincia de Buenos Aires and is the CTO at Scotas.com, a company that specializes in near real-time search solutions using Apache Solr and Oracle. He divides his time between university jobs and external projects related to Oracle and big data technologies. He has worked on several Oracle-related projects, such as the translation of Oracle manuals and multimedia CBTs. His background is in database, network, web, and Java technologies. In the XML world, he is known as the developer of the DB Generator for the Apache Cocoon project. He has worked on the open source projects DBPrism and DBPrism CMS, the Lucene-Oracle integration using the Oracle JVM Directory implementation, and the `https://restlet.com/` project, where he worked on the Oracle XDB Restlet Adapter, which is an alternative to writing native REST web services inside a database resident JVM. Since 2006, he has been part of an Oracle ACE program. Oracle ACEs are known for their strong credentials as Oracle community enthusiasts and advocates, with candidates nominated by ACEs in the Oracle technology and applications communities. He has coauthored Oracle Database Programming using Java and Web Services by Digital Press and Professional XML Databases by Wrox Press, and has been a technical reviewers for several Packt books, such as *Apache Solr 4 Cookbook, ElasticSearch Server* and others.

www.PacktPub.com

For support files and downloads related to your book, please visit `www.PacktPub.com`.

Did you know that Packt offers eBook versions of every book published, with PDF and ePub files available? You can upgrade to the eBook version at `www.PacktPub.com` and as a print book customer, you are entitled to a discount on the eBook copy. Get in touch with us at `service@packtpub.com` for more details.

At `www.PacktPub.com`, you can also read a collection of free technical articles, sign up for a range of free newsletters and receive exclusive discounts and offers on Packt books and eBooks.

`https://www.packtpub.com/mapt`

Get the most in-demand software skills with Mapt. Mapt gives you full access to all Packt books and video courses, as well as industry-leading tools to help you plan your personal development and advance your career.

Why subscribe?

- Fully searchable across every book published by Packt
- Copy and paste, print, and bookmark content
- On demand and accessible via a web browser

Customer Feedback

Thanks for purchasing this Packt book. At Packt, quality is at the heart of our editorial process. To help us improve, please leave us an honest review on this book's Amazon page at `https://www.amazon.com/dp/1786460017`.

If you'd like to join our team of regular reviewers, you can e-mail us at `customerreviews@packtpub.com`. We award our regular reviewers with free eBooks and videos in exchange for their valuable feedback. Help us be relentless in improving our products!

Table of Contents

Preface

Even structured data is useless if it can't help you to take strategic decisions and improve existing system. If you love to play with data, or your job requires you to process custom log formats, design a scalable analysis system, and manage logs to do real-time data analysis, this book is your one-stop solution. By combining the massively popular Elasticsearch, Logstash, Beats and Kibana, ELK Stack has advanced to Elastic Stack that delivers actionable insights in near real time from almost any type of structured or unstructured data.

This book brushes up your basic knowledge of implementing the Elastic Stack and then dives deeper into complex and advanced scenarios. We'll help you with data analytics challenges and take you through practical scenario of an intranet portal to understand utilization of Elastic Stack components. You will be able to grasp advanced techniques for log analysis and visualization. Newly announced features such as Beats and X-Pack are also covered in detail with examples.

Toward the end, you will see how to use the Elastic stack for real-world case studies and we'll show you some best practices and troubleshooting techniques for the Elastic Stack.

What this book covers

Chapter 1, *Elastic Stack Overview*, covers the shift from ELK Stack to Elastic Stack followed by setup of various components of Elastic Stack.

Chapter 2, *Stepping into Elasticsearch*, takes us to how Elasticsearch started as a project, how Elasticsearch works and covering various Elasticsearch API's and Aggregations.

Chapter 3, *Exploring Logstash and Its Plugins*, covers introduction of Logstash along with understanding it's architecture. It also covers the various plugins with suitable examples. At the end, a Logstash configuration file is shown for parsing logs.

Chapter 4, *Kibana Interface*, teaches about the various interfaces present in Kibana in depth along with an example to demonstrate how to combine all the interfaces to create a dashboard.

Chapter 5, *Using Beats*, takes us to introducing the beats, understanding how beat differs from Logstash followed by exploring various beats, their functionalities and setup steps. At the end, we explored how to use Beats in Elastic Stack.

Chapter 6, *Elastic Stack in Action*, covers a real-world use-case of an Intranet Portal server and showcases and how to use Elastic Stack components to solve the problem.

Chapter 7, *Customizing Elastic Stack*, teaches us how to extend each component of Elastic Stack and how to create a plugin for our use-cases.

Chapter 8, *Elasticsearch APIs*, takes us to various Elasticsearch API's along with understanding Elasticsearch modules, Ingest nodes, Discovery pPlugins and how to use Java client to access various Elasticsearch operations.

Chapter 9, *X-Pack: Security and Monitoring*, covers introduction of X-Pack along with installation of X-Pack. It also covers the usage and functionalities provided by Shield, Marvel and Profiler.

Chapter 10, *X-Pack: Alerting, Graph, and Reporting*, teaches us about the usage and functionalities of Watcher, Graph and Reporting features.

Chapter 11, *Best Practices*, takes us to understand why do we need to follow best practices along with listing of various best practices which should be followed which has been categorized into multiple sub-sections.

Chapter 12, *Case Study-Meetup*, covers complete coverage of understanding the problem statement followed by extending Logstash and creating a plugin to fetch required information. It then takes us to understand how to utilize Elastic Stack components to cover end-to-end understanding of Meetup data and showcasing the powerful capabilities of Elastic Stack for data analytics.

What you need for this book

Following table lists all required software and tools needed to execute example in the book. Wherever requires, links to download the software is also present within the chapter as well.

Software	Version	Link
Elasticsearch	5.1.1	https://www.elastic.co/downloads/past-releases/elasticsearch-5-1-1
Logstash	5.1.1	https://www.elastic.co/downloads/past-releases/logstash-5-1-1
Kibana	5.1.1	https://www.elastic.co/downloads/past-releases/kibana-5-1-1

Filebeat	5.1.1	https://www.elastic.co/downloads/past-releases/filebeat-5-1-1
Packetbeat	5.1.1	https://www.elastic.co/downloads/past-releases/packetbeat-5-1-1
Winlogbeat	5.1.1	https://www.elastic.co/downloads/past-releases/winlogbeat-5-1-1
Metricbeat	5.1.1	https://www.elastic.co/downloads/past-releases/metricbeat-5-1-1
Elasticsearch	1.4.0	https://www.elastic.co/downloads/past-releases/elasticsearch-1-4-0
Liferay	6.2CEGA4	https://sourceforge.net/projects/lportal/files/Liferay%20Portal/6.2.3%20GA4/liferay-portal-tomcat-6.2-ce-ga4-20150416163831865.zip/download
Java	8.x	http://www.oracle.com/technetwork/java/javase/downloads/index.html
Elasticray	1.2.0	https://web.liferay.com/marketplace/-/mp/application/41044606
Go	1.7.5	https://golang.org/dl
Ruby	2.4.0	https://www.ruby-lang.org/en
NodeJS	6.9.0	https://nodejs.org/en/download/releases/
Gradle	2.13	https://gradle.org/gradle-download
Python	2.7.10	https://www.python.org
Virtualenv		https://virtualenv.pypa.io/en/stable/
cookiecutter		https://github.com/audreyr/cookiecutter.

Who this book is for

If you have heard the word ELK stack and want to learn more about it's latest development and how it became Elastic Stack, this book is for you. If you use analytics or like to play with visualizations on your data, this book helps you to understand how the components of the stack can help you.

Conventions

In this book, you will find a number of text styles that distinguish between different kinds of information. Here are some examples of these styles and an explanation of their meaning.

Code words in text, database table names, folder names, filenames, file extensions, pathnames, dummy URLs, user input, and Twitter handles are shown as follows: "The next lines of code read the link and assign it to the to the BeautifulSoup function."

A block of code is set as follows:

```
#import packages into the project
from bs4 import BeautifulSoup
from urllib.request import urlopen
import pandas as pd
```

When we wish to draw your attention to a particular part of a code block, the relevant lines or items are set in bold:

```
<head>
<script src="d3.js" charset="utf-8"></script>
  <meta charset="utf-8">
  <meta name="viewport" content="width=device-width">
  <title>JS Bin</title>
</head>
```

Any command-line input or output is written as follows:

```
C:\Python34\Scripts> pip install -upgrade pip
C:\Python34\Scripts> pip install pandas
```

New terms and **important words** are shown in bold. Words that you see on the screen, for example, in menus or dialog boxes, appear in the text like this: "In order to download new modules, we will go to **Files** | **Settings** | **Project Name** | **Project Interpreter**."

Warnings or important notes appear in a box like this.

Tips and tricks appear like this.

Reader feedback

Feedback from our readers is always welcome. Let us know what you think about this book-what you liked or disliked. Reader feedback is important for us as it helps us develop titles that you will really get the most out of. To send us general feedback, simply e-mail feedback@packtpub.com, and mention the book's title in the subject of your message. If there is a topic that you have expertise in and you are interested in either writing or contributing to a book, see our author guide at www.packtpub.com/authors.

Customer support

Now that you are the proud owner of a Packt book, we have a number of things to help you to get the most from your purchase.

Downloading the example code

You can download the example code files for this book from your account at http://www.packtpub.com. If you purchased this book elsewhere, you can visit http://www.packtpub.com/support and register to have the files e-mailed directly to you.

You can download the code files by following these steps:

1. Log in or register to our website using your e-mail address and password.
2. Hover the mouse pointer on the **SUPPORT** tab at the top.
3. Click on **Code Downloads & Errata**.
4. Enter the name of the book in the **Search** box.
5. Select the book for which you're looking to download the code files.
6. Choose from the drop-down menu where you purchased this book from.
7. Click on **Code Download**.

Once the file is downloaded, please make sure that you unzip or extract the folder using the latest version of:

- WinRAR / 7-Zip for Windows
- Zipeg / iZip / UnRarX for Mac
- 7-Zip / PeaZip for Linux

The code bundle for the book is also hosted on GitHub at https://github.com/PacktPublishing/Mastering-Elastic-Stack. We also have other code bundles from our rich catalog of books and videos available at https://github.com/PacktPublishing/. Check them out!

Errata

Although we have taken every care to ensure the accuracy of our content, mistakes do happen. If you find a mistake in one of our books-maybe a mistake in the text or the code-we would be grateful if you could report this to us. By doing so, you can save other readers from frustration and help us improve subsequent versions of this book. If you find any errata, please report them by visiting http://www.packtpub.com/submit-errata, selecting your book, clicking on the **Errata Submission Form** link, and entering the details of your errata. Once your errata are verified, your submission will be accepted and the errata will be uploaded to our website or added to any list of existing errata under the Errata section of that title.

To view the previously submitted errata, go to https://www.packtpub.com/books/content/support and enter the name of the book in the search field. The required information will appear under the **Errata** section.

Piracy

Piracy of copyrighted material on the Internet is an ongoing problem across all media. At Packt, we take the protection of our copyright and licenses very seriously. If you come across any illegal copies of our works in any form on the Internet, please provide us with the location address or website name immediately so that we can pursue a remedy.

Please contact us at copyright@packtpub.com with a link to the suspected pirated material.

We appreciate your help in protecting our authors and our ability to bring you valuable content.

Questions

If you have a problem with any aspect of this book, you can contact us at questions@packtpub.com, and we will do our best to address the problem.

1

Elastic Stack Overview

It's as easy to read a log file of a few MBs or hundreds as it is to keep data of this size in databases or files and still get sense out of it. But then a day comes when this data takes up terabytes, petabytes and grows even faster in future. As data demand pushes, normal text editors or word processing tools would refuse to cope up and would not be able to open such a large dataset. There would be a need to analyze the raw data which can be used to discover insights. You start to find something for huge log management, or something that can index the data properly and make sense out of it. If you Google this, you will stumble upon ELK Stack. Elasticsearch manages your data, Logstash reads the data from different sources, and Kibana makes a fine visualization of it.

Recently, ELK Stack has evolved as Elastic Stack. We will get to know more about it in this chapter, along with setting it up. The following are the points that will be covered in this chapter:

- Introduction to ELK Stack
- The birth of Elastic Stack
- Who uses the Stack
- Stack competitors
- Setting up Elastic Stack
- X-Pack

Introduction to ELK Stack

It all began with Shay Banon, who started an open source project called **Elasticsearch,** successor of **Compass,** which gained popularity as one of the top open source database engines. Later, based on the distributed model of working, **Kibana** was introduced, to visualize the data present in Elasticsearch. Earlier, to put data into Elasticsearch, we had **Rivers,** which provided us with a specific input via which we inserted data into Elasticsearch.

However, with growing popularity, this setup required a tool via which we could insert data into Elasticsearch and have flexibility to perform various transformations on data (to make unstructured data structured and have full control on how to process the data). Based on this premise, **Logstash** was born, which was then incorporated into the Stack, and together these three tools, Elasticsearch, Logstash, and Kibana were named **ELK Stack**.

The following diagram is a simple data pipeline using ELK Stack:

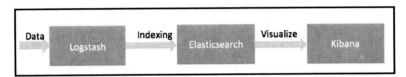

As we can see from the preceding figure, data is read using Logstash and indexed to Elasticsearch. Later, we can use Kibana to read the indices from Elasticsearch and visualize it using charts and lists. Let's understand these components separately, and the role they play in the making of the Stack.

Logstash

As mentioned earlier, Rivers were initially used to put data into Elasticsearch before ELK Stack. For ELK Stack, Logstash is the entry point for all types of data. Logstash has so many plugins to read data from a number of sources, and so many output plugins to submit data to a variety of destinations - one of those is the Elasticsearch plugin, which helps to send data to Elasticsearch.

After Logstash became popular, Rivers eventually got deprecated, as they made the cluster unstable and also performance issues were observed.

Logstash does not just ship data from one end to another; it helps us with collecting raw data and modifying/filtering it to convert it to something meaningful, formatted, and organized. The updated data is then sent to Elasticsearch. If there is no plugin available to support reading data from a specific source, writing the data to a location, or modifying it in your own way, Logstash is flexible enough to allow you to write your own plugins.

Simply put, Logstash is open source, highly flexible, rich with plugins and can read your data from your choice of location. It normalizes data as per your defined configurations, and sends it to a particular destination, as per the requirements.

We will be learning more about Logstash in `Chapter 3`, *Exploring Logstash and Its Plugins* and `Chapter 7`, *Customizing Elastic Stack.*

Elasticsearch

All of the data read by Logstash is sent to Elasticsearch for indexing. Elasticsearch is not only used to index data, it is also full-text search engine, highly scalable, distributed, and offers many more things too. Elasticsearch manages and maintains your data in the form of indices and offers you to query, access, and aggregate the data using its APIs. Elasticsearch is based on **Lucene**, thus providing you all of the features that Lucene does.

We will be learning more about Elasticsearch in `Chapter 2`, *Stepping into Elasticsearch,* `Chapter 7`, *Customizing Elastic Stack,* and `Chapter 8`, *Elasticsearch APIs.*

Kibana

Kibana uses Elasticsearch APIs to read/query data from Elasticsearch indices, to visualize and analyze in the form of charts, graphs and tables. Kibana is in the form of a web application, providing you with a highly configurable user interface that lets you query the data, create a number of charts to visualize, and make actual sense out of the data stored.

We will be learning more about Kibana in `Chapter 4`, *Kibana Interface* and `Chapter 7`, *Customizing Elastic Stack.*

After a robust ELK Stack, as time passed, a few important and complex demands took place, such as authentication, security, notifications, and so on. This demand led to the development of a few other tools such as **Watcher** (providing alerts and notifications based on changes in data), **Shield** (authentication and authorization for securing clusters), **Marvel** (monitoring statistics of the cluster), **ES-Hadoop**, **Curator**, and **Graph**, as requirements arose.

The birth of Elastic Stack

All the jobs of reading data were once done using Logstash, but that's resource consuming. Since Logstash runs on JVM, it consumes a good amount of memory. The community realized the need for improvement and to make the pipelining process resource friendly and lightweight. Earlier, **Packetbeat** was born, a project which was an effort to make a network packet analyzer that could read from different protocols, parse the data, and ship to Elasticsearch. Being lightweight in nature did the trick and a new concept of **Beats** was formed. Beats are written in Go programming language. The project evolved, and now ELK stack was no more just Elasticsearch, Logstash, and Kibana; Beats also became a significant component.

The pipeline now looked as follows:

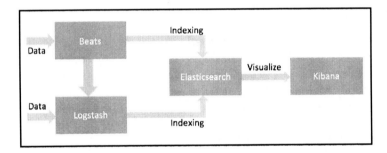

Beat

A Beat reads data, parses it, and can ship it to either Elasticsearch or Logstash. The difference is that they are lightweight, serve a specific purpose, and are installed as agents. There are a few Beats available such as Metricbeat, Filebeat, Packetbeat, and so on, which are supported and provided by the Elastic Team and a good number of Beats are already written by the community. If you have a specific requirement, you can write your own Beat using the `libbeat` library.

In simple words, Beats can be treated as very lightweight agents to ship data to either Logstash or Elasticsearch, offering you an infrastructure using the `libbeat` library to create your own Beats.

We will be learning more about Beats in `Chapter 5`, *Using Beats* and `Chapter 7`, *Customizing Elastic Stack.*

Together Elasticsearch, Logstash, Kibana, and Beats became Elastic Stack, formally known as ELK Stack. Elastic Stack did not just add Beats to its team; they will be using the same version always. The starting version of the Elastic Stack will be 5.0.0 and the same version will apply to all the components.

This version and release method is not only for Elastic Stack, but for other tools of the Elastic family as well. Due to there being so many tools, there was a problem of unification, wherein each tool had their own version, and every version was not compatible with each other, hence leading to a problem. To solve this, all of the tools will now be built, tested, and released together.

All of these components play a significant role in creating a pipeline. While Beats and Logstash are used to collect the data, parse it, and ship it, Elasticsearch creates indices, which is finally used by Kibana to make visualizations. While Elastic Stack helps with a pipeline, other tools add security, notifications, monitoring, and other such capabilities to the setup.

Who uses Elastic Stack?

In the past few years, implementations of Elastic Stack have been increasing very rapidly. In this section, we will consider a few case studies to understand how Elastic Stack has helped this development.

Salesforce

Salesforce developed a new plugin named **ELF (Event Log Files)** to collect Salesforce logged data to, enable auditing of user activities. The purpose was to analyze the data to understand user behavior and trends in Salesforce.

The plugin is available on GitHub at `https://github.com/developerforce/elf_elk_dock er`.

ELF is an abbreviation for **Event Log Files**. This plugin simplifies the Stack configuration and allows to download Event Log Files to get indexed and finally make sense of the data by visualizing it using Kibana. This implementation utilizes Elasticsearch, Logstash and Kibana.

CERN

There is not just one use case that Elastic Stack helped **CERN (European Organization for Nuclear Research)**, but five. At CERN, Elastic Stack is used for the following:

- Messaging
- Data monitoring
- Cloud benchmarking
- Infrastructure monitoring
- Job monitoring

Multiple Kibana dashboards are used by CERN for a number of visualizations.

Green Man Gaming

Green Man Gaming is an online gaming platform where game providers publish their games. The website wanted to make a difference by proving better gameplay. They started using Elastic Stack to carry out log analysis, search, and analysis of gameplay data.

They began with setting up Kibana dashboards to gain insights about the counts of gamers, by the country and currency used by gamers. This helped them to understand and streamline support and help in order to provide an improved response.

Apart from these case studies, Elastic Stack is used by a number of other companies to gain insights into the data they own. Sometimes, not all of the components are used; that is, not all of the times a Beat would be used and Logstash would be configured. Sometimes, only an Elasticsearch and Kibana combination is used.

If we look at the users within the organization, all of the titles who are expected to do big data analysis, business intelligence, data visualizations, log analysis, and so on, can utilize Elastic Stack for their technical forte, for example data scientists, devops, and so on.

Stack competitors

Well, it would be wrong to call for Elastic Stack Competitors because Elastic Stack has been emerged as a strong competitor to many other tools in the market in recent years and is growing rapidly. Few of these are:

- Open source:
    - **Graylog**: Visit `https://www.graylog.org/` for more information
    - **InfluxDB**: Visit `https://influxdata.com/` for more information
- Others:

    - **Logscape**: Visit `http://logscape.com/` for more information
    - **Logcene**: Visit `http://sematext.com/logsene/` for more information
    - **Splunk**: Visit `http://www.splunk.com/` for more information
    - **Sumo Logic**: Visit `https://www.sumologic.com/` for more information

- Kibana competitors:
    - **Grafana**: Visit `http://grafana.org/` for more information
    - **Graphite**: Visit `https://graphiteapp.org/` for more information
- Elasticsearch competitors:
    - **Lucene/Solr**: Visit `https://lucene.apache.org/` or `http://lucene.apache.org/solr/` for more information
    - **Sphinx**: Visit `http://sphinxsearch.com/` for more information

Most of these compare with respect to log management, while Elastic Stack is much more than that. It offers you the ability to analyze any type of data, not just logs.

Setting up Elastic Stack

In this section, we will install all four components of Elastic Stack on two popular operating systems – Microsoft Windows and Ubuntu. As a pre-requisite for installation of Elasticsearch or Logstash, Java should be installed. In case you have Java installed you can skip the Installation of Java section.

Installation of Java

In this section, JDK needs to be installed for accessing Elasticsearch. Oracle Java 8 (Oracle JDK version 1.8.0_73 onwards) should be installed, as it is the recommended version for Elasticsearch 5.0.0 onwards.

Installation of Java on Ubuntu 14.04

Install Java 8 using terminal and apt package in the following manner:

1. Add Oracle Java PPA (Personal Package Archive) to apt repository list:

   ```
   sudo add-apt-repository -y ppa:webupd8team/java
   ```

 In this case, we use a third-party repository. It does not violate the Oracle Java Rules by not including Java binaries; instead this PPA directly downloads Java Binaries from Oracle and installs the binaries.

   You will be prompted to enter a password after running sudo command (unless you are not logged into as root) and you would receive OK on successful addition to repository, which indicates repository has been imported.

2. Update the apt package database to include all the latest files under the packages:

   ```
   sudo apt-get update
   ```

3. Install the latest version of Oracle Java 8:

   ```
   sudo apt-get -y install oracle-java8-installer
   ```

   Also during installation, you will be prompted to accept the license agreement which pops up as shown in the following screenshot:

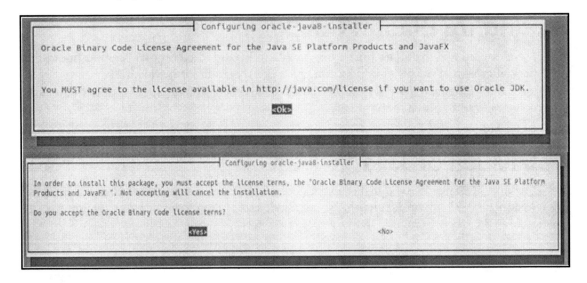

4. To check whether Java has successfully installed, type the following command into the terminal:

```
java -version
```

```
yuvraj@ubuntu:~$ java -version
java version "1.8.0_74"
Java(TM) SE Runtime Environment (build 1.8.0_74-b02)
Java HotSpot(TM) 64-Bit Server VM (build 25.74-b02, mixed mode)
```

The preceding screenshot signifies Java has installed successfully.

Installation of Java on Windows

We can install Java on windows by going through the below steps:

1. Download the latest version of Java JDK from Sun Microsystems site using the following link:

   ```
   http://www.oracle.com/technetwork/java/javase/downloads/index.html
   ```

   Upon opening the link click on the **Download** button of JDK to download.

   You will be redirected to the download page - first click on the **Accept License Agreement** radio button, then click on your Windows version (use x86 for 32-bit or x64 for 64-bit) to download the EXE file.

2. Double click on installation file and it will open as an installer.
3. Click on Next followed by accepting license by reading it, and keep clicking next until it shows JDK has successfully installed.

4. Now for running Java in windows, you need to set the path of JAVA in the environment variable settings of Windows. Firstly open properties of My Computer. Select **Advanced system settings** and then click on the **Advanced** tab wherein you will click environment variables options as shown in the following screenshot:

After opening environment variables, click on **New** (under **System Variables**) and give the variable name as JAVA_HOME and variable value as C:\Program Files\Java\jdk1.8.0_74. (Do check in your system where jdk has been installed and provide that path):

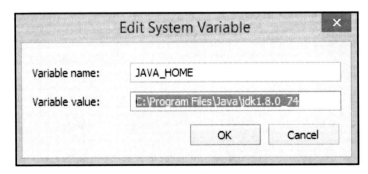

Then double click **Path variable** (under **System Variables**) and move towards the end of the text box – insert a semi colon if not inserted and add the location of the bin folder of JDK such as: `%JAVA_HOME%\bin`. Then click on **OK** to all the windows opened.

 Do not delete anything within the path variable textbox.

5. To validate whether Java is successfully installed, type the following command in command prompt:

```
java -version
```

```
C:\Users\ygupta>java -version
java version "1.8.0_74"
Java(TM) SE Runtime Environment (build 1.8.0_74-b02)
Java HotSpot(TM) 64-Bit Server VM (build 25.74-b02, mixed mode)
```

The preceding screenshot signifies Java has installed successfully.

Installation of Elasticsearch

In this section, Elasticsearch v5.1.1 installation will be covered for Ubuntu and Windows separately.

Installation of Elasticsearch on Ubuntu 14.04

In order to install Elasticsearch on Ubuntu, refer to the following steps:

1. Download Elasticsearch 5.1.1 as a debian package using terminal:

```
wget https://artifacts.elastic.co
/downloads/elasticsearch/elasticsearch-5.1.1.deb
```

2. Install the debian package using following command:

```
sudo dpkg -i elasticsearch-5.1.1.deb
```

 Elasticsearch will be installed in /usr/share/elasticsearch directory. The configuration files will be present at /etc/elasticsearch. The init script will be present at /etc/init.d/elasticsearch. The log files will be present within /var/log/elasticsearch directory.

3. Configure Elasticsearch to run automatically on bootup . If you are using SysV init distribution, then run the following command:

```
sudo update-rc.d elasticsearch defaults 95 10
```

The preceding command will print on screen:

```
Adding system startup for,  /etc/init.d/elasticsearch
```

Check status of Elasticsearch using following command:

```
sudo service elasticsearch status
```

Run Elasticsearch as a service using following command:

```
sudo service elasticsearch start
```

 Elasticsearch may not start if you have any plugin installed which is not supported in ES-5.0.x version onwards. As plugins have been deprecated, it is required to uninstall any plugin if exists in prior version of ES. Remove a plugin after going to ES Home using following command: bin/elasticsearch-plugin remove head

Usage of Elasticsearch command:

```
sudo  service elasticsearch {start|stop|restart|force-
reload|status}
```

If you are using systemd distribution, then run following command:

```
sudo /bin/systemctl daemon-reload
sudo /bin/systemctl enable elasticsearch.service
```

To verify elasticsearch installation open open `http://localhost:9200` in browser or run the following command from command line:

```
curl -X GET http://localhost:9200
```

```
{
  "name" : "xB20COp",
  "cluster_name" : "elasticsearch",
  "cluster_uuid" : "wbXRP_h0QYK8QYNPJbalIA",
  "version" : {
    "number" : "5.1.1",
    "build_hash" : "5395e21",
    "build_date" : "2016-12-06T12:36:15.409Z",
    "build_snapshot" : false,
    "lucene_version" : "6.3.0"
  },
  "tagline" : "You Know, for Search"
}
```

Installation of Elasticsearch on Windows

In order to install Elasticsearch on Windows, refer to the following steps:

1. Download Elasticsearch 5.1.1 version from its site using the following link:

   ```
   https://artifacts.elastic.co/downloads/elasticsearch/elasticsearch
   -5.1.1.zip
   ```

Upon opening the link, click on it and it will download the ZIP package.

2. Extract the downloaded ZIP package by unzipping it using WinRAR, 7-Zip, and other such extracting softwares (if you don't have one of these then download it).

This will extract the files and folders in the directory.

3. Then click on the extracted folder and navigate the folder to reach inside the `bin` folder.
4. Click on the `elasticsearch.bat` file to run Elasticsearch.

If this window is closed Elasticsearch will stop running, as the node will shut down.

5. To verify Elasticsearch installation, open `http://localhost:9200` in the browser:

```
{
  "name" : "3Fqp-HA",
  "cluster_name" : "elasticsearch",
  "cluster_uuid" : "V0u-BkqBTLerMhToip7rGQ",
  "version" : {
    "number" : "5.1.1",
    "build_hash" : "5395e21",
    "build_date" : "2016-12-06T12:36:15.409Z",
    "build_snapshot" : false,
    "lucene_version" : "6.3.0"
  },
  "tagline" : "You Know, for Search"
}
```

Installation of Elasticsearch as a service

After installing Elasticsearch as previously mentioned, open Command Prompt after navigating to the `bin` folder and use the following command:

```
elasticsearch-service.bat install
Usage: elasticsearch-service.bat install | remove | start | stop | manager
```

Installation of Kibana

This section covers installation of Kibana 5.1.1 on Ubuntu and Windows separately, before running Kibana, there are some prerequisites:

- Elasticsearch should be installed and running on port `9200` (default port).
- Make sure the port on which Kibana is running is not being used by any other application. By default, Kibana runs on port `5601`.

Installation of Kibana on Ubuntu 14.04

In order to install Kibana on Ubuntu, refer to the following steps:

1. Before installing Kibana, please check whether your system is 32 bit or 64 bit which can be done using the following command:

```
uname -m
```

If it gives an output as x86_64 it means it is 64-bit system else, if it gives i686 it means it is a 32-bit system.

2. Download Kibana 5.1.1 as a debian package using terminal:
   - For 64-bit system:

```
wget https://artifacts.elastic.co/
downloads/kibana/kibana-5.1.1-amd64.deb
```

   - For 32-bit system:

```
wget https://artifacts.elastic.co/
downloads/kibana/kibana-5.1.1-i386.deb
```

3. Install the debian package using following command:
   - For 64-bit system:

```
sudo dpkg -i kibana-5.1.1-amd64.deb
```

   - For 32-bit system:

```
sudo dpkg -i kibana-5.1.1-i386.deb
```

Kibana will be installed in /usr/share/kibana directory. The configuration files will be present at /etc/kibana. The init script will be present at /etc/init.d/kibana. The log files will be present within /var/log/kibana directory.

4. Configure Kibana to run automatically on bootup . If you are using SysV init distribution, then run the following command:

```
sudo update-rc.d kibana defaults 95 10
```

The above command will print on screen:

```
Adding system startup for /etc/init.d/kibana
```

Check status of Kibana using following command:

```
sudo service kibana status
```

Run Kibana as a service using following command:

```
sudo service kibana start
```

Usage of Kibana command:

```
sudo service kibana {start|force-start|stop|force-
stop|status|restart}
```

If you are using systemd distribution then run following command:

```
sudo /bin/systemctl daemon-reload
sudo /bin/systemctl enable kibana.service
```

 If you want to install any other version of Kibana, you can visit the Elastic Team download site and copy the debian package link and use wget to fetch the package.

5. To verify Kibana installation open http://localhost:5601 in the browser:

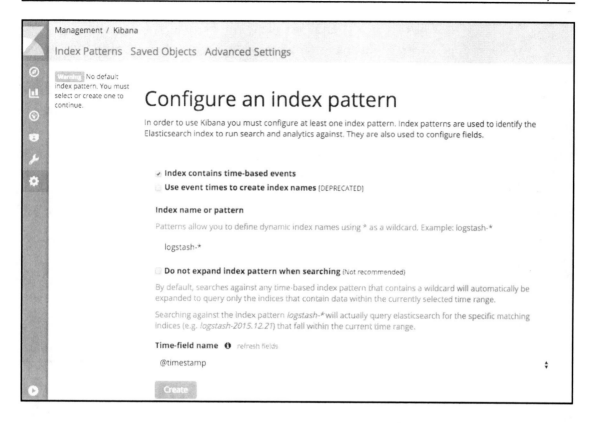

Installation of Kibana on Windows

In order to install Kibana on Windows, refer to the following steps:

1. Download Kibana version 5.1.1 from the Elastic website using the following link:

```
https://artifacts.elastic.co/downloads/kibana/kibana-5.1.1-windows
-x86.zip
```

Upon opening the link, click on it and it will download the ZIP package.

2. Extract the downloaded ZIP package by either it using WinRAR, 7-Zip, or other such software.This will extract the files and folders in the directory.

3. Then click on the extracted folder and navigate the folder to reach inside the `bin` folder.

4. Click on the `kibana.bat` file to run Kibana.

5. To verify Kibana installation, open `http://localhost:5601` in the browser:

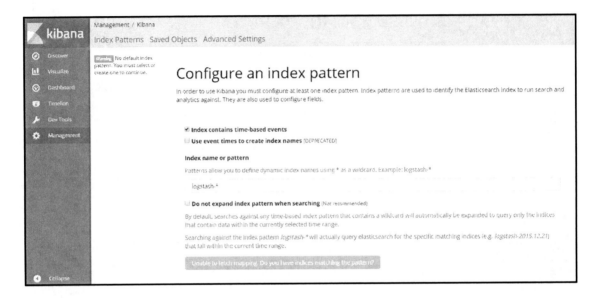

Installation of Logstash

In this section, Logstash will be installed. Logstash 5.1.1 will be installed and this section covers installation on Ubuntu and Windows separately.

Installation of Logstash on Ubuntu 14.04

In order to install Logstash on Ubuntu, refer to the following steps:

1. Download Logstash 5.1.1 as a debian package using terminal:

```
wget https://artifacts.elastic.co
/downloads/logstash/logstash-5.1.1.deb
```

2. Install the debian package using following command:

```
sudo dpkg -i logstash-5.1.1.deb
```

Logstash will be installed in `/usr/share/logstash` directory. The configuration files will be present at `/etc/logstash`. The log files will be present within `/var/log/logstash` directory

3. Check status of Logstash using following command:

```
sudo initctl status logstash
```

Run Logstash as a service using following command:

```
sudo initctl start logstash
```

Logstash is installed in location `/usr/share/logstash`

Installation of Logstash on Windows

In order to install Logstash on Windows, refer to the following steps:

1. Download Logstash 5.1.1 version from the Elastic site using the following link:

```
https://artifacts.elastic.co/downloads/logstash/logstash-5.1.1.zip
```

Upon opening the link click it to download the ZIP package.

2. Extract the downloaded ZIP package by unzipping it using WinRar, 7Zip and other such software.

This will extract the files and folders in the directory.

3. Then click on the extracted folder and navigate the folder to reach inside the bin folder.
4. To validate whether Logstash is successfully installed, type the following command into command prompt after navigating to the `bin` folder:

```
logstash --version
```

This will print the Logstash version installed.

Installation of Filebeat

In this section, Filebeat will be installed. Filebeat 5.1.1 will be installed and this section covers installation on Ubuntu and Windows separately.

Installation of Filebeat on Ubuntu 14.04

In order to install Filebeat on Ubuntu, refer to the following steps:

1. Before installing Filebeat, please check whether your system is 32 bit or 64 bit which can be done using the following command:

```
uname -m
```

If it gives an output as x86_64 it means it is 64-bit system else, if it gives i686 it means it is a 32-bit system.

2. Download Filebeat 5.1.1 as a debian package using terminal
   - For 64-bit system:

```
wget https://artifacts.elastic.co
/downloads/beats/filebeat/filebeat-5.1.1-amd64.deb
```

   - For 32-bit system:

```
wget https://artifacts.elastic.co
/downloads/beats/filebeat/filebeat-5.1.1-i386.deb
```

3. Install the debian package using following command:
   - For 64-bit system:

```
sudo dpkg -i filebeat-5.1.1-amd64.deb
```

   - For 32-bit system:

```
sudo dpkg -i filebeat-5.1.1-i386.deb
```

 Filebeat will be installed in /usr/share/filebeat directory. The configuration files will be present at /etc/filebeat. The init script will be present at /etc/init.d/filebeat. The log files will be present within /var/log/filebeat directory.

4. Configure Filebeat to run automatically on bootup. If you are using SysV init distribution, then run the following command:

```
sudo update-rc.d filebeat defaults 95 10
```

The above command will print on screen:

```
Adding system startup for /etc/init.d/filebeat.
```

Check status of Filebeat using following command:

```
sudo service filebeat status
```

Run Filebeat as a service using following command:

```
sudo service filebeat start
```

Usage of Filebeat command:

```
sudo service filebeat {start|stop|status|restart|force-reload}
```

If you run Filebeat as a service, then it will run the /etc/filebeat/filebeat.yml configuration file.

If you want to install any other version of Filebeat, you can visit the Elastic Team download site and copy the debian package link and use wget to fetch the package.

Installation of Filebeat on Windows

In order to install Filebeat on Windows, refer to the following steps:

1. Before installing Filebeat, please check whether your system is 32 bit or 64 bit which can be done using the following command in command prompt:

```
wmic os get osarchitecture
```

It will give an output as 64-bit or 32-bit.

2. Download Filebeat 5.1.1 version from Elastic site using the following link:

- **For 64-bit system:** `https://artifacts.elastic.co/down loads/beats/filebeat/filebeat-5.1.1-windows-x86_64.zip`
- **For 32-bit system:** `https://artifacts.elastic.co/down loads/beats/filebeat/filebeat-5.1.1-windows-x86.zip`

Upon opening the link, click on it and it will download the ZIP package.

3. Extract the downloaded ZIP package by unzipping it using WinRAR, 7-Zip, or other such software:

This will extract the files and folders in the directory.

4. Open Windows PowerShell as an administrator (install if not present).
5. Navigate to the directory where Filebeat is extracted and stored (such as `C:\Users\username\Desktop`) and run the following command in Windows PowerShell:

`.\install-service-filebeat.ps1`

 If script execution is disabled on your system, you need to set the execution policy for the current session to allow the script to run. For example:

`PowerShell.exe -ExecutionPolicy UnRestricted -File .\install-service-filebeat.ps1.`

This will install Filebeat as a Windows service.

X-Pack

Along with Elastic Stack, there are a few more aspects needed taken care of. These are sensitive points such as security, monitoring, alerts, and so on. **X-Pack** includes five such features:

- Security
- Alerts
- Monitoring
- Graphs
- Reporting

Security, alerts, and monitoring were already there with different names: Shield, Watcher, and Marvel, respectively. Now graphs and reporting are also part of the team, and this team is named X-Pack. Just like tools in Elastic Stack, these will also be developed, built, tested, and released together with the same version.

All of the code files used within the book is available at the following GitHub Repository having branch 5.1.1:
`https://github.com/kravigupta/mastering-elastic-stack-code-fil`
`es/tree/5.1.1`

Summary

This chapter is an introductory chapter for Elastic Stack and its components. We learned about how it progressed, what was changed, what was introduced, and how it became Elastic Stack from ELK stack. We got to know about a few of the case studies where these components helped organizations to meet their requirements.

Later in the chapter, we set up Elasticsearch, Logstash, and Kibana, along with Filebeat as a service. Finally, this chapter introduced X-Pack, which will be covered later in this book.

In the next chapter, we will learn about Elasticsearch in detail, APIs, QueryDSL, and so on.

2
Stepping into Elasticsearch

In the previous chapter, we learned the basics of Elasticsearch, Logstash, Kibana, and Beats, and how to install and configure them to set the pipeline. We came to know the role of Elasticsearch, and the way it worked with other components of the stack. This was just the tip of the iceberg. To get a better idea of how Elasticsearch works, we need to learn about the APIs, modules, and plugins it offers. These topics are divided in two chapters.

We're going to take a deep dive into Elasticsearch in this chapter. These are the topics that we are going to cover:

- The beginning of Elasticsearch
- Understanding the architecture
- Elasticsearch APIs
- Aggregation
- A note for painless scripting

At the end of this chapter, you should have a good idea about how to use aggregations, and the power of APIs. There will be more about Elasticsearch, which will be covered in `Chapter 8`, *Elasticsearch APIs*.

The beginning of Elasticsearch

It all started with **Lucene,** a brilliant project supported by Apache Software Foundation. There is a good list of Lucene-based projects. To name a few – Apache Solr, Elasticsearch, Apache Nutch, Lucene.Net, DocFetcher, and many more. If you ever try to find a search engine kind of solution, you will surely come across Lucene. It's not only available for Java, but also for Delphi, Perl, C#, C++, Python, Ruby, and PHP. A complete list of Lucene implementation is available at `http://wiki.apache.org/lucene-java/LuceneImplementations`.

Lucene is a full text search engine and it creates indices on documents. In a paragraph or blob of text, every string is called a **term** and a sequence of terms is named as a **field,** and a sequence of fields is named a **document.** An **index** contains a sequence of documents and it indexes data as documents.

In books, we usually see an index where all the keywords are written and which helps us to find the actual content. This type of index is called an **inverted-index** where terms or strings are used to index documents.

Lucene is a wonderful project for text-based search engine implementation. It first appeared in 1999 and since then there is a huge list of Lucene-based implementations. An interesting thing to notice is that there are even search engines that use Lucene at the core. These projects extend Lucene by wrapping it, creating an interface for it, adding more features, and so on, thus providing varieties to be utilized for various solutions.

For Java-based projects, Apache Solr and Elasticsearch are a good choice. You can find a number of threads on the Internet discussing the superiority of a search engine.

Before Elasticsearch, *Shay Banon* created **Compass**, which was also built on top of Lucene. Compass made the life of Java developers easy with its seamless integration, XML, JSON support, and ability to integrate with ORM libraries such as Hibernate and JPA. While upgrading to Compass 3.0, Shay felt it would require major changes to address the scalability issue, to upgrade Lucene to version 2.9. Then he thought of a better solution that would address all the issues and thus Elasticsearch came instead of Compass 3.0. In July 2010, on his blog titled *The Future of Compass and Elasticsearch* (`http://thedudeabides.com/articles/the_future_of_compass`), he writes:

> *So, I started out building elasticsearch. It's basically a solution built from the ground up to be distributed. I also wanted to create a search solution that can be used by any other programming language easily, which basically means JSON over HTTP, without sacrificing the ease of use within the Java programming language (or more specially, the JVM).*

Elasticsearch was born at the time and started catching attention among developers in the open source community. As a result, there is a huge list of clients for Elasticsearch. To name a few – GitHub, Quora, Stack Exchange, Mozilla, StumbleUpon, CISCO, and Netflix are the most renowned. A more comprehensive list can be found at the product site here `https://www.elastic.co/use-cases`.

Key features

Elasticsearch can be considered as the most advanced search engine that offers whatever Lucene offers and much more than that. Let's see a few of those features:

- **Just give JSON**: Elasticsearch takes documents, rather structured JSON documents, as input to create indices. All of the field's properties are automatically detected and indexed by default. Elasticsearch creates mappings (strings by default, which we can change) on its own. You don't need to define schema (`schema.xml` as in Solr). Since Elasticsearch utilizes the best of Lucene, it offers full-text search on data that is indexed.

- **RESTful API**: With the RESTful API, when using JSON data most of the necessary actions can be performed. You can send a JSON document to add to index, delete an entry, update an entry, and many more things. We will learn about APIs later in this book.

- **Real-Time Data availability and analytics**: As soon as data is indexed, it is made available for search and analytics. It's all real-time.

- **Distributed**: Elasticsearch allows us to set up as many nodes we need for our requirement. Cluster will manage everything and it can grow horizontally to a large number (1000(s), as they say). To grow the cluster, just start another node in the network with the same cluster name and it will be added to the cluster.

- **Highly available**: The cluster is smart enough to detect a new node or failed node to add/remove from the cluster. As soon as a node is added or removed, data is rebalanced in a manner that it remains available.

- **Safety of your data comes first**: Any change in data is recorded in transaction logs and not only on single, but multiple nodes (just in case of a node failure, it remains available). This way, Elasticsearch tries to minimize the data loss.

- **Multitenancy**: In Elasticsearch, an alias for index can be created. Usually a cluster contains multiple indices. These aliases allow a filtered view of an index to achieve multitenancy.

Understanding the architecture

To understand how Elasticsearch works, it's necessary that we learn about the architecture of it.

To understand how index, types, documents, and fields work together, let's refer to the following figure:

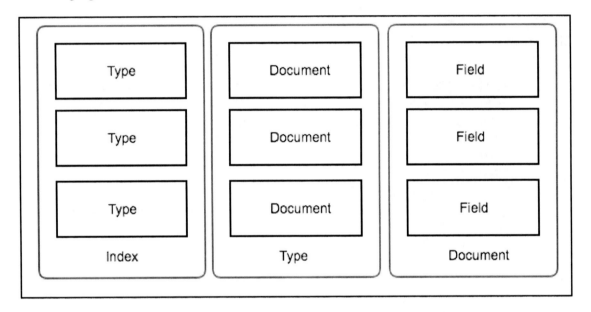

As seen in the preceding figure, an **index** contains one or multiple types. A **type** can be thought of as a table in a relational database. A type has one or more **documents.** There are one or more fields in the document. Fields are key value pairs.

A cluster has one or more nodes. Clusters are identified by their names. By default, elasticsearch is the name of the cluster. In case you have to set up multiple Elasticsearch instances, in the same network, you should keep different names or else all nodes will join the same cluster. Similar to clusters, a node also has a name. We can assign it a name and a cluster name to join. In case we don't provide a cluster name to join, then nodes will automatically search and join the cluster with the name elasticsearch.

If we don't provide a name, a node ID is assigned, which is a random **Universally Unique Identifier (UUID)** and the node will choose its name as the first seven digits of the automatically generated node ID, which will remain unique for each node.

It might happen that an index stores huge data and that it might exceed the hardware size of one node. For such cases, an index can be divided into shards.

There are two types of shards – primary and replica. Each document, when indexed, is first added to the primary shard and then to one or more replica shards. If there are more than one node set up for a cluster, replica shards will be on a different node.

By default, Elasticsearch creates five primary shards and one replica shard for each primary shard. Thus, for an index, if not specified, a total of 10 shards will be created. We can change this configuration and we will learn about it with the Indices API later in this chapter.

Recommended cluster configurations

There are a few configurations that should be taken care of for a proper cluster setup. As we have already discussed, we should provide a cluster name:

```
cluster.name: my-cluster-name
```

Similarly, each node should be given a unique name in order to be easily recognized:

```
node.name: node-1
```

There are other settings as well that are related to data path, discovery of nodes, and so on.

Minimum master nodes

We can specify a property that Elasticsearch evaluates to find out the minimum number of nodes that are needed as master eligible, before it can be called a cluster. Elasticsearch has a default setting for this, but still when you are planning for an Elasticsearch cluster, always consider this setting.

The reason for using this is to prevent data loss. In case of network failure or some other reason it is possible that the cluster chooses another master while the first one is still up, but unreachable. This brings in a situation that is known as split brain and the cluster is divided into two different clusters and causes data loss.

To avoid this problem, *split brain*, use this setting for cluster setup.

The value of this setting can be derived as: *(Total number of nodes / 2) + 1*

So in case you are going to set up a cluster with four nodes, you should keep this value to 3:

```
discovery.zen.minimum_master_nodes: 3
```

All such nodes should also be using the node.master setting with the value true:

```
node.master: true
```

We will be learning more about types of nodes in Chapter 8, *Elasticsearch* APIs modules section.

Local cluster settings

There will be times when you are trying to set multiple instances on the same server. These instances can also share the same data directory that contains indices, shards, cluster metadata, and so on. In order to share the data among instances, each node can use the following code:

```
path.data: /path/to/data/directory
```

Usually, when Elasticsearch is extracted from ZIP/TAR and used, it will use the data folder inside the Elasticsearch directory. As a best practice you should keep the data directory outside the Elasticsearch installation directory.

In case you want a node to behave as a data node you should only set the following:

```
node.data: true
```

And then you should keep node.master as false.

Elasticsearch, by default, will not allow more than one node to share the same data directory. If you want to share the same data, use this setting:

```
node.max_local_storage_nodes: 2
```

The preceding setting code will allow two instances to share the data. You should, however, remember that different type of nodes such as master, data, and so on, should not share the same data directory.

 Setting up multiple instance of Elasticsearch on a single machine is not a recommended configuration for a cluster.

Understanding document processing

As we know, whenever an index is created, shards and replica shards are created. Each shard can have multiple replicas. This complete group is also known as a replication group. In the replication group, the primary shard acts as an entry point for any document indexing operations. The primary shard makes sure that the document and the operation is valid. If everything is alright, the operation is performed and then the primary shard replicates the same operation at the replica shards as well. All of these responsibilities are of the primary shard.

It is not necessary that a document is to be replicated to all replica shards; instead Elasticsearch maintains a copy of who should receive the operation. This list is also called in-sync copies, which is maintained by the master node. By maintaining this list, it is guaranteed that the operation is performed by these shards and the user is also acknowledged. This processing model is also known as the **data-replication model**, which is based on the **primary-backup model**.

In case of a failure of a primary shard, the node that has the primary shard sends a message to the master informing it of this. During this period none of the indexing operation will take place and all shards wait for the master to define a primary shard out of the replicas.

Apart from this, the master node also checks the heath of all shards and it can decide to demote a primary shard based on poor health (probably because of a network failure or disconnection). The master instructs another node to start building a new shard so that the system can be restored to a healthy state, that is, the green statue.

Elasticsearch APIs

There are many APIs available for managing Elasticsearch. These APIs help us to manage cluster, indices, search, and so on. In this section, we will look at each of these APIs in detail.

We can use these APIs through Command Prompt, Console in Kibana, or any tool that can make calls to RESTful APIs.

 By default, Elasticsearch runs on port 9200 to listen to HTTP requests. Kibana uses the same port to connect to Elasticsearch. To learn more about Console, refer to Chapter 4, *Kibana Interface, Exploring Dev tools* section.

Sense is a powerful plugin for Kibana that allows us to make calls to Elasticsearch APIs using a web interface. We will be learning about Sense in `Chapter 8`, *Elasticsearch APIs*. For this chapter, we will be using **cURL**, a Command Prompt utility that allows us to access HTTP requests to access the APIs.

A typical cURL request against ES contains a verb, URL, and message body:

```
$ curl -X{Verb} 'url' -d '{message-body}'
```

Verbs are `GET`, `PUT`, `POST`, `DELETE`, and `HEAD`, and `URL` is either HTTP (by default), or HTTPS. Message body is usually the document we want to index, query we want to perform, or some command we want Elasticsearch to follow.

Document APIs

These APIs allow users to add document(s) to index, get those documents, and edit and delete operations. These APIs are divided into two groups, as discussed in the following sections.

Single document APIs

These APIs are applicable when operations are performed on one document at a time. These can be further divided as follows:

- Index API
- Get API
- Delete API
- Update API

Index API

The **Index** API adds a JSON document to the index. To understand this, let's take an example of a library in which we need to add a book:

```
$ curl -XPUT 'http://localhost:9200/library/book/1?pretty' -d '{
  "author" : "Ravi Kumar Gupta",
  "title" : "Test-Driven Javascript Development",
  "pages" : 240
}'
```

We have used pretty at the end of `uri` to pretty print the JSON output (if any).

This will automatically create an index named `library` if not already present, and add a book to the index. If the index library is already present, it will add the document to it unless there is a document with the same ID present.

Look at the following code pieces:

```
$ curl -XPUT 'http://localhost:9200
/library/book/1?op_type=create&pretty' -d '{
  "author" : "Ravi Kumar Gupta",
  "title" : "Test-Driven Javascript Development",
  "pages" : 240
 }'
```

```
$ curl -XPUT 'http://localhost:9200/library/book/1/_create?pretty' -d
'{
  "author" : "Ravi Kumar Gupta",
  "title" : "Test-Driven JavaScript Development",
  "pages" : 240
 }'
```

In the preceding code and in the first command, we have mentioned `op_type` to set the operation type and set the value as create. We can achieve the same thing by appending `/_create` at the end of the URI. Both will result in the same output and they will add this document to the index. By default, the operation is `create` in case we do not specify (as in the first operation of the previous code listing). Any of the three commands mentioned previously will create an index library if it does not exist and add an entry as provided for author, title, and pages.

When using a create command explicitly either by using the `_create` endpoint or by using the `op_type` parameter, in case the document is already present with the same ID, we will get `version_conflict_engine_exception`.

Let's analyze the output of the preceding code:

```
{
  "_index" : "library",
  "_type" : "book",
  "_id" : "1",
```

```
    "_version" : 1,
    "result" : "created",
    "_shards" : {
      "total" : 2,
      "successful" : 1,
      "failed" : 0
    },
    "created" : true
  }
```

The output shows that the document has been added to an index named `library` and the `type` assigned is `book`. The documents get the `id` specified as 1 with `version` as 1. The value of `result` is set to `created`. The value `true` of `created` shows that the operation was successful. If the same document was already present in the index, while doing the same operation, we will get the value of `result` as `updated`, `_version` will be updated to next, that is, 2 in this case, and the value of `created` would be `false`. The `shard` header tells us that there are total of 2 shards, out of which document got copied to 1 shard successfully. If the value of successful results is at least one, the operation is considered as successful.

There would be five shards by default and one replica for each. Out of five shards, two are chosen for indexing the document. The number of successful shards depends on your cluster settings as well. If there is only one node, then the replica would not be present, and if you notice, the cluster/node health would be yellow. So the value of successful is often less than the total shards. In case you have more than one node set up in the cluster, the value will likely be same. The following is an output of the same call made to a cluster with two nodes:

```
  {
    "_index": "library",
    "_type": "book",
    "_id": "1",
    "_version": 1,
    "result": "created",
    "_shards": {
      "total": 2,
      "successful": 2,
      "failed": 0
    },
    "created": true
  }
```

As we can see, the document was properly replicated. All we need is a positive value of field successful in the output. The document will be copied to multiple shards/replicas as soon as one is available.

Note that we have added an `id1` in the `uri`, `/library/book/1/_create`. In case we want this ID to be generated automatically, we can use the verb `POST` instead of `PUT` for `curl`.

If we use `POST`, then it will automatically create the index along with ID even if index doesn't exist.

Let's add another book:

```
$ curl -XPOST 'http://localhost:9200/library/book?pretty' -d '{
  "author" : "Yuvraj Gupta",
  "title" : "Kibana Essentials",
  "pages" : 210
}'
```

Let's analyze what the output will be now:

```
{
  "_index" : "library",
  "_type" : "book",
  "_id" : "AVSPSXXDxiIiqkaLJfTy",
  "_version" : 1,
  "result" : "created",
  "_shards" : {
    "total" : 2,
    "successful" : 1,
    "failed" : 0
  },
  "created" : true
}
```

This time everything is similar, but the value of `id` is automatically generated by Elasticsearch.

Routing

By default, Elasticsearch, based on the `id` of the document, decides which shard to put a document into. Using the `id` of the document, it calculates a hash and makes a decision to select one or more shards. Instead of Elasticsearch making a decision based on id, we can provide a value that will be used to calculate the hash. This process of *shard allocation* is called *routing*. We can use a query parameter `routing` with the `uri`, as shown in the following command:

```
$ curl -XPOST 'http://localhost:9200/library/book?pretty&routing=books' -d
'{
  "author" : "Yuvraj Gupta",
  "title" : "Kibana Essentials",
  "pages" : 210
```

```
}'
```

In the preceding example, the `Kibana Essentials` book will be placed into a shard based on the hash calculated using the `books` routing parameter.

Get API

The Index API helped us to add a document into the index and the Get API is used to get a document using the ID of the document. Let's try to get the document we stored with `id1`:

```
$ curl -XGET 'http://localhost:9200/library/book/1?pretty'
```

We used the `GET` verb to get a document and provided the `uri` with the ID of the document. The output will be as shown in the following code:

```
{
  "_index" : "library",
  "_type" : "book",
  "_id" : "1",
  "_version" : 1,
  "found" : true,
  "_source" : {
    "author" : "Ravi Kumar Gupta",
    "title" : "Test-Driven Javascript Development",
    "pages" : 240
  }
}
```

We can see that the output includes information related to the document including index name, type, ID, and version. The value of `found` shows whether the document exists with the ID or not. `Source` contains the actual document we indexed.

To check if a document exists or not, we can use the `HEAD` verb as well. Let's see the operations:

```
$ curl -XHEAD -i 'http://localhost:9200/library/book/2'
HTTP/1.1 404 Not Found
Content-Type: text/plain; charset=UTF-8
Content-Length: 0


$ curl -XHEAD -i 'http://localhost:9200/library/book/1'
HTTP/1.1 200 OK
Content-Type: text/plain; charset=UTF-8
Content-Length: 0
```

The source header in the result while getting a document shows the actual document we used. If you are familiar with Kibana Console and try the same command, you might see an error. This is a known issue only for Kibana Console and it is filed here – `https://github.com/elastic/kibana/issues/9141`. We will be learning about Kibana Console, in `Chapter 4`, *Kibana Interface*.

There might be situations where we don't want to retrieve the whole content and only a few of the fields are needed. Or sometimes, we don't want the source at all:

```
curl -XGET 'http://localhost:9200/library/book/1?_source=false'
```

The preceding code will exclude the source from the output. To skip some fields – for example, if we don't want to get pages of the book:

```
curl -XGET 'http://localhost:9200/library/book/1?_source_exclude=pages'
```

To include only authors and skip all other fields:

```
curl -XGET
'http://localhost:9200/library/book/1?_source_include=author'
```

We can use both `_source_include` and `_source_exclude` together. This is helpful when there are documents with many fields and you want to reduce the network overhead by requesting fewer fields. To understand this, add a book with categories:

```
curl -XPUT "http://localhost:9200/library/book/4/_create?pretty" -d'
{
  "author" : "Ravi Kumar Gupta",
  "title" : "Test-Driven JavaScript Development",
  "pages" : 240,
  "category" : [
    {"name":"Technology","subcategory": "javascript"},
    {"name":"Methodology","subcategory": "development"}
    ]
}'
```

Now if we want to get the document with category and skip subcategory, use the following command:

```
curl -XGET http://localhost:9200/library/book/4?
_source_include=category&_source_exclude=*.subcategory
```

The response to the preceding command will be as follows:

```
{
  "_index": "library",
  "_type": "book",
```

```
      "_id": "4",
      "_version": 1,
      "found": true,
      "_source": {
        "category": [
          {
            "name": "Technology"
          },
          {
            "name": "Methodology"
          }
        ]
      }
    }
```

When we need to use only _source_include, we can also use the following:

```
curl -XGET 'http://localhost:9200/library/book/1?_source=author'
```

This will include only the author excluding all others.

Sometimes we might only want the source, in that case use the following:

```
curl -XGET 'http://localhost:9200/library/book/1/_source'
```

We can use _source_include and _source_exclude here as well to exclude or include some fields of the source. Also with the same uri, with HEAD verb, you can find out if a document exists or not.

Sometimes, we may not be worried about a type to which a document belongs and we want to retrieve the document with id. For such cases, we can specify _all for the type and we will get the first document that matches the ID in any type:

```
curl -XGET 'http://localhost:9200/library/_all/1/_source'
curl -XGET 'http://localhost:9200/library/_all/1'
```

While creating an index, we can explicitly specify which fields are to be stored. For example – if we create a library index with the following mappings:

```
curl -XPUT "http://localhost:9200/library" -d'
{
    "mappings": {
        "book": {
            "properties": {
                "author": {
                    "type": "keyword",
                    "store": true
                },
```

```
            "pages": {
                "type": "integer",
                "store": false
            }
        }
    }
}'
```

Please note that the preceding command will throw an
index_already_exists_exception exception in case an index library is already present.
After this we add a book with id 1, similar to what we added previously. Now this will
allow us to get stored fields as an array when passing a stored_field parameter with the
following call:

```
curl -XGET "http://localhost:9200/
library/book/1?stored_fields=author,pages"
```

We will get the following output:

```
{
  "_index": "library",
  "_type": "book",
  "_id": "1",
  "_version": 1,
  "found": true,
  "fields": {
    "author": [
      "Ravi Kumar Gupta"
    ]
  }
}
```

All of the stored fields will be returned as arrays.

Delete API

The **Delete** API helps us to delete a document from the index. We can use the DELETE verb
for this purpose:

```
curl -XDELETE 'http://localhost:9200/library/book/1?pretty'
```

This will result in the following JSON:

```
{
  "found" : true,
  "_index" : "library",
```

```
        "_type" : "book",
        "_id" : "1",
        "_version" : 2,
        "result" : "deleted",
        "_shards" : {
          "total" : 2,
          "successful" : 1,
          "failed" : 0
        }
    }
```

If the document exists, the value of found will be true and it will delete the document.

Every write operation, including delete, will increase the version.

Update API

The **Update** API helps us to update a document. The update happens using a script that we provide. While updating, it gets the document from the index, runs the script on the document, and indexes back. Let's try to add a category to our book that we added earlier:

```
curl -XPOST 'http://localhost:9200/library/book/1/_update?pretty' -d '{
    "script" : {
        "inline" : "ctx._source.category = \"category\"",
        "lang": "painless",
        "params" : {
        "category" : "Technical"
      }
    }
}'
```

Earlier versions of Elasticsearch used groovy language for scripting by default. With the latest versions of Elasticsearch, such as 5.x, a new language for scripting is developed and embedded to Elasticsearch by default. This language is named as Painless and it has a similar syntax as groovy. We will be learning more about this later in this chapter. Wherever we need to use script, we can simply specify field lang with value as painless. We will be using painless script by default throughout the chapter.

In case you get a document missing error, it may be because you deleted the book with `id` 1 while trying previous operations in the *Delete API* section. Just add a book again to try this out.

Here, we are running an inline script that will add a `category` field if none exists. If a category field exists, it will update the field:

```
"inline" : "ctx._source.category = category"
```

In the preceding command, we are assigning `_source.category`. It will take value from the `param` category in `params`:

The `ctx` map contains `_index`, `_type`, `_id`, `_version`, `_routing`, `_parent`, `_timestamp`, `_ttl`, and `_source` variables.

Running the preceding command will result in the following JSON:

```
{
  "_index" : "library",
  "_type" : "book",
  "_id" : "1",
  "_version" : 2,
  "result" : "updated",
  "_shards" : {
    "total" : 2,
    "successful" : 1,
    "failed" : 0
  }
}
```

Now the book with `id` 1 will have `category` as `Technical`. In case, we need to delete a field, we can do so by using `ctx._source.remove()`:

```
$ curl -XPOST 'http://localhost:9200/library/book/1/_update?pretty' -d
' {
"script" : "ctx._source.remove("category")",
"lang" : "painless"
}
```

We can even put a condition and then do an update:

```
"inline" : "ctx._source.category.contains(category) ?
 ctx.op = "delete" : ctx.op = "none"
```

As per the preceding command, it will first check whether the category field contains a category named Technical, and if it does, then it will delete that document, otherwise do nothing.

We can also update a document partially and in this case, we need to provide only the field that we want to update:

```
$ curl -XPOST 'http://localhost:9200/library/book/1/_update?pretty' -d
'{
    "doc" : {
    "pages" : 250
  }
}'
```

The preceding code will update only the pages in the type book with id 1. The value is merged in this case. In case both script and doc are present, doc will be ignored and only script will run.

A document will be re-indexed only if source differs from the old one. If we want to always update the document even if source did not change, we can use detect_noop and set it to false:

```
$ curl -XPOST 'http://localhost:9200/library/book/1/_update?pretty' -d
'{
  "doc" : {
    "pages" : 250
  },
  "detect_noop" : false
}'
```

Refer to the following code:

```
$ curl -XPOST 'http://localhost:9200/library/book/3/_update?pretty' -d
'{
  "script" : {
    "inline" : "ctx._source.category = "category"",
    "lang": "painless",
    "params" : {
      "category" : "Technical"
        }
    },
     "upsert" : {
       "category" : "Technical"
    }
}'
```

If the document does not exist with the ID (3 in this case) supplied, then a new document will be created with values inside the `upsert`. We can also use `scripted_upsert` in which the script handles the initialization of the document instead of `upsert`. We should use `scripted_upsert` as `true`.

We can skip adding an `upsert` in case we want to use the content of `doc` as a new document. For this, we can set `doc_as_upsert` to `true` and skip adding `upsert` in the operation:

```
$ curl -XPOST 'http://localhost:9200/library/book/5/_update?pretty' -d
'{
    "doc" : {
     "pages" : 250
     },
    "doc_as_upsert" : true
  }'
```

Multi-document APIs

These APIs support operations on multiple documents. Similar to single document APIs, these can also be divided. Let's take a look at each of these.

Multi-get API

As the name suggests, this API helps us to get multiple documents at a time. We need to provide `index`, which is mandatory, `type`, which is optional, and `id`. If we want to get documents with ID 1 and 5, this is how we can do so:

```
$ curl -XGET 'http://localhost:9200/_mget?pretty' -d
'{
    "docs" : [
  {
    "_index" : "library",
  "_id" : 1
    },
   {
    "_index" : "library",
    "_id" : 5
    }
  ]
}'
```

We provide an array to the docs and as a result we get an array of documents. If we know that all the documents are going to be from the same index, then we can specify the index name in uri and use 'http://localhost:9200/library/_mget?pretty' instead of 'http://localhost:9200/_mget?pretty'.

And similarly for type as well. We can use 'http://localhost:9200/library/book/_mget?pretty instead of 'http://localhost:9200/_mget?pretty.

Now there is only _id, which is repeated. In such cases we can further change the request to include the ids parameter, which will contain an array of _id(s):

```
curl -XGET 'http://localhost:9200/library/_mget?pretty' -d  '{
  "ids" : [1, 5]
}'
```

Or as follows:

```
curl -XGET 'http://localhost:9200/library/book/_mget?pretty' -d '{
  "ids" : [1, 5]
}'
```

If we don't want to specify type field then we can either leave that empty or use _all, in which case it will bring the first document in the all type matching the specified ids.

In the result set, all documents will contain the source field as well. In case we want to skip source or want some fields only, we can use _source, _source_include, and _source_exclude as URL parameters as we did in the Get API on a single document. Possible usage for the source can be as shown in the following code:

```
curl -XGET 'http://localhost:9200/library/book/_mget?pretty' -d '{
  "docs" : [
  {
    "_index" : "library",
    "_id" : 1,
    "_source" : ["author"]
  },
  {
    "_index" : "library",
    "_id" : 5,
    "_source" : {
      "include" : ["author"],
      "exclude" : ["pages"]
         }
    }
  ]
```

```
        }'
```

In the first one we are trying to get only authors and excluding all others. The second example is also similar in a way as we are including only author and excluding pages.

Similarly, we can pass fields as well and an array of fields as value. Only `stored_fields` supplied in the array will be returned. We can even set a default list of `stored_fields` to be returned in the url and for each document as well:

```
$ curl 'http://localhost:9200/library/book/_mget?stored_fields=author'
-d '{
"docs" : [
{
    "_id" : 1
},
{
    "_id" : 5,
    "stored_fields":["pages"]
}
 ]
}'
```

The preceding operation will get the `author` field for all those documents for which fields are not defined explicitly. For a document with an `id` of `5`, only the `pages` field will be returned provided that the `pages` field is mapped as a stored field.

Bulk API

There are times when we need to do operations on a good amount of documents, the **Bulk** API comes in handy for such situations. We can do index, create, delete, and update with this API. We can use this API on:

```
/_bulk
/index/_bulk
/index/type/_bulk
```

Search APIs

These APIs help users to search into one or more indices. Let's get into these APIs in more detail.

Search API

This API allows us to search on one or more indices and zero or more types. The search operation can be done in two ways – putting query parameters in the search uri or by using the **Domain Specific Language (DSL)** query in the request body. The operation returns the number of hits, which shows the number of results.

Query parameters

Using this way, we use q= to specify the search parameters. For example, if we want to search for all the books with author containing gupta we can use the GET verb:

```
$ curl -XGET
'http://localhost:9200/library/_search?q=author:gupta&pretty'
```

This will result in the following JSON:

```
{
  "took" : 4,
  "timed_out" : false,
  "_shards" : {
    "total" : 5,
    "successful" : 5,
    "failed" : 0
  },
  "hits" : {
    "total" : 2,
    "max_score" : 0.37158427,
    "hits" : [ {
      "_index" : "library",
      "_type" : "book",
      "_id" : "AVSPSXXDxiIiqkaLJfTy",
      "_score" : 0.37158427,
      "_source" : {
        "author" : "Yuvraj Gupta",
        "title" : "Kibana Essentials",
        "pages" : 210
      }
    }, {
      "_index" : "library",
      "_type" : "book",
      "_id" : "1",
      "_score" : 0.2972674,
      "_source" : {
        "author" : "Ravi Kumar Gupta",
        "title" : "Test-Driven JavaScript Development",
        "pages" : 250,
```

```
        "category" : "Technical"
      }
    } ]
  }
}
```

As we can see, we got two hits for `Kibana Essentials` and `Test-Driven Javascript Development`.

Unlike `POST`/`PUT` operations, results from `GET` operations will be returning the total number of shards in the `_shards` section of the result.

In the previous call, we did not specify any type and if we want to, we can call the following:

```
$ curl -XGET 'http://localhost:9200/
library/book/_search?q=author:gupta&pretty'
```

If there are multiple indices or multiple types, we can search those using the following:

```
$ curl -XGET 'http://localhost:9200/
library,users/_search?q=author:gupta&pretty'
$ curl -XGET 'http://localhost:9200/
library/book,journal/_search?q=author:gupta&pretty'
```

> In case an index is not present, the `index_not_found_exception` exception will be thrown.

If we want to search into all indices and all types, we can skip specifying any in the `uri`:

```
$ curl -XGET 'http://localhost:9200/_search?q=author:gupta&pretty'
```

We can provide as many indices and types (comma separated) as we want.

Search shard API

This API helps us to get the indices and shards against which a search will be executed. While searching we can provide comma separate indices and types. To understand this, let's see the following `uri`:

```
$ curl -XGET 'http://localhost:9200/library/_search_shards?pretty'
```

This will return us all the shards available for searching and indexing. We can provide a routing value as well:

```
$ curl -XGET
'http://localhost:9200/library/_search_shards?pretty&routing=gupta'
```

Now we will get a short list because we have specified the routing value. We can specify multiple routing values (comma separated).

Multi-search API

This API allows us to do multiple search operations at a time. We need to provide a file that contains the header and body part of a search request. The header part specifies index, type to search on, `search_type`, preference, and routing. The body part contains the query, from, size, aggregations, and so on. For example, consider the following:

```
{"index" : "library", "type" : "book" }
{"query" : {"term" :{"author" : "gupta"}} }
```

In the preceding code, the first line is the header and the second line is the body part. There can be as many pairs as we want in the file. Once we have the queries ready, we can run the operation using the GET verb. Let's assume that we put all of our queries in a file named `queries`:

```
$curl -XGET 'http://localhost:9200/_msearch?pretty' --data-binary
@queries; echo
```

Using `--data-binary`, we can specify the file containing all headers and bodies. `@queries` is the filename.

Count API

As the name suggests, this API call results in the number of matches for a query. We can use the `_count` endpoint to get the number of results:

```
$ curl -XGET 'http://localhost:9200/library/book/_count?pretty' -d '{
"query" : {
"term" : {"author" : "gupta"}
}
}'
```

And the outcome of this operation will be as follows:

```
{
   "count" : 2,
   "_shards" : {
     "total" : 5,
```

```
        "successful" : 5,
        "failed" : 0
    }
}
```

The result shows that there are two matches across five shards.

Validate API

If we are running a query on sensitive data or it is going to be taking too much time or some other reason, what if we could validate the query first and then run it. This API helps us to know whether the query is a valid one before executing the query.

To use this API we can use the /_validate/query endpoint:

```
$ curl -XGET
'http://localhost:9200/library/book/_validate/query?pretty' -d '{
    "query" : {
      "term" : {"author" : "gupta"}
        }
}'
```

The operation will result in true or false for the valid field.

Explain API

This API explains the score calculation for a query and a specific document. We can use the /_explain endpoint for this purpose. In this operation we need to provide a single index and single type:

```
$ curl -XGET 'http://localhost:9200/library/book/1/_explain?pretty' -d
'{
   "query" : {
     "term" : {"author" : "gupta"}
   }
}'
```

We executed this on book with id 1 and for query where we expect gupta to be in author name.

Profile API

Sometimes we might encounter a slow-running query and this API can help us with the low level detail, to find which component of the query is taking time so that we can analyze and take action. This API is still an experiment in ES 5.x. To enable a profile on a call, use the following:

```
$ curl -XGET
"http://localhost:9200/library/_search?q=author:gupta&pretty" -d'
    {
       "profile": true
    }'
```

In the results, we usually have hits along with basic information, but now there will also be detailed profiling information. This will do profiling for each shard of the index being searched for the query we made. This contains the complete query execution details.

X-Pack also offers a profiler that can be referred to in Chapter 9, *X-Pack: Security and Monitoring* under the *Understanding Profiler* section.

Field stat API

This API gives us the statistics about one or more fields. We use the _field_stats endpoint for this purpose. For example:

```
$ curl -XGET 'http://localhost:9200/_field_stats?pretty&fields=pages'
```

The preceding operation is performed at the cluster level by default. Similar to fields, we can also use a level to define whether it will be cluster level or indices level. This results in how many shards, count, minimum value, maximum value, density, and so on:

```
{
  "_shards": {
    "total": 5,
    "successful": 5,
    "failed": 0
  },
  "indices": {
    "_all": {
      "fields": {
        "pages": {
          "type": "integer",
          "max_doc": 2,
          "doc_count": 2,
          "density": 100,
```

```
            "sum_doc_freq": -1,
            "sum_total_term_freq": 2,
            "searchable": true,
            "aggregatable": true,
            "min_value": 210,
            "min_value_as_string": "210",
            "max_value": 240,
            "max_value_as_string": "240"
          }
        }
      }
    }
  }
```

If you see any value as -1 that means the measurement for that field is not available for one or more shards.

This API is helpful for you to find out min, max values, count of terms, and so on. This API is also experimental and can be removed in future releases.

Indices APIs

The Indices API helps us to build and manage indices, settings, mappings, aliases, and templates. In this section, we will take a closer look at what it offers.

Managing indices

This section introduces the endpoints that help us to create, update, and delete indices and settings.

Creating an index

To create an index, we use the PUT verb with curl. While creating an index we can specify settings such as shards, mapping, aliases, and so on. To create an index with all default settings, we can use the following:

```
$ curl -XPUT 'localhost:9200/library'
```

This will try to create an index named library and if it can, the output will be:

```
{"acknowledged":true}
```

This operation will create five primary and five replica shards (one for each primary shard) for this index. We can change these settings, including mappings and aliases. Let's see a more complex example:

```
$ curl -XPUT 'http://localhost:9200/library' -d '{
"settings" : {
  "number_of_shards" : 2,
  "number_of_replicas" : 1
}
}'
```

This will create two primary shards and one replica for each primary shard for this index.

 If an index is already created and you try to create it again, you are likely to get index_already_exists_exception.

Checking if an index exists

We can use the HEAD verb with curl to check if an index exists. For example, if we want to check if a library index exists:

```
$ curl -XHEAD -i 'http://localhost:9200/library'
```

```
HTTP/1.1 200 OK
Content-Type: text/plain; charset=UTF-8
Content-Length: 0
```

If the status code is 404, that means the index does not exist.

Getting index information

We can get information about the index using the following:

```
$ curl -XGET 'localhost:9200/library?pretty'
```

This will show information about the library index, which includes aliases, mappings, settings, and warmers. Settings contain shard information, creation time, version, and so on:

```
{
  "library": {
    "aliases": {},
    "mappings": {
      "book": {
        "properties": {
```

```
        "author": {
          "type": "keyword",
          "store": true
        },
        "pages": {
          "type": "integer"
        },
        "title": {
          "type": "keyword",
          "store": true
        }
      }
    }
  },
  "settings": {
    "index": {
      "creation_date": "1484693593662",
      "number_of_shards": "5",
      "number_of_replicas": "1",
      "uuid": "kW1tscieT6OaWClNnhguAQ",
      "version": {
        "created": "5010199"
      },
      "provided_name": "library"
    }
  }
}
```

If there is no information available, an empty array will be returned as it did for aliases.

> If an index is not present and you try to get any information, you are likely to get index_not_found_exception.

Managing index settings

If we want to get just settings, we can use /{index}/_settings:

```
$ curl -XGET 'http://localhost:9200/library/_settings?pretty'
```

{index} can also take multiple indices as comma separated. We can also use wildcards to match indices.

We can also update settings after an index is created. We can use the same endpoint {index}/_settings with the PUT verb. The settings will be updated dynamically. *If we do not specify any, it will update settings for all indices*:

```
$ curl -XPUT 'http://localhost:9200/library/_settings?pretty' -d '{
  "index" : {
  "number_of_replicas" : 2
}
}'
```

The preceding operation will set two replica shards for each primary shard on the library index.

So far, we have seen operations on creating, editing, opening, and closing. For an index, we can also monitor the indices by checking statistics, shard stores, recovery info, and segments.

Getting index stats

This operation helps us to get stats about an index. It will show information about documents, index size, indexing stats, search, fielddata, flush, merge, request cache, refresh, suggest, translog, warmer, and other statistics. To get stats of an index, run the following:

```
$ curl -XGET 'http://localhost:9200/library/_stats?pretty'
```

We can supply comma separated multiple indices to get stats for multiple indices at a time. We can also specify which specific stats to get, as shown in the following command:

```
$ curl -XGET 'http://localhost:9200/library/_stats/docs,search?pretty'
```

Getting index segments

Using the _segment endpoint on one or more indices, we can get low-level segment information of an index:

```
$ curl -XGET 'http://localhost:9200/library/_segments?pretty'
```

Getting index recovery information

This API provides us information about index shard recoveries. This provides a very detailed view for each shard of an index. We can use the _recovery endpoint on one or more indices:

```
$ curl -XGET 'http://localhost:9200/library/_recovery?pretty'
```

Getting shard stores information

This API helps us to get shard stores for one or more indices. To get shard stores, we can use the _shard_stores endpoint:

```
$ curl -XGET 'http://localhost:9200/library/_shard_stores?pretty'
```

This will affect all of the shards and the following is one such shard:

```
"0" : {
        "stores" : [ {
          "re4j45-yTp6VZgMN7dP2Sg" : {
            "name" : "xB20COp",
        "ephemeral_id" : "SK9sdPOnRPuCKs51VtvNqg",
            "transport_address" : "127.0.0.1:9300",
            "attributes" : { }
          },
        "allocation_id" : "9I_4rywATD6CV8lqvFIFaA",
          "allocation" : "primary"
        }
          ]
        }
```

It shows the stores with node name, address, attributes, version, and allocation type for each store. *If you are running only one node, information about replica shards will not be present.*

Index aliases

Aliases are just like what we have in Unix OS. In Unix, they are for commands, here they are for indices.

We can create an alias for single or multiple indices. Once an alias is set and we use it instead of indices names in the API calls, Elasticsearch will replace the alias with the actual indices names and execute the operations. Aliasing is useful when we have many indices and we have a reason to group them.

For example, we have a production server set up that includes database, web, and application servers, and we have set up elastic stack to collect logs from all of those to put in Elasticsearch. Now there are other indices as well, but we want to perform some operation on all logs related indices. We can use an alias for all those indices, for example, prod_logs and then whatever operations we want to perform we can do so by simply using prod_logs in place of indices rather than typing in all of the indices. We can create aliases using the _aliases endpoint.

We can add and remove aliases for an index, as in the following snippet:

```
$ curl -XPOST 'http://localhost:9200/_aliases' -d '{
  "actions" : [
    { "add" : { "index" : "library", "alias" : "alias1" } },
    { "remove" : { "index" : "library", "alias" : "alias1" } }
  ]
}'
```

We can provide as many actions as we want. The first action we called for is to add an alias alias1 for index library and the second action removes it.

An alias name cannot be the same as an index name.

Mappings

When we add a document to an index, based on data inside the document, Elasticsearch creates mappings. These mappings help us identify and define whether the field should be a full text field, numeric, or date.

In Elasticsearch, to divide documents within an index into logical groups, every index has one or more mapping types. Every mapping types has meta-fields (_index, _type, _id, _source) and a list of fields for the type. Every field has a data type. These data types can be string, long, double, date, boolean, ip (IP address), object, nested, and specialized types related to geo locations – geo_point, geo_shape.

We can get mappings of an index using the _mapping endpoint on an index:

```
$ curl http://localhost:9200/library/_mapping?pretty
```

If there are multiple types and we want to get mappings for a specific type, use the {index}/_mapping/{type} endpoint:

```
$ curl http://localhost:9200/library/_mapping/book?pretty
```

This will output a properties map containing all of the fields:

```
{
  "library": {
    "mappings": {
      "book": {
        "properties": {
          "author": {
            "type": "text",
            "fields": {
              "keyword": {
                "type": "keyword",
                "ignore_above": 256
              }
            }
          },
          "pages": {
            "type": "long"
          },
          "title": {
            "type": "text",
            "fields": {
              "keyword": {
                "type": "keyword",
                "ignore_above": 256
              }
            }
          }
        }
      }
    }
  }
}
```

The book type contains these three fields and we can see that for each field there is a type defined along with other relevant properties.

We can also get mapping for specific field(s) using
{index}/_mapping/{type}/field/{fields}. Multiple fields can be supplied comma separated:

```
$ curl localhost:9200/library/_mapping/field/title?pretty
```

We can also check if a type exists using the HEAD verb:

```
$ curl -XHEAD -i 'http://localhost:9200/library/_mapping/book'
```

```
HTTP/1.1 200 OK
Content-Type: text/plain; charset=UTF-8
Content-Length: 0
```

Status code `200` acknowledges that the type exists, if it doesn't exist it would be `404`.

We can also add mappings using the *Put Mappings API*, which allows us to add a new type or new field.

To add a new type to an index, for example, `paper` to `library`, run the following:

```
$ curl -XPUT 'http://localhost:9200/library/_mapping/paper' -d'
{
      "properties": {
        "abstract": {
          "type": "string"
        }
      }
}'
```

Executing this will acknowledge `true` if it was successfully created. This will create a `paper` type with an `abstract` field to a `paper` mapping type.

Closing, opening, and deleting an index

Sometimes, we might want to stop read/write for a specific index for maintenance or recovery purpose. When an index is closed, it has no overhead on the cluster except maintaining its metadata. We can close/open index using `/{index}/_close` and `/{index}/_open`, respectively. To do so, we use the `POST` verb with `curl`:

```
$ curl -XPOST 'http://localhost:9200/library/_close'
$ curl -XPOST 'http://localhost:9200/library/_open'
```

If we don't want an index at all, we can also delete it using the `DELETE` verb:

```
$ curl -XDELETE 'http://localhost:9200/library'
```

This will delete the index from cluster like it was never there. We can also use wildcard to delete multiple indices, for example, to delete all indices with the name `textXXX`:

```
$ curl -XDELETE 'http://localhost:9200/test*'
```

This would see if there are any indices with a name starting with `test`, it will delete all those. In case there is no index present with the name `test` and we are using wildcards, we won't get any errors, but an acknowledgement:

```
{
    "acknowledged": true
}
```

But if we delete an index without wildcards and the index does not exist, we will get an exception – index_not_found_exception.

Other operations

There are more operations that this API supports such as clearing the cache, upgrading Elasticsearch indices, force merge, refresh, and flushing:

- **Clearing Cache**: The _cache/clear endpoint helps us to clear cache for one or more indices:

```
$ curl -XPOST "http://localhost:9200/library/_cache/clear"
```

- **Flush**: Using _flush helps us to free memory from one or more indices by clearing the transaction logs and by flushing data to index storage:

```
$ curl -XPOST "http://localhost:9200/library/_flush"
```

- **Refresh**: This API provides the _refresh endpoint to refresh one or more indices:

```
$ curl -XPOST "http://localhost:9200/library/_refresh"
```

- **Upgrade API**: This API helps us to upgrade indices from older Elasticsearch versions to new versions. We can use the _upgrade endpoint to upgrade one or more indices. This process will usually take time:

```
$ curl -XPOST 'http://localhost:9200/library/_upgrade?pretty'
```

This will give us the following output:

```
{
  "_shards": {
    "total": 15,
    "successful": 10,
    "failed": 0
  },
  "upgraded_indices": {
    "library": {
      "upgrade_version": "5.1.1",
      "oldest_lucene_segment_version": "6.3.0"
```

```
              }
          }
      }
```

As we can see, the library index was upgraded successfully and the version it is upgraded to is specified.

Cat APIs

This API helps us to print information nodes, indices, fields, tasks, and plugins in a human readable format rather than a JSON. It can also be visualized how tables are printed on console.

We will learn more about cat APIs in `Chapter 8`, *Elasticsearch APIs*, *The cat APIs* section.

Cluster APIs

These APIs allows us to know about cluster state, health, statistics, node statistics, and node information. We will learn about Cluster APIs in `Chapter 8`, *Elasticsearch APIs*, *The cluster APIs* section.

Query DSL

In this manner, we need to provide a request body with the `uri` just like we have been using for Document APIs. We can rewrite our author search query as follows:

```
$ curl -XGET 'http://localhost:9200/library/book/_search?pretty' -d '{
    "query" : {
      "term" : {"author" : "gupta"}
    }
}'
```

This query will return the same result. Whatever query parameters we defined using q=, we define them in `term`. To learn more about Query DSL, refer to
`https://www.elastic.co/guide/en/elasticsearch/reference/5.1/query-dsl.html`.

Aggregations

This framework is a very important part of Elasticsearch. As the name suggests, this framework helps us to do aggregations and generate analytic information on result of a search query. Aggregations help us to get better insight of the data. For example, if we take our library index into account, we can get answers to: How many books in a specific year, which technology, average book per year, and many more.

These aggregations show their power when it comes to gaining insight of system data on a dashboard. Most often system dashboards have aggregated data in form of charts. We will also be using aggregations in later chapters and those aggregations will help Kibana to generate useful visualizations.

There are two types of core aggregations: metrics and buckets. We will learn about these in this section.

Bucket

These aggregations create buckets of documents based on a criterion. These types of aggregations can also hold sub-aggregations. We will learn about sub-aggregations in this section.

To understand bucket aggregations, let's add another index for stones and a type named diamonds. The dataset is available at
`https://vincentarelbundock.github.io/Rdatasets/datasets.html`.

For your convenience, the used dataset is also bundled with this chapter and it is available with code files. If you want to try out the unmodified dataset, you can get it here
`https://vincentarelbundock.github.io/Rdatasets/csv/Ecdat/Diamond.csv`. A few samples from the dataset are as follows:

Carat	Cut	Color	Clarity	Price
0.23	Ideal	E	SI2	326
0.21	Premium	E	SI1	326
0.23	Good	E	VS1	327
0.29	Premium	I	VS2	334
0.31	Good	J	SI2	335

A row in this table shows data about one diamond. We have carat, cut, color, clarity, and price. There are other fields as well, but we have omitted those here for the sake of simplicity.

The Logstash config file to store this data into Elasticsearch is as follows:

 Logstash will be covered in `Chapter 3`, *Exploring Logstash and Its Plugins*.

```
input{
  file{
    path =>"/opt/elk/datasets/diamonds.csv"
    start_position =>"beginning"
  }
}
filter{
    csv{
      columns =>
                ["caret", "cut", "colour", "clarity", "depth",
"table", "price", "x", "y", "z"]
      separator => ","
    }
    mutate {
            convert => ["caret","float"]
            convert => ["depth","float"]
            convert => ["table","integer"]
            convert => ["price","integer"]
            convert => ["x","integer"]
            convert => ["y","integer"]
            convert => ["z","integer"]
    }
}
output {
        elasticsearch {
            index => "stones"
            document_type => "diamond"
            hosts => "localhost"
        }
}
```

In the preceding configuration, we have added a mutate section to convert fields to proper types. If we do not convert, Elasticsearch will set the string type for all the fields. Also, notice that we have added an index name as `stones` (a new index will be created for this name automatically if it does not exist already) and document type as `diamond`. This will create an index in Elasticsearch with the name stones and a type diamond to that index. If the index and type are already present, it will add data to those. We have not provided a port for Elasticsearch here and it will take a default port `9200`. To run Logstash using this configuration, run the following (assuming that the configuration file is named `logstash-diamond.conf` and placed inside the `conf` directory):

```
$ ./bin/logstash -f conf/logstash.diamonds.conf
```

The last command will create an index upon which we will be trying out the aggregations.

With our search query, if we add an aggregation, it will look like this:

```
"aggs" : {
  "<aggregation-name>" : {
    "<aggregation-type>" : {
      "field" : "<field-name>"
    }
  }
}
```

This is how we define an aggregation – using the `aggs` parameter (if we put aggregations instead of `aggs`, that'll work too). Apart from the `aggs` parameter, we need to provide a name for aggregation, a type we want to use, and finally we need to provide a field against which the data should be aggregated.

Let's create our first bucket aggregation – and in this, we want to put diamonds in buckets by clarity:

```
$ curl -XGET 'http://localhost:9200/stones/diamond/_search?pretty'
-d '{
  "aggs" : {
    "diamonds_by_clarity" : {
      "terms" : {
        "field" : "clarity"
      }
    }
  }
}'
```

You might get an `illegal_argument_exception` saying that Fielddata is disabled on text fields by default. Set fielddata=true on [clarity] in order to load fielddata in memory by uninverting the inverted index. Note that this can however use significant memory.

To enable fielddata on a field, for example, on `clarity`, use the following:

```
$ curl -XPUT "http://localhost:9200/stones/_mapping/diamond" -d'
{
  "properties": {
    "clarity": {
      "type":      "text",
      "fielddata": true
    }
  }
}'
```

This will create buckets of clarity and the output will be as follows:

```
"aggregations" : {
    "diamonds_by_clarity" : {
        "doc_count_error_upper_bound" : 0,
        "sum_other_doc_count" : 0,
        "buckets" : [ {
          "key" : "si1",
          "doc_count" : 13065
        }, {
          "key" : "vs2",
          "doc_count" : 12258
        }, {
          "key" : "si2",
          "doc_count" : 9193
        }, {
          "key" : "vs1",
          "doc_count" : 8171
        }, {
          "key" : "vvs2",
          "doc_count" : 5066
        }, {
          "key" : "vvs1",
          "doc_count" : 3655
        }, {
          "key" : "if",
          "doc_count" : 1790
        }, {
          "key" : "i1",
          "doc_count" : 741
        } ]
    }
```

}

As we can see, there are buckets for each unique value of clarity and the value becomes the key and count of all documents that appear as doc_count for each bucket.

Let's make it more complex by adding a metric aggregation as child aggregation of this:

```
$ curl -XGET 'http://localhost:9200/stones/diamond/_search?pretty' -d
'{
  "aggs" : {
    "diamonds_by_clarity" : {
      "terms" : {
        "field" : "clarity"
      },
      "aggs" : {
        "max_price" : {
          "max" : {
            "field" : "price"
          }
        }
      }
    }
  }
}'
```

To add a child aggregation, we just add one more aggs parameter inside the aggregation we created. max is a metric aggregation that we will learn about in the next section. Let's analyze the output of this one:

```
"buckets" : [ {
        "key" : "si1",
        "doc_count" : 13065,
        "max_price" : {
          "value" : 18818.0
        }
      }, {
        "key" : "vs2",
        "doc_count" : 12258,
        "max_price" : {
          "value" : 18823.0
        }
      },
   . . .
  ]
```

Each of the buckets will now contain max_price of the documents inside that bucket.

Let's take another example where we will use price range to analyze the data. As we can see, the price goes to max <19k, based on this let's define our price ranges from 0-5k, 5-10k, 10-14k, 14-16k, and 16-19k. The aggregation that we will use this time is the range aggregation:

```
$ curl -XGET 'http://localhost:9200/stones/diamond/_search?pretty' -d
'{
  "aggs" : {
    "price_ranges" : {
      "range" : {
        "field" : "price",
        "ranges" : [
          { "to" : 5000 },
          {"from" : 5000, "to" : 10000 },
          {"from" : 10000, "to" : 14000 },
          {"from" : 14000, "to" : 16000 },
          {"from" : 16000, "to" : 19000 }
        ]
      }
    }
  }
}'
```

We need to define ranges as well for this aggregation. The output will now contain buckets according to ranges defined:

```
"aggregations" : {
    "price_ranges" : {
      "buckets" : [ {
        "key" : "*-5000.0",
        "to" : 5000.0,
        "doc_count" : 39212
      }, {
        "key" : "5000.0-10000.0",
        "from" : 5000.0,
  "to" : 10000.0,
        "doc_count" : 9504
      }, {
        "key" : "10000.0-14000.0",
        "from" : 10000.0,
        "to" : 14000.0,
        "doc_count" : 3064
      }, {
        "key" : "14000.0-16000.0",
        "from" : 14000.0,
        "to" : 16000.0,
        "doc_count" : 1017
      }, {
```

```
                    "key" : "16000.0-19000.0",
                    "from" : 16000.0,
                    "to" : 19000.0,
                    "doc_count" : 1142
                }   ]
            }
        }
```

We can see that documents are now divided as per the ranges defined.

Before we do more with aggregations, let's put some more data into Elasticsearch. We are going to add a new type named movies to our library index. We will use the IMDB dataset, which can be downloaded from this URL:

https://vincentarelbundock.github.io/Rdatasets/csv/ggplot2/movies.csv.

We have removed the first column, which is S.No. in the CSV, and loaded the rest of the data using Logstash. This is the configuration file loaded:

```
        input{
          file{
            path =>"/ opt/elk/datasets/movies.csv"
            start_position =>"beginning"
          }
        }
        filter{
            csv{
              columns =>
                ["title", "year", "length", "budget", "rating", "votes",
  "r1votes", "r2votes", "r3votes", "r4votes", "r5votes", "r6votes",
  "r7votes", "r8votes", "r9votes", "r10votes", "mpaaRating", "action",
  "animation", "comedy", "drama", "documentary", "romance", "short"]
                separator => ","
              }
          mutate {
                  convert => ["year","integer"]
                  convert => ["budget","integer"]
                  convert => ["votes","integer"]
                  convert => ["rating","integer"]
                  convert => ["action","integer"]
                  convert => ["animation","integer"]
                  convert => ["comedy","integer"]
                  convert => ["drama","integer"]
                  convert => ["documentary","integer"]
                  convert => ["romance","integer"]
                  convert => ["short","integer"]
              }
          }
        }
```

```
output {
    elasticsearch {
        index => "library"
        document_type => "movies"
        hosts => "localhost"
    }
}
```

We can run this configuration just like we did for stones. The only change is that we have kept the index name the same as library and `document_type` as movies :

```
$ ./bin/logstash -f conf/logstash.movies.conf
```

Metrics aggregations

At the time of indexing, there are some numbers or values extracted and metrics aggregations compute those metrics from documents. There are single-valued and multi-valued numeric metrics. There are a number of aggregations available in this class, and in this section, we will learn about important metrics aggregations.

Avg aggregation

This single-value aggregation takes numeric values into account to calculate the average for aggregated documents. The values can be taken from specific fields or can also be a result of some script. This is a single-value metrics. For example, if we want to see average votes, we can use the following:

```
$ curl -XGET 'http://localhost:9200/library/movies/_search?pretty' -d
'{
  "aggs" : {
    "avg_votes" : { "avg" : { "field" : "votes" } }
  }
}'
```

This will return a number of records with the aggregation result:

```
{
  ...
  "aggregations" : {
      "avg_votes" : {
      "value" : 632.1034394774443
      }
    }
}
```

Min aggregation

This single-value aggregation returns the minimum value extracted from aggregated documents. For example, to find the minimum rating, use the following:

```
{
    "aggs" : {
        "min_rating" : { "min" : { "field" : "rating" } }
    }
}
```

Max aggregation

This single-value aggregation returns the maximum value extracted from aggregated documents. For example, to find the maximum rating, use the following:

```
{
  "aggs" : {
    "max_rating" : { "max" : { "field" : "rating" } }
  }
}
```

Percentiles Aggregation

It is a multi-value aggregation that generates percentile over a numeric field. For example, we are getting percentiles on a rating field.

To get percentile for rating, use the following:

```
{
  "aggs" : {
    "rating_percentiles" : {
      "percentiles" : { "field" : "rating" }
    }
  }
}
```

This will result in the following:

```
{
    ...
    "aggregations" : {
      "rating_percentiles" : {
        "values" : {
                "1.0" : 1.0,
```

```
                        "5.0"  :  3.0,
                        "25.0" :  5.0,
                        "50.0" :  6.0,
                        "75.0" :  7.0,
                        "95.0" :  8.0,
                        "99.0" :  9.0
                    }
                }
            }
        }
```

Sum aggregation

It is a single-value aggregation. This aggregation returns the sum of the extracted values on a field. For our dataset, we want to find the number of comedy movies:

```
$ curl -XGET 'http://localhost:9200/library/movies/_search?pretty' -d
'{
  "aggs" : {
    "total_comedy_movies" : { "sum" : { "field" : "comedy" } }
  }
}'
```

The preceding code will result in the following:

```
"aggregations" : {
    "total_comedy_movies" : {
        "value" : 17271.0
    }
}
```

Value count aggregation

It is a single-value aggregation. This aggregation results in the number of documents for that search and the field. For example, to get the count of the movies released in 2000, run the following:

```
$ curl -XGET
'http://localhost:9200/library/movies/_search?pretty&q=year:2000'
    -d '{
    "aggs" : {
      "total_rated_movies" : { "value_count" : { "field" : "rating" } }
    }
}'
```

Cardinality aggregation

This is also a single-value metrics aggregation. This can be visualized as a distinct query on a relational database. Let's say if we want to get the number of unique clarity in the movies index, we can use this aggregation:

```
$ curl 'http://localhost:9200/library/movies/_search?pretty' -d '{
  "aggs" : {
    "years" : {
      "cardinality" : {
        "field" : "year"
      }
    }
  }
}'
```

This will result in a count of unique clarity in the index:

```
"aggregations" : {
    "years" : {
      "value" : 68
    }
}
```

Stats aggregation

When calculated, this multi-valued aggregation returns min, max, sum, count, and avg on that field.

To calculate status on votes, run the following:

```
$ curl -XGET 'http://localhost:9200/library/movies/_search?pretty' -d
'{
  "aggs" : {
    "stats_votes" : { "stats" : { "field" : "votes" } }
  }
}'
```

This will result in the following output:

```
"aggregations" : {
    "stats_votes" : {
      "count" : 58787,
      "min" : 5.0,
      "max" : 149494.0,
      "avg" : 629.4601357442972,
      "sum" : 3.7004073E7
```

```
            }
        }
```

Extended stats aggregation

This multi-valued aggregation extends stats aggregation. Apart from min, max, count, sum, and avg, this aggregation adds `sum_of_squares`, `variance`, `std_deviation`, and `std_deviation_bounds`. For example, let's calculate extended stats on votes:

```
$ curl -XGET 'http://localhost:9200/library/movies/_search?pretty' -d
'{
  "aggs" : {
    "extended_stats_votes" : { "extended_stats" : { "field" : "votes" }
  }
}'
```

This will result in the following output:

```
"aggregations" : {
    "extended_stats_votes" : {
        "count" : 58787,
        "min" : 5.0,
        "max" : 149494.0,
        "avg" : 629.4601357442972,
        "sum" : 3.7004073E7,
        "sum_of_squares" : 8.60820897863E11,
        "variance" : 1.4246828534358414E7,
        "std_deviation" : 3774.4971233739752,
        "std_deviation_bounds" : {
            "upper" : 8178.4543824922475,
            "lower" : -6919.534111003653
        }
    }
}
```

We will be learning more about these aggregations in the following chapters with examples, for example, we will be using geolocation related aggregation in Chapter 12, *Case Study-Meetup* along with term, range aggregations, and much more.

A note for painless scripting

There are times when we use scripts, update data, scripted fields, and many more use cases. Prior to version 5.x, groovy was the default language for your scripts. We even did not specify which scripts we wanted to use back then. Since these scripts were executed remotely security was always a concern that Elastic Team had to address. This became the reason for designing **Painless**.

Painless is both secure and efficient when it comes to performance. It has a similar syntax as of Groovy so it is also easy to learn and use. For most of the cases, you don't need to make changes to your previously written scripts. All you need to add is a parameter called `lang` and specify the value as `painless`.

To define a variable in painless, simply use the following:

```
def myVar = 'my-value';
```

We don't need to specify any type. At runtime, the type of variable will be detected whatever suits appropriate. Painless supports all variable types defined by Java.

To define an array, use the following:

```
int[]
```

To define a list, use the following:

```
def nums = [1, 2, 3, 4, 5]
nums[0] // 1st element
nums[-1] // last element of the list
```

Similarly, map can also be defined:

```
def book = ['name': 'Java', 'pages': 450];
book.name // refers to Java
```

To loop through, use the following:

```
for(item:nums) { .. }
```

To further understand how to use this, we will use our index library, which has books. Let's consider that five pages are added to each book at the end for advertisement purposes. All the books in the library must be updated to add five more pages in the page count. To achieve this, we can use the `update_by_query` endpoint from the Document API:

```
curl -XPOST "http://localhost:9200/library/book/_update_by_query" -d'
{
```

```
    "script": {
      "inline": "ctx._source.pages += 5",
      "lang": "painless"
    },
    "query": {
      "match_all": {
      }
    }
}
```

In this simple example, we have just taken `ctx._source` and updated the pages to add five pages for each book by querying using `match_all`.

Let's add some more complexity to it. If all of the books had a publication field as well, similar to the book in the following document:

```
curl -XPUT "http://localhost:9200/library/book/41/_create?pretty" -d'
{
  "author" : "Ravi Kumar Gupta",
  "title" : "Test-Driven JavaScript Development",
  "pages" : 240,
  "publication" : "packt"
}'
```

Now, if we want to update pages by adding five more, but only for those books that were published by Packt, then we can use the following condition:

```
curl -XPOST "http://localhost:9200/library/book/_update_by_query" -d'
{
  "script": {
    "inline": "if(ctx._source.publication == \"packt\"))"
    ctx._source.pages += 5",
    "lang": "painless"
  },
  "query": {
    "match_all": {
    }
  }
}'
```

Similarly, loop and other facilities provided by Painless can be utilized as script. A complete documentation for Painless scripting can be found at – https://www.elastic.co/guide/en/elasticsearch/reference/5.1/modules-scripting-painless.html.

Summary

In this chapter, we learned about Elasticsearch architecture and the way Elasticsearch was born. Later we got familiar with Elasticsearch APIs – Search, Indices, and Document. With the help of these APIs we learned how to add documents to Elasticsearch, how to query those documents, managing the indices. At the end of the chapter, aggregations show how to effectively search documents. We will be practicing these concepts in the next chapters with more examples.

In the next chapter, we will learn about Logstash, and how to configure Logstash for complex data types, and Logstash plugins.

3

Exploring Logstash and Its Plugins

In the previous chapter, we learned a lot about Elasticsearch, its features, its architecture, and the various APIs it provides. We learned in detail about how to use the APIs exposed and the functionalities provided by the APIs. Now that we have explored Elasticsearch, let us explore another popular component, namely, Logstash. In this chapter, we will focus on exploring the various components of Logstash. We will understand the need for Logstash, Logstash flow architecture, and the usage of various plugins.

By the end of this chapter, you will understand the need for Logstash, the Logstash workflow, the configuration and the various plugins present.

In this chapter, we will cover the following topics:

- Introduction to Logstash
- Logstash Plugin Architecture
- Logstash Configuration File Structure
- Types of Plugins
- Exploring Input Plugins
- Exploring Filter Plugins
- Exploring Output Plugins
- Exploring Codec Plugins
- Plugins Command-Line Options
- Logstash Command-Line Options

- Logstash Configuration for Parsing Logs
- Monitoring APIs

Introduction to Logstash

Logstash started as a brainchild project of Jordan Sissel, who has a background in operations and system administration. He was always challenged to find insights from logs. Once, he wanted to stream a large number of logs per second, however, he was unable to find a suitable free tool or project fit for his use case. At that time, he took the challenge into his hands and started building Logstash to provide a tool for users to handle the streaming of large numbers of logs per second; and combined it with powerful functionalities to fetch relevant information from the logs. One of the premises of Logstash was to build a centralized system to gather logs from multiple systems so that managing logs from multiple sources became easy for further processing and aggregating the logs.

Logstash started as an individual product but later, as Elasticsearch was growing, Jordan Sissel joined Elastic. to develop Logstash actively. Since then, there has been no looking back, as Logstash has become a core component of Elastic Stack, creating a comprehensive platform for collecting data from multiple sources, logging data, analyzing log data, storing the data, and visualizing the data as a single pipeline connected with multiple components. Logstash has some powerful functionalities and real-time data collection capabilities, which makes it a comprehensive tool for processing logs. Logstash is an open source log-management tool that is part of Elastic Stack, providing a fully open source solution for end-to-end log management.

Why do we need Logstash?

Logstash mainly started as a project for managing logs, but it has since been extended to analyze any type of data, be it event data, timestamped data, application logs, transactional data, CSV data, file input, and so on. Data can be structured, unstructured, or semi-structured, which makes it difficult to convert the data into a proper format. To manage logs of different types coming in from different systems, we require a tool which is powerful in handling the various different types of log data and analyzing it in near-real-time to generate insights from the log data. Logstash helps you to collect data from multiple systems into a central system wherein data can be parsed and processed as required. Also, Logstash helps you to gather the data from multiple systems and store the data in a common format, which is easily used by Elasticsearch and Kibana.

Logstash allows you to pipeline data, which can be extracted, cleansed, transformed, and loaded to gain valuable insights from the data. In such a way, Logstash does the work of **Extract, Transform, and Load** (ETL) , a popular term used in data warehousing and business intelligence domains. Logstash extracts the data from multiple systems, performs some operations to process or transform the log, such as filtering data, removing fields, adding fields, grokking data, and so on, followed by loading the processed data.

Logstash is often referred to as a *Swiss Army knife*, as it can process any type of data and, due to the fact that it contains a wide range of inputs for inputting data from different sources, filters to transform the data, and outputs to store the data, making Logstash a go-to tool for all your data.

Let's have a look at some of the key features of Logstash.

Features of Logstash

Among the various features of Logstash, we will have a look at the key features that differentiate Logstash other log management tools:

- **Open source**: Logstash is completely free to use and is an open source tool whose source code is available freely on GitHub.
- **Seamless integration with Elasticsearch, Beats, and Kibana**: This is a powerful data processing pipeline which is tightly coupled to fetch data from multiple systems using Beats, store the data for real-time search capabilities in Elasticsearch, and visualize the stored data using Kibana.
- **Extensibility**: Logstash provides a variety of inputs, filters, and outputs to use for processing logs of different types. It provides flexibility to create and develop inputs, filters, or outputs for Logstash, which are easy to create and developer-friendly.
- **Interoperability**: Logstash provides the interoperability to use it with various other components and tools. Logstash can fetch data from various different tools and output the data into various different tools, making it easier to use Logstash as part of a complex workflow.
- **Pluggable data pipeline architecture**: Logstash contains over 200 plugins developed by Elastic. and the community which can be used. Logstash is designed as a generic framework wherein you mix and match the inputs or filters or output and it will process the data accordingly. It uses a format of configuration file to use various plugins.

It is the crux and the heart behind the architecture of Logstash as it provides greater flexibility. To understand it better, let's take a look at the following example:

Suppose there is a new tool or software that you use to store data. Logstash currently doesn't support an output connector to store your data in that. Having a pluggable architecture, you can easily develop a plugin wherein you write a piece of code to store data in the required tool using a set of parameters. After creating a plugin, you can use that plugin directly in Logstash. Without a need to go through the Logstash source code, you have easily developed a plugin, which has extended Logstash, and you can leverage its processing capabilities.

Logstash Plugin Architecture

The Logstash pipeline consists of input, filter, and output plugins. Let's have a look at the following diagram to understand how Logstash uses the plugins:

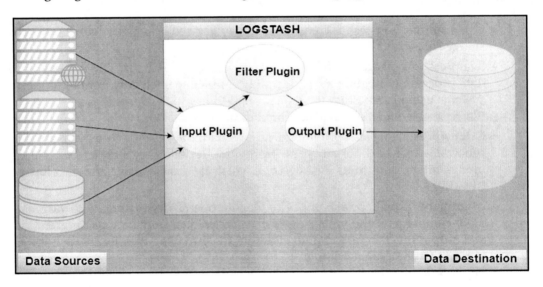

In the preceding architecture, we can see that there can be multiple data sources from which data is collected, which constitutes as Logstash **Input Plugin**. After getting input, we can use the **Filter Plugin** to transform the data and we can store output or write data to a destination using the **Output Plugin**.

Logstash uses a configuration file to specify the plugins for getting input, filtering data, and storing output. The **Input Plugin** and **Output Plugin** are mandatory to specify in the configuration file whereas the **Filter** plugin is optional to use. If you have input data and without transforming or modifying the data, you can directly store the data in the destination, then in this case filter plugin is not required.

The architecture can be simplified as shown in the following diagram:

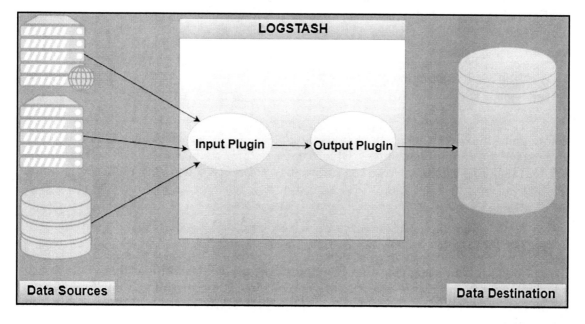

Now that we understand the Logstash architecture, let's have a look at the configuration file, wherein we define the various plugins to use for input, filter, and output.

Logstash Configuration File Structure

A Logstash configuration file contains three sections for specifying each type of plugin we want to use. The three sections are input, filter, and output. Consider the following example:

```
input {

    }
filter {

    }
```

```
output {

    }
```

Each section contains the configuration for single or multiple plugins. To configure a plugin, provide the plugin name inside the section, followed by the settings or parameters of that plugin. It is specified in terms of key => value pair. **For each section, if you define multiple plugins, then the order of execution is the order in which they appear in the configuration file.** Each plugin has its own set of settings, which needs to be used with the plugin name.

 The => sign is an assignment operator which assigns the value to the key in the configuration file.

Before going into depth about the various plugins available in each of the sections, let's understand the various value types, which can be defined as the value of the settings in the configuration file, and how to use conditions for conditional statements in the configuration file.

Value types

Every Logstash plugin contains a set of settings to be used. Some settings that are mandatory to specify are marked as required fields. For each setting, we define a value, which is as per the different value types supported by Logstash. The various available value types are discussed in the following sections.

Array

This is a collection of one or more values.

For a single value, the syntax is as follows:

```
Key => "value"
```

For multiple values, the syntax is as follows:

```
Key => ["value1","value2","value3"]
```

If you specify the same settings multiple times in an array, the values get appended to the array, as shown here:

```
Key => "value"
Key => "value1"
Key => ["value2","value3","value4"]
```

The key will contain all the five values, that is, `value`, `value1`, `value2`, `value3`, and `value4`.

Boolean

This is used to specify the value as either `true` or `false`.

For example:

```
Key => true
Key1 => false
```

> The value of a Boolean type, that is, `true` or `false`, must not be disclosed in quotes.

Bytes

A byte is a string type field (enclosed in double quotes), which is used to represent a unit of bytes. It uses both the **International System of Units (SI Units)** (kB, MB, or GB) and binary units (KiB, MiB, or GiB) to calculate the bytes. It is used to define the value followed by the unit. It is case insensitive and also accepts a space between the value of the key and the unit. Also, SI units are based on base-1000, whereas binary units are based on base-1024, that is to say, 1 kB = 1000 bytes, whereas 1 KiB = 1024 bytes.

For example:

```
size => "2467KiB"
size => "9872miB"
Key => "452 GB"
```

> If no unit is specified, then the value represents the number of bytes.

```
Key => "1234"
```

Codec

A `codec` is not a value type but is used to represent the data. It is used to decode the data coming from the input and encode the data before going to the output. It eliminates the need to have an additional filter to specify how the data is:

```
codec => "plain"
```

Comments

This is not a value type but is used to define a comment in the configuration file. Its syntax is the same as that used in Perl, Python, or Ruby. It is specified by #. It can appear anywhere in the line:

```
Key => "value" #It is string value type
#Hope you are learning
```

Hash

A hash is a collection of key-value pairs, wherein both the key and the value are specified within double quotes. Multiple entries of key-value pairs are not separated by commas, but are instead separated by spaces:

```
match => {
   "field1" => "value1"
   "field2" => "value2"
   ...
}
```

Number

A number must contain valid numeric values of either an integer or float type:

```
number => 44
amount => 1.28
```

String

A string contains a value which can be enclosed either in single or double quotes. If the string value contains the same quote as the string specifier, then it needs to be escaped with a backslash:

```
name => "yuvraj"
escape => "value"ue"
single => 'Hello It's nice you are reading it'
```

Use of Conditionals

Conditionals are used to check for conditions based on which action can be taken. In the case of configuration files, we can check for conditions in the plugins based on which settings or configuration will be used. It is handled in a similar way to other programming languages and it supports if, else, and else if statements.

The structure of the configuration file is as follows:

```
if EXPRESSION {
    ...
} else if EXPRESSION {
    ...
} else {
    ...
}
```

Expressions contain operators such as comparison operators, Boolean operators, and unary operators. The comparison operators are subdivided into equality operators, regex operators, and inclusion operators:

- **Equality operators**: Equality operators contain the following list of operators: ==, !=, <, >, <=, and >=
- **Regex operators**: Regex operators contain the following list of operators: =~ and !~
- **Inclusion operators**: Inclusion operators contain the following list of operators: in and not in
- **Boolean operators**: Boolean operators contain the following list of operators: and, or, nand, and xor
- **Unary operators**: Unary operators contain the following list of operators: !

We will have a look at how to use these operators in the examples set out throughout this chapter.

As described previously, Logstash configuration is divided into multiple sections. Let's have a look at the various plugins available for use within these sections.

Types of Plugins

Let's have a look at some of the plugins in the following sections.

Input plugins

The various `input` plugins available in Logstash are shown in the following figure:

Refer to the link: `https://www.elastic.co/guide/en/logstash/5.1/input-plugins.html`

Filter plugins

The various `filter` plugins available in Logstash are as follows:

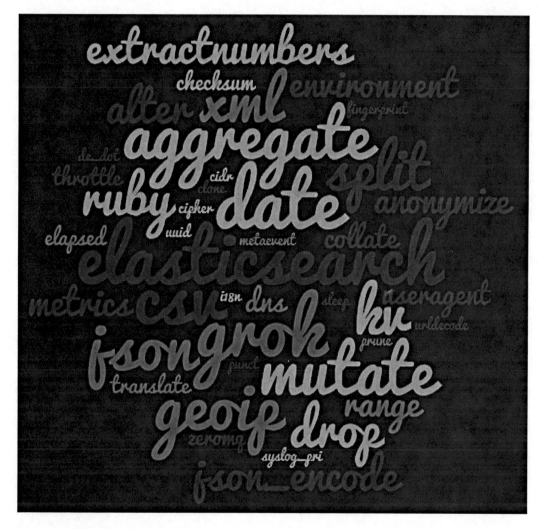

Refer to the link: `https://www.elastic.co/guide/en/logstash/5.1/filter-plugins.html`

Output plugins

The various `output` plugins available in Logstash are as follows:

Refer to the link: `https://www.elastic.co/guide/en/logstash/5.1/output-plugins.html`

As we have covered the different sections of plugins available in configuration file i.e. Input, Filter and Output Plugin. But, there is another set of plugin which doesn't have a different section altogether but it is part of Input and Output Plugin.

Codec plugins

The `Codec` plugins are part of the input or output that change the representation of data of an event. They can be called stream-filters, as they provide ways to encode or decode the data flowing in or out of Logstash.

The various codec plugins available in Logstash are as follows:

Refer to the link: `https://www.elastic.co/guide/en/logstash/5.1/codec-plugins.htm l`

Exploring Input Plugins

An input plugin is used to get data from a source or multiple sources and to feed data into Logstash. It acts as the first section, which is required in the Logstash configuration file. Some of the input plugins are described in the following sections.

stdin

The stdin is a fairly simple plugin, which reads the data from a standard input. It reads the data we enter in the console, which then acts as an input to Logstash. This is mostly used to validate whether the installation of Logstash is done properly and whether we are able to access Logstash.

The basic configuration for stdin is as follows:

```
stdin {
}
```

In this plugin, no additional settings are mandatory. If we use the preceding configuration, whatever we write in the console will be taken as input, without any additional parameters.

The additional configuration settings are as follows:

- add_field: This is used to add a field to the incoming data.
- codec: This is used to decode the incoming data and to interpret in what format the data is coming as input. Possible values of codec are all the codec plugins that are present.
- enable_metric: It is used to get metric values from each plugin for reporting of a plugin.
- id: It is used to provide a unique identifier to a plugin which can be used to track information of a plugin and can be used for debugging.
- tags: This is used to add a tag to the incoming data, which can be used for processing. For similar types of events, data from a given source can be tagged for processing. It is mostly used with conditionals, which helps to perform various sets of actions as per the tags.
- type: This is used to add a type field for the incoming data. It is very useful when we have data coming in from different sources wherein we can mention the type to differentiate the data among the sources. It is mainly used while filtering, wherein we can mention different logic for different sources of data while using the type field.

The value type and default values for the settings are as follows:

Setting	Value type	Default value
add_field	Hash	{}
codec	Codec	"line"
enable_metric	Boolean	true
id	String	No default value
tags	Array	No default value
type	String	No default value

Configuration example:

```
input {
        stdin {
                add_field => {"current_time" => "%{@timestamp}" }
                codec => "json"
                tags => ["stdin-input"]
                type => "stdin"
                  }
        }
```

In the preceding configuration, we have mentioned the codec as JSON; therefore, our input has to be in JSON format. When we enter anything in JSON, it will be parsed as per the key-value pair and will add a field called current_time, whose value will be that of a timestamp field, which is a metadata field. If we input in any other format apart from JSON, then it will give us _jsonparsefailure in tags, along with the stdin-input tag.

file

The file plugin is one of the most common plugins used for getting inputs from a file. It streams the data from a file or files similar to using tail -f, but with additional capabilities. It is a powerful plugin as it keeps track of any changes in the files, the last location from which the file was read, sends updated files with data, detects file rotations, and provides options to read a file from the beginning or end.

It keeps information about the current position from which it fetched data from the files in a file called `sincedb`. By default, it is placed in the `$HOME` directory, but the location can be changed using the `sincedb_path` setting. The frequency for tracking files can be changed using the `sincedb_write_interval` setting.

The basic configuration for `file` is as follows:

```
file {
    path => ...
}
```

In this plugin, only the `path` setting is mandatory.

path

This specifies the location of either the directory or the filename from where files will be read. You can provide either the name of the directory, the name of a particular file, or the filename patterns to find. You can specify single or multiple patterns/locations to find.

The `path` plugin defined must be absolute and not relative.

The additional configuration settings are as follows:

- `add_field`: This is used to add a field to the incoming data.
- `close_older`: This is used to close the input file if it was last modified more than the specified settings. It frees the file I/O operations and it repeatedly checks the file for changes. If a file is being tailed and data is not coming and crosses the specified settings limit, then the file will be closed so that other files can be opened. It will be queued and reopened whenever the file is updated or modified.
- `codec`: This is used to decode the incoming data and to interpret in what format the data is coming as input.
- `delimiter`: This is used as a separator to identify different lines.
- `discover_interval`: This is used to define the setting that determines how often the `path` will be expanded to search for new files created inside the `path`.
- `enable_metric`: This is used to get metric values from each plugin for the reporting of a plugin.

- `exclude`: This is used to exclude any file or file patterns that will not be read as an input.
- `id`: This is used to provide a unique identifier to a plugin which can be used to track information of a plugin and can be used for debugging.
- `ignore_older`: This is used to ignore reading the files that have not been modified since the time as mentioned in the settings. Even if the file is ignored, it is read as if files have been modified or updated with new content.
- `max_open_files`: It is used to define the maximum number of files which can be opened at a time. If there are more files to be read than the specified number, then use `close_older` to close the files which have not been modified lately. Setting the value of this property as very high will cause OS performance issues.
- `sincedb_path`: This is used to define the file location for writing `sincedb` files for tracking log files.
- `sincedb_write_interval`: This specifies the time interval in which `sincedb` files will be written, to include the current position read for tracking multiple log files.
- `start_position`: This is used to determine whether to read the file from the **beginning or the end**. It is initially used only when the file is being read for the first time and does not have an entry in the `sincedb` file. If your file contains older data, then you can read the file by specifying the start position as beginning.
- `stat_interval`: This is used to check whether files have been modified or not. Increasing the interval will lead to fewer calls made by the system, but it will increase the interval to track changes in the log files.
- `tags`: This is used to add a tag to the incoming data, which can be used for processing. It is mostly used with conditionals, which helps to perform various sets of actions, as per the `tags`.
- `type`: This is used to add a `type` field for the incoming data. It is very useful when we have data coming in from different sources wherein we can mention the `type` to differentiate the data among the sources. It is mainly used while filtering, wherein we can mention different logic for different sources of data while using the `type` field.

The value type and default values for the settings are as follows:

Setting	Value type	Default value
add_field	Hash	{}
close_older	Number	3600
codec	Codec	"plain"
delimiter	String	"n"
discover_interval	Number	15
enable_metric	Boolean	true
exclude	Array	No default value
id	String	No default value
ignore_older	Number	No default value
max_open_files	Number	No default value
path	Array	No default value
sincedb_path	String	$HOME/.sincedb*
sincedb_write_interval	Number	15
start_position	String	"end"
stat_interval	Number	1
tags	Array	No default value
type	String	No default value

Configuration example:

```
input {
        file {
                path => ["/var/log/elasticsearch/*","/var/messages/*.log"]
                add_field => ["[location]", "%{longitude}" ]
                add_field => ["[location]", "%{latitude}" ]
                exclude => ["*.txt"]
                start_position => "beginning"
                tags => ["file-input"]
                type => "filelogs"
                }
        }
```

In the preceding configuration, we have mentioned a couple of paths from which files will be read. It will read all the files present within the elasticsearch directory and read files ending with a LOG extension present within the messages folder. Assuming the file contains latitude and longitude, add a location field, which will contain the values of longitude and latitude (the format in which Kibana reads geoip). We are excluding all the text files. We are telling Logstash to read the files from the beginning as they already contain data we want to read.

The preceding configuration can be divided into two different files wherein path values will be different, based on which we can specify the different tags and the different types, as shown in the following code snippet:

```
input {
        file {
                path => "/var/log/elasticsearch/*"
                tags => ["elasticsearch"]
                type => "elasticsearch"
                 }
        file {
                path => "/var/messages/*.log"
                tags => ["messages"]
                type => "message"
                 }

        }
```

udp

The udp plugin is one which reads the data as messages over the network using the UDP protocol. It lists the port from which it reads the event.

The basic configuration for udp is as follows:

```
udp {
     port => ...
}
```

In this plugin, only the port setting is mandatory:

- port: This is the port on which Logstash will listen to the incoming events or messages.

If using a port number less than `1024`, then it will require root privileges to use.

The additional configuration settings are as follows:

- `add_field`: This is used to add a field to the incoming data.
- `buffer_size`: This is used to define the maximum packet size to read from the network.
- `codec`: This is used to decode the incoming data and to interpret in what format the data is coming in as input.
- `enable_metric`: This is used to get metric values from each plugin for reporting of a plugin.
- `host`: This is used to specify the hostname Logstash will listen to.
- `id`: This is used to provide a unique identifier to a plugin which can be used to track information of a plugin and can be used for debugging.
- `queue_size`: This is used to specify the maximum number of unprocessed packets that can be held in memory. If the number of packets becomes greater than `queue_size`, then the data will be lost.
- `receive_buffer_bytes`: This is used to specify the receiving buffer size in bytes. If not set, then the OS default value will be used.
- `tags`: This is used to add a tag to the incoming data, which can be used for processing. It is mostly used with conditionals, which helps to perform various sets of actions, as per the `tags`.
- `type`: This is used to add a `type` field for the incoming data. It is very useful when we have data coming in from different sources wherein we can mention the `type` to differentiate data among sources. It is mainly used while filtering, wherein we can mention different logic for different sources of data while using the `type` field.
- `workers`: This is used to define the number of threads that will process the packets at once.

The value types and default values for the settings are as follows:

Setting	Value type	Default value
`add_field`	Hash	{}
`buffer_size`	Number	65536

codec	Codec	"plain"
enable_metric	Boolean	true
host	String	"0.0.0.0"
id	String	No default value
port	Number	No default value
queue_size	Number	2000
receive_buffer_bytes	Number	No default value
tags	Number	No default value
type	Array	No default value
workers	String	2

Configuration example:

```
input {
        udp {
                host => "192.168.0.6"
                port => 5000
                workers => 4
                 }
        }
```

In the preceding configuration, we have mentioned the host and port from which Logstash will read the events. Also, we specified workers as 4, which means there will be 4 threads which will process the packets in parallel.

Exploring Filter Plugins

A filter plugin is used to perform transformations on the data. If your input fetches data based on what you want to process the data, then a filter plugin will help you to do so before sending the output. It acts as the intermediate section between input and output, which is required in the Logstash configuration file.

Let's have a look at few of the filter plugins.

grok

The `grok` plugin is the most commonly used filter in Logstash and has powerful capabilities to transform your data from unstructured to structured data. Even if your data is structured, you can streamline the data using this pattern. Due to the powerful nature of the grok pattern, Logstash is referred to as a Swiss Army Knife. Grok is used to parse the data and structure the data in the way you want. It is used to parse any type of log that is in human-readable format. It combines the text patterns into a structure that helps you to match the logs and group them into fields. Logstash ships with more than 120 grok patterns, which you can readily use, and you can even create your own patterns to match with grok.

 Grok patterns can be found at
`https://github.com/logstash-plugins/logstash-patterns-core/tree/master/patterns`. They are also present within the Logstash installation folder and can be found by searching for the grok patterns file.

The basic syntax for a grok pattern is as follows:

```
%{SYNTAX:SEMANTIC}
```

Here, SYNTAX is the name of the pattern that matches the data and SEMANTIC is the identifier or the field name that provides you with a matched pattern, as defined in the syntax.

With grok, you can use the regular expressions, or you can even create custom patterns. The regular expression library used is **Oniguruma**, whose regex syntax is available at `https://github.com/kkos/oniguruma/blob/master/doc/RE`. You can even create a custom patterns file, which contains your custom-created patterns to match the data. Grok matches the data from left to right and matches the pattern one by one.

Let's have a look at a few log lines and apply grok patterns to them.

Pick a sample log line:

```
Log line: Jun 19 02:11:30 This is sample log.
```

Let us use existing grok patterns to create a matching grok pattern for the preceding log line:

```
%{CISCOTIMESTAMP:timestamp} %{GREEDYDATA:log}
```

Now let's have a look at their specified patterns to understand them:

```
CISCOTIMESTAMP %{MONTH} +%{MONTHDAY}(?: %{YEAR})? %{TIME}
GREEDYDATA .*
```

This looks so tough to come up with. How do I know which pattern matches my data?

I agree, it's difficult to know which patterns are available and which patterns to match. But don't worry; your friends will help you to discover your pattern initially on which you can modify as per requirement. You can visit either of the following two websites for help related to building patterns to match the data:

- http://grokdebug.herokuapp.com
- http://grokconstructor.appspot.com/

The basic configuration for `grok` is as follows:

```
grok {
}
```

In this plugin, no settings are mandatory. The additional configuration settings are as follows:

- `add_field`: This is used to add a field to the incoming data.
- `add_tag`: This is used to add a tag to the incoming data. Tags can be static or dynamic based on keys present in the incoming data.
- `break_on_match`: This is used to exit searching for filters or patterns if it is set as `true`. It will finish the filter on successful match of the pattern. If set as `false`, it will match all the grok patterns.
- `keep_empty_captures`: This is used to keep event fields which are empty if set as `true`.
- `match`: This is used to match the field with the value. The value is provided as a pattern or multiple patterns, which can be provided as an array.
- `named_captures_only`: This is used to keep only the fields which have been defined using the grok pattern, if set as `true`.
- `overwrite`: This is used to overwrite the value of the field. It will overwrite the existing field value.
- `patterns_dir`: This is used to mention the directory in which you have custom-created patterns defined. You can mention a single directory or multiple directories.

- `patterns_files_glob`: This is used to select all the files from the directory as specified in `patterns_dir`.
- `periodic_flush`: This is used to call the `flush` method at regular intervals.
- `remove_field`: This is used to remove a field from the incoming data.
- `remove_tag`: This is used to remove a tag from the incoming data.
- `tag_on_failure`: This is used to create a tag with a failure message if the event was not able to match the grok pattern or there is no successful pattern match with the value.
- `tag_on_timeout`: This is used to create a tag if the grok regular expression gets timed out.
- `timeout_millis`: This is used to terminate the regular expression if it takes more than the time specified in this setting. It is applicable to each pattern if there are multiple patterns for grok. It is in milli-seconds.

The value type and default values for the settings are as follows:

Setting	Value type	Default value
`add_field`	Hash	{}
`add_tag`	Array	[]
`break_on_match`	Boolean	true
`keep_empty_captures`	Boolean	false
`match`	Hash	{}
`named_captures_only`	Boolean	true
`overwrite`	Array	[]
`patterns_dir`	Array	[]
`patterns_files_glob`	String	"*"
`periodic_flush`	Boolean	false
`remove_field`	Array	[]
`remove_tag`	Array	[]
`tag_on_failure`	Array	["_grokparsefailure"]
`tag_on_timeout`	String	"_groktimeout"
`timeout_millis`	Number	2000

Configuration example:

```
filter {
        grok {
                add_field => {"current_time" => "%{@timestamp}" }
                match => { "message" => "%{CISCOTIMESTAMP:timestamp}
                %{HOST:host} % {WORD:program}: [%{NUMBER:duration}]
                %{GREEDYDATA:log}" }
                remove_field => ["host "]
                remove_tag => ["grok","test"]
        }
    }
```

In the preceding configuration, we are matching the data with the pattern defined as a message. It will match the data with this pattern and if the pattern does not match, it will add a `_grokparsefailure` tag. It will also remove the field `host` from the message.

mutate

The `mutate` filter is used to perform various mutations on the field such as renaming the field, joining the field, converting the field to uppercase or lowercase, splitting the string or converting the datatype of the field, and so on.

The basic configuration for `mutate` is as follows:

```
mutate {
    }
```

In this plugin, no settings are mandatory. The additional configuration settings are as follows:

- `add_field`: This is used to add a field to the incoming data.
- `add_tag`: This is used to add a tag to the incoming data. Tags can be static or dynamic based on keys present in incoming data.
- `convert`: This is used to convert the datatype of the field. You can convert the field value into integer, string, Boolean, date, or float.

 All fields stored to Elasticsearch are of the `string` datatype. To change the datatype of the field, use `convert` to change the datatype for that field.

- gsub: This is used to search and replace a value of the field using a regular expression. It is similar to the sed command in Unix. It takes its input as three parameters, namely, fieldname, search pattern, and replace by. It can only be applied to fields whose datatype is a string.

 Do not forget to escape the backslash for the search pattern.

- join: This is used to join the values of an array by a character as defined. It is only applied on the fields whose datatype is an array.
- lowercase: This is used to convert the value of the string to lowercase.
- merge: This is used to merge two fields with a datatype array or hash. It will not merge two fields with a datatype array and hash. Also, fields with datatype string are converted into an array so that you can merge the string with the array.
- periodic_flush: This is used to call the flush method at regular intervals.
- remove_field: This is used to remove a field from the incoming data.
- remove_tag: This is used to remove a tag from the incoming data.
- rename: This is used to rename the field name.
- replace: This is used to replace the value of the field.
- split: This is used to split the field using a separator, which splits the field into an array. It only works on fields with a datatype string.
- strip: This is used to remove the whitespace from the field.
- update: This is used to update the value of an existing field. If the field doesn't exist, update will not work.
- uppercase: This is used to convert the value of the string to uppercase.

The value type and default values for the settings are as follows:

Setting	Value type	Default value
add_field	Hash	{}
add_tag	Array	[]
convert	Hash	No default value
gsub	Array	No default value
join	Hash	No default value

lowercase	Array	No default value
merge	Hash	No default value
periodic_flush	Boolean	false
remove_field	Array	[]
remove_tag	Array	[]
rename	Hash	No default value
replace	Hash	No default value
split	Hash	No default value
strip	Array	No default value
update	Hash	No default value
uppercase	Array	No default value

Configuration example:

```
filter {
      mutate {
              convert => {"field1" => "float" }
              gsub => ["field2","!","+"]
              lowercase => ["field2"]
              rename => {"field1" => "newfield"}
              strip => ["field1", "field2"]
              update => {"field2" => "It's easy to update"}
          }
      }
```

In the preceding configuration, we are showcasing a few of the mutations applied on the fields.

CSV

csv is used to perform various operations on received CSV input data. It is used for parsing the CSV type of data separated by commas. Although it is a csv filter, it is worth mentioning that it can parse the data with any separator.

The basic configuration for csv is as follows:

```
csv {
}
```

In this plugin, no settings are mandatory. The additional configuration settings are as follows:

- add_field: This is used to add a field to the incoming data.
- add_tag: This is used to add a tag to the incoming data. Tags can be static or dynamic based on keys present in the incoming data.
- autogenerate_column_names: This is used to autogenerate the names of the columns, if set to true. If a header is present, it will be used as a column name.
- columns: This is used to define the name of the columns that appear in the file. If the names of the columns are not specified, then default column names are used, which are "column1", "column2", and so on. If there is a larger number of columns than those defined, the columns are auto-numbered. It is useful to define when there is no header in the file.
- convert: This is used to convert the datatype of the field. You can convert the field value into either an integer, string, Boolean, date, or float.
- periodic_flush: This is used to call the flush method at regular intervals.
- quote_char: This is used to specify the character that quotes the values of the CSV fields.
- remove_field: This is used to remove a field from the incoming data.
- remove_tag: This is used to remove a tag from the incoming data.
- separator: This is used to specify the separator that separates the column.
- skip_empty_columns: This is used to specify whether to skip the empty columns or not.
- source: This is used to expand the value of the source field.
- target: This is used to specify the target field in which data will be stored.

The value types and default values for the settings are as follows:

Setting	Value type	Default value
add_field	Hash	{}
add_tag	Array	[]
autogenerate_column_names	Boolean	true
columns	Array	[]
convert	Hash	{}
periodic_flush	Boolean	false
quote_char	String	"'''"
remove_field	Array	[]
remove_tag	Array	[]
separator	String	","
skip_empty_columns	Boolean	false
source	String	"message"
target	String	No default value

Configuration example:

```
filter {
        csv {
                columns => ["id","name","money"]
                convert => {"id" => "integer", "money" => "float"}
                quote_char => "#"
                separator => "    "
        }
    }
```

In the preceding configuration, we mentioned the names of the columns. We converted the datatype of the fields and changed the value of the quote character. We also specified the separator to separate the columns by a tab.

Exploring Output Plugins

The output plugin is used to send data to a destination. It acts as the final section required in the Logstash configuration file. Some of the most used output plugins are as follows.

stdout

This is a fairly simple plugin, which outputs the data to the standard output of the shell. It is useful for debugging the configurations used for the plugins. This is mostly used to validate whether Logstash is parsing the input and applying filters (if any) properly to provide output as required.

The basic configuration for stdout is as follows:

```
stdout {
}
```

In this plugin, no settings are mandatory. The additional configuration settings are as follows:

- codec: This is used to encode the data before sending it as an output. You can use codec as JSON to display the output data in JSON format, or use codec as rubydebug to display the output data using the Ruby Awesome Print library.
- workers: This is used to define the number of threads that will process the packets for output.

The value types and default values for the settings are as follows:

Setting	Value type	Default value
codec	Codec	"line"
workers	Number	1

Configuration example:

```
output {
        stdout {
                codec => rubydebug
                workers => 2
        }
}
```

In the preceding configuration, we have mentioned the `codec` as `rubydebug` and it will print the output to the current shell as a standard output.

file

The `file` plugin is used to write the output to a file. It helps to create a file in which output is stored that can be used later on as well. By default, it writes one event per line written in JSON format and can be modified using the `codec`.

The basic configuration for `file` is as follows:

```
file {
    path => ...
}
```

In this plugin, only the `path` setting is mandatory:

- `path`: This specifies the location of either the directory or the filename where files will be written. You can provide the name of the file either directly, or using field name values to create a file.

The additional configuration settings are as follows:

- `codec`: This is used to encode the data before sending it as an output.
- `create_if_deleted`: This is used to create a file even if the file has been deleted. Whenever an input will be parsed, the output will be stored to a file, and if the file is deleted, it will be re-created.
- `dir_mode`: This is used to define the mode of the directory access to be used.
- `file_mode`: This is used to define the mode of the file access to be used.
- `filename_failure`: If the path provided is incorrect, then all the output will be written to the file, as specified in the configuration for this field.
- `flush_interval`: This is used to determine the time (in seconds) for writing to the file at a specified interval.
- `gzip`: This is used to gzip the output before writing it and storing it as a file.
- `workers`: This is used to define the number of threads that will process the packets for output.

The value types and default values for the settings are as follows:

Setting	Value type	Default value
codec	Codec	"json_lines"
create_if_deleted	Boolean	true
dir_mode	Number	-1
file_mode	Number	-1
filename_failure	String	"_filepath_failures"
flush_interval	Number	2
gzip	Boolean	false
path	String	No default value
workers	Number	1

Configuration example:

```
output {
        file {
                create_if_deleted => true
                file_mode => 777
                filename_failure => "failedpath_file"
                flush_interval => 0
                path => "/usr/share/logstash/file.txt"
        }
    }
```

In the preceding configuration, we are mentioning the mode of file access as well as specifying the option to recreate the file if deleted. The flush_interval is specified as 0, that is, it will write output to the file for every event as and when it is received. We have also specified the path within which the file, which will store the output, will be created.

elasticsearch

The elasticsearch output plugin is used to send the output from Logstash to Elasticsearch, where data will be stored. It is one of the most commonly used output filters for sending data to Elasticsearch. If you want to visualize data in Kibana, you will need to send your data to Elasticsearch. Kibana uses the data stored in Elasticsearch to create visualizations.

The basic configuration for `elasticsearch` is as follows:

```
elasticsearch {
}
```

In this plugin, no settings are mandatory.

This output plugin has various additional configuration settings; however, we will look at a few of them in more detail here:

- `action`: This is used to perform various operations on the documents stored in Elasticsearch. The various operations are: `index` (used to index a document), `delete` (used to delete a document based on the ID), `create` (used to create and index the document, where the ID is unique) and `update` (used to update the document based on the ID).
- `cacert`: This is used to provide the absolute path of the `.cer` or `.pem` file, which is used as a certificate to validate the server certificate for secured access.
- `codec`: This is used to encode the data before sending it as an output.
- `doc_as_upsert`: This is used to enable the update mode for each document. It is an `upsert` mode, wherein if a document contains an ID that has already been processed, then it will update the value of that ID. If the document ID doesn't exist, then it will create the document with that ID.
- `document_id`: This is used to specify the ID for the document, which acts as a unique specifier. Generally, it's advised to keep it auto-incremental.
- `document_type`: This is used to provide the type wherein the document will be stored. As discussed in the previous chapter, an `index` can contain multiple types. So to send the output to a specific type or different type, this property needs to be specified.
- `hosts`: This is used to specify the host IP address to communicate with the Elasticsearch node. It will specify which `hosts` should be connected to while sending data. You can specify single or multiple `hosts` at once. By default, the port is `9200`.

 Do not include the dedicated master node of Elasticsearch in the `hosts` property, otherwise it will send input data to the master nodes.

- `index`: This is used to specify the name of the index in which data will be written. The index name can be either static or dynamic when derived from a field value or using regex.

- `path`: This is used when you are using a proxy to connect to the Elasticsearch node. For that you can specify the `path` wherein Elasticsearch is reachable.
- `proxy`: This is used to specify the proxy address while connecting to the Elasticsearch node.
- `ssl`: This is used to enable the **Secured Socket Layer (SSL)** transmission or **Transport Layer Security (TLS)**, which creates a secured communication channel with the Elasticsearch node or cluster.

The value types and default values for the settings are as follows:

Setting	Value type	Default value
action	String	"index"
cacert	Filesystem path	No default value
codec	Codec	"plain"
doc_as_upsert	Boolean	false
document_id	String	No default value
document_type	String	No default value
hosts	Array	["127.0.0.1"]
index	String	logstash-%{+YYYY.MM.dd}
path	String	/
proxy	<<,>>	No default value
ssl	Boolean	No default value

Configuration example:

```
output {
        elasticsearch {
                cacert => "/usr/share/logstash/cert.pem"
                doc_as_upsert => true
                document_type => "elasticsearch"
                hosts => ["localhost:9200","127.0.0.3:9201"]
                index => "logstash"
                ssl => true
        }
}
```

In the preceding configuration, we have specified the certificate path and enabled the `upsert` functionality for the document. We have mentioned the `type` wherein it should store the output data. We have also specified the nodes of the Elasticsearch cluster to connect and write output data within the `index` Logstash, as mentioned.

Exploring Codec Plugins

Codec plugins are used to encode/decode the data. The input data can come in various formats, hence, to read and store the data of different formats, we use codec. Some of the codec plugins are as follows.

rubydebug

The `rubydebug` codec is a fairly simple plugin that outputs the data to the standard output of the shell, which prints the data using the Ruby Awesome Print library.

The basic configuration for `rubydebug` is as follows:

```
rubydebug {
}
```

In this plugin, no settings are mandatory. The additional configuration settings are as follows:

- `metadata`: This is used to specify whether or not to include the metadata while printing the output to the shell.

The value type and default values for the settings are as follows:

Setting	Value type	Default value
metadata	Boolean	false

Configuration example:

```
codec {
        rubydebug { metadata => true }
    }
```

json

The `json` codec plugin is a simple plugin which encodes or decodes the data in JSON format. It is used when data consists of JSON records.

 If the JSON records are delimited by n, then use the `json_lines` codec.

The basic configuration for `json` is as follows:

```
json {
}
```

In this plugin, no settings are mandatory. The additional configuration setting is as follows:

- `charset`: This is used to determine the character encoding set used for the data. This value is set as per standard UTF-8 or as per the encoding in which data is coming as an input.

The value type and default value for the setting is as follows:

Setting	Value Type	Default value
charset	String	UTF-8

Configuration example:

```
codec {
        json { charset => "UTF-8-MAC" }
    }
```

avro

The `avro` plugin is used to read input data that is in `avro` format. It is used to encode or decode the `avro` format records. It is mostly used with Kafka input, as Kafka sends the data in `avro` compressed format. Kafka is a highly scalable message queue to handle real-time streaming data.

`avro` is a community-maintained plugin and may not be present in Logstash plugins.

The basic configuration for `avro` is as follows:

```
avro {
    schema_uri => ...
}
```

In this plugin, only the `schema_uri` setting is mandatory.

- `schema_uri`: This is used to specify the schema file, which `avro` requires to read the data. It can be specified as a local file or a file present in an HTTP URL.

The value type and default value for the setting is as follows:

Setting	Value Type	Default value
schema_uri	String	No default value

Configuration example:

```
codec {
        avro {
        schema_uri => "/usr/share/logstash/input-schema.avsc"
    }
}
```

multiline

The `multiline` plugin is a very important codec, which is used to merge multiple events into one. It was created to capture the Java exception and stack trace messages as a single event instead of multiple events. It is mostly used when monitoring logs or performing log analysis. We can use various regular expressions to determine which multiple lines are part of which event.

 The `multiline` filter has been deprecated in favor of `multiline` codec.

The basic configuration for `multiline` is as follows:

```
multiline {
    pattern => ...
    what => ...
}
```

In this plugin, the `pattern` and `what` settings are mandatory.

- `pattern`: This is used to specify the pattern for which it will match the pattern with the event. You can use either regex patterns or grok patterns to match with the events.
- `what`: This is used to specify that the matched pattern will be part of the previous event or the next event. It determines that the pattern which has been matched will belong to which event. Its value can be either `previous` or `next`.

The additional configuration settings are as follows:

- `auto_flush_interval`: This is used to specify the time interval in which multiple lines will be converted to the events if they match the specified pattern or no new data has been received. If specified, then the events will be pushed to the output after the specified number of seconds.
- `charset`: This is used to determine the character encoding set used for the data. This value is set as per standard UTF-8 or as per the encoding in which data is coming as an input.
- `max_bytes`: This is used to specify the maximum size in bytes before Logstash writes the captured `multiline` events to the output.
- `max_lines`: This is used to specify the maximum number of lines before Logstash writes the captured `multiline` events to the output.
- `multiline_tag`: This is used to add a tag to the `multiline` events that match the pattern.
- `negate`: This is used to determine whether the event matching the pattern will be part of the `multiline` event and the value under what setting will be used.
- `patterns_dir`: This is used to mention the directory in which you have custom-created patterns defined. You can mention a single directory or multiple directories. It is used only when you have created custom patterns.

The value types and default values for the settings are as follows:

Setting	Value type	Default value
`auto_flush_interval`	Number	No default value
`charset`	String	UTF-8
`max_bytes`	Bytes	10 MiB
`max_lines`	Number	500
`multiline_tag`	String	multiline
`negate`	Boolean	`false`
`pattern`	String	No default value
`patterns_dir`	Array	[]
`what`	String	No default value

Configuration example:

```
codec {
        multiline {
        multiline_tag => "multiline-event"
        pattern =>"^["
        negate => "true"
        what => "next"
    }
 }
```

In the preceding configuration, we have specified the codec as multiline and mentioned to tag all the multiline events with the tag name as multiline-event. We specified to search a pattern wherein the line starts with a square bracket ([). We have mentioned what as next, which tells us that the matched multiline event should be part of the next event, and mentioned negate as true, which searches the pattern in the logs and until the pattern is found, it is considered to be part of a single event.

In this chapter, we have mentioned that there are over 200 plugins available for use with Logstash, which are developed by Elastic and the community. Now you may question whether, if a new plugin is created and available with the latest version of Logstash, a person using an older version of Logstash will be able to use the latest plugin.

Yes. They will. If your plugin is compatible with the older version of Logstash, you can install the plugin. Let's have a look at how to list plugins and install/update/remove a plugin available in Logstash.

Plugins Command-Line Options

As we have already discussed the various type of plugins available in Logstash, let's understand how to list/install/update/remove a plugin using the `logstash-plugin` script, which is present within the `bin` folder of Logstash.

The usage of the `plugin` command-line option is as follows:

```
bin/logstash-plugin [OPTIONS] SUBCOMMAND [ARG]
```

The various subcommands are `list`, `install`, `remove`, `update`, `pack`, `unpack`, and `generate`.

`list` is used to list the installed plugins, `install` is used to install a plugin, `remove` is used to remove a plugin, `update` is used to update a plugin, `pack` is used to package already installed plugins and `unpack` is used to unpack packaged plugins.

Listing of Plugins

To list all the plugins available in Logstash:

```
bin/logstash-plugin list
```

The various options available for list can be viewed using:

```
bin/logstash-plugin list --help
```

It displays options such as `--installed`, `--verbose`, `--group NAME`.

To find an installed plugin using its name:

```
bin/logstash-plugin list kafka
```

To display the version of the installed plugin:

```
bin/logstash-plugin list --verbose logstash-input-kafka
```

To display the installed plugins for a group (Input, Filter, Output or Codec):

```
bin/logstash-plugin list --group filter
```

Installing a plugin

The various options available for `install` can be viewed using the following command:

```
bin/logstash-plugin install --help
```

It displays options such as `-version`, `--[no-]verify`, `--preserve`, `--development`, and `--local`.

To install a plugin, use the following command:

```
bin/logstash-plugin install logstash-filter-dissect
```

Kindly use root access to perform command line options for plugins.

To install a specific version of the plugin, use the following command:

```
bin/logstash-plugin install --version 1.0.8 logstash-filter-dissect
```

To verify the plugin validity before installation, use the following command:

```
bin/logstash-plugin install --verify logstash-filter-dissect
```

To install the plugin without verifying the plugin validity, use the following command:

```
bin/logstash-plugin install --no-verify logstash-dilter-dissect
```

To install the plugin locally, use the following command:

```
bin/logstash-plugin install --local logstash-filter-dissect
```

Removing a plugin

The various options available for removing a plugin can be viewed using:

```
bin/logstash-plugin remove --help
```

It does not contain any additional options.

To uninstall a plugin:

```
bin/logstash-plugin remove logstash-filter-dissect
```

Updating a plugin

The various options available for update can be viewed using the following command:

```
bin/logstash-plugin update --help
```

This displays options such as --[no-]verify and --local.

To update all the installed plugins, use the following command:

```
bin/logstash-plugin update
```

To update a specific plugin, use the following command:

```
bin/logstash-plugin update logstash-filter-dissect
```

To verify the plugin validity before updating, use the following command:

```
bin/logstash-plugin update --verify logstash-filter-dissect
```

To update the plugin without verifying the plugin validity, use the following command:

```
bin/logstash-plugin update --no-verify logstash-filter-dissect
```

To update the plugin locally, use the following command:

```
bin/logstash-plugin update --local logstash-filter-dissect
```

Packing a plugin

The various options available for pack can be viewed using:

```
bin/logstash-plugin pack --help
```

It displays options such as --tgz, --zip, --[no-]clean, and --overwrite.

To package a plugin in GZipped TAR format, use the following command:

```
bin/logstash-plugin pack --tgz
```

To package a plugin in ZIP format, use the following command:

```
bin/logstash-plugin pack --zip
```

To delete the generated dump of plugins, use the following command:

```
bin/logstash-plugin pack --clean
```

To not delete the generated dump of plugins, use the following command:

```
bin/logstash-plugin pack --no-clean
```

To overwrite a previously generated package file, use the following command:

```
bin/logstash-plugin pack --overwrite
```

Unpacking a plugin

The various options available for unpack can be viewed using the following command:

```
bin/logstash-plugin unpack --help
```

This displays options such as --tgz and --zip.

To unpack a packaged GZipped TAR file, use the following command:

```
bin/logstash-plugin unpack --tgz filename
```

To unpack a packaged ZIP file, use the following command:

```
bin/logstash-plugin unpack --zip filename
```

Let's discover some more command line options related to Logstash.

Logstash command-line options

There are various command-line options to use with Logstash. The various command-line options can be viewed using the following command:

```
bin/logstash --help
```

This displays various options, which are described here.

To specify the name of Logstash instance:

```
bin/logstash --node.name NODENAME
```

To run Logstash using a configuration file or directory containing configuration files, use the following commands:

```
bin/logstash -f CONFIGPATH
```

Or use the following command:

```
bin/logstash --path.config CONFIGPATH
```

To run Logstash by specifying the configuration directly in the command line, use the following command:

```
bin/logstash -e "input { stdin { type => stdin } }"
```

To specify the number of workers to run to process in parallel, use the following command:

```
bin/logstash -w 12 or bin/logstash --pipeline.workers 12
```

The default value is 8.

To specify the maximum number of events a worker will connect before executing filters and output plugins, use the following command:

```
bin/logstash -b 50 or bin/logstash --pipeline.batch.size 50
```

The default value is 125.

To specify the time to wait before checking for new events (delay in ms), use the following command:

```
bin/logstash -u 10
```

Or:

```
bin/logstash --pipeline.batch.delay 10
```

The default value is 250 ms.

To force Logstash to exit in shutdown even if it contains events in memory, use the following command:

```
bin/logstash --pipeline.unsafe_shutdown
```

To specify the directory in which Logstash will store data, use the following command:

```
bin/logstash --path.data PATH
```

The default value is $LS_HOME/data.

To specify the path to find custom plugins in Logstash, use the following command:

```
bin/logstash -p PATH or bin/logstash --path.plugins PATH
```

PATH is defined as PATH/logstash/TYPE/NAME.rb, where TYPE is the group name (Inputs, Outputs, Filters, Codecs) and NAME is the name of the plugin.

To write logs in a directory for running Logstash, use the following command:

```
bin/logstash -l PATH or bin/logstash --path.logs PATH
```

To specify the log level for the logs emitted by Logstash, use the following command:

```
bin/logstash --log.level LEVEL
```

Possible values for LEVEL are: fatal, warn, error, debug, info (default value) and trace.

To print the compiled config ruby code as a debug log:

```
bin/logstash --config.debug
```

To use --config.debug, --log.level=debug must be enabled.

To display the version of Logstash:

```
bin/logstash -V or bin/logstash --version
```

To verify that the Logstash configuration file is correct:

```
bin/logstash -f file.conf --config.test_and_exit or bin/logstash -f
file.conf -t
```

Grok patterns are not verified. Only valid syntax is validated.

To enable auto-reload of Logstash configuration file:

```
bin/logstash -f file.conf -r or bin/logstash -f file.conf --
config.reload.automatic
```

The default value is `false`.

To specify the reload interval for checking the Logstash configuration file for changes (in secs):

```
bin/logstash -f file.conf --config.reload.interval 5
```

the default value is 3 sec.

To specify the directory containing the settings file for Logstash:

```
bin/logstash --path.settings SETTINGS_DIR
```

Default value is `$LS_HOME/config`.

Logstash Tips and Tricks

There are a few tips related to Logstash, which are described in the following sections.

Referencing fields and Its values

In the Logstash configuration file, you can refer to a field by its name and can subsequently pass the value of a field into another field. If you want to refer to a `top-level field`, use the field name directly. If you want to refer to a `nested field`, use the `[top-level field][nested field]` syntax. To refer the field, Logstash uses the `sprintf` format, which helps us to refer to the field values.

The `sprintf` format is as follows:

```
%{[top-level field][nested field].....}
```

For example:

```
output {
        elasticsearch {
                document_type => "%{@version}"
                index => "logstash_%{type}_%{+YYYY-MM-dd-H}"
    }
}
```

 The `index` name cannot contain the following special characters: , /, *, ?, ",
<, >, |, or ,. Also, the `index` name must be in lowercase only.

Adding custom-created grok patterns

As discussed previously, we can create our own grok patterns, which we can use directly.
We can use existing defined grok patterns and modify them as per our data, or we can even
define new grok patterns using regular expressions.

The basic syntax of a grok pattern is as follows:

```
%{SYNTAX:SEMANTIC}
```

The basic syntax of defining a pattern in a grok file using the regular expression is as
follows:

```
PATTERNNAME Regular-Expression_Syntax
```

For example:

```
ALPHANUMERIC ([a-zA-Z0-9-]+)
```

The basic syntax of defining a pattern in a grok file using an existing defined grok pattern is
as follows:

```
PATTERNNAME %{EXISTING_GROK-PATTERN)
```

For example:

```
RECORDTIME %{TIME}
```

We will explore more custom created grok patterns later in this chapter in the *Logstash Configuration for Parsing Logs* section.

Logstash does not show any output

This is one of the common issues we face while running Logstash. In this case, Logstash runs the configuration but we are unable to see any output printed in the standard output. This issue can occur in a few scenarios, as mentioned in the following subsections.

When an input file has already been completely read

In this scenario, we are using the `input` plugin as a file and have specified a file or files from which to read the data, as the file input uses a mechanism of creating `sincedb` files, which helps Logstash know how much the input file has been processed and parsed. So in this scenario, if the input file has already been read completely, then running Logstash again for the same set of input files will not display any output.

Let's have a look at the content of a `sincedb` file:

```
948594 0 2049 47484
```

Its columns are inode (Unix) or identifier (Windows), major device number, minor device number, and byte offset.

The inode column, along with the major and minor device numbers, helps to refer to the file that is being read by the `file` input plugin. Byte offset determines the number of bytes read in the file.

There are a couple of solutions to solve this:

- **Solution 1**: Delete the `sincedb` file that is present in `$HOME/.sincedb_*` and run Logstash again with the configuration file. This time, it will display the output as well.
- **Solution 2**: Use the setting or parameter of `sincedb_path` and specify its value as follows:

```
sincedb_path => "/dev/null"
```

It will fool Logstash into believing that it has never parsed the input file.

 Solution 2 is not recommended, as whenever Logstash restarts, the complete file will be parsed from the beginning, which will lead to duplicate data.

When an input file is not modified since 1 day

In this scenario, we use the input plugin as a file and specify a file as an input. When the input file has not been modified for 86,400 seconds, or 1 day, then Logstash will run but will not display any output.

There are a couple of solutions to solve this:

- **Solution 1**: Modify the file so that it will be read by Logstash.
- **Solution 2**: Use the `touch` command (UNIX) to change the timestamp. This solution will only work if the `sincedb` path is `/dev/null`.

Logstash Configuration for Parsing Logs

In this section, we will explore how to use Logstash to parse a file that contains different types of logs. It will utilize the knowledge gained in this chapter, which will be put into action. We will use custom created grok patterns to parse the data, as per our requirements.

Let's have a look at the data.

The log file contains millions of records with a combination of Tomcat logs and Catalina logs. The log file also contains application exceptions, errors, and stack trace messages. The log file contains log events of various log levels, such as `INFO`, `WARN`, `ERROR`, `DEBUG`, and `FATAL`.

Sample Catalina logs

Have a look at the following logs:

```
    Mar 10, 2016 10:04:37 PM org.apache.catalina.startup.Catalina load
INFO: Initialization processed in 433 ms
    Mar 10, 2016 10:04:37 PM org.apache.catalina.core.StandardService
startInternal INFO: Starting service Catalina
```

Sample Tomcat logs

Have a look at the following logs:

```
    2016-03-10 22:04:40,892  INFO localhost-startStop-1
support.AnnotationConfigWebApplicationContext:208 - Registering annotated
classes: [class matrix.api.config.RESTConfig]
    2016-03-10 22:05:07,248 ERROR http-bio-8080-exec-1
handler.ExceptionHandlerAdvice:57 - We have encountered an internal error.
org.springframework.dao.EmptyResultDataAccessException: Incorrect result
size: expected 1, actual 0
  at org.springframework.dao.support.DataAccessUtils (Support.java:71)
  at org.springframework.jdbc.core.Jdbc.queryForObject(Jdbc.java:489)
  at org.impl.HealthCheckDaoImpl.getResult(HealthCheckDaoImpl.java:30))
  at org.springframework.web.Handler.invokeForRequest(Handler.java:132)
```

Let us create custom grok patterns to match the Catalina logs and Tomcat logs. We will create a file named `grok-pattern` inside the `/usr/share/logstash/patterns`.

Grok pattern for Catalina logs

Let's have a look at the pre-defined and custom grok patterns used for parsing of Catalina logs:

```
MONTH
b(?:Jan(?:uary)?|Feb(?:ruary)?|Mar(?:ch)?|Apr(?:il)?|May|Jun(?:e)?|Jul(?:y)
?|Aug(?:ust)?|Sep(?:tember)?|Oct(?:ober)?|Nov(?:ember)?|Dec(?:ember)?)b
MONTHDAY (?:(?:0[1-9])|(?:[12][0-9])|(?:3[01])|[1-9])
YEAR (?>dd){1,2} HOUR (?:2[0123]|[01]?[0-9])
MINUTE (?:[0-5][0-9])
SECOND (?:(?:[0-5][0-9]|60)(?:[:.,][0-9]+)?)
DURATION (AM|PM)
CATALINA_DATESTAMP %{MONTH} %{MONTHDAY}, %{YEAR}
%{HOUR}:?%{MINUTE}(?::?%{SECOND}) %{DURATION}
JAVACLASS (?:[a-zA-Z0-9-]+.)+[A-Za-z0-9$]+
JAVALOGMESSAGE (.*)
LOGLEVEL ([A-
a]lert|ALERT|[T|t]race|TRACE|[D|d]ebug|DEBUG|[N|n]otice|NOTICE|[I|i]nfo|INF
O|[W|w]arn?(?:ing)?|WARN?(?:ING)?|[E|e]rr?(?:or)?|ERR?(?:OR)?|[C|c]rit?(?:i
cal)?|
CRIT?(?:ICAL)?|[F|f]atal|FATAL|[S|s]evere|SEVERE|EMERG(?:ENCY)?|[Ee]merg(?:
ency)?)
CATALINALOGLEVEL %{CATALINA_DATESTAMP:datestamp}s*%{JAVACLASS:class}
%{JAVALOGMESSAGE:loginfo} %{LOGLEVEL:level}: %{JAVALOGMESSAGE:logmessage}
```

Grok pattern for Tomcat logs

Let's have a look at the pre-defined and custom grok patterns used for parsing of Tomcat logs:

```
MONTHNUM (?:0?[1-9]|1[0-2])
TOMCAT_DATESTAMP %{YEAR}-%{MONTHNUM}-
%{MONTHDAY}s*%{HOUR}:?%{MINUTE}(?::?%{SECOND})
REQUEST (?:[a-zA-Z0-9-]+-)+[A-Za-z0-9$]+ LOGLINE (?:[a-zA-Z0-9-]+.)+(?:[a-zA-Z0-9-]+:)+[A-Za-z0-9$]+
TOMCATLOG %{TOMCAT_DATESTAMP:datestamp}s*%{LOGLEVEL:level}
%{REQUEST:request} %{LOGLINE:line} - %{JAVALOGMESSAGE:logmessage}
```

> The patterns common for the Catalina and Tomcat logs will be defined only once in the `grok-pattern` file as the file is common for parsing both of the patterns.

Logstash configuration file

The Logstash Configuration file to be used is shown in the following code snippet:

```
input   {
     file  {
          path => "/usr/share/tomcat/logs/catalina.out"
          type => "tomcat"
          start_position => "beginning"
          codec => multiline  {
               patterns_dir => "/usr/share/logstash/patterns"
               pattern =>
          "(^%{TOMCAT_DATESTAMP}|^%{CATALINA_DATESTAMP})"
               negate => true
               what => "previous"
          }
        }
     }
}
filter   {
     mutate   {
          gsub => ['message', "n", " "]
          gsub => ['message', "t", " "]
     }
     grok   {
          patterns_dir => "/usr/share/logstash/patterns"
          match => [ "message", "%{TOMCATLOG}","message",
   "%{CATALINALOGLEVEL}"]
     }
```

```
    date    {
        match => [ "timestamp", "yyyy-MM-dd HH:mm:ss,SSS","MMM dd,
yyyy HH:mm:ss a"]
        }
    if "_grokparsefailure" in [tags]  {
      drop { }
    }
}
output    {
    elasticsearch  {
        hosts => "localhost:9200"
        index => "logs"
        document_type => "logs"
    }
    stdout { codec => rubydebug }
    if [level] == "ERROR"  {
    email  {
        address => "smtp.gmail.com"
        port => "587"
        username => "gupta.yuvraj"
        password => "password123"
        use_tls => "true"
        from => "<gupta.yuvraj@gmail.com>"
        subject => "Error status"
        to => "<kravi.gupta@gmail.com>"
        htmlbody => "<h2>%{request}</h2><br/><br/><h3>Full
        Event</h3><br/><br/><div
        align='center'>%{message}</div>"
        }
    }
}
```

Let's look at the preceding configuration to understand what it is doing.

 All the previously mentioned grok-patterns and logstash configuration file is present at: `https://github.com/kravigupta/mastering-elastic-stack-code-files/tree/5.1.1/Chapter03`

In the preceding configuration file, we have used the input plugin as a file, where we have specified the filename and given it a type, which we will use to parse data. Also, we have specified to read the file from the start. We have then used multiline codec, as the log contains exceptions and stack traces, where we have specified the pattern along with the pattern directory, as it is a custom created pattern. We have mentioned negate as true, which searches the pattern in the logs and until the pattern is found, it is considered to be part of a single event. Using what as previous, it indicates that the matched multiline event should be part of a previous event itself.

In the filter plugin, we are using multiple types of filters to transform the data. We have used the mutate filter, wherein we are substituting all the new lines and tab-separated logs by a space. We have used grok to indicate that it should match the message field as per %{TOMCATLOG} and %{CATALINALOGLEVEL}, which are custom created grok patterns and therefore defined by the property patterns_dir. We have used a date filter to tell Logstash to match the timestamp field as per the timestamp pattern specified. At the end of this filter, we have mentioned not to include any event that fails the grok match.

In the output plugin, we are using three types of output, namely, output to elasticsearch, output to standard output (stdout), and output to email.

In the output as elasticsearch plugin, we have specified the elasticsearch node to connect to along with the index and type name.

In the output as stdout plugin, we have specified to print the logs as per the Ruby Awesome Print library.

In the output as email plugin, we are using conditionals. You should see this plugin only when the value of the level field is equal to ERROR. We have provided the settings of the mail server, such as address and port, and specified the username and password to connect to the mail server. We have set use_tls as true, as we are using the port that is set when secured communication is enabled. We have then mentioned the e-mail ID of the sender, the e-mail ID of the recipient, the subject of the e-mail, and the content to be sent in the e-mail.

To run the Logstash Configuration use the following command after navigating to Logstash Directory:

```
bin/logstash -f log-config.conf
```

You may face an error when you run the configuration file as email output plugin could be missing. To install email output plugin use following command after navigating to Logstash directory:- `bin/logstash-plugin install logstash-email-output`

If you want to run the Logstash Configuration file using Logstash service then you would need to put the Logstash Configuration file in following path:

`/etc/logstash/conf.d/`

It will run the configuration files present within this directory whenever logstash runs as a service.

Whenever you will run Logstash (5.x onwards), it will open a Logstash API endpoint at port `9600`.

After reading the above note, you must be wondering why does Logstash open an API endpoint. Let's understand it in following section.

Monitoring APIs

In this section, we will have a look at the various APIs currently exposed in Logstash to retrieve runtime metric information.

By default, API binds to `127.0.0.1` and picks up the first available port in the range of `9600-9700`. But if another instance of Logstash is running, let's say at port `9600`, then you would need to specify the new port on which Logstash will run using following command:

```
bin/logstash --http.port 9602
```

You can get basic information when Logstash runs by opening `http://localhost:9600` in your browser or run the following command from the command line:

```
curl -X GET http://localhost:9600?pretty
```

The response of the preceding command is as follows:

```
{
    "host": "ubuntu",
    "version": "5.1.1",
    "http_address": "127.0.0.1:9600"
    "id" : "6d32ec3e-700b-48eb-bbc3-6a48b2b00f9e",
    "name" : "ubuntu",
    "build_date" : "2016-12-06T13:17:53+00:00",
    "build_sha" : "aa36c4f4b702c6d379e5a97c22627933bca04f68",
    "build_snapshot" : false
}
```

Node info API

This provides information about the node, such as the node OS level information, node JVM level information, and pipeline related information.

You can get all the Node information at once by running the following command:

```
curl -X GET http://localhost:9600/_node/?pretty
```

OS Info

This provides the OS level information of the node such as OS name, architecture, version, and available processors.

```
curl -X GET http://localhost:9600/_node/os?pretty
```

The response is as follows:

```
{
  "os": {
    "name": "Linux",
    "arch": "amd64",
    "version": "4.2.0-27-generic",
    "available_processors": 4
  }
}
```

JVM info

This provides JVM level information of the node such as the JVM process ID, version, VM info, memory usage, and garbage collectors.

```
curl -X GET http://localhost:9600/_node/jvm?pretty
```

The response is as follows:

```
{
"jvm" : {
    "pid" : 6340,
    "version" : "1.8.0_74",
    "vm_name" : "Java HotSpot(TM) 64-Bit Server VM",
    "vm_version" : "1.8.0_74",
    "vm_vendor" : "Oracle Corporation",
    "start_time_in_millis" : 1481599754165,
    "mem" : {
      "heap_init_in_bytes" : 268435456,
      "heap_max_in_bytes" : 1038876672,
      "non_heap_init_in_bytes" : 2555904,
      "non_heap_max_in_bytes" : 0
    },
    "gc_collectors" : [ "ParNew", "ConcurrentMarkSweep" ]
}
```

Pipeline Info

The provides pipeline information for the node such as the number of workers, batch size, batch delay, and configuration information.

```
curl -X GET http://localhost:9600/_node/pipeline?pretty
```

The response is as follows:

```
{
"pipeline" : {
    "workers" : 4,
    "batch_size" : 125,
    "batch_delay" : 5,
    " config_reload_automatic" : false,
    " config_reload_interval" : 3
    }
}
```

Plugins Info API

This provides information about all the plugins that are installed in Logstash. It is nothing more than the output of following command:

```
bin/logstash-plugin list --verbose
```

You can get all the plugin information by running the following command:

```
curl -X GET http://localhost:9600/_node/plugins?pretty
```

The response is as follows:

```
{
  "total": 94,
  "plugins": [
    {
      "name": "logstash-codec-cef",
      "version": "4.1.0"
    },
    {
      "name": "logstash-codec-collectd",
      "version": "3.0.2"
    },
    {
      "name": "logstash-codec-dots",
      "version": "3.0.2"
    },
    .
    .
    .
  ]
```

Node stats API

This provides runtime statistics about the node, such as the node JVM stats, process stats, memory usage stats, and pipeline stats.

You can get all the node information at once by running the following command:

```
curl -X GET http://localhost:9600/_node/stats?pretty
```

JVM stats

This provides information about the node's threads, memory usage, and garbage collectors. Use the following command to get the JVM stats:

```
curl -X GET http://localhost:9600/_node/stats/jvm?pretty
```

Process stats

This provides information about the file descriptors, memory info, and CPU info. You can use the following command to get the process stats:

```
curl -X GET http://localhost:9600/_node/stats/process?pretty
```

Pipeline stats

This provides information about the pipeline events, plugins, and reload information. You can use the following command to get the pipeline stats:

```
curl -X GET http://localhost:9600/_node/stats/pipeline?pretty
```

Hot threads API

This provides the list of all the hot threads running for Logstash, that is, Java threads that use higher CPU resources and execute for a longer duration of time.

You can get the hot thread information by running the following command:

```
curl -X GET http://localhost:9600/_node/hot_threads?pretty
```

There are a few parameters associated with hot threads, as described next.

Threads

This provides the number of threads to return as a response. By default, it is 3, you can use the following command to get thread information:

```
curl -X GET http://localhost:9600/_node/hot_threads?threads=1
```

Human

If set as `true`, this provides the response in plain text instead of JSON. By default, it is false. Use the following command:

```
curl -X GET http://localhost:9600/_node/hot_threads?human=true
```

Ignore idle threads

If set as true, this does not provide response of idle threads. By default, it is `true`. You can use the following command to ignore idle threads:

```
curl -X GET
http://localhost:9600/_node/hot_threads?ignore_idle_threads=false
```

Summary

In the chapter, we learned about Logstash, its need and its features. We covered the basics of Logstash Flow and the structure of the Logstash Configuration. Later we explored in detail the various types of plugins available along with the settings of few of the plugins were explained in detail. We also covered the Plugin Command Line Arguments along with Logstash Command Line Options. It was followed by Logstash tips and tricks and also, covered the example of application logs which had Tomcat and Catalina logs and we discovered how to create/run a Logstash Configuration file to perform ETL operations on the logs. At the end of the chapter, we had a look at the various monitoring APIs exposed to end-user to get relevant information of Logstash which was earlier appeared like a black box full of secret.

In the next chapter, we will learn about Kibana, its features and will explore the various interfaces provided by Kibana in detail.

4
Kibana Interface

After exploring Elasticsearch and Logstash, it's time for Kibana, which provides us with an interface to visualize the data we collect and store. In this chapter, we will focus on the Kibana interface, providing all the important details. We will also learn about Lucene query searches, aggregations, and so on, and understand the role they play.

At the end of this chapter, you will understand the new features of Kibana, the functionality of various tabs and their components along with how to create visualizations, dashboards, and customize Kibana settings. Also you will understand how to insert data into Elasticsearch, create an index pattern, and visualize the data, followed by how to create dashboards and share and embed them.

In this chapter, we will cover the following sections:

- Kibana and its offerings
- Exploring the discover interface
- Querying and searching data
- Exploring the visualize interface
- Understanding aggregations
- Exploring the dashboard interface
- Understanding Timelion
- Exploring Dev Tools
- Exploring the management interface
- Putting it all together

Kibana and its offerings

Kibana is a visualization tool that is used for visualizing data (structured or non-structured) stored in Elasticsearch. Kibana acts an over-the-top layer of Elasticsearch which is used to search, view, analyze data, and create visualizations on the data that is
stored in Elasticsearch indices. Kibana and Elasticsearch are Elastic products, but both use the Apache license, which uses the powerful capabilities
of Elasticsearch (Lucene query syntax, aggregations) and is based
on Apache Lucene. Kibana provides the ability to do analysis of data, visualize the data in forms of different charts such as the Area Chart, Line Chart, Bar Chart, Pie Chart, Tile map, Metrics, and Data table, and create dashboards that can even be shared or embedded. Dashboards provide a unified way to showcase all your
visualizations in one place. All the searches/visualization/dashboard are stored as JSON and the underlying has JSON documents. The JSON files for searches/visualization/dashboards are stored within Elasticsearch. It has the ability to handle and analyze large volumes of data in near real time. With the help of the auto-refresh functionality, your visualizations/dashboard will change dynamically, which provides real-time insights. It is simple to set up and easy to use with its browser-based interface.

Kibana requires a web server to work (incorporated in Kibana 4 and onwards)and any modern browser that supports the industry standards and renders the content in a similar way across all web browsers to work seamlessly. Kibana interacts with Elasticsearch using the REST-based API exposed by Elasticsearch, which provides simple HTTP calls to request and receive information. REST is a stateless protocol that uses the HTTP protocol for communication between multiple systems instead of using the complex implementation of CORBA, SOAP, WSDL, RPC, and so on. REST uses HTTP to provide CRUD (create, read, update, and delete) operations.

The following is the figure from `Chapter 1`, *Elastic Stack Overview*, which showcases a typical and high-level architecture of the Elastic Stack:

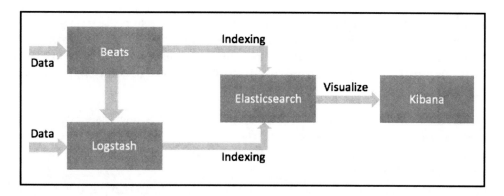

We can observe that Kibana is the endpoint for users. Whatever is collected by Logstash or Beats and stored in Elasticsearch can be viewed and analyzed using the Kibana interface.

Kibana interface

The Kibana interface typically looks as shown in the following screenshot:

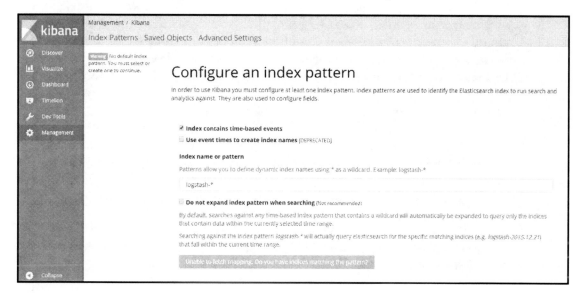

The interface is a welcoming change from the earlier Kibana versions, bringing in a completely new UI. The interface has been redesigned, keeping minimalistic things as required. You can collapse the left-pane to show the names along with the icons or only the icons of various tabs. The interface mainly consists of six tabs as present on the left-side pane, which can be described as follows:

- **Discover**: This page provides an overview of the data, such as name of the selected index, a list of fields in the data, and the text stored in the fields as data. It provides the ability to search data, query data, filter data, analyze data, and display search results.

- **Visualize**: This page provides an overview of the various types of visualizations, steps to create a new visualizations from either a new or saved search, and open a saved visualization. It also provides the ability to create, view, update, and delete custom created visualizations.

- **Dashboard**: This page provides a single view page for all the saved visualizations and searches. It provides the ability to edit, move, resize, and remove the visualizations. It helps to find insights easily by combining multiple visualizations and displaying them at once.

- **Timelion**: This page is the newest addition to the Kibana interface. It is used for visualizing time-series data. Inspired by the word "timeline", it provides the ability to co-relate multiple sources of data into a single time-series based visualization. It accesses the data using easy-to-use simple expressions that will be a learning curve initially. It has been born out of Elastic Lab's research project that focusses on the next big thing.

- **Dev Tools**: As part of Kibana itself, Dev Tools consists of a Console. Console provides a simple yet intuitive UI to interact with the REST API of Elasticsearch using a web browser. Dev Tools also consists of Profiler, which is available as part of X-Pack. We will cover it in *Understanding Profiler* section in `Chapter 9`, *X-Pack: Security and Monitoring*.

- **Management**: This page provides an overview of all of the configurations used in Kibana. It is used to configure a new index or indices pattern, modify existing configuration parameters, export and import saved objects (searches, visualizations, and dashboards), version details of Kibana, and build/commit details of Kibana.

Exploring the discover interface

The Discover page helps you to play around with the data by easily analyzing the indexed documents. It allows you to perform different types of searches on the data, helping you to understand what the data means or how the data can be used to create visualizations. It provides the ability to choose different index names by changing the index pattern without leaving the Discover page. You can easily perform search queries, use filters, and view documents matching the queries and filters.

A **Discover** page interface typically looks like the following:

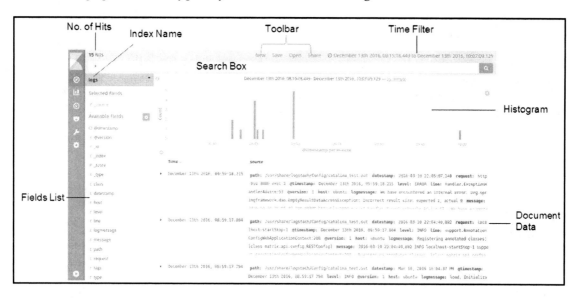

The Discover page uses the following components:

- **Time Filter**: This filters the data for a specific time range
- **Search Box**: This is used to search and query the data
- **Toolbar:** This contains options such as new search, save search, open saved search, and share
- **Index Name**: This displays the name of the selected index
- **Fields List:** This displays the name of all the fields that are present within the selected index
- **Number Of Hits**: This displays the total number of documents as per the time interval specified and corresponding to the search query matching documents result

- **Histogram**: This displays the information of the number of documents per time
- **Document Data**: This displays the documents with the entire data

Histogram is only displayed in the **Discover** page when the index contains time-based events.

Now let us have a look at each of the components individually.

Time Filter

This is used to drill down the data based on time. It provides the flexibility to search/query/filter the data on any time period as required. It makes it easier to analyze data of a specific time period or customize the time period as per the requirement. It also provides various options for setting the Time Filter.

By default, the Time Filter is set as the last 15 minutes, which means it displays data of the previous 15 minutes only.

Upon clicking on the Time Filter, we can find various sub-options as mentioned in the following sections.

Quick time filter

This provides numerous time range options to quickly use the Time Filter for viewing data such as today, this week, year to date, this day last week, previous month, last 30 minutes, last 24 hours, last 90 days, last 5 years, and so on.

Relative time filter

It is used to filter the data based on the relative time with respect to the current time. It provides a From and a To box to specify the relative time from Now. The various options to specify a relative time include Seconds, Minutes, Hours, Days, Weeks, Months and Years ago.

It also provides a small checkbox to round the relative time to its nearest second, minute, hour, day, week, month, and year.

Absolute time filter

This is used to provide the starting date/time in the From field and the ending date/time in the To field time range as per the date and time format. The date and time format is *YYYY-MM-DD HH:mm:ss.SSS*, where:

- *YYYY* defines the year in four digits (like, 2017)
- *MM* defines the month in two digits (from 01-12)
- *DD* defines the day in two digits (from 01-31)
- *HH* defines the hours in two digits (from 00-23)
- *mm* defines the minutes in two digits (from 00-59)
- *ss* defines the seconds in two digits (from 00-59)
- *SSS* defines milliseconds in three digits (from 000-999)

Auto-refresh

It is used to automatically refresh the page after a specified time interval, such as 5 seconds, 1 minute, 12 hour, 1 day, and so on. It is mostly used to analyze real-time streaming data as it provides the updated data on-the-go. The **Auto-Refresh** option will appear to the left side of the Time Filter upon clicking the Time Filter bar.

The Time Filter can also be set by clicking on any of the bars of Histogram or by clicking and dragging the cursor of the mouse to select the time range.

Querying and Searching data

The search box is used to perform various types of queries that fetch the matching documents. Upon searching, the whole Discover page along with its components gets automatically refreshed. Kibana uses the underlying powerful capabilities of Lucene query syntax using the data that is queried. As Kibana utilizes the functionality of the underlying Elasticsearch, Lucene queries provide the ability to perform various types of searches ranging from simple to complex queries.

Lucene queries provide a number of ways to search data. Let's look at these one by one.

Full-text searches

This is used to search for a term within the complete text. The different ways to search for full-text are shown as follows:

- Search for the single term:

  Example: To search for a phrase, type `elasticsearch kibana` in the search bar.

- Search for a phrase (group of words):

  Example: To search for a single term, type kibana in the search bar.

> By default, phrases use, OR Boolean operator to search for phrases.

- Search for an exact term or phrases:

  Example: To search for terms within a field, type the fieldname followed by a colon and search a term such as text: kibana.

- Search for a term within a specific field:

  Example: To search for an exact term or phrase use double quotes to enclose the search word within and type `elasticsearch kibana` in the search bar.

Range searches

To perform range searches, the common syntax is fieldname followed by colon and using brackets [] or {} to specify the starting range TO end range. TO is a keyword that has to be used as it is and specified in capital letters to search the range:

- Date Range Search: For example, to search for a date range, type `modified_date: [2016-04-01 TO 2016-06-30]`
- Number Range Search: For example, to search for a number range, type `no_of_tweets: [100 TO 1000]`
- String Range Search: For example, to search for text range, type `text: [elasticsearch TO kibana]`

Square brackets [] provide an inclusive range query, that is, they will include the mentioned keywords for the search. Curly brackets {} provide exclusive range query, that is, they will not include the mentioned keywords for the search.

Boolean searches

A Boolean search is a type of search that provides the use of operators as shown:

- OR operator: This is used to combine multiple terms and search for any of the terms:

  Example: Type elasticsearch OR kibana where OR is the keyword

  You can even use the OR operator by typing, elasticsearch || kibana where the double pipe (||) is the keyword

  Also, OR is the default operator when specifying multiple words such as elasticsearch kibana which means elasticsearch or kibana.

- AND operator: This is used to combine multiple terms and search for all of the terms:

  Example: Type elasticsearch AND kibana where AND is the keyword

  You can even use the AND operator by typing, elasticsearch && kibana where the double ampersand (&&) is the keyword.

- NOT operator: This is used to exclude terms occurring after NOT in search:

  Example: Type elasticsearch NOT kibana where NOT is the keyword

Proximity search

This is used to find the terms that are at a definite distance from each other. It uses the tilde symbol (~) as a keyword.

For example, type "java elasticsearch"~50, which will provide documents in which Java and Elasticsearch terms are at a maximum distance of 50 words.

Wildcard searches

These are used to search for matching patterns using the wildcard expressions, as shown in the following list:

- Single character search: This is used to replace the single character in the wildcard search

  Example: Type `?ac`, which will provide results such as `mac`, `sac`, and `tac`. The question mark (`?`) is the keyword.

- Multiple character search: This is used to replace zero or more characters in the wildcard search

  Example: Type `m*c`, which will provide results such as `mac`, `magic`, `macintosh`, `machine`, `music`, and so on. The asterisk (`*`) is the keyword.

Regular expressions search

This is used to find the terms, phrases, or fields that are following a specific pattern. It uses a slash (`/`) and square brackets (`[]`) to specify patterns.

For example, type `/mu[dgm]/ AND /ma[cdnp]/`, which will provide documents containing terms such as mud, mug, and mum combined with terms such as mac, mad, man, and map.

Grouping

This is used to create complex queries to search by combining multiple terms, phrases, and different types of operators.

For example, type `(elasticsearch OR kibana) AND (Logstash OR "Lucene query")`.

Fields and filters

The field list is used to provide the list of all the fields that are used in the data. It is useful in analyzing the dataset to learn what the fields are and what type of information the field contains. Fields are categorized under selected fields and available fields wherein the name of each field is arranged in alphabetical order.

It also provides the option of knowing about the data present in the field, the top five values of the field, and its percentage breakdown for the documents containing the value. Such information is available by clicking on any of the fields from the Fields List. Also you can add the fields to view the data of that field for all the documents by clicking on **Add**, which is present beside the field name. It will move the field name under selected fields, which will provide you with the information of the values present in the field.

Filtering the field

This is used to filter the search results on the basis of the values of the field. Field searches can also be indirectly done by filtering using the fields. There are two types of filters provided:

- **Positive filter**: This is denoted by the plus symbol (+) magnifier. It will display the documents that will contain that value of the field.
- **Negative filter**: This is denoted by the minus symbol (–) magnifier. It will exclude all the documents that will contain that value of the field.

Filters can be added in the following two ways:

- Adding positive and negative filters by clicking on the field name (under the fields list) and selecting the value of the field for which you want to include or exclude documents
- Adding positive and negative filters by clicking on the field value present in the document data by expanding the data and selecting the value for which you want to include or exclude documents

After the addition of filters, let's take a look at the functionalities of the filters.

Functionalities of filters

Filters provide an easy way to analyze data by filtering as required. It helps to drill into the data by applying different ways of filters, as described in the following list:

- **Enable filter**: This is used to enable the filter and it will display the documents that match the filter. It is similar to the positive filter and it is always displayed in a green color.
- **Disable filter**: This is used to disable the filter. It will display all the documents without filtering. It is displayed in a striped shaded color.
- **Pin filter**: This is used to pin the filter that will persist across Kibana pages. For example, if you are using a filter in the Discover page and pin the filter, then even if you move to any other page in Kibana the filter will be present.
- **Unpin filter**: This is used to unpin the existing pinned filters. These filters will not persist across Kibana pages.
- **Invert filter**: This is used to invert the filter, which means if it's a matching filter, then it's inverted and it will display the documents that do not contain the filter. After inverting it again it will display the documents matching the filter.
- **Toggle filter**: This is used to toggle the state of the filter. Enabled filters are depicted using a green color, whereas disabled filters are depicted using a red color. On toggling the filter, the enabled filter becomes a disabled filter and vice versa.
- **Remove filter**: This is used to remove the filter completely. It will delete the existing added filter.
- **Custom filter**: This is used to customize the added filter. The JSON representation of the filter is provided and it can be customized. It can also be used to provide an alias for the filter that can be reused.

All of the preceding mentioned filters can be viewed in the Kibana UI, as shown in the following screenshot:

Discovery page options

In the toolbar along with the search bar, there are other options, such as:

- **New Search**: This is used to create a new search query by erasing any present search query.
- **Save Search**: This is used to save the search query along with the selected index.
- **Open Saved Search**: This is used to load the existing saved search queries with the specified index. It will open the saved search query and the index with which it was saved.
- **Share:** This is used to share the search query via a link for which a short URL can also be generated or shared directly. It can also be used to share the saved search.
- **Adding fields to the Document Data**: Fields can be easily added to the document data by clicking the **Add** button, which is present beside the field name under the fields list upon hovering of the mouse cursor.
- **Removing fields from the Document Data**: Fields can be easily removed from the document data by clicking the **Remove** button, which is present beside the field name under the Fields List upon hovering of the mouse cursor.
- **Viewing Data**: Data from the document data can be easily viewed by clicking the ▸ symbol, which is present in the left of the document data starting column.
- **Sorting Documents:** Added fields to the document data can be sorted by clicking on the sort symbol present beside the column name.
- **Moving fields:** Added fields to the document data can be rearranged and moved either to the left side or right side by clicking on (>>) or (<<) present beside the symbol for removing the field from the document data.

Exploring the visualize interface

Visualization is the heart of Kibana and it is one of the sole reasons behind the creation of Kibana to provide users the capability to visualize large volumes of data. As the adoption of Elasticsearch and Logstash was increasing day by day, the ability to directly visualize data stored in Elasticsearch was missing and users were unable to make sense of the data. Then came the savior, Kibana, which solved the problem and provided a simple yet intuitive interface. It solved the challenge of visualizing huge volumes of data in near real time. It is the core component that makes Kibana a functionally rich open source software.

The **Visualize** page helps to visualize all the data that has been stored in Elasticsearch. After understanding the data using the **Discover** page, the Visualize page takes it a step further and provides the ability to build visualizations with ease. Visualizations help to understand the data instead of going through tons of raw data, which you may not make any sense of. The **Visualize** page is where you can create, view, modify, and delete the custom created visualizations.

The Visualize page interface typically looks like the following screenshot:

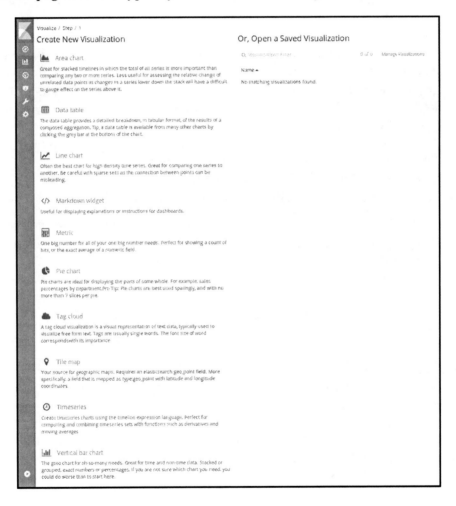

Using the Visualize page is a little tricky as there are four steps to follow for designing visualization:

1. Selecting the type of visualization for creating a new visualization.
2. Selecting the name of the index.
3. Selecting the search data source.
4. Visualization Canvas.

Steps *1*, *2*, and *3* are pretty straightforward and provides the option to select which type of visualization you want to create, select which index to choose, and determine whether it will use a saved search source or a new search source. However, step *4* opens up an interface that could be alien to people at first. Visualization Canvas is the core part wherein you create, edit, configure, and delete visualizations. Its interface upon opening looks like the following:

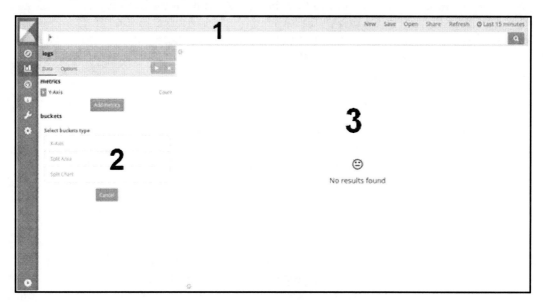

 By default, the Time Filter is set to **Last 15 minutes**.

The Visualization Canvas consists of three main sections:

- Toolbar (marked as number **1**)
- Aggregation Designer (marked as number **2**)
- Preview Visualization (marked as number **3**)

Before having a look at how to build visualizations, let's understand the underlying component of Elasticsearch aggregations, which is used to build visualizations.

Understanding aggregations

Visualization uses Elasticsearch aggregations to provide simple and complex representation of data using a variety of charts, maps, and so on. Aggregations form the driving engine for creating visualizations in Kibana and follow the aggregations logic in Elasticsearch. They have grown from the facets module of Elasticsearch. Aggregations are nothing but collection of data that allow faster querying of data and easy aggregation of data. The aggregations are primarily categorized into two categories: bucket and metrics.

Bucket aggregations

Bucketing is used to distribute the various documents among various bucket(s) based on one or more criterion/criteria. They are used to group the various documents and evaluate them against a criteria to define which document will fit into which bucket. Whenever aggregation has to be done, all the documents are evaluated to find which bucket will hold which document. The process is followed as it is until all the documents fit into the buckets as evaluated. They also compute the documents in the buckets and return the number of documents present in each bucket.

Bucket aggregations provide flexibility as they can combine with metric aggregations or you can create sub-aggregations. Sub-aggregations will compute the documents for each bucket as generated by the parent aggregation. Also, the bucketing strategies of different bucket aggregators are different as some use single bucket strategy, some use a multiple buckets strategy, and some dynamically create buckets while aggregating data. Buckets represent the x-axis in visualizations.

The different bucket aggregators present in Kibana are:

- **Date Histogram**: This aggregation is used with fields having a datatype as date, which is automatically extracted by Kibana if the index contains time-based events. It requires a field of datatype date and an interval parameter to aggregate data on. It groups documents matching the criteria of buckets that are specified by the interval parameter. The available interval parameters Auto, Second, Minute, Hourly, Daily, Weekly, Monthly, Yearly, and Custom.

  For example, the documents contain a field having multiple dates. If you specify the date type field and interval parameter as monthly, then all the documents will be grouped based on months, and those documents having a date from 1ˢᵗ July to 31ˢᵗ July will fall in the bucket of July, and so on.

- **Histogram**: This aggregation is used with fields containing numbers or numeric values. It requires a field of the datatype number and any interval having a numeric value to aggregate data on. It dynamically creates buckets based on the specified interval. It groups documents matching the criteria of buckets that are specified by the interval parameter.

> Histogram is similar to the Date Histogram aggregation except that Histogram uses number type data, whereas Date Histogram uses date type data.

  For example, for documents that contain a numeric value field having values from 1 to 1,000, the interval is specified as 100. It will aggregate all the documents and will group them based on bucket values whose keys are 100, 200, and so on.

- **Range**: This aggregation is used with fields containing numeric values. It requires a field of datatype numbers and the interval needs to be specified in numeric value to aggregate data on. It creates buckets based on the range mentioned. It groups documents matching the criteria of buckets that are specified by the range.

> Range is similar to Histogram aggregation except that Histogram creates buckets dynamically, whereas in Range buckets are specified in interval in `From` and `To date`

- **Date Range**: This aggregation is used with fields containing date type values. It requires a field of datatype date and the interval needs to be specified in accepted date formats to aggregate data on. It creates buckets based on the range mentioned. It groups documents matching the criteria of buckets that are specified by the range.

 Date Range is similar to Date Histogram aggregation except that Date Histogram creates buckets dynamically, whereas in Date Range buckets are specified in intervals in the From and To date. Also, date range includes FROM values in buckets, but excludes TO values.

- **IPv4 Range**: This aggregation is used with fields containing IP type values. It requires a field of datatype IP and the interval needs to be specified to aggregate data on. It creates buckets based on the IP range provided. It groups documents matching the criteria of buckets that are specified by the range.
- **Terms**: This aggregation creates buckets based on the values of a field in the documents. It dynamically creates buckets. It is similar in usage with the GROUP BY statement of SQL. It creates buckets as the field values and puts in documents containing that field. It allows you to order the field by selecting either Top N or Bottom N results.

  For example: The documents contain a field named countries. You want to group the data by countries to find the top five or bottom five countries.

- **Filters**: This aggregation creates buckets based on the search queries. It uses search queries, which act as filters and are also the key for the buckets.

  For example: You can choose a query such as countries:India, which will create a bucket for the same and fits the documents into it matching the search query.

- **Significant terms**: This aggregation is mostly used to find the uncommonly common terms in the data. It compares the foreground set, which contains the result and the background set that contains data in the index. They provide results that have taken a significant change between foreground and background sets.
- **GeoHash:** This aggregation is used with fields containing geo_point values. It dynamically creates buckets. It groups documents matching the geo_points into buckets. It is available only in TileMap visualization. The Bucket aggregators are displayed in Kibana, as shown in the following screenshot:

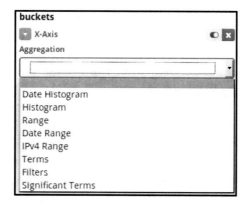

Metric aggregations

Metric aggregations represent the computation of metrics over the documents that are present in buckets. They compute the metrics such as count, average, sum, median, min, max, standard deviation, unique count, percentiles, and percentile ranks of the fields present in the documents. Metric aggregations are used on top of bucket aggregations. After the buckets are aggregated with the documents, metrics are computed such as counting the number of documents, the average of a field in all the documents, and the min or max values of a field in all the documents to provide a single value result of each bucket. In chart visualizations, metrics represent the *y*-axis in the Area Chart, Line Chart, or Vertical Bar Chart.

The different metric aggregators present in Kibana are:

- **Count**: This aggregation is mostly used and is the most important to calculate the number of documents present in each bucket and return the number as a value. This value can be used to extract the count from any fields present in the document.

  For example: To find out the number of users visiting your website, you can use the website name field for bucket aggregation and use metric aggregation to count the number of users visiting the website.

- **Average**: This aggregation is used to calculate the average value of a numeric field present in the documents that are stored in the buckets.

- **Sum**: This aggregation is used to calculate the sum of a numeric field present in the documents that are stored in the buckets.

- **Median**: This aggregation is used to calculate the middle number that separates the higher half values from lower half values. It can also be considered as the 50th percentile.
- **Min**: This aggregation is used to calculate the minimum value of a numeric field present in the documents that are stored in the buckets.
- **Max**: This aggregation is used to calculate the maximum value of a numeric field present in the documents that are stored in the buckets.
- **Standard Deviation**: This aggregation is used to calculate the dispersion of values present in the documents that are stored in the buckets. It quantifies the variation between the values of the fields.
- **Unique Count**: This aggregation is used to calculate the number of unique values of a field present in the documents that are stored in the buckets. Its functionality is similar to the `COUNT (DISTINCT fieldname)` functionality of SQL.
- **Percentile**: This aggregation is used to calculate the percentiles of a numeric field present in the documents that are stored in the buckets. It falls under the category of multi-value metrics aggregation as it stores multiple values per bucket. The percentile results in the value for which specified the percentage of documents lie.
- **Percentile Ranks**: This aggregation is used to calculate the percentile ranks of a numeric field present in the documents that are stored in the buckets. It falls under the category of multi-value metrics aggregation as it stores multiple values per bucket. It specifies the percentage of the values that occur for buckets.

All metric aggregators are displayed in Kibana, as shown in the following screenshot:

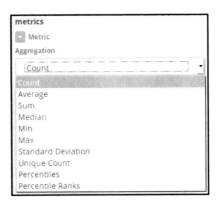

After understanding the underlying aggregations that are used to create visualizations, let's have a look at how to build various visualizations provided by Kibana.

Visualization Canvas

The Visualization Canvas consists of three main sections:

- **Toolbar**: This provides various options such as **New Visualization, Save Visualization, Open Saved Visualization, Share Visualization**, and **Refresh**.
- **Aggregation Designer**: This comprises of two tabs: **Data** and **Options**. The **Data** tab is used for defining the metrics and bucket aggregations on the basis of which visualizations are created. The **Options** tab is used to define the additional options provided for the visualizations, which can be customized as required.
- **Preview Visualization**: This is used for previewing the visualizations that have been created using the Aggregation Designer. It provides a single view page to customize, edit, or modify the visualizations and get a preview instantly.

Now, let's go through the types of visualizations.

Area chart

This is used to display the distribution of data (documents) over a period of time. It is useful for creating stacked timelines. It is mostly used to show trends over time wherein the area is filled with colors to depict the data.

Data table

This is used to display aggregated data in a tabular format. It provides the results in a text form. It is used to display any type of data stored within the documents in an aggregated way for better understanding.

 It can be used to export the data table in either a raw or formatted format.

Line chart

This is used to display a distribution of data (documents) over a period of time in the form of lines. It is useful for creating time-series charts. It is mostly used to show trends over time or comparing multiple time-series charts.

Bubble chart

This is an extension of a Line Chart wherein instead of the lines, each data point is displayed as a bubble. Line charts can be extended/converted to Bubble Charts by adding other metrics in the *y*-Axis and selecting the metrics type as the dot size.

Markdown widget

This is used to display instructions, information, or explanations in a text-based input. It is a GitHub flavored markdown wherein you can display any text, links, tables, or code-blocks. It is useful for information pertaining to a dashboard.

Metric

This is used to display a single number for all your analysis. It displays the number for metric aggregations based on the data. It does not involve any bucketing.

Pie chart

This is used to display the proportion of the whole quantity. It is represented using slices where each slice contributes to the total contribution and shows the percentage contribution against the whole. Mostly, it's preferred to use this visualization only when you want to display fewer slices.

Tag clouds

These are used for giving a visual representation to the data. They are used to provide importance of a word by font color and font size. The font size is determined by the type of metric aggregation used. If count is used, then the most occurring word has the biggest font size and the least occurring word has the smallest font size.

Tile map

This is used to display the geographical locations based on the geo coordinates that are represented through latitude and longitude. It uses the GeoHash bucket aggregation to map the points with its location.

Time series

This is used to create time-series based charts using Timelion expression language. It is helpful in deriving statistics, moving averages, and a host of other mathematical functions. You can skip to the *Learning Timelion* section to learn more about this visualization.

Vertical bar chart

This is a general purpose chart used for displaying a variety of data. It is used with both time-based and non-time based data. It uses the bar to represent data wherein the size of the bars is determined by their value. The higher the size of the bar, the more value, and the lower the size of the bar, the lesser the value.

The following is a list of various **Data** tabs and **Options** tabs provided by Kibana for the different visualizations.

Data tab visualizations are as follows:

Type of Visualization	Metrics	Bucket
Area Chart	*y*-axis	X-Axis, Split Area, Split Chart
Data Table	Metric	Split Rows, Split Table
Line Chart	*y*-axis	X-Axis, Split Lines, Split Chart
Metric	Metric	–
Pie Chart	Slice Size	Split Slices, Split Chart
Tag Clouds	Tag Size	Tags
Tile Map	Value	Geo Coordinates
Vertical Bar Chart	*y*-axis	X-Axis, Split Bars, Split Chart

Options tab visualizations are as follows:

Type of Visualization	View Options
Area Chart	Chart Mode (Stacked, Overlap, Percentage, Wiggle, Silhouette), Smooth Lines, Set Y-Axis Extents, Scale Y-Axis to Data Bounds, Order buckets by descending sum, Legend position, Show Tooltip
Data Table	Per Page, Show metrics for every bucket/level, Show Partial Rows, Calculate metrics for every bucket/level, Show total, Total function

Line Chart	Y-Axis Scale (Linear, Log, Square Root), Smooth Lines, Show Connecting lines, Show Circles, Set Y-Axis Extents, Scale Y-Axis to Data Bounds, Order buckets by descending sum, Legend position, Show Tooltip
Metric	Font Size
Pie Chart	Donut, Legend Position, Show Tooltip
Tag Cloud	Text Scale (Linear, Log, Square Root), Orientation (Single, Right angled, Multiple), Font Size, Show label
Tile Map	Map Type (Scaled Circle Markers, Shaded Circle Markers, Shaded Geohash Grid, Heatmap), Legend Position, Show Tooltip, Desaturate Map Tiles, WMS compliant map server
Vertical Bar Chart	Bar Mode (Stacked, Percentage, Grouped), Y-Axis Scale (Linear, Log, Square Root), Set Y-Axis Extents, Scale Y-Axis to Data Bounds, Order buckets by descending sum, Legend Position, Show Tooltip

Exploring the Dashboard interface

Dashboard provides a unified view of displaying all your visualization in one place. Dashboard provides a collection of multiple visualizations or searches that can be arranged in any way and it allows the ability to resize, move, edit, or remove any visualization added to the dashboard. The dashboard provides real time insights to the streaming data as all visualizations are updated in the dashboard in real time. Updating the visualization reflects instantly across the dashboards using that visualization. Dashboard also provides the ability to use search queries that update the visualizations present in the dashboard as per the search result.

 For creating a dashboard, visualizations/searches need to be saved.

The **Dashboard** page interface typically looks like the following screenshot:

The **Dashboard** interface is fairly simple to understand as it displays the main Kibana header, which is the same across all pages in Kibana that contain the Time Filter.

The toolbar consists of several options, such as:

- **Search Bar**: This is used for querying the dashboards similar to querying in the **Discover** page.
- **New Dashboard:** This is used to create a new dashboard.

 If you have created a dashboard and added visualizations to it, and you haven't saved the dashboard and you click on New Dashboard, then the unsaved dashboard will be emptied and the added visualizations will disappear.

- **Add**: This is used to add saved visualizations and searches to the dashboard.
- **Save Dashboard**: This is used to save the dashboard that includes added visualizations.
- **Open Dashboard**: This is used to load the saved dashboards with visualizations.
- **Share**: This is used to share the dashboard either by sharing the link or embedding it within a web page using the link provided. Also, it allows you to share the link by generating a short URL.

- **Options**: This is used to select the theme for the dashboard, that is, a dark theme or light theme.

Understanding Timelion

Timelion is the latest addition to the Kibana UI with the introduction of Elastic Stack. Timelion is used for analysis and visualizations of time-series data. It provides the ability to combine multiple data sources into a single visualization and gives a range of mathematical calculations that can be used, such as cumulative sum, derivative, moving averages, and so on.

Timelion is present in the left-pane of the Kibana UI between icons of **Dashboard** and **Dev Tools**. It has its own language and expressions when using it, which makes it difficult to start with. However, it has a great built-in documentation and tutorial to guide you on how to start using Timelion.

When you click on Timelion, you will be greeted with a screen similar to the following screenshot:

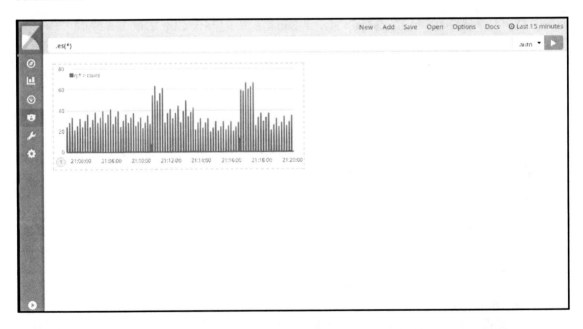

In the preceding screenshot, you see that there has been a default expression that has already been added, .es(*),which means it is querying all the data present in Elasticsearch within all the indices. It represents the count of documents present in Elasticsearch.

You can query a particular index such as logs by changing the expression from `.es(*)` to `.es(index=logs)`. It will then show the count of documents present in the logs index in Elasticsearch.

Let's understand the Timelion interface in brief:

- **New**: This is used to create a new Timelion page for creating visualizations.
- **Add**: This is used to add charts within the same Timelion page.
- **Save**: This is used to save the Timelion page. It provides two options, which are to save the Timelion sheet or save the current expression as a Kibana dashboard panel.
- **Open**: This is used to open the saved Timelion sheet.
- **Options**: This provides the option of specifying the number of rows and columns.
- **Docs**: This provides the documentation to start with Timelion.

Other options include:

- **Time Filter**: This provides the time-filter options for filtering the data.
- **Search Box**: This provides the usage for using language and expressions for analyzing the data.
- **Time Interval**: This specifies the time interval to be defined. If auto, it picks the time interval on its own as per the Time Filter described. It can be set as `1s`, `1m`, `1d`, `1y`, or custom. It is present next to the Search box.

To start learning how to use Timelion, let's click on the **Docs** options present in the Toolbar beside the Time Filter option. Upon clicking it, you will be greeted with functional reference information, which describes all the functions available in Timelion. You will see a screen similar to the following:

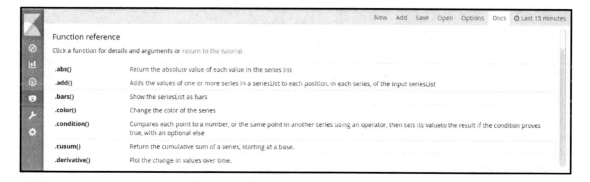

You can scroll down to view more functions as there are close to 50 functions available. It also provides functions to fetch data from third-party sites such as Quandl and the World Bank whose data is available in the form of API calls.

Also, you can see in the preceding screenshot that there is a reference to a tutorial that goes through a deeper understanding of Timelion as documented. To go through the tutorial, click on the **return to the tutorial** link, which will take you to the **Welcome to Timelion** page.

It will look like the following screen:

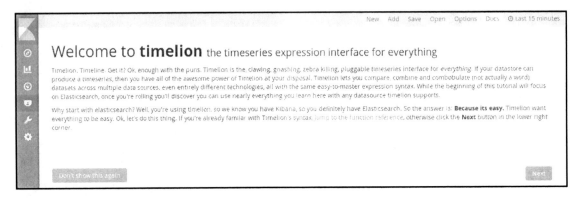

You can go through the tutorial to learn about Timelion by clicking on the **Next** button, which is present in the lower-right level of the tutorial page.

Let's have a look at a few options that appear after scrolling on the added charts:

- **Remove**: This is used to remove a chart from the Timelion sheet
- **Drag to Order**: This is used to re-order the positions of various charts
- **Full Screen**: This is used to display the visualization created in a full screen

Exploring Dev Tools

Dev Tools refers to the development tools that aid the developer. In Kibana, it is used for the Console UI, which provides a simple yet clean interface to access API queries using the REST API exposed by the Elasticsearch client. Console allows us to make any API call from a web browser. Its interface gives us a clean way to make a call and generates JSON in a pretty print format, which allows you to view results in a neat way. It works on top of an HTTP layer of an Elasticsearch cluster.

Upon clicking **Dev Tools**, you will be greeted with the Console UI, as shown in the following screenshot:

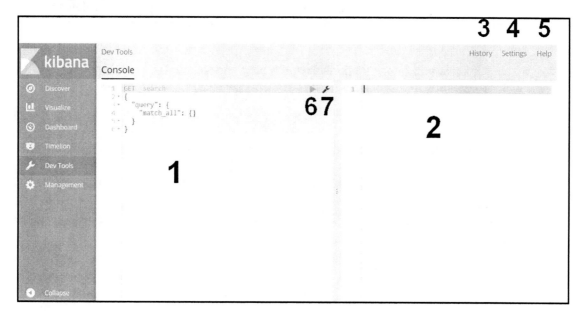

For a better understanding all of the available options are marked in the screenshot from number 1 to 7, which are described this section:

1. Editor Pane: This is the area where we write our request. It uses commands in cURL similar syntax and presents it in a simpler way. For example, by default, a query displayed in Console is:

```
GET _search
{
  "query": {
    "match_all": {}
  }
}
```

It can be interpreted as the following query of Elasticsearch –

```
curl -XGET "http://localhost:9200/_search" -d'
{
  "query": {
    "match_all": {}
  }
}'
```

GET is the verb we want to use and _search is the endpoint to search for all the indices present in Elasticsearch. This area also provides autocomplete and auto suggestions for APIs, indices, types, and so on. We can also paste complete cURL commands and they will automatically be translated to syntax adopted by console.

Console will query the Elasticsearch host address that Kibana is connected to Elasticsearch. By default, it is localhost:9200.

2. Response Pane: Whatever we request, Console will request it to Elasticsearch and the result is pretty printed in JSON format in this area.
3. This option shows us the request history. It stores the history of the last 500 requests.
4. Using this option, we can change the font properties, autocomplete settings, and so on.
5. This is a help option for users showing a sample request, and it lists all the keyboard shortcuts.
6. Whatever request we type in, we can run that by clicking the green run button.
7. This wrench icon provides us with the option to copy the request as the cURL command and to set it if the text should be auto indent or not. If the request has been properly formatted and if you select auto indent, Console will collapse the complete request into a single line, which is useful for debugging purposes.

You can mention multiple requests in the editor pane, which will be executed one by one in the order as specified.

Exploring the Management interface

Settings provide a way to customize and tweak various Kibana related properties.

This page has been categorized into multiple options to understand the various settings involved with each of the options. The options are displayed as shown in the following screenshot:

Let us have a closer look at the various settings provided by each of the options.

Index patterns

This option provides us with the ability to configure an index or indices pattern to be used with Kibana. It provides the various indices patterns that have already been configured to use with Kibana along with the ability to view the information related to various fields present in an index.

You can configure various types of index, such as:

- **Index Name**
- **Index Patterns**

Index patterns are divided into the following two search categories:

- **Wildcard Searches:** `logstash-*` will fetch all indices names starting with `logstash-`
- **Event Time Based:** `[logstash-]YYYY-MM-DD` will fetch all indices following a pattern wherein the index name starts with `logstash-` followed by the event date/time

For additional settings of the index, click on the index to view more information, such as:

- Listing of fields within the index
- Properties of fields such as type, format, searchable, aggregatable, analyzed, excluded, and controls
- Option of setting the index as a default index
- Refreshing the fields list within the index
- Removing the index pattern from Kibana
- Managing field properties such as changing the format of the field

Upon clicking the index name, you get additional settings as tabs apart from fields, such as:

- Scripted fields: It is used to create on-the-fly fields to compute information.
- Source filters: It is used to exclude fields from the _source field. As the _source field contains all the fields, some of the fields may not be of importance. Hence, you can exclude the fields from the _source field directly.

Saved objects

This option is used for managing the various saved objects such as saved searches, visualizations, and dashboards. It is used to view, edit, export, import, and delete objects. It also provides the ability to export all the objects saved as searches, visualizations, or dashboards to be exported all at once.

Advanced Settings

This option contains the advanced settings that are experimental, undocumented, or unsupported. It provides additional capability to tweak the settings and controls of Kibana. It is mainly for advanced users to play around with, which if used incorrectly can cause unexpected behavior. Also deleting any settings from this tab will delete the setting from the Kibana configuration.

Let's have a look at some of the settings provided in this tab:

- **dateFormat**: Used to change the date format present in the documents.

  For example, the default setting: MMMM Do YYYY, HH:mm:ss.SSS (*July 27th 2016, 12:46:01.000*) can be changed to: MMMM DD YYYY (*July 27 2016*).

- **dateFormat:tz**: Used to change the date format as per the specified time zone.

  For example, the default setting: Browser - IST (*July 27th 2016, 12:45:25.000*) can be changed to: Asia/Singapore (*June 27th 2016, 15:15:25.000*).

- **doc_table:highlight**: Used for mentioning whether to highlight results or not.

  Default setting: True (in the **Discover** and **Saved** searches dashboards).

- **history:limit**: Used for showing the recent values of query inputs.

    Default setting: `10`.

- **savedObjects:perPage**: Used to display the number of saved objects per page using the loading dialog.

    Default setting: `5`.

- **timepicker:timeDefaults**: Used to set the default Time Filter of Kibana.

    Default setting: `{ "from": "now-15m", "to": "now", "mode": "quick" }` can be changed: `{ "from": "now-30m", "to": "now-15m", "mode": "relative" }`.

    It will change the default Time Filter and will show results from `30` minutes ago to `15` minutes ago.

- **dashboard:defaultDarkTheme**: Used to set the default theme of the **Dashboard** page.

    The default setting: `false` can be changed to `true`. It will always display the dashboard in the dark theme whenever the dashboard page is opened.

After understanding the various options provided by Kibana, if we look closely there is another option available that gives minimal information about Kibana. Click on the Information icon present above the options in the top-right corner, which provides you with the following information:

- Build number
- Commit SHA Hash Code

Also, the version number is mentioned between the **Management** interface heading the and Kibana settings options.

Sometimes there could be some issues due to which Kibana may not start or may not show any data in the Discover page. To learn if Kibana has started properly, you can go to the following URL:

```
http://localhost:5601/status
```

Where localhost is the host address of your Kibana server.

The preceding URL gives following information as mentioned in the following sections:

Status

This is used to provide the status of the Kibana server along with other information, such as:

- Heap total
- Heap used
- Load
- Response time average
- Response time max
- Requests per second
- Status breakdown of the installed plugins of Kibana along with their names and status

Putting it all together

After learning about Elasticsearch, Logstash, and Kibana, let's use these components to create an end-to-end pipeline to parse data from Logstash to Elasticsearch and visualize it using Kibana. We will use a CSV file as input data, which will be used to analyze and create visualizations out of the data.

This will help us to quickly get started by using all the three components together to create an end-to-end pipeline. While using this example in this chapter, we assume that you have successfully installed Elasticsearch, Logstash, and Kibana as described in Chapter 1, *Elastic Stack Overview*.

Let's have a look at the input data.

Input data

We will be using the input data provided by **United States Department of Agriculture Economic Research Service (USDA ERS)**, which is about educational attainment for the U.S and counties, 1970-2014. It provides information about the attainment of education, people who have less than a high school diploma, a high school diploma only, those who have completed some college (1-3 years) degree, or four years of a college degree. All this information is all showcased for each decade from 1970-2014. It represents the number of people and percentage of people who have attained education, which is divided by state and area name. This dataset also provides information about the Rural-Urban Continuum Code and the Urban Influence Code for 2003 and 2013. The file format is .csv.

From author, use this subset of data

This data is available at: `http://www.ers.usda.gov/data-products/coun` `ty-level-data-sets/download-data.aspx`. Information about the Urban Influence Code is available at: `http://www.ers.usda.gov/data-products` `/urban-influence-codes/documentation.aspx`. Information about the Rural-Urban Continuum Code is available at: `http://www.ers.usda.gov/data-products/rural-urban-continuum-code` `s/documentation.aspx`.

New link to data from author

The file contains lots of headers (columns). We will use some of the headers to analyze data and create visualizations.

Let us have a look at the workflow that will be used for inserting input data using Logstash with output being stored in Elasticsearch, which will then be used by Kibana for analyzing the data.

The workflow is as follows:

1. Create a Logstash configuration file and perform the following steps:

   i. Use the file input plugin to insert data into Logstash.

   ii. Use a csv filter to name the columns and change the datatype of fields from string to an appropriate datatype.

   iii. Use the Elasticsearch output plugin to store data into Elasticsearch. Also use the stdout output to display logs on the screen.

2. Create an index pattern in Kibana.
3. Analyze the data and create visualizations in Kibana.

Creating a Logstash configuration file

As we are already aware of various Logstash plugins used for Input, Filters, and Output. For easy understanding, we will show the configuration file as per Input, Filter, and Output plugins.

Use the `Input` plugin by implementing the following code:

```
input{
  file{
    path =>"/usr/share/logstash/InputData/Education.csv"
    start_position =>"beginning"
  }
```

```
}
```

In the preceding `Input` plugin, we are using the file input plugin, mentioning the path from where to read the input data and mentioning to read the data starting from the beginning.

Use the `Filter` plugin by implementing the following code:

```
filter
{
  csv{
  columns=>
    [
    "State",
    "AreaName",
    "2003Rural-urbanContinuumCode",
    "2003UrbanInfluenceCode",
    "2013Rural-urbanContinuumCode",
    "2013UrbanInfluenceCode",
  "Lessthanahighschooldiploma,1970", "Highschooldiplomaonly,1970",
    "Percentofadultswithlessthanahighschooldiploma,1970",
    "Percentofadultswithlessthanahighschooldiploma,2010-2014",
    "Percentofadultswithahighschooldiplomaonly,2010-2014",
    "Percentofadultscompletingsomecollegeorassociate'sdegree,2010-2014",
    "Percentofadultswithabachelor'sdegreeorhigher,2010-2014"
    ]
  }
mutate {
    convert => ["2003Rural-urbanContinuumCode","integer"]
    convert => ["2003UrbanInfluenceCode","integer"]
    convert => ["2013Rural-urbanContinuumCode","integer"]
    convert => ["2013UrbanInfluenceCode","integer"]
    convert => ["Lessthanahighschooldiploma,1970","integer"]
    convert => ["Highschooldiplomaonly,1970","integer"]
    convert =>
    ["Percentofadultswithlessthanahighschooldiploma,1970","float"]
    convert =>
    ["Percentofadultswithlessthanahighschooldiploma,2010-2014","float"]
    convert =>
    ["Percentofadultswithahighschooldiplomaonly,2010-2014","float"]
    convert =>
["Percentofadultscompletingsomecollegeorassociate'sdegree,2010-2014","float
"]
    convert =>
["Percentofadultswithabachelor'sdegreeorhigher,2010-2014","float"]
  }
}
```

In the preceding `Filter` plugin, we are using the CSV filter plugin, mentioning the column names in the CSV and using mutate to change the datatype of fields from `string` to `float` or `integer`.

 By default, column names in csv are named as `column 1`, `column 2`, and so on. Also by default, Logstash parses the columns as a datatype `String`.

Use the `Output` plugin by implementing the following code:

```
output{
  elasticsearch {
    hosts => "localhost:9200"
    index => "education"
  }
  stdout { codec => rubydebug }
}
```

In the preceding `Output` plugin, we are storing the data in Elasticsearch by mentioning properties such as hosts, index name, and document type. Also we are using `stdout`, which prints the output to the `STDOUT` of the running Logstash shell.

Let us save the previously created Logstash configuration in the `/usr/share/logstash` folder with the name `education.conf`. Run the logstash configuration file after navigating to the Logstash folder, using the following command:

$ sudo bin/logstash -f education.conf

 Make sure before running Logstash with the configuration file that Elasticsearch is running as mentioned in `Chapter 1`, *Elastic Stack Overview*.

Logstash will run and parse the configuration file for each input and store the input in the education index in Elasticsearch. You will see the logs in the console, which will show how your data is being stored in Elasticsearch. You will see the following output:

```
Settings: Default pipeline workers: 4
Logstash startup completed
{  "message" => "US,UnitedStates,,,,,"523,73,312","341,58,051",47.7,
13.7,28.0,29.1,29.3
"@version" => "1",
"@timestamp" => "2017-02-16T05:02:31.878Z",
"path" => /usr/share/logstash/InputData/Education.csv
```

```
"host" => "ubuntu",
"State" => "US",
"AreaName" => "UnitedStates",
"2003Rural-urbanContinuumCode" => nil,
"2003UrbanInfluenceCode" => nil,
"2013Rural-urbanContinuumCode" => nil,
"2013UrbanInfluenceCode" => nil,
"Lessthanahighschooldiploma,1970" => "523,73,312",
"Highschooldiplomaonly,1970" => "341,58,051",
"Percentofadultswithlessthanahighschooldiploma,1970" => "47.7",
"Percentofadultswithlessthanahighschooldiploma,2010-2014" => "13.7",
"Percentofadultswithahighschooldiplomaonly,2010-2014" => "28.0",
"Percentofadultscompletingsomecollegeorassociate'sdegree,2010-2014" =>
"29.1",
"Percentofadultswithabachelor'sdegreeorhigher,2010-2014" => "29.3"
}
```

Using Kibana

After pushing the data from Logstash to Elasticsearch, let's have a look at the data stored in Elasticsearch. You can run Kibana, as explained in Chapter 1, *Elastic Stack Overview*, either as a service or using the bat file (Windows users).

The following command is used to start kibana as a service using the Terminal:

```
sudo service kibana start
```

Or, the following command is used to start Kibana after navigating to the Kibana installed directory (Ubuntu):

```
bin/kibana
```

Or, you can click directly on the kibana.bat file present in the Kibana installation directory to start Kibana in Windows.

Now let's verify that Kibana has started by entering the following URL in the browser:

```
http://localhost:5601
```

You will be greeted with **Configure an index pattern,** as shown in the following screenshot:

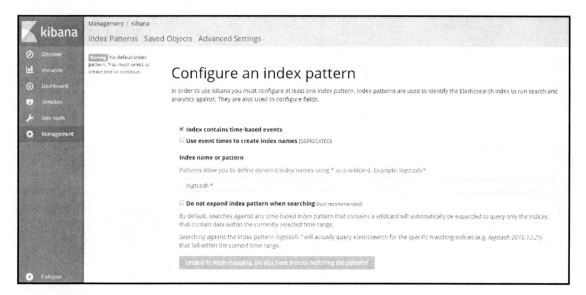

Let's configure the index pattern by mentioning the index name or pattern as education. Also, untick the option **Index contains time-based events** as there are no time-based related fields in the data. Click on the Create button to configure the index.

After clicking on the **Create** button, let's verify that the data is indexed and populated with correct field names and its datatype. Go to the **Management** page and click on the education index name under the index pattern present in the left side of **Index Patterns** option. It will then list the fields in the index and provide details such as name, datatype, format, and whether the fields are searchable, aggregatable, analyzed, or excluded. Let's go to the **Discover** page to discover the data. Click on the Discover page and on the left-side pane check the index name. If the index name is education, then you can use the page to discover data or else select the index name as education by clicking on the arrow button beside the index name.

You will see the data in the **Discover** page, as shown in the following screenshot:

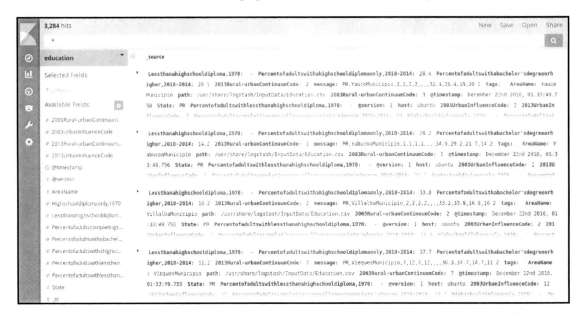

Let's understand the data by viewing the data associated with each field to get a better understanding of what the field conveys along with the values contained in the fields. We can find the values for fields such as `State` and `AreaName`. Also, you can click on the available fields to see the popular values for that field. It is easier to analyze data by adding fields for which you want to view data.

Now let's build visualizations after analyzing the data. We will create visualizations and save them, which will be used to create a dashboard. Let's build visualizations for the following scenarios:

- Top states based on 2003 RUCC
- Top states based on 2003 UIC
- Top five area names with less than high school diploma 1970
- Top five area names with high school diploma 1970

- Percentage of adults having less than high school diploma in 1970 by area and state
- Top states as per their count and their top 2013 RUCC
- Insights such as total records, total number of 2013RUCC codes present, total number of 2013 UIC present, total number of states, total number of area names, average percentage of adults without high school diploma (2010-2014), with high school diploma only, with college or associate degree, and with bachelor's degree or higher

Top states based on 2003 RUCC

In this scenario, we want to create a bar chart that displays the top five RUCC values used along with the state count for the RUCC:

1. Click on the **Visualize** tab and select the vertical bar chart to create a new visualization.
2. Select the search source from a new search, mentioning the index name as `education` (in case of multiple configured indices in Kibana).
3. Select the *y*-axis as **Count** in the metrics section. In the buckets aggregation, select the *x*-axis as terms aggregation on the field named `2003Rural-urbanContinuumCode`, which is ordered by the `metric:Count` displayed in descending order with the size 5.
4. Then select **Split Bars** with the sub-aggregation of terms on the `State.keyword` field, which is ordered by the `metric:Count` displayed in descending order with the size 5.

5. Finally, click on **Apply** to view the visualization, as shown in the following screenshot:

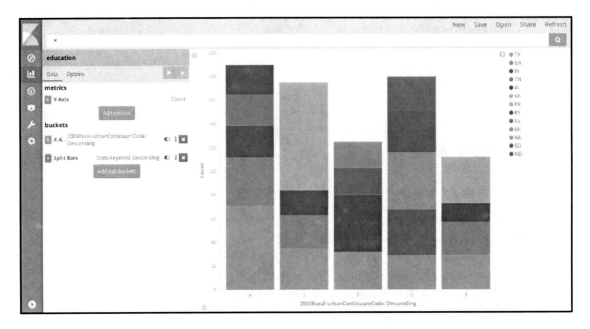

Save the visualization as `TopStatesBasedon2003RUCC`, which will be used while creating a dashboard.

Top states based on 2003 UIC

In this scenario, we want to create a bar chart that displays the top five states as per count along with the top three values of the 2003 UIC based on states:

1. Click on the **Visualize** tab and select the vertical bar chart to create a new visualization.

2. Select the search source from a new search, mentioning the index name as education (in case of multiple configured indices in Kibana).

3. Select the **Y-axis** as **Count** in the **metrics** section. In the **buckets** aggregation, select the **X-axis** as the terms aggregation on the field named State.keyword, which is ordered by the metric:Count displayed in descending order with the size 5.

4. Then select **Split Bars** with the sub-aggregation of terms on the 2003UrbanInfluenceCode field, which is ordered by the metric:Count displayed in descending order with the size 3.

5. Finally, click on **Apply** to view the visualization, as shown in the following screenshot:

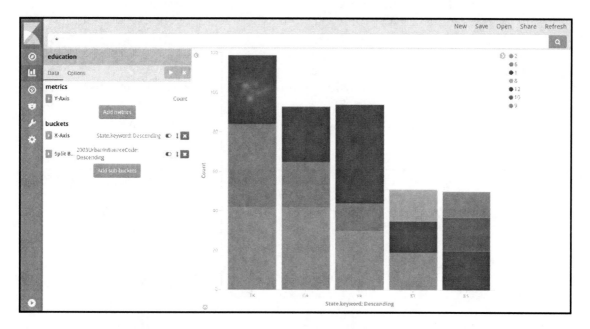

Save the visualization as TopStatesBasedon2003UIC, which will be used while creating a dashboard.

Top five area names with less than high school diploma 1970

In this scenario, we want to create a bar chart that displays the top five values of the
LessthanHighSchoolDiploma1970 field along with the area name for which it occurs:

1. Click on the **Visualize** tab and select vertical bar chart to create a new
   visualization.
2. Select the search source from a new search, mentioning the index name as
   education (in case of multiple configured indices in Kibana).
3. Select the **Y-axis** as **Count** in the **metrics** section. In the **buckets** aggregation,
   select the **X-axis** as the terms aggregation on the field named
   LessthanHighSchoolDiploma, 1970, which is ordered by the term displayed in
   descending order with the size 5.

4. Then select **Split Bars** with the sub-aggregation of terms on the
   AreaName.keyword field, which is ordered by the metric:Count displayed in
   descending order with size 5.
5. Finally, click on **Apply** to view the visualization, as shown in the following
   screenshot:

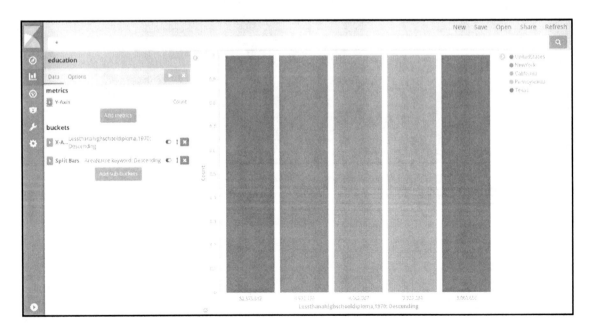

Save the visualization as `Top5AreaNamewithLessthanHSD1970`, which will be used while creating a dashboard. In this visualization, we see the value of `AreaName` as `UnitedStates`, which is the sum for all the values of the field, which we will exclude in other visualizations.

Top five area names with high school diploma 1970

In this scenario, we want to create a bar chart that displays the top five values of the `HighSchoolDiploma1970` field along with the area name for which it occurs:

1. Click on the **Visualize** tab and select the vertical bar chart to create a new visualization.
2. Select the search source from a new search, mentioning the index name as `education` (in case of multiple configured indices in Kibana).

3. Select the **Y-axis** as **Count** in the **metrics** section. In the **buckets** aggregation, select the **X-axis** as terms aggregation on the field named `HighSchooldiplomaonly,1970`, which is ordered by the term displayed in descending order with the size 5.
4. Then select **Split Bars** with the sub-aggregation of terms on the field `AreaName.keyword`, which is ordered by the `metric:Count` displayed in descending order with the size 5. As we need to exclude search results of `AreaNameunitedstates`, click on **UnitedStates**, mentioned in the legend. Upon clicking it, click on the positive filter symbol, which will add the filter. Then go to filter actions and select invert, which will show results for all `AreaNames` except `UnitedStates`.

4. Finally, click on **Apply** to view the visualization, as shown in the following screenshot:

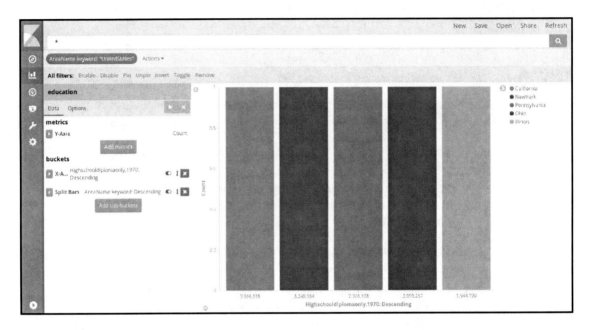

Save the visualization as `Top5AreaNamewithHSD1970`, which will be used while creating a dashboard.

Percentage of adults having less than high school diploma in 1970 by area and state

In this scenario, we want to create a pie chart that displays the top five values depicting the highest percentage of adults with the less than high school diploma 1970 field along with the area name and state for which it occurs:

1. Click on the **Visualize** tab and select Pie chart to create a new visualization.
2. Select the search source from a new search, mentioning the index name as `education` (in case of multiple configured indices in Kibana).
3. Select **Slice Size** as **Count** in the **metrics** section. In the **buckets** aggregation, select **Split Slices** as the terms aggregation on the field named `Percentofadultswithlessahighschooldiploma,1970`, which is ordered by the term displayed in descending order with the size 5.

2. Then select **Split Splices** with sub-aggregation of terms on the `State.keyword` field, which is ordered by the term displayed in descending order with the size 5.

3. Then select **Split Splices** with the sub-aggregation of terms on the field `AreaName.keyword`, which is ordered by the term displayed in descending order with the size 5.

4. Finally, click on **Apply** to view the visualization, as shown in the following screenshot:

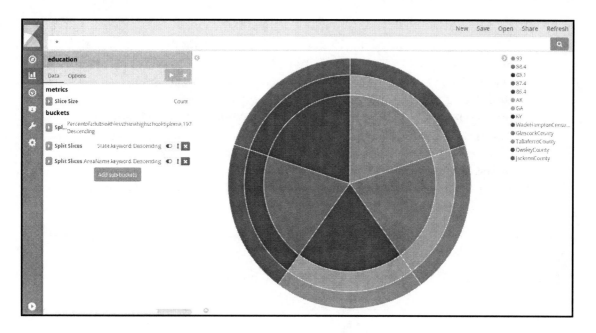

Save the visualization as `%AdultslessthanHSD1970ByArea&State`, which will be used while creating a dashboard.

Top states as per their count and their top 2013 RUCC

In this scenario, we want to create a data table that displays the top five values of the state field along with the top five values of its 2013 RUCC for which it occurs:

1. Click on the **Visualize** tab and select **Data table** to create a new visualization.
2. Select the search source from a new search, mentioning the index name as `education` (in case of multiple configured indices in Kibana).
3. Select **Metric** as **Count** in the **metrics** section. In the **buckets** aggregation, select **Split Rows** as the terms aggregation on the field named State.keyword, which is ordered by `metric:Count` displayed in descending order with the size 5.
4. Then select **Split Rows** with the sub-aggregation of terms on the `2013Rural-urbanContinuumCode` field, which is ordered by the `metric:Count` displayed in descending order with the size 5.
5. Finally, click on **Apply** to view the visualization, as shown in the following screenshot:

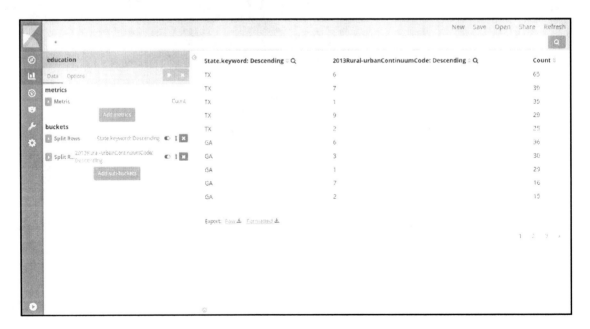

Save the visualization as `Topstateswith2013RUCCCodes`, which will be used while creating a dashboard.

Insights

In this scenario, we want to create a metric that displays various numbers in one place. We will see the total number of records, unique count of 2013 RUCC, unique count of 2013 UIC, total number of states, total number of `AreaNames`, average percentage of adults with less than high school diploma, with high school diploma only, with some college or associate degree, and with bachelor's degree or higher:

1. Click on the **Visualize** tab and select **Metric** to create a new visualization.
2. Select the search source from a new search, mentioning the index name as `education` (in case of multiple configured indices in Kibana).
3. Select **Metric** as **Count**. Select metric with a unique count aggregation on the `2013Rural-urbanContinuumCode` field.
4. Select metric with a unique count aggregation on the `2013UrbanInfluenceCode` field.
5. Select metric with a unique count aggregation on the `State.keyword` field.
6. Select metric with a unique count aggregation on the `AreaName.keyword` field.
7. Select metric with a average aggregation on the `Percentofadultswithabachelor'sdegreeorhigher,2010-2014` field.
8. Select metric with a average aggregation on the `Percentofadultscompletingsomecollegeorassociate'sdegree,2010-2014` field.
9. Select metric with a average aggregation on the `Percentofadultswithabachelor'sdegreeorhigher,2010-2014` field.

10. Select metric with a average aggregation on the
    `Percentofadultswithahighschooldiplomaonly,2010-2014` field.

11. Select metric with a average aggregation on the
    `Percentofadultswithlessthanahighschooldiploma,2010-2014` field.
    Change the **Font Size** to 35 from the **Options** tab to display all the information
    together.

12. Finally, click on **Apply** to view the visualization, as shown in the following
    screenshot:

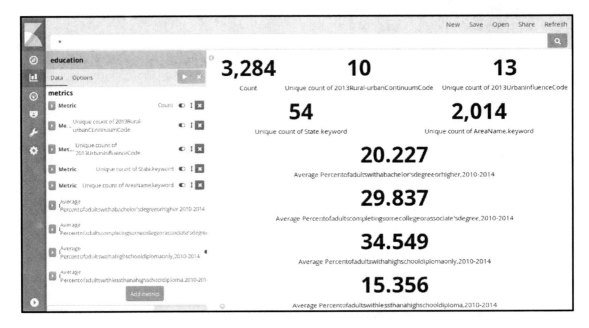

Save the visualization as `Insights-Metric`, which will be used while creating a
dashboard.

Creating a dashboard in Kibana

Now let's add all the saved visualizations to the dashboard. To add saved visualizations to **Dashboard**, go to the **Dashboard** page and click on **Add**. After adding all the visualizations along with moving and resizing them, you get a dashboard that looks like the following screenshot:

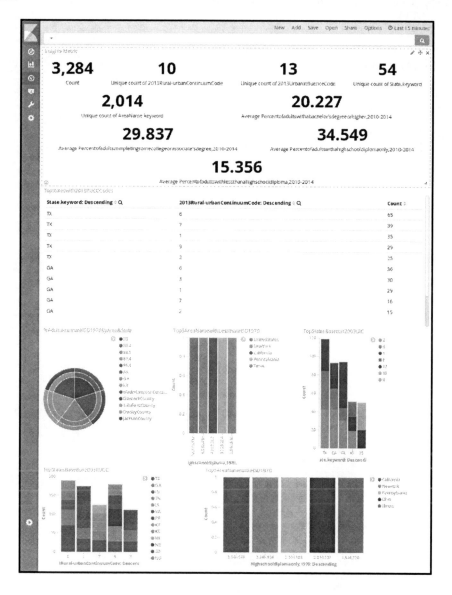

Summary

In this chapter, we learned about Kibana, its interfaces, and got a glimpse of what it is capable of. Using examples, we created several types of visualizations to analyze the data. Kibana is becoming very popular among analytics tools these days for its offerings. We will be learning more in the following chapters where we will see the real-time datasets, log analysis on production servers, and so on.

In the next chapter, we will learn about Beats, which is a new component of Elastic Stack. We will see the types of Beats, their usage, and the role they play in Elastic Stack with examples.

5

Using Beats

In the previous chapters, we explored the former ELK Stack components, along with the basics of each component and how they function together. Now, as the Stack expands and grows rapidly, let's familiarize ourselves with the newest component in the Elastic Stack.

In this chapter, we will understand the basic foundation of Beats and cover various other sections focusing entirely on Beats. We will cover from the basics to the advanced level, showcasing the ability of different types of Beats and how Beats fits into the Elastic Stack.

In this chapter, we will cover the following sections:

- Introduction to Beats
- How Beats differs from Logstash
- How Beats fits into Elastic Stack
- An overview of the different types of Beats
- Exploring Elastic Team Beats
- Exploring Community Beats
- Beats in action with Elastic Stack

Introduction to Beats

Before learning about Beats, let's understand how Beats first came into existence. Beats was not started as a project within Elastic, the company behind the ELK Stack. It all started with the Packetbeat project, wherein they wanted access to statistics between communications among various servers, providing them information.

They wanted to develop a solution which would store data in Elasticsearch, but would not consume high memory or resources. They faced the problem of using a Logstash agent on each server from which information was required, which used JVM and consumed a lot of memory and resources. Packetbeat became popular due to its ability to provide lightweight shippers, which ship the data to Elasticsearch without consuming much memory and CPU resources. Following its popularity, Elastic acquired Packetbeat and created the Beats Platform. The Beats Platform contains a number of Beats which have been developed by Elastic; this also contains Community Beats, which have been developed by developers for which infrastructure and libraries have been exposed.

Beats is the latest component to be added to the Elastic Stack. Beats does not have any out-of-the box functionality like each component of the ELK Stack, which used Elasticsearch to search and analyze the data, Logstash to process the logs, and Kibana, which provides the functionality of visualizing the data, as a visualization tool. However, Beats is a platform that provides various beats that have the ability to collect logs from different sources, parse the logs, and ship them to Logstash or Elasticsearch, which can then be visualized in Kibana. Thus, Beats are lightweight open source data shippers that collect the data from the machine/server and send different types of operational data to Elasticsearch/Logstash. You can send the data directly from Beats to Elasticsearch, or you can send data from Beats to Logstash, where you can process and parse the data for different purposes before sending the data to Elasticsearch. Beats can also be understood as a collection of lightweight daemons that collect data and ship it to either Elasticsearch or Logstash. Being lightweight in nature, these do not leave heavy footprints on the system.

The Beats platform contains a number of Beats that have been developed for different purposes. If you want to solve a specific use case, create a Beat for your use case, which will provide you with flexibility and that you can later contribute to the community. To simplify the process of developing your own beats, the Beats Platform provides you with all the options and usage of an API so that you can develop the Beat focusing only on the logic specific to your Beat and everything else is taken care of by the platform. The platform provides you with a common framework that handles various services and provides a unified infrastructure for everyone to use and develop the Beats. The Beats Platform is written using the Go language, which makes Beats more efficient by using fewer resources and less memory, which is, in turn, beneficial while shipping the data via an agent.

How Beats differ from Logstash

From what we have understood about Beats, it looks fairly similar to Logstash, wherein we have input plugins that are used to parse the data. So, how does Beats differ? Beats are data shippers shipping data from a variety of inputs such as files, data streams, or logs whereas Logstash is a data parser. Though Logstash can ship data, it's not its primary usage. In a nutshell, Beats and Logstash are similar in functionality, but there are glaring differences between them both in terms of how they are developed and the underlying technology used.

Let's look at the differences between them:

- Logstash consumes a lot of memory and requires a higher amount of resources, whereas Beats requires fewer resources and consumes low memory.
- Logstash is heavy to install on all the systems from which you want to collect the logs, whereas Beats are lightweight data shippers that will ship your data from multiple systems.
- If you are collecting logs from multiple systems, then you do not need to run the Logstash service on every system, whereas Beats can run across all systems from which you want to ship the data.
- Logstash is based on Java requiring JVM, whereas Beats are created based on the Go language.
- In scenarios where you just need to parse your logs without doing any type of processing with multiple filter plugins, you would write a Logstash configuration, for which you would need to learn how to write the configuration, which requires you to learn about another component before storing data in Elasticsearch. However, in Beats it's recommended that you use it where you plan to collect the logs, avoiding processing and shipping it directly into Elasticsearch without involving another component, which adds complexity.

As per the preceding explanation, it becomes clear that Logstash is heavy to install across the system, requires a lot of memory, and consumes high system resources. However, for this purpose, we had Logstash-forwarder, which was built on the same premises as Beats, wherein Logstash-forwarder is lightweight and doesn't require many resources. Is Logstash-forwarder the same as Beats, then?

While it's correct that Logstash-forwarder was built for the same use cases as Beats, it is one of the only lightweight solutions built for shipping data from multiple sources to Elasticsearch or Logstash. Additionally, it was neglected within the community and lagged behind in terms of enriching features, improving the existing features, and fixing bugs. Now, as the time arises when Elastic Stack is being used more and more by organizations and enterprises, there is an ever-growing need of being able to create customized data shippers that are lightweight and provide the functionality of shipping logs to Elasticsearch or Logstash.

One of the beats, that is, Filebeat, is based on the Logstash-forwarder project and uses the existing project code. The existing project code has been repackaged in the Go language and developed as a beat by following the common infrastructure provided, and also using the common framework used to develop any other beat. The core features of Logstash-forwarder have been used in Filebeat, such as when an acknowledgement after a message has been received, which prevents the loss of data, and the Lumberjack protocol, which has been used even in Filebeat. The Beats framework service makes it easier to run the beats as a Windows service.

With this, a question may arise: will Beats replace Logstash in the future? The answer to this is, simply, no, as Logstash is similar to a Swiss Army knife, providing the capabilities of loading data from multiple sources, processing the logs using powerful functionalities provided by different filter plugins, and providing the ability to store output in multiple sources. In short, Logstash provides capabilities of ETL (Extract, Transform, and Load), whereas Beats are lightweight shippers that ship the data, as it is, to either Logstash or Elasticsearch, without performing any transformations on the data.

How Beats fits into Elastic Stack

Having used the ELK Stack, which has been in existence for some time, we ask: is there space for another component in the Stack?

This is one of the biggest questions we think you'll have: where and how will Beats fit into the Elastic Stack? As we have already covered what Beats are, we have your answer covered, and this section that will provide you the answer to your question.

Beats has been added among the core components of the Stack due to the endless opportunities it creates when you use it. In the ELK Stack, you are bounded by the input plugins provided, via which only you can read the data. If you want to index operational data within Elasticsearch, such as transaction level information between multiple systems, Docker container statistics, Tomcat JMX metrics, or system-wide process level statistics, you would need to write a Logstash input plugin, which would then be used for such scenarios. For scenarios where you have multiple systems and you want to fetch logs from each of them, you can use Beats to fetch the data across the systems to a centralized Logstash server from which data can be parsed, processed, and stored. Using this scenario, there will be no requirement of using a system with high memory and resources, as Beats are lightweight shippers. In addition, for scenarios where you just need to parse the data as it is without processing, Beats will come into play, as you can directly store the data in Elasticsearch and you would not be required to use Logstash.

Let's have a look at an overview of the Elastic Stack:

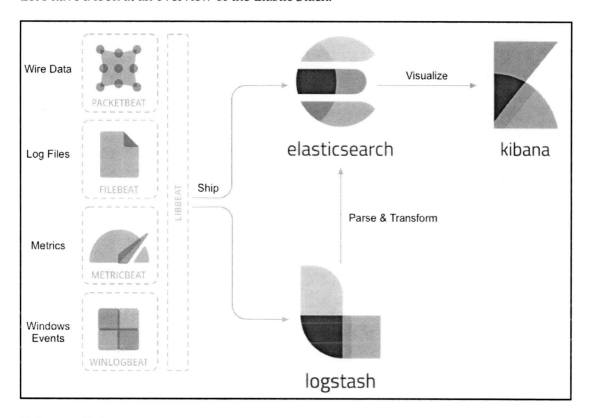

Reference link: https://www.elastic.co/guide/en/beats/libbeat/5.1/images/beats-platform.png

In the preceding diagram, you can see that the Beats platform consists of different beats as developed by Elastic. Beats has the responsibility of collecting and shipping data either to Logstash or Elasticsearch for further processing or storing of data. Then, the data can be used to analyze operational data or to create visualizations/dashboards using Kibana.

After understanding Beats, let's take a look at the various beats developed by Elastic and by the community.

An overview of the different types of Beats

In this section, we will look at some of the beats that have been developed and are in use by enterprises for development and production purposes. Beats are being developed and enhanced by Elastic as well as by the community.

The following are some of the beats developed by Elastic:

- Packetbeat
- Metricbeat
- Filebeat
- Winlogbeat
- Libbeat

The following are some of the beats developed by the open source community:

- Apachebeat
- Dockbeat
- Elasticbeat
- Execbeat
- Httpbeat
- Lmsensorsbeat
- MySQLbeat
- Twitterbeat and more

 Elastic does not provide any support for the open source community developed Beats.

Beats by Elastic Team

As mentioned earlier, we will take a look at the different types of beats provided by Elastic Team in order to understand what each type of beat means and what functionalities they offer.

Packetbeat

Packetbeat is the main beat that started as a project outside Elastic, and the company that Elastic acquired for creating their Beats Platform has become an integral part of Elastic Stack.

Packetbeat, as you might have guessed from its name, is a packet analyzer that provides information related to transactions carried out between the servers of different applications on a network. It provides statistics related to network communication among the different types of application servers.

Metricbeat

Metricbeat is an important beat as it collects metrics from across the systems and from the services running on those system. It is an extension of the top command in Linux systems which provide system level information about the processes, the resources consumed by the processes (amount of memory used, CPU utilizations), and much more.

With additional metrics collection as provided by the top command in Linux, this beat will ship all this information to Elasticsearch or Logstash and this can then be analyzed using Kibana in the form of beautifully created visualizations. Metricbeat is a lightweight shipper that fetches metrics and ships the fetched information of the systems and relevant information of the services running on the system at regular time intervals.

Filebeat

Filebeat is inspired by the Logstash-forwarder project, which has been used by enterprises in their production environments for a long time. Repackaging the Logstash-forwarder in a new way lays the path for Filebeat.

Filebeat is an open source log shipping agent that ships logs from multiple systems by consuming minimal resources. It ships log files from systems to either Elasticsearch or Logstash. It provides the ability to ship logs from multiple systems to a centralized system/server, from which the logs can be parsed and processed. It does not have any dependencies or any plugins to manage.

Winlogbeat

Winlogbeat is the latest addition to the group of Elastic Beats. This beat came into existence due to the requirement of having a beat dedicated towards getting Windows event logs. Having a beat that helps you to get a variety of event logs from different types of Windows events was a major draw, as it can be easily used.

Winlogbeat is an open source shipping agent that ships Windows events in logs from multiple systems. The log files can be shipped to either Elasticsearch or Logstash, as per your requirements. It can be installed as a service on Windows XP or later versions.

Libbeat

Libbeat does not offer any functionality like the other beats we mentioned previously. It is a library created by Elastic Team that acts as a common framework or architecture, where you can develop beats. The library is written in the Go language, which exposes APIs that can be directly used by all Beats, thereby reducing development effort and ensuring that all Beats behave in a similar way so that they are easy to package and run with common tools.

The common parts for developing beats are present in the Libbeat library, which contains various packages providing functionalities such as forwarding data to Elasticsearch or Logstash, implementing logging, configuring input options, handling signals, handling Windows services, and so on. Enhancing the Libbeat library will benefit all the Beats, as they can use the new libraries provided instead of rewriting the code.

Beats by community

In this section, we will look at some of the beats that have been developed by the community and have contributed to the Beats Platform. We will take a look at a couple of beats to understand what the Beats do and what functionality is offered by them.

Dockbeat

Dockbeat has been contributed by the open source community due to the ever-growing popularity of using Docker for containerizing applications. It is becoming more popular with the usage of CI tools. While Docker is being used more and more in production, it's necessary to have monitoring tools that provide statistics related to the container. However, if you use Elastic Stack, which provides a common framework for the beats platform, why would there be a need to create a separate tool from scratch that handles everything that is handled by the Elastic team and provided in the Libbeat library?

Dockbeat provides container statistics, such as container attributes, CPU usage, network statistics, memory consumption statistics, I/O operations access statistics, and Dockbeat status information. As with other beats, it's a lightweight agent installed across multiple systems that reads the Docker container statistics periodically and indexes the information in Elasticsearch, from which we can visualize the information using Kibana.

Lmsensorbeat

Lmsensorbeat is an amazing yet simple beat that uses the lm-sensors library to provide information about the systems through information from sensors, which are loaded by the kernel modules (it can be done after installing the lm-sensors library, which provides a command to detect various sensors present in the system).

Lmsensorbeat monitors various types of sensors to collect information, such as the CPU or motherboard temperature, voltages, fan speeds, and so on. This is basic information that is usually ignored, but we can now easily monitor and properly index that information in Elasticsearch.

Exploring Elastic Team Beats

As we already covered the different types of beats provided by the Elastic Team, in this section, we will explore those beats and understand their features, learn how to set them up, and how to configure the beats with the various configuration options as provided. This section will provide you with all the necessary information you will need for understanding beats in detail.

Understanding Filebeat

As discussed, Filebeat is an open source log shipping agent that has been inspired by the Logstash-forwarder project, and it's based on the Logstash-forwarder source code. Filebeat is used for monitoring logs (files or directories) and forwards those logs to either Logstash, for further processing, or to Elasticsearch, for data indexing.

Let's understand how Filebeat works with the help of its architecture, as displayed below:

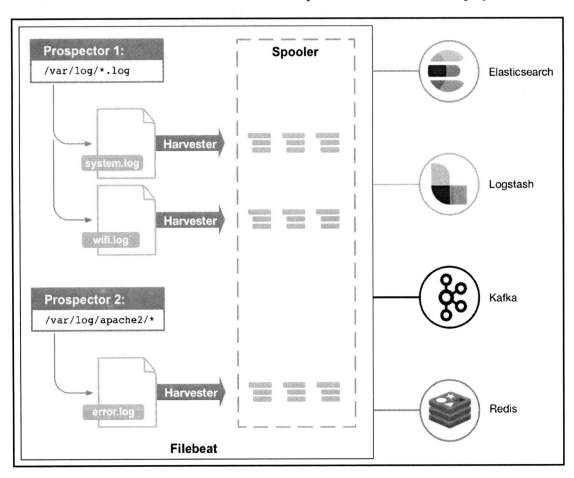

Link: https://www.elastic.co/guide/en/beats/filebeat/5.1/filebeat-overview.html

In the preceding image, there are a lot of new terms to understand, such as **Prospector**, **Harvester**, and **Spooler**. So, let's try to decode the terms and their meanings:

- **Prospector**: This contains a list of all the paths from where logs are to be read. These paths are configured using a configuration file.
- **Harvester**: This is started by Filebeat once logs are captured using the Prospector. The role of Harvester is to read the log file that is provided and to detect any new content created in the file, which it then sends to Spooler.
- **Spooler**: This receives input from the Harvester. Spooler is a central location, wherein all the logs are accumulated and aggregated. The aggregated data is then sent ahead to the output of the Filebeat, as configured in the configuration file.

Whenever Filebeat is started, it creates a single or multiple Prospectors that then start to find the log files mentioned in the path. It finds all the sources to read data from. For every file found by the prospector, corresponding harvester is started. Every harvester reads the content of a single file only. If multiple files are found, then multiple Harvesters are started. Every Harvester then reads the file (line by line) associated with and sends the content on to the Spooler. Then, the Harvester waits for new content (if any) in the log file associated with it. Upon finding new content, it then sends the new log file data to the Spooler. The Spooler is responsible for aggregating the data from multiple Harvesters, and the aggregated data is then sent to the configured output of Filebeat.

 The Harvester is responsible for opening and closing of files. Also, if a file is removed or renamed while it's harvested it is still read by Filebeat which keeps the disk space reserved until the Harvester is closed.

After understanding how Filebeat works, let's set up Filebeat in order to use it.

You can refer to section *Installation of Filebeat* of `Chapter 1`, *Elastic Stack Overview* to install Filebeat.

Let's have a look at the configuration file of Filebeat to understand the different sections of the Filebeat file to configure it for use.

The `filebeat.yml` file is divided into following sections:

- Filebeat Prospectors
- Filebeat Global Options
- Processors Configuration
- Output Configuration
- Paths Configuration
- Logging Configuration

The *Filebeat Prospectors* section lists the prospectors from which data will be fetched along with their configuration. The Filebeat Global Options contains common properties that are common for Filebeat. The Processors Configuration section contains all the properties related to the processor. The Output Configuration section contains the configuration of various outputs available to send data from Beats such as Elasticsearch, Logstash, Kafka, Redis, File, and Console. The Paths section provides default configuration of path files for Filebeat installation. The Logging Configuration section provides various settings to get log-level information for debugging purposes.

Let's explore the configuration properties of a few of the aforementioned sections.

Filebeat Prospectors Configuration

The sample configuration file contains a lot of properties. Let us take a look at a few of them:

```
filebeat.prospectors:
- input_type: log
  paths:
    - /var/log/*.log
  #encoding: plain
  #exclude_lines: ["^DBG"]
  #include_lines: ["^ERR", "^WARN"]
  #document_type: log
  #scan_frequency: 10s
  #max_bytes: 10485760
```

 By default, all properties starting with # contain the same values as predefined in the `filebeat.full.yml` configuration file. If you wish to modify the property value, remove the # before the property name and mention the value.

Let's try to decode what each property means so that you can easily get accustomed to the properties:

- `input_type`: This determines how the input needs to be read. It is used to specify the type of input which publishes events to Elasticsearch or Logstash. It contains value as log (read every line of the file) and stdin (read the standard input). By default its value is log.

- `paths`: Filebeat initially requires a path, from under which it will search for log files, where each path acts as a Prospector from which log files are searched for. For every log file found, the Prospector creates a Harvester, which then reads the data from the file. The path defines the directory where Filebeat will search for `.log` files, as mentioned in the `paths` property. Multiple path directories can be specified by simply adding `-`, followed by the directory name in a new line. Each line can specify a single path.

- `encoding`: Encoding determines the file encoding that it follows. It is used to read the files containing international characters. Encoding names used over here are recommended by **W3C (World Wide Web Consortium)**. Examples of encoding that can be specified are UTF-8, big5, latin1, plain, and so on.

- `exclude_lines`: This is used to specify to Filebeat the type of lines to ignore from the file, which can be specified using regular expressions. They can also be specified as multilines, where the messages of multiple lines are combined into a single line before being filtered by `exclude_lines`. In the configuration file, its value is ^DBG, wherein Filebeat will ignore the lines starting with "DBG".

- `include_lines`: This is used to specify to Filebeat the type of lines to include from the file that can be specified using regular expressions. They can also be specified as multilines, where the messages of multiple lines are combined into a single line before being filtered by `exclude_lines`. In the configuration file, its value is `["^ERR", "^WARN"]`, wherein Filebeat will include lines starting with either "ERR" or "WARN".

 `include_lines` is always executed first by Filebeat, and, after that, it executes `exclude_lines`.

- `document_type`: This is used to specify the index type if the output is Elasticsearch. The value of the property, as specified, will be the name of the type for the index. The default value is log.

- `scan_frequency`: This is used to specify the time interval after which the Prospector checks for any new files and the Harvester checks the file for new content. It scans the directory as mentioned in the path for any files that have been created. The default value is 10s.

- `max_bytes`: This specifies the maximum size of a single event log that can be received by Filebeat. The default value is specified as 10485760, that is, 10 MB. If any single event log size is more than the specified number of bytes, then the additional bytes are discarded and are not captured by Filebeat.

Processors configuration

The Libbeat library provides a common platform of processors which can be used across the various Beats seamlessly. Processors are nothing new but filters with additional functionality.

Processors are used for:

- Reducing the number of exported fields in the output
- Enhancing events with metadata and additional processing capabilities

Every processor is given an event as an input on which processor conditions/actions are executed and finally an event is provided as an output and so on multiple processors can be defined and used.

> Filters have been renamed as processors. The processor is different in functionality from the Ingest Node processor in Elasticsearch.

Defining a processor

For defining a processor, you are require to mention the name of the processor, the conditions (which is optional), and the parameters to apply in the processor, syntax is:

```
processors:
 - <processor_name>:
      when:
          <condition>
      <parameters>
```

> You can mention one or many processors. It will be executed in the order they are defined in the configuration file.

The supported conditions are:

- `equals`: This checks whether the value matches the specified field value. It accepts only integer or string values.
- `contains`: This checks whether the value is part of the field as mentioned. It accepts only string values in a either string field or an array of strings field.
- `regexp`: This checks whether the regular expression is part of the field as mentioned. It accepts only string values.

- `range`: This checks whether the field is between the range of values as specified. It supports `lt`, `gt`, `lte`, and `gte` conditions. It accepts only integer or float values.

There are a few operators that use the conditions as mentioned in the previous section, that is, `OR`, `AND`, and `NOT` operators. They are used to specify multiple conditions at once.

Supported Processors are:

- `add_cloud_metadata`: This processor is used to add metadata information from the supported cloud providers (EC2, Digital Ocean, and GCE) on which ever application is hosted. The syntax is as follows:

  ```
  processors:
  - add_cloud_metadata:
  ```

- `decode_json_fields`: This processor is used to decode the JSON strings. The syntax is as follows:

  ```
  processors:
  - decode_json_fields:
      fields: ["field1", "field2", ...]
      process_array: false
      max_depth: 1
  ```

Here, fields is the mandatory setting and the rest are optional.

- `drop_event`: This processor is used to drop the event if a Condition matches. A condition is required, otherwise all the events will be dropped. The syntax is as follows:

  ```
  processors:
  - drop_event:
        when:
          condition
  ```

- `drop_fields`: This processor is used to drop the fields from the event if a condition matches. If the condition is missing then all the fields mentioned will always be dropped. The syntax is as follows:

  ```
  processors:
  - drop_fields:
        when:
          condition
        fields: ["field1", "field2", ...]
  ```

The @timestamp and type fields cannot be dropped even if it is specified under the fields.

- include_fields: This processor is used to include the fields from the event if a condition matches. If the condition is missing then only the specified fields will be exported. You can specify one or many include_fields under the processors section. The syntax is as follows:

```
processors:
  - include_fields:
        when:
          condition
        fields: ["field1", "field2", ...]
```

 The @timestamp and type fields will be included even if not specified under fields.

Output Configuration

The Output Configuration section contains the option to send output of data to an output component. One or many output components can be specified. As mentioned previously, you can send output to Elasticsearch, Logstash, Kafka, Redis, File, and Console.

Elasticsearch Output Configuration

Some of the options of Elasticsearch output are mentioned here:

```
output.elasticsearch:
  #enabled: true
  hosts: ["localhost:9200"]
  #index: "filebeat-%{+yyyy.MM.dd}"
  #proxy_url: http://proxy:3128
  #max_retries: 3
```

Let's try to decode what each property means so that you can easily get accustomed to the properties:

- enabled: This is used to enable or disable the output module specified.

- `hosts`: This is used to specify the address of `elasticsearch` nodes to connect with. You can connect to single or multiple elasticsearch nodes as required. The log events are distributed in round robin order if there are multiple `elasticsearch` nodes. Each `elasticsearch` node can be defined as IP: PORT. If the port is not defined, then by default the port is used as 9200. You can define multiple `elasticsearch` nodes separated by commas.

- `index`: This is used to specify the index name to which Filebeat will write events to in Elasticsearch. By default, the index name is `[filebeat-]YYYY.MM.DD`.

- `proxy_url`: This is used to specify the address of the proxy URL to connect to the Elasticsearch nodes.

- `max_retries`: This is used to specify the maximum number of retries done to send an event before it fails. Once an event fails that event is dropped.

 Some beats such as Filebeat ignore the `max_retries` setting and retries until all events are sent.

Logstash Output Configuration

Some of the options of the Logstash output are mentioned in the following sections:

```
output.logstash:
  #enabled: true
  hosts: ["localhost:5044"]
  #index: "filebeat"
  #loadbalance: true
  #worker: 1
```

Let's try to decode what each property means so that you can easily get accustomed with the properties:

- `hosts`: This is used to specify the address of Logstash servers to connect with. If the port is not defined, then by default the port is used as 5044. You can define multiple `logstash` nodes separated by commas.

- `index`: This is used to specify the index name to which Filebeat will write events. By default, the index name is `filebeat`.

- `loadbalance`: This is used to balance the load across multiple Logstash servers hosts. If false, it will send data to random Logstash hosts if multiple hosts are mentioned.

- `worker`: This is used to specify the number of workers to be used to send events to Logstash. It is best to modify when the load balance is set as true.

Logging Configuration

Some of the options of the Logging Configuration are mentioned in the following section:

```
#logging.level: info
#logging.to_syslog: true
logging.to_files: true
logging.files:
  #path: /var/log/filebeat
  #name: filebeat
```

Let's try to decode what each property means so that you can easily get accustomed with the properties:

- `logging.level`: This is used to specify the log level for which logging will be done. It can contain values such as `critical`, `error`, `warning`, `info`, and `debug`. By default, it is set to `info`.
- `logging.to_syslog`: This is used to send all the logging output to the system log if its value is set as true. By default, it is set to false.
- `logging.to_files`: This is used to write all the logging output to a file. To enable logging to a file, its value should be specified as true.
- `path`: This is used to specify the directory location where logging output files will be stored.
- `name`: This is used to specify the name of the file where logging output files will be stored.

Understanding Metricbeat

As discussed earlier, Metricbeat is an open source lightweight shipper which reads system wide statistics and provides process level information such as the CPU, memory used per processes of a system, and the various services used by the system. It is responsible to collecting all the statistics and sending them to various such as Elasticsearch, Logstash, Kafka, Redis, File, and Console.

Metricbeat provides lots of statistics and metrics by monitoring the server and collecting information from the system as well as the supported services.

Some of the supported services are as follows:

- Apache
- Couchbase
- Docker
- Kafka
- MySQL
- Nginx
- PostgreSQL
- Redis
- System
- Zookeeper

Let's explore the System Module, which can be easily derived using Metricbeat.

System Module

The System Module contains metricsets of various statistics which have been divided into various sections providing information such as CPU-level statistics, file-level statistics, memory-level statistics, network-level statistics, and process-level statistics.

Let's explore the various metricsets present within the System module:

CPU metricset

This covers the following metrics for CPU:

- Percentage and amount of CPU time spent idle
- Percentage and amount of CPU time spent on waiting for I/O disk operations
- Percentage and amount of CPU time spent on handling hardware interrupts
- Percentage and amount of CPU time spent on low-priority processes
- Percentage and amount of CPU time spent on handling software interrupts
- Percentage and amount of CPU time spent waiting by the virtual CPU while another process was being serviced by the Hypervisor (available only for Unix systems)
- Percentage and amount of CPU time spent in kernel space
- Percentage and amount of CPU time spent in user space

This metricset is available for Linux, Windows, OpenBSD, FreeBSD, and Darwin OS.

 Core metricset provides similar information about the CPU at each core level.

Disk I/O metricset

This covers the following metrics for the disk I/O:

- Total number of milliseconds spent on performing I/O operations
- Name of the disk
- Total number of bytes read successfully by the disk (on Linux it is equivalent to the number of sectors read * 512, which is the assumed sector size)
- Total number of reads completed successfully
- Total number of milliseconds spent by all read operations
- Total number of bytes written successfully to the disk (on Linux it is equivalent to the number of sectors read * 512, which is the assumed sector size)
- Total number of writes completed successfully
- Total number of milliseconds spent by all write operations

This metricset is available for Linux, Windows, and FreeBSD (amd64).

Filesystem metricset

This covers the following metrics for the filesystem statistics:

- Total available disk space to an unprivileged user
- Name of the disks
- Total number of file nodes present across the filesystem
- Total disk space available
- Total number of free file nodes present across the filesystem
- Mounting location of the disks
- Used disk space along with its percentage

This metricset is available for Linux, Windows, OpenBSD, FreeBSD, and Darwin OS.

FsStat metricset

This covers the following metrics for the mounted filesystem statistics:

- Count of filesystems present
- Total number of files present
- Total free space
- Total used space
- Total space available (free + used)

This metricset is available for Linux, Windows, OpenBSD, FreeBSD, and Darwin OS.

Load metricset

This covers the following metrics providing load statistics:

- Average system load for the last 1 minute
- Average system load for last 15 minutes
- Average system load for the last 5 minutes
- Average system load normalized by the number of cores for the last 1 minute
- Average system load normalized by the number of cores for last 15 minutes
- Average system load normalized by the number of cores for the last 5 minutes

This metricset is available for Linux, OpenBSD, FreeBSD, and Darwin OS.

Memory metricset

This covers the following metrics providing memory statistics:

- Actual free memory
- Actual used memory in bytes along with its percentage
- Total free memory
- Available swap memory
- Total swap memory
- Used swap memory in bytes along with its percentage
- Total memory
- Used memory in bytes along with its percentage

This metricset is available for Linux, Windows, OpenBSD, FreeBSD, and Darwin OS.

Actual free memory is based on OS. For Linux, it is free memory and memory of caches and buffers. For OSX, it is free memory and inactive memory. For Windows, it is equal to total free memory.

Network metricset

This covers the following metrics for the network statistics:

- Total number of bytes received and sent
- Total number of incoming packets that were dropped
- Total number of outgoing packets that were dropped
- Total number of errors while receiving and sending
- Total number of packets received and sent
- Name of the interface

This metricset is available for Linux, Windows, FreeBSD and Darwin OS.

Process Metricset

This covers the following metrics for the process-level statistics:

- Process in the command line used to start the process
- Time when the process was started by the CPU
- Percentage of CPU time spent by the process (similar to %CPU of the top command)
- Hard and soft limit on the number of **File-Descriptors** opened by the process
- Total number of File-Descriptors opened by the process
- Percentage and total amount of memory occupied by the process in RAM
- Total shared memory and virtual memory used by the process
- Name of the process
- Process group ID, process parent ID and Process ID
- Process state
- Username that started the process (if username is not found, it contains UID)

This metricset is available for Linux, Windows, FreeBSD, and Darwin OS.

After understanding some of the statistics provided by Metricbeat, let's set up Metricbeat in order to use it.

Installation of Metricbeat

This section covers installation of Metricbeat 5.1.1 on Ubuntu and Windows separately.

Installation of Metricbeat on Ubuntu 14.04

In order to install Metricbeat on Ubuntu, refer to the following steps:

1. Before installing Metricbeat, please check whether your system is 32 bit or 64 bit which can be done using the following command:

   ```
   uname -m
   ```

   If it gives an output as x86_64 it means it is 64-bit system else, if it gives i686 it means it is a 32-bit system.

2. Download Metricbeat 5.1.1 as a debian package using terminal:

   For 64-bit system-

   ```
   wget https://artifacts.elastic.co
   /downloads/beats/metricbeat/metricbeat
   -5.1.1-amd64.deb
   ```

   For 32-bit system-

   ```
   wget https://artifacts.elastic.co/downloads
   /beats/metricbeat/metricbeat-5.1.1-i386.deb
   ```

3. Install the debian package using following command:

   For 64-bit system-

   ```
   sudo dpkg -i metricbeat-5.1.1-amd64.deb
   ```

   For 32-bit system-

   ```
   sudo dpkg -i metricbeat-5.1.1-i386.deb
   ```

 Metricbeat will be installed in /usr/share/metricbeat directory. The configuration files will be present at /etc/metricbeat. The init script will be present at /etc/init.d/metricbeat. The log files will be present within /var/log/metricbeat directory.

4. Configure Metricbeat to run automatically on startup. If you are using SysV init distribution, then run the following command:

```
sudo update-rc.d metricbeat defaults 95 10
```

The above command will print on screen – Adding system startup for /etc/init.d/metricbeat.

Check status of Metricbeat using following command:

```
sudo service metricbeat status
```

Run Metricbeat as a service using following command:

```
sudo service metricbeat start
```

Usage of Metricbeat command:

```
sudo service metricbeat {start|stop|status|restart|force-reload}
```

 If you run Metricbeat as a service, then it will run the /etc/metricbeat/metricbeat.yml configuration file.

 If you want to install any other version of Metricbeat, you can visit the Elastic Team download site and copy the debian package link and use wget to fetch the package. Installation of Metricbeat on Windows is mentioned at https://github.com/kravigupta/mastering-elastic-stack-code-files/wiki/Appendix.

Understanding Packetbeat

Packetbeat is the main beat that lays down the beats platform. After Elastic acquired Packetbeat due to its immense popularity, Beats as a platform was conceptualized and born. As discussed earlier, Packetbeat is an open source lightweight packet analyzer that monitors various systems and applications present over the network. Packetbeat captures network level information among different application servers.

Packetbeat works by getting traffic between different application servers, and after that, decodes the protocols used by the application servers, correlating the request with the responses so that all the information is recorded in the form of a transaction. Packetbeat can easily provide you with interesting information such as issues with your applications that occur due to bugs, or performance-related issues.

In addition, it makes troubleshooting easier and speeds up the fixing process, as root-cause analysis can be easily done with the stored information.

Some of the protocols supported by Packetbeat are as follows:

- HTTP
- MySQL
- MongoDB
- Redis
- ICMP
- DNS
- PostgreSQL
- Thrift
- Memcache

After decoding the protocols and messages, Packetbeat correlates the request with responses that are known as **transactions**. Every transaction is stored in Elasticsearch as a JSON document if the output is to Elasticsearch. Packetbeat provides network traffic information using Elasticsearch and Kibana, in which instances can even be used to analyze various log files using Filebeat stored in Logstash. Using this, we can perform network traffic analysis and log file analysis on the same system.

Installation of Packetbeat

In this section, Packetbeat 5.1.1 will be installed, and the section covers installation on Ubuntu and Windows separately.

Installation of Packetbeat on Ubuntu 14.04

In order to install Packetbeat on Ubuntu, refer to the following steps:

1. Before installing Packetbeat, please check whether your system is 32 bit or 64 bit which can be done using the following command:

```
uname -m
```

If it gives an output as x86_64 it means it is 64-bit system else, if it gives i686 it means it is a 32-bit system.

2. Download Packetbeat 5.1.1 as a debian package using terminal:

For 64-bit system-

```
wget https://artifacts.elastic.co/
downloads/beats/packetbeat/
packetbeat-5.1.1-amd64.deb
```

For 32-bit system-

```
wget https://artifacts.elastic.co/
downloads/beats/packetbeat/
packetbeat-5.1.1-i386.deb
```

3. Install the debian package using following command:

For 64-bit system-

```
sudo dpkg -i packetbeat-5.1.1-amd64.deb
```

For 32-bit system-

```
sudo dpkg -i packetbeat-5.1.1-i386.deb
```

 Packetbeat will be installed in /usr/share/packetbeat directory. The configuration files will be present at /etc/packetbeat. The init script will be present at /etc/init.d/packetbeat. The log files will be present within /var/log/packetbeat directory.

4. Configure Packetbeat to run automatically on startup. If you are using SysV init distribution, then run the following command:

```
sudo update-rc.d metricbeat defaults 95 10
```

The above command will print on screen – Adding system startup for /etc/init.d/packetbeat.

Check status of Packetbeat using following command:

```
sudo service packetbeat status
```

Run Packetbeat as a service using following command:

```
sudo service packetbeat start
```

Usage of Packetbeat command:

```
sudo service packetbeat {start|stop|status|restart|force-reload}
```

 If you run Packetbeat as a service, then it will run the `/etc/packetbeat/packetbeat.yml` configuration file.

 If you want to install any other version of Packetbeat, you can visit the Elastic Team download site and copy the debian package link and use `wget` to fetch the package. Installation of Packetbeat on Windows is mentioned at `https://github.com/kravigupta/mastering-elastic-stack-code-files/wiki/Appendix`.

Exploring Community Beats

As Elastic Stack components are parts of an open source initiative, Beats have been embraced by the community, which is actively contributing to the creation of different types of Beats. There are many new beats being developed by the community that follow the Beats platform. Let us have a look at a community beat, explore it, set it up, and understand the configuration options provided for the beat.

Understanding Elasticbeat

This is a community-developed beat that provides simple yet useful functionalities. This beat provides Elasticsearch cluster related information. It provides statistics of `elasticsearch` clusters, `elasticsearch` nodes, and the health of `elasticsearch` nodes using the API. It requests various types of statistics from the `elasticsearch` cluster, which are exposed via the `elasticsearch` API.

Let's set up Elasticbeat in order to use it.

Installation of Elasticbeat

In this section, Elasticbeat will be installed, and this section covers installation on Ubuntu and Windows. Elasticbeat has been developed using the Go language, which will be required in order to set up and use Elasticbeat.

Installation of Elasticbeat on Ubuntu 14.04

In order to install Elasticbeat on Ubuntu, refer to the following steps:

1. Install GO language package by downloading using following command:

   ```
   wget https://storage.googleapis.co
   m/golang/go1.7.1.linux-amd64.tar.gz
   ```

2. Extract the archive and move to custom location such as /usr/local:

   ```
   tar -xvzf go1.7.1.linux-amd64.tar.gz -C /usr/local/
   ```

   Use the above command with sudo access.

3. Add the following variables related to GO to your ~/.bashrc file:

   ```
   export GOROOT="/usr/local/go"
   export GOPATH="$HOME/go"
   export PATH="$GOROOT/bin:$PATH"
   ```

   Make changes reflect in bashrc file using following command:

   ```
   source ~/.bashrc
   ```

4. Verify Go language is installed by using the following command:

   ```
   go version
   ```

   It will print the version of Go language as: go version go1.7.1 linux/amd64

5. Navigate to the workspace and create a directory using the following commands:

   ```
   mkdir -p $GOPATH
   cd $GOPATH
   mkdir -p src/github.com/radoondas
   ```

6. Navigate to the directory and clone the elasticbeat repository using the following command:

   ```
   cd $GOPATH/src/github.com/radoondas
   git clone https://github.com/radoondas/elasticbeat.git
   ```

Note: Install git if not installed using following command:
sudo apt-get install -y git

7. Build elasticbeat by using the following command:

```
cd $GOPATH/src/github.com/radoondas/elasticbeat
make
```

If you are facing errors after running make command, make sure that GO installed is greater than version 1.5.

8. Run elasticbeat using the following command:

```
./elasticbeat  -e -v -d elasticbeat -c elasticbeat.yml
```

If you are unable to run elasticbeat, then check your elasticbeat.yml file and comment template settings if uncommented and again run.

This will run elasticbeat successfully and will start gathering information related to the Elasticsearch nodes and indices them in Elasticsearch as per its configuration file.

Installation of Elasticbeat on Windows is mentioned at https://github.com/kravigupta/mastering-elastic-stack-code-files/wiki/Appendix.

Elasticbeat configuration

The sample configuration file contains the following properties:

```
input:
   period: 10
   urls:
      - http://127.0.0.1:9200/
   stats:
      cluster: true
      nodes: true
      health: true
```

Let's try to decode what each property means so that you can easily get accustomed to the properties:

- `period`: This specifies the time interval (in seconds) in which Elasticbeat fetches the information. By default, it is 10, that is, Elasticbeat will read statistics every 10 seconds.
- `urls`: This specifies the list of URLs from the Elasticsearch server from which statistics need to be read.
- `cluster`: This is used to fetch the statistics related to the cluster using the Elasticsearch API of `_cluster/stats`.
- `nodes`: This is used to fetch the statistics related to the node using the Elasticsearch API of `_nodes/stats/process`, `jvm`, `os`, `fs`, `thread_pool`, `transport`, `http`, `breaker`, and `script`.
- `health`: This is used to fetch the statistics related to the cluster using the Elasticsearch API of `_cluster/health`.

Beats in action with Elastic Stack

After learning about the various kinds of beats, their functionality, and the information provided, we will learn about how to get started with Beats in order to use it along with Elastic Stack. We will cover the following use cases, showcasing an end-to-end flow for the following cases:

- Using Metricbeat to directly send data to Logstash, which will process and store logs in Elasticsearch so that they can then be visualized in Kibana
- Using Elasticbeat to index data in Elasticsearch and visualize it using Kibana

In this section, you will understand how to get started with simple processing and how to connect multiple components with ease. The objective of this section is not to show you the powerful processing capabilities of Logstash, or how Beats will optimize performance across various systems; it is just to show you how we can connect multiple components so that data flows from each component, and we can correlate the input from Beats to visualize the output in Kibana.

Exploring Metricbeat with Logstash and Kibana

As discussed earlier, we will use Metricbeat to gather the statistics and send the data to Logstash. Logstash will then parse the logs as per requirement and index the data by storing it in Elasticsearch. Using data in Elasticsearch, Kibana will visualize the data and will use an existing created dashboard for Metricbeat, which will provide you with direct access to common visualizations created by the Beats Team. Let's try to simplify the steps to follow for better understanding the workflow in this section.

We will use Metricbeat and store its output to Logstash. To send the output to Logstash, we will configure the Logstash output as provided in the Metricbeat configuration file. We will then create a Logstash configuration file, which will take input from Metricbeat and store the data as output to Elasticsearch. For this, we will download and install the beats input plugin provided for Logstash (if not present) so that we can read input data from Metricbeat.

Also, we will configure the output plugin in Logstash to index the data in Elasticsearch. Afterwards, we will use the Beats dashboard provided by the Elastic team, which will be then used to import saved searches, visualizations, indices, and dashboards in Kibana.

 Make sure that Metricbeat has been installed on your system.

Step 1–Configuring Metricbeat to send data to Logstash

In this step, we will modify the Metricbeat configuration file named `metricbeat.full.yml` to `metricbeat.yml`, which is present in the `/etc/metricbeat` directory. We will specify the output as Logstash and console.

Specifying the output as console will help to understand whether beats is able to send data to Logstash. By default, Logstash is configured with the host as localhost and the port as `5044`.

The configuration file needs to be modified so that `elasticsearch` output can be commented out and logstash output will be uncommented. Also, console output will be uncommented along with its option of pretty print as true. If we remove all the comments from the file along with newlines, the configuration file will look like the following:

```
metricbeat.modules:
- module: system
  metricsets:
```

```
                - cpu
                - load
                - core
                - diskio
            - filesystem
            - fsstat
            - memory
            - network
            - process
            enabled: true
            period: 2s
            processes: ['.*']
    output.logstash:
        enabled: true
        hosts: ["localhost:5044"]
    output.console:
        enabled: true
        pretty: true
    logging.level: info
    logging.to_files: true
    logging.files:
        rotateeverybytes: 10485760 # = 10MB
```

Run Metricbeat using the following command:

```
sudo /usr/share/metricbeat/bin/metricbeat -c
/etc/metricbeat/metricbeat.yml
```

If you are able to view the logs, then your configuration is correct.

The mentioned Metricbeat command runs the process in the foreground which should only be used to verify that your data is being populated. Once verified, you should stop the foreground process.

To run Metricbeat in the background, run the following command:
`sudo service metricbeat start`
Check Metricbeat is able to parse logs by running the following command:
`tailf /var/log/metricbeat/metricbeat`

Step 2–Creating a Logstash configuration file

In this step, we will create a Logstash configuration file that will read the Beats' input and will store output in Elasticsearch. Before creating the Logstash configuration file, you should verify that the beats-input plugin is present within your Logstash.

To verify the beats-input plugin in Ubuntu, use the following command:

```
/usr/share/logstash/bin/logstash-plugin list | grep beats
```

If present, it will show `logstash-input-beats` as the output. If not present, install `beats-input-plugin` using the following command:

```
/usr/share/logstash/bin/logstash-plugin install logstash-input-beats
```

 The usage of bin/plugin has been deprecated. It has been replaced with `bin/logstash-plugin`.

To verify `beats-input-plugin` in Windows, use the following command in the Command Prompt:

```
bin\logstash-plugin list
```

If present, it will list all the plugins available and check for `logstash-input-beats` plugin.

If not present, install `beats-input-plugin` using the following command in the Command Prompt:

```
bin\logstash-plugin plugin install logstash-input-beats
```

The Logstash configuration file will look as follows:

```
output {
  elasticsearch {
    hosts => "localhost:9200"
    template_name => "metricbeat"
    template => "/etc/metricbeat/metricbeat.template.json"
    template_overwrite => false
    index => "%{[@metadata][beat]}-%{+YYYY.MM.dd}"
    document_type => "%{[@metadata][type]}"
  }
  stdout { codec => rubydebug }
}
```

As you can see in the preceding configuration file, we are specifying the template so that all the fields captured by beats are stored correctly in Elasticsearch on which the sample beats dashboard will be imported.

Let's save the created Logstash configuration in the `/usr/share/logstash` folder with the `metricbeat.conf` name. Run the Logstash configuration file after navigating to the `logstash` folder using the following command:

```
$ bin/logstash -f metricbeat.conf
```

Logstash will run and parse the configuration file for each input and store the input in the metricbeat-YYYY.MM.dd (YYYY.MM.dd corresponds to the current year, month, and date) index in Elasticsearch. You will see the logs in the console, which will show the data along with various fields in which your data is being stored in Elasticsearch.

The previously mentioned Logstash command runs the process in the foreground, which should only be used to verify that your data is being populated. Once verified, you should stop the foreground process.

Once you are able to view the data in terms of logs from Logstash, copy the metricbeat.conf file to the /etc/logstash/conf.d directory. We can run both the processes as a service, which will run it in the background by using the following command:

```
sudo service metricbeat start
sudo service logstash start
```

This will run the Metricbeat and Logstash processes, which will ultimately store data by creating indices in elasticsearch.

Another way to verify that data is being stored in Elasticsearch after running Logstash is as follows.

Before running the Logstash service and Metricbeat, use the following command:

```
curl -XGET localhost:9200/metricbeat-*
```

The preceding command will give an output error of the index_not_found_exception type.

After running the Logstash and Metricbeat service, use the following command:

```
curl -XGET localhost:9200/metricbeat-*
```

The previous command will give as the output the index name and its metadata.

Step 3–Downloading and loading the sample Beats dashboard

In this step, we will download the sample Beats dashboard provided by Elastic Team to directly monitor the servers. It is provided just as an example for you to quickly get started with; however, you can customize and create searches, visualizations, and dashboards as per your requirements.

To load the dashboards in Kibana, you need to run a load script that will create index patterns in Kibana, such as `metricbeat-*`. This will also load the sample searches, visualizations, and dashboards that have been created.

To load the Beats dashboard in Ubuntu, use the following commands:

```
cd /usr/share/{beat-name}
```

where for Metricbeat full path will be – `/usr/share/metricbeat`

Run the following command to download and load the sample beats dashboard:

```
./scripts/import_dashboards
```

It will load Beats dashboard in Kibana.

 Before running import dashboard scripts, make sure Elasticsearch is running. Loading the Beats dashboard in Windows is mentioned at `https://github.com/kravigupta/mastering-elastic-stack-code-files/wiki/Appendix`.

By default, the import dashboard script assumes that elasticsearch is running on default host and port `{localhost:9200}`. If you are running elasticsearch on different configuration, you can use the –es option to load such as:

```
./scripts/import_dashboards -es http://192.168.1.12:9200
```

Other configuration parameters can also be used. To view them, visit `https://www.elastic.co/guide/en/beats/libbeat/5.1/import-dashboards.html`.

Step 4–Viewing the sample Beats dashboard

After loading the sample dashboard, you can start Kibana. You will see that index patterns have been created as `metricbeat-*`. You can also navigate to **Management | Saved Objects** to view all the dashboards, searches, and visualizations loaded into Kibana.

Go to the Kibana **Visualize** tab and select the visualization from the option under **Or, open a saved visualization**, which will list all the visualizations stored in Kibana. We will select various visualizations that appear in the Metricbeat-Dashboard. You will view the various visualizations as depicted in the following sections.

The Metricbeat dashboard section displays some basic information such as CPU Usage, System Load, and Total Hosts by CPU Usage over a period of time.

Let's have a view of each of the visualizations separately:

- **CPU Usage**: The following screenshot shows the **CPU Usage** screen:

- **System Load**: The following screenshot shows the **System Load** screen:

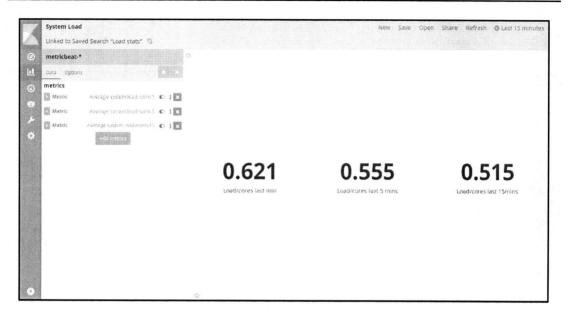

- **CPU Usage over time**: The following screenshot shows the **CUP usage over time screen**:

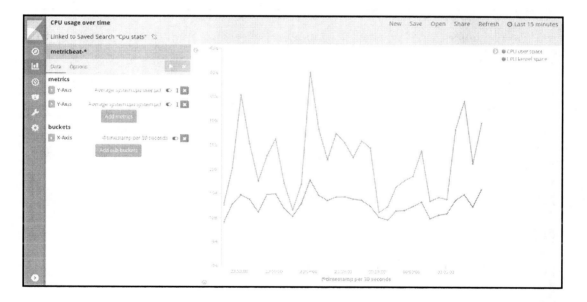

- **System Load over time**: The following screenshot shows the **System Load over time** screen:

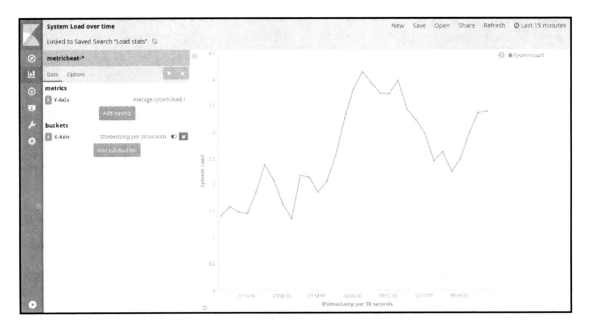

- **Top hosts by CPU usage**: The following screenshot shows the **Top hosts by CPU usage** screen:

Let's have a look at some of the other visualizations present:

- **Top hosts by Memory usage**: The following screenshot shows the **Top hosts by Memory usage** screen:

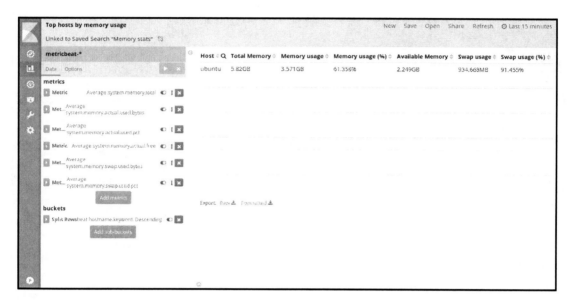

- **Memory Usage over Time**: The following screenshot shows the **Memory Usage over Time** screen:

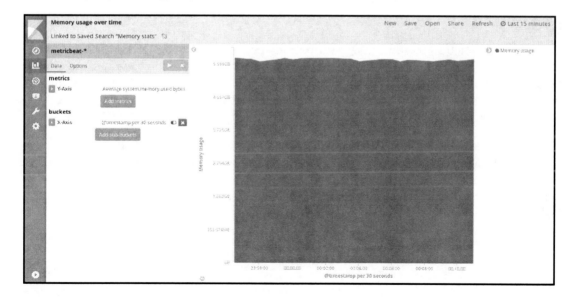

- **Disk space overview**: The following screenshot shows the **Disk Space overview** screen:

Exploring Elasticbeat with Elasticsearch and Kibana

We will use Elasticbeat to gather the information and send the data as output to Elasticsearch which will index the data. Using data in Elasticsearch, Kibana will visualize the data and will use a sample dashboard for Elasticbeat which will provide you with the access to view the data as per visualizations created by the Elasticbeat community. Let's try to simplify the steps to follow for better understanding the workflow in this section.

We will use Elasticbeat and store its output in Elasticsearch. To send the output to Elasticsearch, we will configure the output as provided in the Elasticbeat configuration file. Afterwards, we will download the Beats dashboard provided by the Elasticbeat community, which will be then used to import saved searches, visualizations, indices, and dashboards in Kibana.

Make sure that Elasticbeat has been installed on your system.

Step 1–Configuring Elasticbeat to send data to Elasticsearch

In this step, we will modify the Elasticbeat configuration file named `elasticbeat.yml`, which will be saved in `$GOPATH/src/github.com/radoondas/elasticbeat`. We will specify the output as Elasticsearch. By default, Elasticsearch is configured with the host as localhost and the port as `9200`.

If we remove all the comments from the file along with newlines, the configuration file will look like the following:

```
input:
  period: 1
  urls:
    - http://127.0.0.1:9200
  stats:
    cluster: true
    nodes: true
    health: true
output:
  elasticsearch:
    hosts: ["localhost:9200"]
shipper:
logging:
  files:
    rotateeverybytes: 10485760 # = 10MB
```

Navigate to the following directory using this command:

cd $GOPATH/src/github.com/radoondas/elasticbeat

Run Elasticbeat using the following command:

./elasticbeat -e -v -d elasticbeat -c elasticbeat.yml

You should view the information that every 1 second it is fetching information for Cluster stats, Nodes stats, and Cluster health.

Step 2–Downloading and loading the Elasticbeat dashboard

In this step, we will download the sample Elasticbeat dashboard. It is provided just as an example for you to quickly get started with; however, you can customize and create searches, visualizations, and dashboards as per your requirement.

To load Elasticbeat dashboard in Ubuntu, use the following commands:

```
cd $GOPATH/src/github.com/radoondas/elasticbeat/kibana
curl -L -O
https://github.com/elastic/beats-dashboards/blob/master/load.sh
chmod u+x load.sh
./load.sh
```

It will load the Elasticbeat dashboard in Kibana.

 Before running load scripts, make sure Elasticsearch is running. Loading the Elasticbeat dashboard in Windows is mentioned at `https://github.c om/kravigupta/mastering-elastic-stack-code-files/wiki/Appendix` .

Step 3–Viewing the sample Beats dashboard

After loading the sample searches, visualizations, and dashboards, you can start Kibana. You will see that the Index pattern of `elasticbeat-*` has been created. You can also go to **Management** | **Saved Objects** to view the dashboards, searches, and visualizations loaded into Kibana.

Go to the Kibana **Visualize** tab and select the visualization from the option under **Or, open a saved visualization** which lists down all the visualizations stored in Kibana. We will select various visualizations which appear in the Elasticbeat dashboard. You will view the various visualizations as depicted in the following sections:

- **Cluster document count**: This visualization displays the count of documents present in the cluster over a period of time for each cluster:

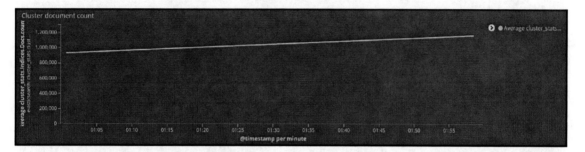

- **Cluster health shards**: This visualization displays the count of health of the initializing shards, active primary shards, primary shards, unassigned shards, and relocating shards over a period of time for each cluster:

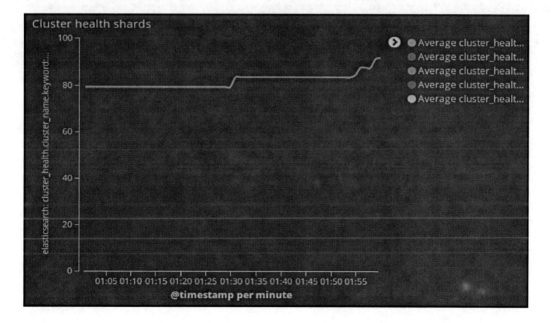

- **Cluster status**: This visualization displays the average number of cluster status nodes present in the cluster over a period of time for each cluster:

- **Cluster OS CPU**: This visualization displays the average percentage of CPU used by the nodes present in the cluster over a period of time for each cluster:

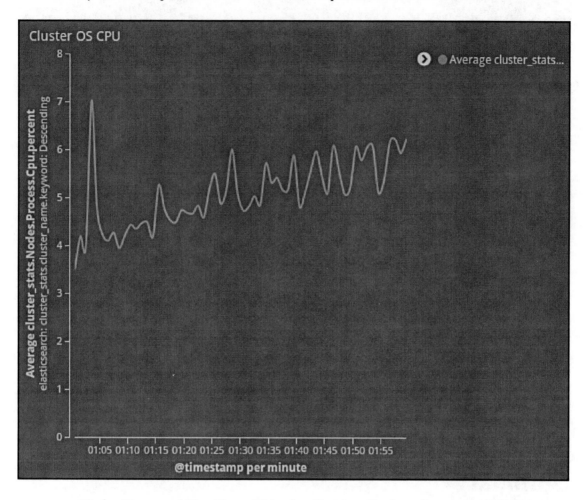

- **Nodes Heap and NonHeap**: This visualization displays the average JVM heap memory, JVM heap memory used, JVM non-heap memory, and JVM non-heap memory used by the nodes in the cluster over a period of time for each cluster:

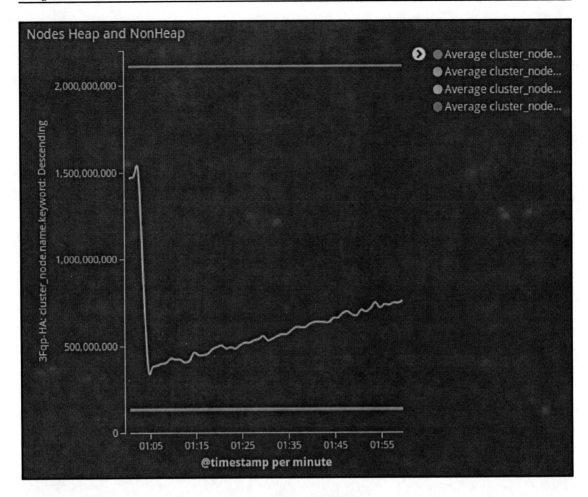

Summary

In the chapter, we learned about Beats which is the newest addition to the Elastic Stack. We covered the basic premises for why Beats was developed or came into existence along with differentiating Beats with Logstash. We explored the role of Beats in Elastic Stack and the importance of Beats for extending former ELK Stack. Later, we explored the different kind of Beats available with an explanation of the Beats, their functionalities, roles, and the configuration options provided. Also how to install and configure the Beats were detailed in this chapter. At the end of the chapter, we covered the example of how Beats can be used in Elastic Stack.

In the next chapter, we will cover a real-time production-like environment wherein we will be solving a particular problem statement. We will explore how Elastic Stack comes to the rescue of the problem statement and will showcase the powerful capabilities of Elastic Stack.

6
Elastic Stack in Action

Elastic Stack has served a number of organizations to solve their problems. A very common scenario where Elastic Stack components are utilized is enterprise intranet solutions. We will pick one such scenario in this chapter. So far, we have learned about setting up Elasticsearch, Logstash, Beats, and Kibana to work together. We will utilize all these components for our use case.

Our use case is a simple implementation, which includes a portal server, a web server, database server, and a search engine. We will analyze all types of logs generated by these servers along with node statistics.

In this chapter, we will cover the following topics:

- Understanding problem scenario
- Preparing Elastic Stack pipeline
- Configuring Elastic Stack components
- Setting up Kibana Dashboards

Understanding problem scenario

One very popular use case of Elastic Stack is to do log management and analysis. Elastic Stack has helped a number of deployments with this scenario. For our example, we will also consider a company intranet, which includes several modules to help employees with the events and processes of the company. These modules are as follows:

- **Employee information system**: This module helps us with user registration and acts as an information provider.
- **Training**: This module helps us with setting up training, training registration, keeping record of attendance, and so on.

- **Performance management system**: This manages all evaluation cycles and appraisals done for all employees.
- **Leave management**: Employees use this module to apply, approve, or reject leaves. This module also allows us to set up default leave types and their count, holiday list, and so on.
- **Blog**: This is the internal blog, which is utilized by the company employees to share their knowledge.
- **Forum**: This is the internal forum that contains categories for technologies, where employees put their queries and also find answers.
- **Wiki**: This is the company wiki, which lists sharable information of projects, processes, policies, and so on.
- **Documents library**: This keeps all the necessary documents of the company at one place, with relevant permissions.
- **Several other modules**: These will help in delivering the content to employees including notifications, birthdays, anniversaries, and so on.

Usually modules like these are developed and set up using an enterprise portal server. For our requirements, we have utilized **Liferay** portal server, which stands among portal leaders. More details about Liferay can be gathered from `https://www.liferay.com/`. Liferay already offers a good amount of **portlets** (modules), and a company portal can utilize them with no, or minimal, changes. We have used blogs, forum, wiki, documents and media, and web content modules for collaboration along with custom-developed modules, that is, employee information, leave management, training, performance management, and so on.

This was all about the enterprise portal server. A portal deployment is usually clustered and is supported by a web server, load balancer, search engine, a database server etc. In the next section, we will see how the architecture is set up to harness the benefit of all of these servers. The version of Liferay chosen is v6.2, which is the most recent and stable version. Liferay 7 is also out in the market, but it would take some more time for it to be stable and bug free.

With all these servers in place, we will have logs spread across the machines (expecting the servers to be on different machines). These logs will have different formats. In case of any event (error or fault) that requires attention, we would need to read and sync logs from different machines and troubleshoot the error or defect.

Of course, the application and server logs are not the only thing we should collect and store, we should collect and store machine-related information as well. These logs can be event logs, runtime RAM, processes, or processor information.

With log management and analysis using Elastic Stack, we plan to keep the logs centralized in one common format and in one place, to analyze the data we can gather.

Understanding the architecture

Since a portal server receives enough traffic to put load on one server, we would always want to keep two portal servers along with a load balancer. There are other tools as well to contribute to the architecture:

- **Liferay**: The portal server that serves as a platform to host all our modules
- **OpenDJ**: The LDAP server
- **MySQL**: The database server
- **Nginx**: The load balancer
- **Elasticsearch**: Liferay portal will use this to store indices, and all search requests will be made against this server

The following diagram showcases the architecture this application follows along with the IP addresses of the node:

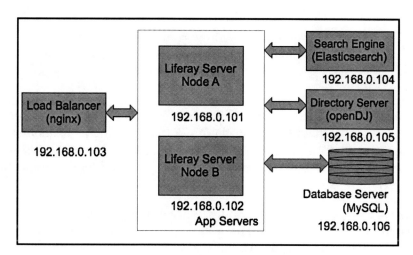

From the network architecture diagram, we can see that there are two nodes for the main application server for which load is balanced using **nginx**, which is acting as a load balancer. The load balancing script for **nginx** is as follows:

```
upstream app_liferay_mes {
  server 192.168.0.101:8080 ;    #Liferay Tomcat Node 1
  server 192.168.0.102:8080 ;    #Liferay Tomcat Node 2
  ip_hash;
}
server {
  listen 80;
  server_name lportal.com;
  access_log /var/log/nginx/lportal.local.log;
  location / {
    proxy_set_header X-Real-IP $remote_addr;
    proxy_set_header X-Forwarded-For $proxy_add_x_forwarded_for;
    proxy_set_header Host $http_host:$server_port;
    proxy_set_header X-NginX-Proxy true;
    proxy_pass http://app_liferay_mes/;
    proxy_read_timeout      180s;
    proxy_connect_timeout   10s;
  }
}
```

 Both of the Liferay nodes run on port number 8080, and we use the lportal.com domain to connect to both nodes balanced by nginx.

We added an upstream and used for proxy. For load balancing, we have chosen to use ip_hash mechanism, which will be using client's IP to determine which node to send the request to. There are other mechanisms as well: round-robin and least-connected. Using ip_hash will ensure that a request stays on the same server and there is no session-related issues in the future.

All the servers are installed on different nodes. Since our app server will be taking a huge amount of search queries, we have a separate server for search engine, and Elasticsearch is used for that. Liferay v6.2 and earlier are shipped with lucene, by default, for content indexing purpose. For support of Elasticsearch, there is a plugin called Elasticray (https://web.liferay.com/marketplace/-/mp/application/41044606), which can be utilized. This plugin is tuned to used Elasticsearch v1.4, so this is the version we will use with Liferay.

Liferay v7 onward uses Elasticsearch, by default, for its search engine capabilities and the Elasticsearch version 2.2 is embedded. We can use a stand-alone server for Elasticsearch also, but the version should be 2.2.

All the users are managed using a directory server, and OpenDJ (formally known as OpenDS) is a good fit. Last node, for database server we have MySQL database server.

The following table lists all the nodes that are part of the system along with their versions:

Server Node	Version
Nginx Load Balancer	nginx/1.10.1
Liferay Server Nodes	6.2
MySQL Database Server	5.7.10
OpenDJ LDAP Server	3.0.0
Elasticsearch Server – For Liferay	1.4.0

Covering installation and setup of all of the components and understanding each of these are out of scope for the book, and it's assumed that you have similar software setup. Your setup may not be utilizing Liferay and other mentioned tools for your use case, but would be serving similar purpose. The main purpose is to understand how Elastic Stack can help us with content storage, visualization, and analysis. For any intranet portal setup, similar sets of tools are required. There would be a load balancer, a database, app server, authentication, and a user store. What we want to cover is to understand which components of Elastic Stack can be used to capture our data and do the necessary processing for us so that we can visualize the data and help ourselves and the organization to take necessary actions and decisions.

However, to help you out with the setup, a wiki is created at `https://github.com/kravigupta/mastering-elastic-stack-code-files/wiki/LiferaySe tup`; this wiki page covers Liferay setup steps.

Preparing Elastic Stack pipeline

We have a scenario for which we want to do data and log analysis covered in the preceding section. To do analysis, we want to use Elastic Stack components to help us. Those components will be installed on different nodes and will be submitting data to one central Elasticsearch node or to an Elasticsearch cluster. In order to set this up, we need to update our architecture to include elastic stack components, such as Logstash, Beats, Elasticsearch, and Kibana.

What to capture?

First thing, before we start updating our architecture, we need to understand what we want to capture and how that is going to help us. The following are few things we want to capture for our requirements:

- Logs generated by the following:
    - Liferay, MySQL
    - Nginx
    - OpenDJ
    - Elasticsearch node, which is used by Liferay
- System statistics for each node:
    - All nodes for Liferay, MySQL, Nginx, OpenDJ, and Elasticsearch
- Network Traffic for each node:
    - Includes HTTP, MySQL protocols, and so on

Updated architecture

We need to update the system setup by adding suitable Beats, Elasticsearch, Kibana, and Logstash. There should be one Elasticsearch node or cluster, which will receive all the data read by Beats/Logstash and one server for Kibana to analyze the recorded data. The most important part is to choose the beat you want to install and on which machine or server.

Let's analyze for each server and come to a conclusion of selected beat:

- **Nginx**: We need to capture access and error logs, running status, and the CPU/memory metrics. For logs, we need Filebeat, and for CPU/memory metrics, we can utilize Metricbeat. We would also like to sniff the network packets using Packetbeat for HTTP protocol.
- **Liferay Nodes**: These are our main servers, which will be serving the actual requests of users. We need to capture logs of the app servers, memory, and cpu usage; Filebeat and Metricbeat will help us here.
- **OpenDJ**: This is our LDAP server, which is responsible for authentication. For logs and other system-related metrics, we would need Filebeat and Metricbeat here as well.

- **Elasticsearch server for Liferay**: This Elasticsearch is to provide search capability for Liferay and this has version 1.4.0. We would want to capture memory and CPU stats, and logs, so Metricbeat and Filebeat would be needed.
- **MySQL Server**: We can capture MySQL-related specific packets here using Packetbeat. Like any other server, we can also capture logs and system stats using Filebeat and Metricbeat.

"Elasticsearch server for Liferay" is different than Elasticsearch in Elastic Stack. The one in Elastic Stack will help us to store data captured and processed by beats and Logstash. Another difference is in the version, Elastic Stack has version 5.1.1 while other has 1.4.0 as supported by Liferay plugin.

The following table specifies which Beats are installed for which server to capture relevant data:

Server Node	Beats Installed
Nginx Load Balancer	Filebeat, Metricbeat, and Packetbeat
Liferay Server Nodes	Filebeat and Metricbeat
MySQL Database Server	Filebeat, Metricbeat, and Packetbeat
OpenDJ LDAP Server	Filebeat and Metricbeat
Elasticsearch Server – For Liferay	Filebeat and Metricbeat

Since we have to read logs for all servers, and the logs will be in files (`.log` files mostly), we will need Filebeat to read logs. For network-related traffic, we will need Packetbeat, and for system statistics, we can utilize Metricbeat.

The data read by Filebeat will be sent to Logstash in order to do some processing and then Logstash will send it to Elasticsearch. Logstash will help us to parse the logs and break the entire log message into multiple fields. For example, an Nginx access log contains the IP of the visitor, referrer, user agent, and many more fields. If we do not break it to multiple fields, we will surely be missing lot of good insights. For additional processing and parsing of log messages, using Logstash is preferred, as it provides flexibility. For Metricbeat and Packetbeat, we will use Elasticsearch as output.

Configuring Elastic Stack components

In this section, we will configure all the tools for capturing the data. The components we will use are Elasticsearch, Logstash, Kibana, Filebeat, Metricbeat, and Packetbeat. Our pipeline would look like the following diagram:

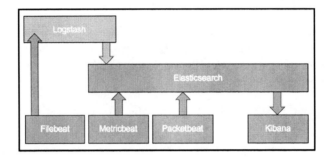

All of the components share the same version, that is, 5.1.1. We will read logs using Filebeat, push those logs to Logstash for processing, and then add them to Elasticsearch for indexing. For our setup, Logstash is used at `192.168.0.112`, Kibana is installed at `192.168.0.111` and Elasticsearch instance is set up at `192.168.0.110`. This Elasticsearch instance is different than what we installed for Liferay search engine capability. The one used for Liferay is a lower version, v1.4.0, because that is the one supported by Elasticray plugin of Liferay.

On the other hand, we will use Metricbeat and Packetbeat to collect data and send it directly to Elasticsearch. Finally, we can visualize the data using Kibana.

Setting up Elasticsearch

Depending on the requirements, we can set up Elasticsearch as a stand-alone node or in a cluster. Refer to `Chapter 11`, *Best Practices* to understand the number of nodes in a cluster, in case you are willing to set up a cluster.

Once you get the archive of elasticsearch extracted on your machine, set the properties for node name, logs path, and so on. Let's modify the configuration file `config/elasticsearch.yml`:

```
node.name: es-node-stack
path.data: /var/lib/elasticsearch
path.logs: /var/log/elasticsearch
network.host: 192.168.0.110
http.port: 9200
```

In case you want to set cluster, give the Elasticsearch cluster a name::

```
cluster.name: es-stack
```

Once Elasticsearch is configured, run the nodes. Navigate to the directory where you kept the extracted Elasticsearch and run:

./bin/elasticsearch.

 Best practice is to install Elasticsearch as a service and use. To learn, refer to installation section of `Chapter 1`, *Elastic Stack Overview*.

This should make our Elasticsearch node/cluster up and running. Elasticsearch is now ready to receive data for each node sent by beats/Logstash.

Setting up agents/Beats

We need to set up Packetbeat, Metricbeat, and Filebeat for our requirements. As defined in the table, Beats corresponding to each node in section – *Updated architecture*, let's install respective beat on each server.

Packetbeat

Let's modify Packetbeat configuration file packetbeat.yml as per our requirements. We need to capture data for HTTP and MySQL protocol, so we need to configure ports for each of the protocol. We need to choose a network interface to capture packets from, and we will capture data from Ethernet, so we will choose `en0`, which is also a default value for the interface devices, as follows:

```
packetbeat.interfaces.device: en0
```

We need to set port numbers for MySQL and HTTP protocols:

```
packetbeat.protocols.http:
  ports: [80, 8080, 8000, 5000, 8002]
packetbeat.protocols.mysql:
  ports: [3306]
```

We will send this data directly to Elasticsearch, and our Elasticsearch cluster IP is `192.168.0.110`, with a default port number:

```
output.elasticsearch:
    hosts: ["192.168.0.110:9200"]
    template.name: "packetbeat"
    template.path: "packetbeat.template.json"
    template.overwrite: false
```

The template is used to set mappings in Elasticsearch. We can leave all other properties to default and start Packetbeat on each of the machines.

Metricbeat

To capture system and server-related stats, we need to configure Metricbeat on each server in our topology. Let's modify the configuration file metricbeat.yml as per our requirements.

For each server, we need to capture system information and statistics, so let's configure `metricbeat.yml`:

```
metricbeat.modules:
- module: system
    metricsets:
        - cpu
        - load
        - core
        - diskio
        - filesystem
        - fsstat
        - memory
        - network
        - process
    enabled: true
    period: 10s
    processes: ['.*']
```

For Nginx server, we can also configure to check the status:

```
- module: nginx
  metricsets: ["stubstatus"]
  enabled: true
  period: 10s
  hosts: ["http://192.168.0.103"]
```

For MySQL server, we can check status using:

```
- module: mysql
    metricsets: ["status"]
    enabled: true
    period: 10s
    hosts: ["root@tcp(192.168.0.106:3306)/"]
```

For hosts configuration, MySQL data source name should be setup as the format below:

```
[username[:password]@][protocol[(address)]]/
```

In case, we do not specify username and password in data source name, the these should be provided using:

```
username: <username>
password: <password>
```

Finally, let's configure the output properties to point to the correct address of the Elasticsearch node:

```
output.elasticsearch:
    hosts: ["192.168.0.110:9200"]
```

Filebeat

Finally, let's set up Filebeat to read logs from all servers by modifying `filebeat.yml` configuration file. There will be different locations to read files from, so we need to set different prospectors for each Filebeat installation.

First, let's set up the common configuration for all instances: output to Logstash, which is set up at `192.168.0.112`:

```
output.logstash:
    hosts: ["192.168.0.112:5044"]
```

Now, for each instance, we will set prospectors (each prospector will start with a – (*hyphen*)) – for Liferay servers, which are installed at /usr/servers on each instance:

```
- input_type: log
  paths:
    - /usr/servers/liferay-portal-6.2-ce-ga4/logs/*.log
  document_type: lrlogs
```

We could also use Filebeat tags to tag events with custom name. For example, if we want to differentiate logs from both `liferay`, we use the tag name `liferay-node-x`, where x refers to the number of node, for example, 1, 2, and so on:

```
- input_type: log
  paths:
     - /usr/servers/liferay-portal-6.2-ce-ga4/logs/*.log
  tags: ["liferay-node-1"]
  document_type: lrlogs
```

In the preceding configuration, we set `liferay-node-1` as tag for the first node of the liferay cluster. For another node, we can set tag as `liferay-node-2`.

Since Liferay is a Java-based server-and there will also be Java stack trace in logs – so in that case, we need to put configuration for multiline logs also. For example, the log entries in the following listing show that liferay's auto deploy scanner tries to scan a zip file but fails because the ZIP file is either corrupt or the file cannot be opened due to a permission issue:

```
10:50:42,357 ERROR
[com.liferay.portal.kernel.deploy.auto.AutoDeployScanner][AutoDeployDir:220
] com.liferay.portal.kernel.deploy.auto.AutoDeployException:
java.util.zip.ZipException: error in opening zip file
com.liferay.portal.kernel.deploy.auto.AutoDeployException:
java.util.zip.ZipException: error in opening zip file
    at                 `
com.liferay.portal.kernel.deploy.auto.BaseAutoDeployListener.isMatchingFile
(BaseAutoDeployListener.java:104)
    at
com.liferay.portal.kernel.deploy.auto.BaseAutoDeployListener.isHookPlugin(B
aseAutoDeployListener.java:46)
    ...
Caused by: java.util.zip.ZipException: error in opening zip file
    at java.util.zip.ZipFile.open(Native Method)
    at java.util.zip.ZipFile.<init>(ZipFile.java:215)
    at java.util.zip.ZipFile.<init>(ZipFile.java:145)
    at java.util.zip.ZipFile.<init>(ZipFile.java:159)
    at
com.liferay.portal.kernel.deploy.auto.BaseAutoDeployListener.isMatchingFile
(BaseAutoDeployListener.java:89)
    ... 6 more
```

For these types of logs, we need to specify Filebeat configuration with a pattern in order to match and keep all subsequent lines of the log entry merged with the leading log line. For such logs, following is the multiline configuration:

```
multiline.pattern: '^([0-9]{2}:[0-9]{2}:[0-9]{2},[0-9]{3})'
multiline.negate: true
```

```
multiline.match: after
```

Now, with the multiline configuration added, such exception content will be part of one log entry. This pattern will match lines with a time at the start and consider for a new log entry, otherwise a non-matching line will be part of the previously matched line.

Apart from these log entries, there are logs generated by app server, which have the following format:

```
Nov 15, 2016 8:53:28 AM org.apache.catalina.startup
.HostConfig deleteRedeployResources
INFO: Undeploying context [/notification-portlet]
```

For such log entries, following is the multiline configuration:

```
multiline.pattern: '^([A-Z]{1}[a-z]{2} [0-9]{1,2}, [0-9]{4}
[0-9]{1,2}:[0-9]{2}:[0-9]{2} (AM|PM))'
multiline.negate: true
multiline.match: after
```

Here, we are trying to match the date pattern with *MMM dd, yyyy HH:mm:ss*. To keep things simple and give us flexibility over logs, we will add liferay logs in two types-**lrlogs** and **lrcatalinalogs** for liferay software logs and app server-related logs, respectively. Our final configuration on `node-1` will be similar to this:

```
- input_type: log
  paths:
    - /usr/servers/liferay-portal-6.2-ce-ga4/logs/*.log

  tags: ["liferay-node-1"]
  document_type: lrlogs
  multiline.pattern: '^([0-9]{2}:[0-9]{2}:[0-9]{2},[0-9]{3})'
  multiline.negate: true
  multiline.match: after

- input_type: log
  paths:
    - /usr/servers/liferay-portal-6.2-ce-ga4
      /tomcat-7.0.42/logs/catalina*.log
  tags: ["liferay-node-1"]
  document_type: lrcatalinalogs
  multiline.pattern: '^([A-Z]{1}[a-z]{2} [0-9]{1,2}, [0-9]{4}
[0-9]{1,2}:[0-9]{2}:[0-9]{2} (AM|PM))'
  multiline.negate: true
  multiline.match: after
```

Files for both log types are located at different places. Liferay-related logs are found in the `LIFERAY_HOME/logs` directory, whereas app server-related logs are inside the `tomcat-xx-xx/logs` directory. In this case, `LIFERAY_HOME` is the directory where Liferay is extracted, and `/usr/servers/liferay-portal-6.2-ce-ga4` is the directory where tomcat is present.

Filebeat configuration on Nginx instance would be simple and similar to the following:

```
- input_type: log
  paths:
    - /usr/local/var/log/nginx/access.log
  document_type: nginxaccesslogs
```

The same for the OpenDJ LDAP server instance will be as follows:

```
- input_type: log
  paths:
    - /usr/servers/opendj/logs/*
  document_type: ldaplogs
```

OpenDJ log entries are not multiline in nature, and thus do not need a multiline filter.

For Elasticsearch instance:

```
- input_type: log
  paths:
    - /usr/servers/elasticsearch-liferay/logs/*.log
  document_type: elasticsearchlogs
```

Setting up Logstash

As soon as Filebeat starts capturing logs, we can start Logstash so that we can receive the logs, parse, process, and index to Elasticsearch. Why do we need Logstash? Filebeat is capable of sending logs directly to Elasticsearch, as they appear with no change.

By processing the data with Logstash, we get a closer look at the data and processed fields, and logs can give us a better analysis opportunity. For example, if we break the Nginx logs to find out geo locations, it will give us a clear idea of locations from which most users access our server. To break the logs into multiple fields, we can use grok patterns.

In the preceding section, when we configured Filebeat, we added logs of these types: nginx logs, liferay logs, elasticsearch logs, and ldap logs. Out of these, let's use grok for nginx, liferay, and openDJ logs. We will create a directory inside `logstash-5.1.1/conf` with name patterns to store all patterns needed:

grok for nginxlogs

Create a file in `logstash-5.1.1/conf/patterns` with the name `nginx.pattern` for this pattern. A sample nginx access log looks as follows:

```
27.109.15.3 - - [02/Jan/2017:13:10:56 +0000] "GET /dashboard HTTP/1.1" 200
4755 "http://google.co.in/" "Mozilla/5.0 (Windows NT 6.1; WOW64)
AppleWebKit/537.36 (KHTML, like Gecko) Chrome/55.0.2883.87 Safari/537.36"
```

This log entry is a typical nginx access log, which has IP, user, auth, timestamp, request verb, a relative URL called, HTTP response code, content length, referrer, and agent. For such log entry, our grok pattern will be:

```
NGUSER [a-zA-Z\.\@\-\+_%]+
NGINXACCESSLOG %{IPORHOST:clientip} %{NGUSER:user} %{NGUSER:auth}
\[%{HTTPDATE:timestamp}\] "%{WORD:verb} %{URIPATHPARAM:request}
HTTP/%{NUMBER:httpversion}" %{NUMBER:response} (?:%{NUMBER:bytes}|-)
(?:"(?:%{URI:referrer}|-)"|%{QS:referrer}) %{QS:agent}
```

This will add a pattern for nginx with the name NGINXACCESSLOG, which we can use in Logstash.

grok for liferaylogs

Our Liferay setup runs on Tomcat. There are server-related logs stored in catalina logs, and our custom logic/liferay-related logs are stored in liferay logs. A typical log for liferay looks like this:

```
08:15:29,024 INFO  [http-bio-8080-exec-1718][TimeEntryHelperImpl:267]
Getting Project Task List
```

This log has information about time, log level, thread, Java class, line number, and log message. For this, our custom grok pattern would look like this:

```
TOMCAT_DATESTAMP %{HOUR}:?%{MINUTE}(?::?%{SECOND})
LOGTHREAD   ([A-Za-z0-9_. -]+)
TOMCAT_LOG %{TOMCAT_DATESTAMP:timestamp} %{LOGLEVEL:level}\s*
\[%{LOGTHREAD:logThread}\]\[%{LOGTHREAD:class}:%{INT:line}\]\s*%{GREEDYDATA
:message}
```

This log pattern will read the liferay logs and store it in fields accordingly. Another type of logs is catalina logs, which are mostly related to portlet deployments to the Liferay portal. A typical log entry might look like this:

```
Nov 15, 2016 8:53:28 AM org.apache.catalina.startup.HostConfig
deleteRedeployResources
INFO: Undeploying context [/notification-portlet]
```

In the preceding log, notification `portlet` is being undeployed. To read such logs, our grok pattern would be:

```
CATALINA_DATESTAMP %{MONTH} %{MONTHDAY}, %{YEAR}
%{HOUR}:?%{MINUTE}(?::?%{SECOND}) (?:AM|PM)
JAVALOGMESSAGE (.*)
CATALINALOGMESSAGE %{CATALINA_DATESTAMP:datestamp}
%{DATA:class}%{LOGLEVEL:level}:\s* %{JAVALOGMESSAGE:message}
```

This log contains a multiline log. Our Filebeat and Logstash configurations will allow us to read multiline logs and use the above grok pattern to correctly break the fields out of log lines. We will see the complete configuration in the next section.

grok for openDJ logs.

The following are the sample log messages:

```
[29/Sep/2016:15:47:53 +0530] CONNECT conn=72 from=127.0.0.1:60395
to=127.0.0.1:1389 protocol=LDAP
[29/Sep/2016:15:47:53 +0530] BIND REQ conn=72 op=0 msgID=1 version=3
type=SIMPLE dn="cn=Directory Manager"
[29/Sep/2016:15:47:53 +0530] BIND RES conn=73 op=0 msgID=1 result=0
authDN="cn=Directory Manager,cn=Root DNs,cn=config" etime=0
[29/Sep/2016:15:47:53 +0530] SEARCH REQ conn=72 op=1 msgID=2
base="dc=rkg,dc=test" scope=sub filter="(objectClass=inetOrgPerson)"
attrs="uid"
[29/Sep/2016:15:47:53 +0530] SEARCH RES conn=73 op=1 msgID=2 result=0
nentries=1 etime=1
[29/Sep/2016:15:47:53 +0530] SEARCH RES conn=72 op=1 msgID=2 result=0
nentries=1000 unindexed etime=343
[29/Sep/2016:16:13:34 +0530] DISCONNECT conn=73 reason="Client Disconnect"
[20/Nov/2016:13:15:56 +0530] DISCONNECT conn=0 reason="Server Error"
msg="LDAP Request Handler 0 for connection handler Administration Connector
0.0.0.0 port 4444 was unable to register this client connection with the
selector: java.nio.channels.ClosedChannelException"
[28/Sep/2016:09:33:40 +0530] category=UTIL severity=NOTICE
msgID=org.opends.messages.runtime.21 msg=Installation Directory:
/usr/servers/opendj
```

OpenDJ logs are not simple. They don't share a common format, thus grok for all such log messages are different. Only the starting timestamp has the same format. There are logs for connection information, bind information, and search along with generic logs. The following are a complete set of grok for such log messages:

```
TIMESTAMP_TZ
\[%{MONTHDAY}/%{MONTH}/%{YEAR}:%{HOUR}%{MINUTE}(?:%{SECOND})\s*%{ISO8601_TI
MEZONE}?\]

OPENDJACESSSEARCHRES %{OPENDJACESSUNBIND} result=%{NUMBER:result}
nentries=%{NUMBER:numberOfEntries}
%{RESULTTYPE}\s*etime=%{NUMBER:eventTime}

RESULTTYPE (%{WORD:resultType})?

OPENDJACESSSEARCHREQ %{OPENDJACESSUNBIND} base=%{GREEDYDATA:baseInfo}
scope=%{GREEDYDATA:scope} filter=%{GREEDYDATA:filterCondition}

OPENDJACESSBINDRES %{OPENDJACESSUNBIND} result=%{NUMBER:result}
authDN=%{GREEDYDATA:authDetails} etime=%{NUMBER:eventTime}

OPENDJACESSBINDREQ %{OPENDJACESSUNBIND} version=%{NUMBER:versionNumber}
type=%{WORD:bindType} dn=%{GREEDYDATA:directoryName}

OPENDJACESSUNBIND %{TIMESTAMP_TZ:timestamp} %{GREEDYDATA:requestType}
conn=%{NUMBER:connID} op=%{NUMBER:opID} msgID=%{NUMBER:messageID}

OPENDJACESSDISCONNECT %{TIMESTAMP_TZ:timestamp} %{WORD:requestType}
conn=%{NUMBER:connID}
reason="%{DATA:reason}"(\smsg="%{GREEDYDATA:messageInfo})?

OPENDJACESSCONNECT %{TIMESTAMP_TZ:timestamp} %{WORD:requestType}
conn=%{NUMBER:connID} from=%{IPORHOST:fromIP}:%{NUMBER:fromPort}
to=%{IPORHOST:toIP}:%{NUMBER:toPort} protocol=%{WORD:protocolName}

OPENDJLOGS %{TIMESTAMP_TZ:timestamp} category=%{WORD:categoryName}
severity=%{WORD:severityLevel} msgID=%{GREEDYDATA:messageID}
msg=%{GREEDYDATA:message}

OPENDJACESSUNBIND %{TIMESTAMP_TZ:timestamp} %{GREEDYDATA:requestType}
conn=%{NUMBER:connID} op=%{NUMBER:opID} msgID=%{NUMBER:messageID}
```

These grok cover all formats of log messages for openDJ. Let's save these patterns in `logstash-5.1.1/conf/patterns/opendj.pattern` file.

Config File

Let's take a look at the configuration file to be used to process logs from liferay, nginx, and OpenDJ nodes:

```
input {
    beats {
       port => 5044
       codec => multiline {
          patterns_dir => "./conf/patterns/"
          pattern => "(^%{TOMCAT_DATESTAMP}|
                      ^%{CATALINA_DATESTAMP}|
                      ^%{TIMESTAMP_TZ})"
          negate => true
          what => "previous"
       }
   }
}

filter{
  if [type] == "lrlogs" {
    mutate {
       gsub => ['message', "\n", " "]
       gsub => ['message', "\t", " "]
    }
    grok {
      patterns_dir => "./conf/patterns"
      match => [ "message", "%{TOMCAT_LOG}"]
    }
  }
  if [type] == "lrcatalinalogs" {
    mutate {
       gsub => ['message', "\n", ""]
       gsub => ['message', "\t", " "]
    }
    grok {
      patterns_dir => "./conf/patterns"
      match => [ "message", "%{CATALINALOGMESSAGE}"]
    }
  }
  if [type] == "nginxaccesslogs" {
    grok{
      patterns_dir => "./conf/patterns"
      match => { "message" => "%{NGINXACCESSLOG}" }
    }
    geoip {
          source => "clientip"
    }
```

```
      }
  if [type] == "ldaplogs" {
    grok{
      patterns_dir => "./conf/patterns"
      match => { "message" => [ "%{OPENDJLOGS}",
                 "%{OPENDJACESSCONNECT}",
                 "%{OPENDJACESSDISCONNECT}",
                 "%{OPENDJACESSBINDREQ}",
                 "%{OPENDJACESSBINDRES}",
                 "%{OPENDJACESSSEARCHREQ}",
                 "%{OPENDJACESSSEARCHRES}",
                 "%{OPENDJACESSUNBIND}" ] }
    }
  }
}

output {
  elasticsearch {
    hosts => "192.168.0.110:9200"
    document_type => "%{[@metadata][type]}"
  }
}
```

 The path to `patterns_dir` can also be added as an absolute path.

Let's understand what we are trying to do here. At the input section, we are listening to Filebeat. The input from Filebeat is passed through a multiline codec. For multiline log messages, this process adds \n for line break and \t as tabs for space before a line starts in Java stack trace. We are mutating the logs to remove \n and \t by space so that all log lines are considered a single line before we pass it through the grok filter. After the filter, logs are broken into their respective fields and then stored to Elasticsearch.

In case of nginx logs, we do not need to specify codec in input section and mutate in filters. Also, we can use the NGINXACCESSLOG pattern to match the logs. Additionally, we will use geoip so that we can find out geo location-related data using a visitor's IP. This will add a location field, which has latitude and longitude values. If we do not specify any index name in the output section, the index name will be logstash- %{+YYYY.MM.dd}. The mapping templates provided and already loaded into logstash for Elasticsearch plugin will automatically convert location field to geo_point, which can be used for tile map-like visualization.

For OpenDJ log messages, we have provided an array of grok patterns. It will pick the first grok matching the message.

Once we have the configuration file ready, let's say with the name as `portal.conf`, run the command to start logstash:

```
./bin/logstash -f conf/portal.conf
```

This will start sending logs read by Filebeat to Elasticsearch, which can be viewed using Kibana.

Setting up Kibana

Our IP address for Kibana is `192.168.0.111`, and for Elasticsearch, it is `192.168.0.110`. Let's keep the name of the kibana host machine as `kibana-node-stack`. Our `config/kibana.yml` would be as follows:

```
server.host: "192.168.0.111"
server.port: 5601
elasticsearch.url: "http://192.168.0.110:9200"
server.name: "Kibana-node-stack"
```

Once kibana is set up and configured, let's start Kibana to visualize the incoming data. Run the following command in the directory where you installed kibana:

```
$ ./bin/kibana
```

After Kibana is started, set up the index patterns. For example, for log-related patterns, all indices are going to be matched by the `logstash*` pattern.

Setting up Kibana Dashboards

For all of the Beats, there are few sample dashboards already created. We can import those dashboards using a script provided with each beat. Let's take a look at dashboards for each beat.

PacketBeat

Import the dashboards for Packetbeat by running the following command in the Packetbeat directory:

```
./scripts/import_dashboards -es http://192.168.0.110:9200
```

This will import all dashboards for Packetbeat and in Kibana. We can see these dashboards by navigating to Kibana **Web Interface** | **Dashboard** | **Open**, and you should see a list of pre-set dashboards:

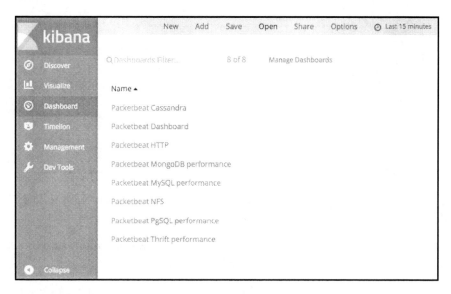

By default, all of the dashboards will be imported. In case we do not want to keep a dashboard, we can delete it using the **Manage Dashboards** link.

MetricBeat

Import the dashboards for MetricBeat by running the following command in the MetricBeat directory:

```
./scripts/import_dashboards -es http://192.168.0.110:9200
```

This will import all dashboards for MetricBeat, and in Kibana. We can see these dashboards by navigating to Kibana **Web Interface** | **Dashboard** | **Open**, and you should see a list of pre-set dashboards:

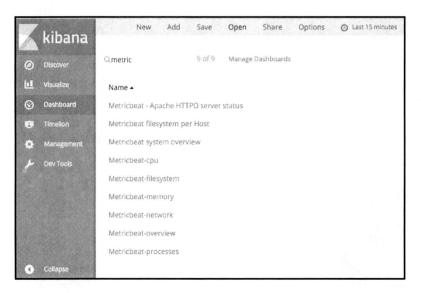

By default, all of the dashboards will be imported. In case we do not want to keep a dashboard, we can delete it using **Manage Dashboards** link.

There are no default dashboards available for Filebeat, and we need to create one for what we want to capture.

Now, when all of the things are set up and running, and data is being captured, we are ready to visualize and catch any critical issues that might occur. If I were supposed to monitor my servers, I would be interested to know the memory statistics of each machine, processor usages, if there is any critical error occurring. For database statistics, I would be keen to know if there are any slow queries, which queries are used most frequently, response times, throughput, and so on. Fortunately, you need very little or no efforts to visualize most of these stats. When we imported the dashboards, all such visualizations were preloaded into Kibana dashboards.

Checking DB (MySQL) Performance

For MySQL, we can see the DB methods that are used with counts, response time, errors, reads vs writes, throughput, and so on, as seen in the following screenshot; this dashboard can be seen by navigating to **Kibana** | **Dashboard** | **Open** | **Packetbeat MySQL Performance**:

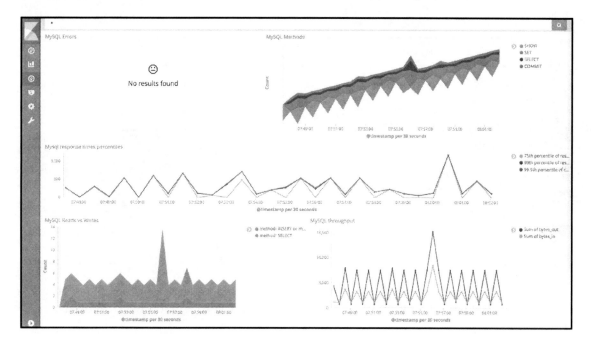

Along with these, the same dashboard also lists the most frequent queries and slow MySQL queries. This is often helpful to take decisions to improve performance. You will want to cache the results of the queries that are most frequently used for some time and decrease DB transactions count. For queries that are slow, you will want to optimize the queries to improve response time. The following is a screenshot of the two lists: the first one shows the most frequent queries, and the second one lists all slow queries with an average response time:

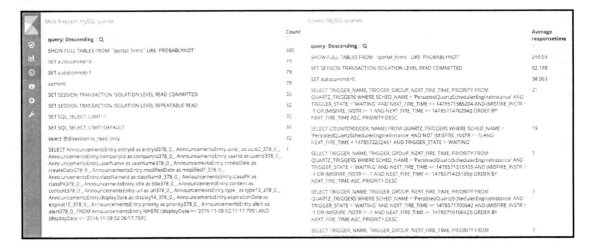

Apart from these charts and listings, there are other stats available in Packetbeat: Overview Dashboard, which also lists Web transactions, latency, error versus successful transactions, and so on.

In case we need to add more visualizations, we can do so by creating visualizations and adding them to the dashboard. Similarly, we can remove the unnecessary or irrelevant visualization from dashboard as well.

Analyzing CPU usage

Using Metricbeat dashboards, we can see CPU usage and system loads using Metricbeat – CPU dashboard:

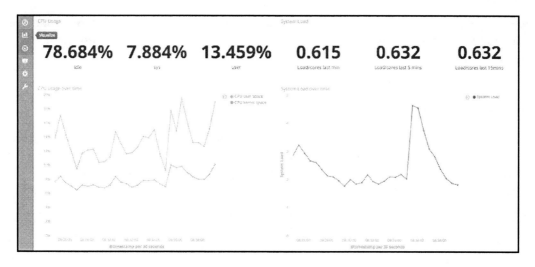

Apart from this, the same dashboard also lists the CPU stats for each machine, where Metricbeat is set up and running.

Keeping an eye on memory

Similar to CPU stats, Metricbeat also offers a dashboard with memory-related statistics. This dashboard shows data for memory usage, available memory, swap usage, along with top hosts by memory usage:

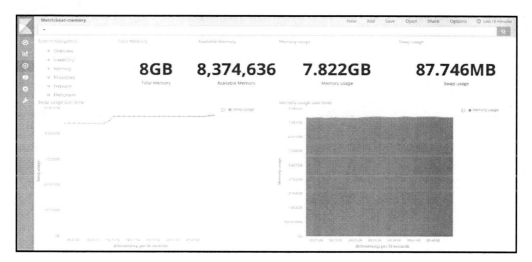

There are other dashboards available, which help us to visualize process-related data. We can see top processes by memory and CPU usage, charts with CPU usage and memory usage per process.

Checking logs

When Filebeat is run, it will crawl all logs files for changes and send them to Elasticsearch to be indexed after parsing them by Logstash. By navigating to **Kibana | Discover**, we can see all of the logs for index pattern we set for **logstash***. The following is a sample representation of the logs listed:

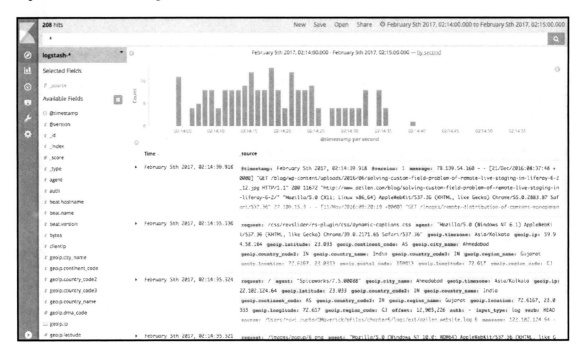

We can search logs using different parameters (fields, listed on the left menu under **Available Fields**). Usually, in the production environment, there are too many logs when there is a good amount of concurrent users. This leads to even thousands of logs per second or minute. Finding an error in logs is not easy, and in such cases, tools such as Kibana help a lot by providing such a feature where we can search into log entries. To gather useful information from too many logs is not an easy task. Categorization helps in such cases-like we did using document type while setting Filebeat prospectors. Additionally, we added tags as well for our main app server nodes. The following is an image of filtered logs using type for **nginxaccesslogs**:

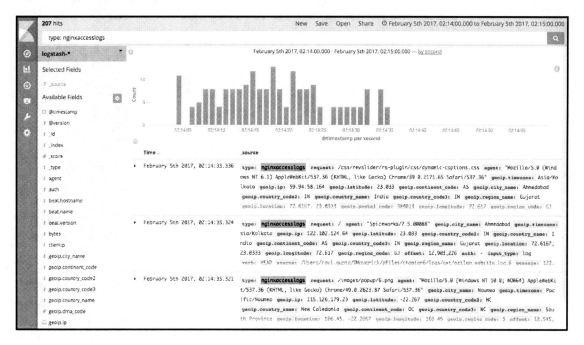

We used type: nginxaccesslogs to filter the logs. As we can see, logs for only the **nginxaccesslogs** type are displayed; this view gives us a specific, targeted view and list of the logs we are looking for.

Similarly, we can try for tags as well. We can select logs for only **liferay node 1** using the tag we specified in Filebeat configuration.

For a given time frame, we can also see the classification of logs by clicking on a filed under available fields on left side. We can see the count of logs for each category. For example, if we want to know the count of logs for each node of liferay, we can see it under **tags** as shown in the following screenshot:

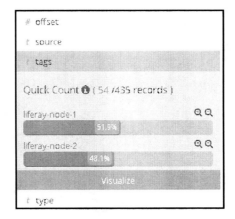

We can quickly create visualization from here. If you click on the visualize button under the log counts, it will take you to a vertical bar chart, where liferay nodes will be on x-axis and counts will be on y-axis.

Similar to these stats and logs, we can also keep an eye on all of the nodes and servers including app server (Portal in our case), HTTP server, LDAP Server, search engine, and so on.

Finding most visited pages

If you are serving to a good number of users, you would always want to know the most visited pages in order to serve better content and user experience. The Packetbeat HTTP dashboard lists all such web pages' URLs along with the counts:

Top 10 HTTP requests	
query: Descending ⚲	Count ⌄
POST /group/mint/time-sheet	8,027
GET /group/mint/project-dashboard	6,013
GET /group/mint/projects	6,013
GET /	4,024
GET /group/mint/employee-listing	4,022
POST /poller/receive	2,068
GET /mint-theme/images/portlet/draggable_borderless.png	2,017
GET /group/mint/dashboard	2,013
GET /c	2,012
POST /web/guest/home	2,012
Export: Raw ⬇ Formatted ⬇	

In the preceding image, we can see a list of URLs along with the request type and count. We can clearly see that people are more interested to get information about the projects and accessing their timesheet. There can be many conclusions based on this data, and that purely depends on the organization's need.

Visitors' map

It's always a curious fact to know where the visitors are from. Also, if that can appear on a map, it is a pleasure to look. Google Web analytics-like platform shows this visualization and helps to know visitors count of a region. With help of Kibana, tile maps, we can build a similar visualization provided we have the location, that is, latitude and longitude. While setting up Logstash, we added a grok pattern to break the logs and used mutate to add two more fields to build a `geo_point` field. Using this, we can draw points on our map; let's create a visualization for this use case:

1. Navigate to **Kibana** | **Visualize** | **New** | **Tile Map** and select index pattern as **logstash***
2. For the metrics, keep value as aggregation count
3. Select the only available sub-bucket-**Geo Coordinates**
4. From the fields, select **geoip.location**

5. Go to options and change the map type to `heatmap` and click on Run; you should see a heatmap of all visitors:

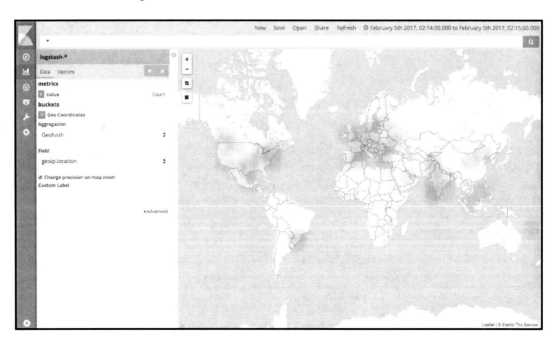

6. Change the map type to scaled circle markers and zoom in to a region or country, for example, India; it gives a better idea along with a legend:

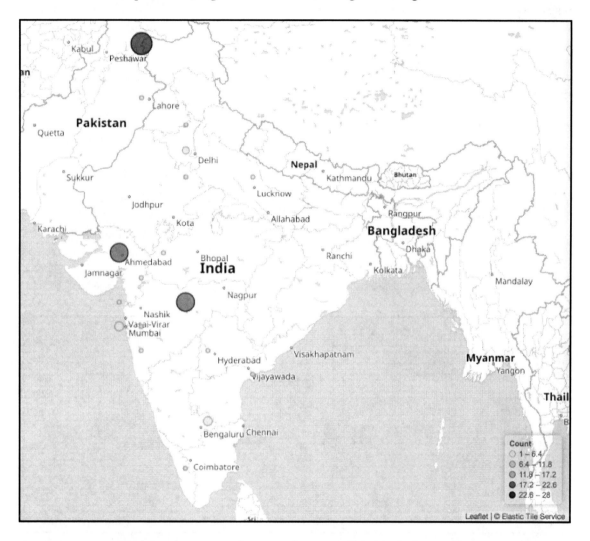

As we can see, our visitors are spread across the map. This kind of visualizations helps us to understand the geography of visitors and serve them content in a better and familiar-to-them manner.

Number of visitors in a time frame

It's always a fun fact and important at the same time to look at the current visitors on our website. We can set a metric to find out the number of unique visitors in a given time frame. These kinds of metrics can help a lot to understand time frames for which there are maximum visitors or minimum visitors. If we need to take our website down for some time and make a decision of maintenance or downtime window, we can see when there are minimum visitors:

1. Select a time range of your choice
2. Navigate to **Kibana | Visualize | New | Metric** and select index pattern as **logstash***
3. For metric, keep aggregation as count, and change the custom label to **Total Hits**
4. Add another metric, keep aggregation to **Unique Count**, choose field as **clientip.keyword,** and set label to **Unique Count of Visitors**
5. Similarly, you can add more metrics for unique count of countries using **geoip.country_name.keyword,** and for unique cities count, use **geoip.city_name.keyword**
6. Click on run, and you should see metrics for your desired time range:

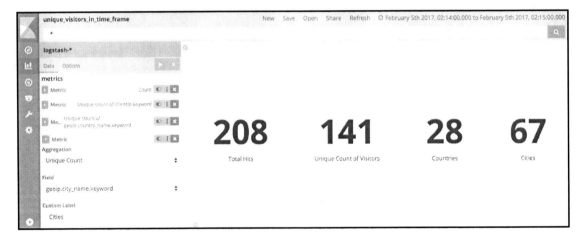

As we can see, **141** unique visitors from **67 Cities** of **28 Countries** made total **208** hits. At a moment, we can get such data to see the traffic on the website.

Request Types

Let's do another visualization for all types of request verbs: GET, PUT, POST, and so on. This is another important fact to know and understand. Most often, POST requests are fired when there is an action performed. This kind of data can be helpful to understand the behavior of the visitors:

1. Navigate to **Kibana | Visualize | Data Table**, and select index pattern as **logstash***
2. In the metrics, keep aggregation as count
3. Add a bucket of type split rows and choose aggregation on Terms
4. Choose `verb.keyword` for field and change the label to **Request Type**
5. Click on run and, a data table will be generated similar to this:

Request Type Q	Count
GET	3,290
POST	202
HEAD	66

As we can see, most of the requests are made for getting the data as compared to POST request.

Error type-log levels

Similar to request types, we can also set up a data table for log levels. For this visualization, we can set a filter for `lrlogs` and then a data table similar to request types data table with field as `level.keyword`. Since we are interested to know the log levels only for logs generated for app server nodes - that is, liferay nodes -we should create a filter for `lrlogs`. To create a filter, perform the following steps:

1. Navigate to **Kibana | Discover**, and click on type under available fields

2. From the types, click on lens icon with + for lrlogs. This will add a filter for type as lrlogs:

This filter has definition as follows:

```
{
  "query": {
    "match": {
      "type": {
        "query": "lrlogs",
        "type": "phrase"
      }
    }
  }
}
```

3. Pin this filter, and this will be available for us in visualize mode; we will use this for error type visualization:

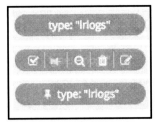

The first image is the default when we added the filter. The second image is when we mouse over on it, and last is when we click on pin to pin this filter.

Now, when we have the filter set up, we can do our visualization for log levels in liferay logs; follow these steps to get this visualization done:

1. Navigate to **Kibana | Visualize | Data table**, and select index pattern as **logstash***.
2. Keep the metric as count.
3. Add bucket for split rows and choose aggregation as Terms and field as level.keyword.
4. Change the label to **Log Level**, size to **10**, and click on run. A data table will be generated with log levels with the count as occurrence:

Log Level Q	Count
INFO	127
SEVERE	39
WARNING	2

You can change the time range as per your needs. Knowing log levels is not enough, and you would want to do more-for example, whenever an error occurs, you get a notification of some kind. We will use logstash's capability of e-mailing for this purpose later in this chapter.

Top referrers

It's good to know which are the referrers to your website. This is an important factor to understand and utilize for SEO purpose. Being referred from a genuine and popular website is a big deal, and you would want more of such references. Let's find out the top referrers:

1. Remove the existing filter, if there is any.
2. Navigate to **Kibana > Visualize > Data table**, and select index pattern as **logstash***.
3. Similar to other data tables, just change the field for terms aggregation as `referrer.keyword`.
4. Change the size to **10**; click on Run, and you will get the top **10** referrers along with the count.

Top agents

Knowing top agents can help you to understand the changes needed for the best user experience for your visitors. Similar to top referrers data table, create a data table visualization for agents by keeping field for terms aggregation as `agent.keyword`. You should have a visualization similar to the following:

Agent Name Q	Count
"Mozilla/5.0 (Macintosh; Intel Mac OS X 10_11_2) AppleWebKit/537.36 (KHTML, like Gecko) Chrome/47.0.2526.106 Safari/537.36"	121
"Mozilla/5.0 (Windows NT 6.1; WOW64) AppleWebKit/537.36 (KHTML, like Gecko) Chrome/51.0.2704.103 Safari/537.36"	85
"Mozilla/5.0+(compatible; UptimeRobot/2.0; http://www.uptimerobot.com/)"	78
"Mozilla/5.0 (Windows NT 6.1; WOW64) AppleWebKit/537.36 (KHTML, like Gecko) Chrome/50.0.2661.102 Safari/537.36"	53
"Mozilla/5.0 (Windows NT 6.1; WOW64) AppleWebKit/537.36 (KHTML, like Gecko) Chrome/49.0.2623.112 Safari/537.36"	48
"Mozilla/5.0 (Windows NT 6.1; rv:40.0) Gecko/20100101 Firefox/40.0"	46
"Mozilla/5.0 (Windows NT 6.1; WOW64) AppleWebKit/537.36 (KHTML, like Gecko) Chrome/55.0.2883.87 Safari/537.36"	43
"Pingdom.com_bot_version_1.4_(http://www.pingdom.com)"	41
"Mozilla/5.0 (Windows NT 6.1) AppleWebKit/537.36 (KHTML, like Gecko) Chrome/50.0.2661.102 Safari/537.36"	36

You can see that most of the requests are made from Mac OSX.

Alerting using Logstash e-mail capability

Alerting is a key aspect of analytics. You cannot continuously monitor logs or any other stats 24×7, and you need to be alerted when some specific event happens. For example, if there is any error occurring in logs, you would always want to be notified of it. Nobody can tolerate an error on a production server.

Let's use the e-mail capability of Logstash for e-mail notifications whenever some errors occur. For this, we will use e-mail output plugin of logstash. This plugin is not part of logstash packaging, but we can install it using:

```
bin/logstash-plugin install logstash-output-email
```

Once the plugin is installed, we can use it in the output section. Add the following configuration to the output section to configure your Gmail account to send an e-mail:

```
if [level] == "ERROR" {
  email {
    address => "smtp.gmail.com"
    port => "587"
    username => "mes.packt"
    password => "<password>"
    use_tls => "true"
```

```
        from => "<mes.packt@gmail.com>"
        subject => "Error status"
        to => "<to-email>"
        htmlbody => "<h2>Some error occurred on %{host} for %{type}</h2>
                    <h6>Log File Name</h6>
                    <div>%{source}</div>
                    <h6>Java Class</h6>
                    <div>%{class}</div>
                    <h6>Line Number</h6>
                    <div>%{line}</div>
                    <h6>Full Event</h6><div>%{message}</div>"
    }
  }
```

In the preceding listing, we will check whether the log level was error. This field is added by `grok` filter. Replace the `<password>` with actual password and change to to-e-mail to an actual e-mail address. Whenever an error occurs, an e-mail will be sent to the specified e-mail.

For example, refer to the following screenshot for an e-mail triggered because of an error log:

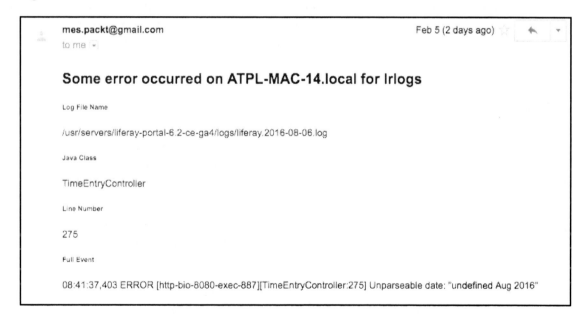

X-Pack provides a way to be notified using watcher, and we will learn about watcher later in `Chapter 10`, *X-Pack: Alerting, Graph, and Reporting* and `Chapter 12`, *Case Study: Meetup.*

Using a message broker

The traffic on production servers is supposed to be high at times. When this happens, log entries and statistics data become very critical and the amount of such data in total is also high. All of the Beats will be doing their work and will be sending respective data to Elasticsearch, but it is possible that some of the packets/data are lost while processing. It may happen because of a network failure, very high peaks of data, or any other possible reason. The point is, the data being indexed must not be lost in any case.

To address this problem, using a message broker or buffer is a good choice. There are many tools that can be evaluated for your choice of the message broker. For Open Source, there are two good tools available:

- **Redis**: `http://redis.io/`
- **Kafka**: `https://kafka.apache.org/`

Sometimes, it seems that message broker is a must for a production environment, but there might be cases when we don't need any message broker at all. When we use Filebeat, it acts as a temporary buffer. Logs generated will definitely be indexed, but it might take some time and their search might have some latency. If that latency is okay, there is no need to use a broker for logs. It will save another hardware or server to monitor in production environment. Using a buffer/message broker purely depends on the system requirements.

Summary

In this chapter, we analyzed how components from Elastic Stack can be made useful for a production environment. More or less, similar architectures and arrangement is done for most of the production environment. We should be careful while choosing the Beats for servers. Sometimes, we may put Beats to read data, which is not that critical and can be managed otherwise.

Later in the chapter, we saw how predefined dashboards help us with the information we need. Although these dashboards provide most of the useful information, we can still customize them as per our convenience and requirements.

In the next chapter, we will learn how to customize each component of the stack. We will learn the way they can be customized and modified as per our need.

7
Customizing Elastic Stack

One point to check whether a tool is great, is to find the answer of the following question: how much can it be customized? If you are selling your product, and if you have answer to that question like – *Yes, and these are the ways*. You already sold the product. This is an era of open source products, and level of customization of the product, plays a major role in deciding whether a product should be utilized for our requirement or not. There are many things your buyer would want to do with your setup, such as writing custom plugins, modifying existing things in product, modifying the UI for your branding, and much more.

In this chapter, we will learn how to customize the Elastic Stack by extending or modifying the components. The following is a list of topics that we will capture in this chapter:

- Extending Elasticsearch
- Extending Logstash
- Extending Beats
- Extending Kibana

Extending Elasticsearch

Elasticsearch is a rich-in-feature, stable, and mature project, yet it is growing everyday. Like a good open source project, Elasticsearch offers ways to extend and let users customize Elasticsearch in their own ways. There are many things you would want to achieve through customization, to name a few: you would want to support a new repository to which Elasticsearch can connect and keep data, you might be interested to write your own analyzer, which does some additional tasks as compared to the existing analyzers in Elasticsearch, and so on. For the previous versions of Elasticsearch (prior to v5), developers used to create their own rivers to support a new data source. In fact, using the HTTP and transport modules, there are numerous opportunities of extending Elasticsearch beyond Elasticsearch packaged code and providing something that helps to integrate Elasticsearch with some other tool or technology.

Although not too many attempts were made to customize Elasticsearch by community, the following are the most common and popular methods of customization:

- **Writing a plugin**: Prior to version 5, when the stack was known as ELK stack, three types of plugins were supported: Java, Site, and Mixed. Site and Mixed plugins were used to provide a user interface for Elasticsearch and used a combination of web development technologies and languages for their development. These plugins were mostly used to look into the indices, shards, and relevant information. Java plugins, at the other hand, were used to provide additional feature to Elasticsearch and did not have a user interface. These plugins were mostly developed to add support for discovery of nodes in cloud environments, support for repositories, analyzers, and so on. Starting from naming of Elastic Stack and version 5.0 of Elasticsearch, Site and Mixed plugins are deprecated, and only Java plugins are supported. You can find all the available plugins for Elasticsearch (for versions 5.1.x) at – `https://github.com/e lastic/elasticsearch/tree/5.1/plugins`

- **Extending your application to utilize Elasticsearch**: The second way is to utilize Elasticsearch APIs by creating an application outside and calling APIs using HTTP module or transport module. When we want to call HTTP module, we can do so using simple REST calls. On the other hand, to access using transport protocol and make call to Elasticsearch APIs, we need to add dependency to our project. The JAR file for transport client is available at `https://mvnrepository.c om/artifact/org.elasticsearch.client/transport/5.1.1`. Though site and mixed plugins, which were providing a view of Elasticsearch indices, shards, cluster related data, and so on, are deprecated, you can build your own client to connect it to Elasticsearch cluster and do standard index, search, get, and delete operations.

We will not create any plugin for Elasticsearch, but we will cover how to set things up and the structure of the plugin.

Elasticsearch development environment

To extend Elasticsearch by creating a plugin, we should set up few things to speed up the development. The first thing is to get the source code of Elasticsearch:

```
$ git clone https://github.com/elastic/elasticsearch.git
```

This will checkout the master branch, which is the in-development version, and usually not stable. Let's switch to a version that we will use: 5.1:

```
$ git checkout -b elasticsearch-local origin/5.1
```

 In case, you do not have Git, install it from `https://git-scm.com/`. Similarly, Gradle is available at `https://gradle.org/`.

An Elasticsearch plugin project is a gradle project. To develop and build plugin, we need Java and Gradle. For Elasticsearch, you need Java version 8 and Gradle version 2.13 onwards. You can use a choice of IDE for plugin development, which supports gradle project development. This is pretty much it for the Elasticsearch development environment.

Anatomy of an Elasticsearch Java plugin

The Elastic team has intentionally put an example plugin in the Elasticsearch source. The plugin is named as jvm-plugin that is available at, `https://github.com/elastic/elasticsearch/tree/5.1/plugins/jvm-example`.

The plugin usually contains the directory structure similar to this:

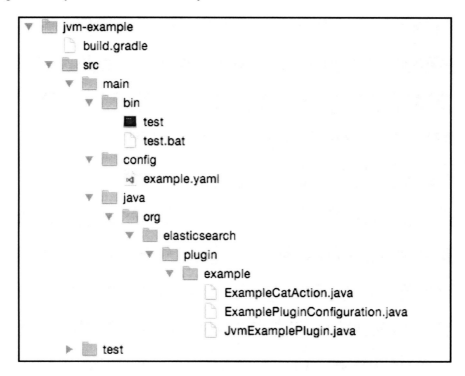

The plugin is usually a Gradle project and contains a configuration and a plugin class. If you are going to develop your own plugin, your plugin directory structure should be similar. Under the `src/main` directory, there should be a `config` directory, which will have the configuration file in a YAML format and a Java directory, which will contain the actual plugin implementation. The configuration file will contain all configuration needed for the plugin to run. The bin and test directories are for binaries and test cases, respectively.

Our main plugin class, which in the example here is `JvmExamplePlugin`, extends `org.elasticsearch.plugins` plugin class, so should every new plugin class.

Gradle plugin `esplugin` helps to build the plugin. In the `build.gradle` file, necessary settings to utilize the plugin are mentioned at the top, similar to this:

```
esplugin {
description 'Demonstrates all the pluggable Java entry points in
elasticsearch'
classname 'org.elasticsearch.plugin.example.JvmExamplePlugin'
}
```

The class name refers to our plugin class name. This should match the exact package and class name as our plugin class.

Every Elasticsearch plugin must contain a `plugin-descriptor.properties` file under the `src/main/resource` directory. You need to create this directory and file. This file helps Elasticsearch to know that this project is a type of plugin. By default, few properties in the descriptor file are enabled, for example, plugin description, plugin version, name, class name, Elasticsearch version, Java version and so on. Since Elastic Stack maintains the same version for all components, your plugin should also share the same version of Elasticsearch for which the plugin is developed. These are mandatory for every plugin:

```
description=Demonstrates all the pluggable Java entry points
version=5.1.1
name=jvm-example
classname=org.elasticsearch.plugin.example.JvmExamplePlugin
java.version=1.8
elasticsearch.version=5.1.1
```

Building the plugin

Once we are done with our plugin code, we can build using the `gradle` standard commands. When we run the `gradle` commands to build the project, plugin descriptor file is automatically created and put into the plugin folder.

To build the source code, navigate to plugin directory and run the following:

gradle clean build

This command will collect all dependencies (at first run), compile the complete source code, and build the project.

To create a JAR file, which is the distribution file for our plugin, use the following command:

gradle jar

The preceding command will generate jar files inside the build directory within our plugin. This command will create five files for distribution similar to the following:

```
jvm-example-5.1.1-SNAPSHOT-javadoc.jar
jvm-example-5.1.1-SNAPSHOT-sources.jar
jvm-example-5.1.1-SNAPSHOT.jar
jvm-example-5.1.1-SNAPSHOT.pom
jvm-example-5.1.1-SNAPSHOT.zip
```

The zip file is the main plugin and contains plugin JAR file, plugin descriptor file, config, and so on. This plugin can be installed to our Elasticsearch setup just like any other plugin.

Being in an open source community, it's always good to share the work you do. If you create your plugin, it's always good to host the plugin code somewhere, probably at Github.com, so that the community can take advantage of the plugin.

Extending Logstash

There are two ways to extend Logstash: either by modifying the core or adding one more plugin to its repository. As we have already learned, there are four types of plugins – Input, Output, Filter, and Codec. Generating plugin in Logstash is very easy and needs only one command to be run; the generated plugin needs only our custom logic for it to be implemented.

Logstash plugins are written in Ruby programming language (`http://www.ruby-lang.org/en/`). These plugins are actually ruby gems. To be able to write effective gems, you should be familiar with Ruby.

In this section, we will develop our own input plugin, which will fetch data from a web service. The complete code of the plugin is available at GitHub at `https://github.com/kravigupta/mastering-elastic-stack-code-files/tree/5.1.1/Chapter07/logstash-input-weather`. The purpose of this exercise is to learn how a plugin can be generated and customized to serve the purpose, along with understanding of structure of the plugin.

If you analyze any scenario that utilizes Elastic Stack components, Logstash plays a big role because of the number of plugins available for each type. If you see a new input data source, and you need to collect the data and put it to either Elasticsearch or some other destination, you create a Logstash plugin, collect the data, and index it. Similarly, if you see complex data coming in, you use filter and codec plugins to break it to chunks and index it accordingly. Similarly, Elasticsearch is not the only output destination when it comes to storing the data. It is possible that we want to capture specific tweets and put them to database so that third-party applications can read the tweets directly from their database. There are so many other use case that you can find, which will make you realize that one Logstash plugin will help you greatly to set up the proper data pipeline.

Generating a plugin

To generate a plugin, Logstash uses the following syntax:

```
./bin/logstash-plugin generate --type plugin-type --name plugin-name --path
plugin-path
```

In the preceding command, we need to provide the type of the plugin, name of the plugin, and the path where we want to generate the plugin.

The type of the plugin can take input from one of the plugin types: Input, Filter, Codec, and Output. In this section, we will create an input plugin to fetch data from `https://openweathermap.org/`. To keep things simple, we will use this plugin to capture weather data for one city at a time.

Let's generate our Logstash input type plugin with name weather:

```
./bin/logstash-plugin generate --type input --name weather --path ../my-
plugins/
```

We have created a my-plugins directory parallel to where Logstash is extracted. This command will automatically prepend `logstash-input-` to the plugin name and will create a directory named `logstash-input-weather` inside the my-plugins directory. The generated plugin is a simple ruby gem project.

Anatomy of the plugin

If you check out the plugin directory, it will be similar to this:

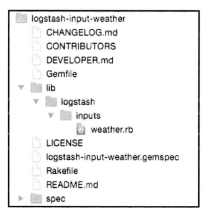

A Logstash plugin consists of the following elements:

- A `gemspec` file that is used to describe the project. In the preceding image, `logstash-input-weather.gemspec` file.
- Inside the `lib/logstash/inputs` directory lies our plugin code in the file usually named as `plugin-name.rb`, which contains a sample implementation of how a plugin file should be.
- The directory spec contains all tests written for the plugin.
- Other relevant files to help build the ruby gem and documentation, for example, Rakefile, README.md and so on.

weather.rb file

This is the main file, which will contain our logic to implement the input plugin. This plugin class is named as `Weather` and extends the `LogStash::Inputs::Base` class. The sample code inside this plugin class generates a repeating event. There are two key methods:

- `run(queue)`: It contains the actual logic. Inside run, there is a while loop, which runs until stop is signaled. This loop sleeps for an interval defined by a variable and defaults to 1 second. This method takes a queue as an argument, and when we have prepared an event, we push that event to the queue.
- `stop()`: It is called once when Logstash shuts down.

Plugin logic implementation

Before we can start the implementation, we need to obtain an API key from `https://openweathermap.org`, which will be used to call the weather API to get data for a city. Register an account on the website and open `https://home.openweathermap.org/api_keys` and generate a key for your usage.

The API call we will make is for getting the current data of a city. To get more details about the API and its response, check out the content at `https://openweathermap.org/current`. We are going to use the call with the city name and the API endpoint is `http://api.openweathermap.org/data/2.5/weather?q=cityName&appid=key`.

To make use of this, we need to replace `cityName` with the city of our interest and key with the API key.

Also, the output of the web service is a JSON object with various details about current weather of the city; a JSON response is similar to:

```
{
    "coord": { "lon": 72.62, "lat": 23.03 },
    "weather": [
      { "id": 800, "main": "Clear",
      "description": "clear sky", "icon": "01d" }
    ],
    "base": "stations",
    "main": {
      "temp": 300.15, "pressure": 1014, "humidity": 18,
      "temp_min": 300.15, "temp_max": 300.15
    },
    "visibility": 6000,
    "wind": {
      "speed": 2.6, "deg": 30
    },
    "clouds": { "all": 0 },
    "dt": 1486643400,
    "sys": {
      "type": 1, "id": 7758, "message": 0.0129, "country": "IN",
      "sunrise": 1486604711, "sunset": 1486645354
    },
    "id": 1279233,
    "name": "Ahmedabad",
    "cod": 200
}
```

The preceding response is for the Ahmedabad city of India. It has information about temperature, sunset/sunrise times, rain, wind-related information along with city metadata, that is, country, and geo-location information.

Let's develop the logic for our plugin's implementation, which will extract all of the fields, and store it in the index. Let's understand the steps involved to write the plugin.

Reading data from API end point

To get data from openweathermap.org, we need to call web service endpoint. For that capability, we need to import the net/http library. Add the following line to top of the weather.rb file:

```
require "net/http" # for calling web service url
```

We should define API URL in a variable, but before we do that, we need to define `cityName` and `key` as a Logstash configuration setting. Let's define these variables as follows:

```
config :cityName, :required => true, :default => ""
config :key, :required => true, :default => ""
```

We are not setting any default value to these two settings and expect users to provide values using Logstash configuration file for pipeline. We are also setting the configurations as required since without these values, the plugin won't be able to start and collect data. Now, we can set up URL as follows:

```
"http://api.openweathermap.org/data/2.5/weather?q="+cityName+"&appid="+key;
```

Now, we can make a web service call using:

```
response = Net::HTTP.get_response(URI.parse(url))
```

If the data call is made correctly, we will have the desired data in `response.body`, which we can use for parsing to JSON:

```
weatherData = JSON.parse(response.body)
```

The `weatherData` variable will have the JSON that has all what we need to index.

Preparing an event

Once we have weather data in a variable, we can prepare an event using the `LogStash::Event.new()` method:

```
event = LogStash::Event.new()
```

The `Event.new()` can also take field as parameters. If we want to put `cityName` as one of the field while initializing the event, the call would be:

```
event = LogStash::Event.new("cityName" => cityName)
```

Now, we can use `event.set()` to add more fields to the event. Consider this example:

```
event.set("cityName", cityName)
```

The response has fields with values as JSON object and array along with simple values, such as numbers or strings. We are breaking JSON response into multiple fields, and we should break such fields as well. So, let's define two more variables with such field names:

```
config :jsonFields, :default => "main,clouds,sys,coord,wind"
config :arrayFields, :default => "weather"
```

These fields are also added as configuration, and default values are set to field names. In case you want to change field names using pipeline configuration, you can do that. Only these fields will be broken further.

Now, let's loop through all of the fields:

```
jsonFieldsKeys = @jsonFields.split(",")
arrayFieldsKeys = @arrayFields.split(",")
weatherData.each do |k,v|
    if(jsonFieldsKeys.include? k)
      v.each do |key, val|
        event.set(k.to_s + "_" +key.to_s, val)
      end
    else
      if(arrayFieldsKeys.include? k)
        v.each do |obj|
          obj.each do |key, val|
            event.set(k.to_s + "_" +key.to_s, val)
          end
        end
      end
      event.set(k.to_s, v)
    end
end
```

This will ensure that all desired fields are broken and stored.

Publish the event

We first decorate the event so that if there are any tags defined, those can be added to the event:

```
decorate(event)
```

After decorating, we push the event to the queue so that it can be published to Elasticsearch:

```
queue << event
```

This ends our custom logic that stays in the while loop of the run(queue) method. This loop sleeps for interval defined by the variable interval which by default is one second. We are all done for coding, and now can proceed to building the plugin, installing it to Logstash and test the data flow in Kibana.

Openweathermap.org allows maximum 60 requests per hour so setting interval to 60 seconds is a fair value for this plugin.

Building and installing a plugin

Once we are done with the implementation, we can now build the plugin as a `ruby gem`, which can later be installed to Logstash like any other plugin. To build the plugin, use `gem` command:

```
gem build logstash-input-weather.gemspec
```

If you get error like:

```
ERROR: While executing gem ... (Gem::InvalidSpecificationException)
"FIXME" or "TODO" is not a description
```

Then, you should update your `gemspec` file with the correct content. Usually, we need to modify the values for summary, description, and home page inside the `logstash-input-weather.gemspec` file. If there are no errors, you should be able to see the output similar to this:

```
Successfully built RubyGem
Name: logstash-input-weather
Version: 0.1.0
File: logstash-input-weather-0.1.0.gem
```

This will create a file with a `.gem` extension and with our plugin name in the plugin directory, which can now be installed to Logstash using bin/plugin command inside logstash:

```
./bin/logstash-plugin install /path/to/logstash-input-weather-0.1.0.gem
```

Now, we can use the plugin to capture data from `openweathermap.org`. To test whether the plugin is installed or not, we can run the following command to list all plugins and search whether our plugin name is there or not:

```
./bin/logstash-plugin list
```

Testing our plugin

Once the plugin is installed, we can test it using a combination of Logstash, Elasticsearch, and Kibana. Let's create a config file for Logstash named `weather.conf`, in which we will put the configuration to collect data from `openweathermap.org` and send it to Elasticsearch. To minimize the complexity, we won't be taking any filter for now. Our simplistic configuration file would be similar to:

```
input {
  weather {
    key => "<your-api-key-here>"
    cityName => "Ahmedabad"
  }
}
output  {
    elasticsearch  {
        index => "weather"
        document_type => "citiesData"
    }
}
```

It is often needed to debug the plugin; for which you can start Logstash in debug mode by setting `log.level` to debug in `logstash-5.1.1/config/logstash.yml`:

```
log.level: debug
```

Another thing is to do is to add `stdout` as an output in pipeline.The `stdout` plugin will show us whatever event is created at console, which we can quickly analyze.

Put your own API key in the place of `<your-api-key-here>`, and we can run logstash using the following:

```
./bin/logstash -f conf/weather.conf
```

We can see the logs in Kibana:

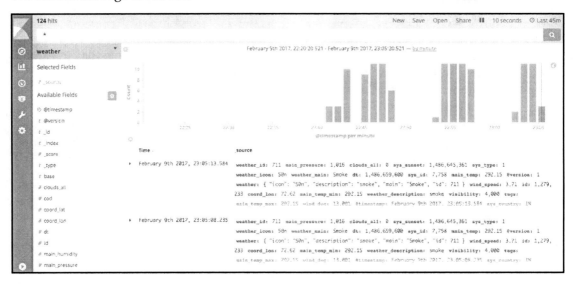

If we run Logstash in debug mode, we can see the logs on console similar to this:

```
[2017-02-09T23:07:13,394][DEBUG][org.apache.http.wire] http-outgoing-0 >>
"{"weather_id":711,"main_pressure":1016,"clouds_all":0,"sys_sunset":1486645
361,"sys_type":1,"weather_icon":"50n","weather_main":"Smoke","dt":148665960
0,"sys_id":7758,"main_temp":292.15,"@version":"1","weather":[{"icon":"50n",
"description":"smoke","main":"Smoke","id":711}],"wind_speed":3.71,"id":1279
233,"coord_lon":72.62,"main_temp_min":292.15,"weather_description":"smoke",
"visibility":4000,"tags":[],"main_temp_max":292.15,"wind_deg":13.0008,"@tim
estamp":"2017-02-09T17:37:13.373Z","sys_country":"IN","sys_sunrise":1486604
705,"coord_lat":23.03,"name":"Ahmadabad","cod":200,"main_humidity":37,"sys_
message":0.1309,"base":"stations"}[\n]"
```

We can see the logs for the event being sent. We can identify the logs using document type (_type in the preceding Kibana screenshot). That ensures that our plugin is working, collecting the data, and sending it to Elasticsearch for proper indexing.

Similar to this, we can write other types of plugins as well. As discussed earlier, knowledge of ruby programming language would help us to develop Logstash plugins.

 We will also create an input plugin for meetup.com to be used in Chapter 12, *Case Study-Meetup*. That plugin is bit more complex than this.

Extending Beats

As we learned through previous chapters, there are four core Beats provided by Elastic Team: Filebeat, Packetbeat, Metricbeat, and Winlogbeat. There is a huge list of community Beats as well available at
`https://www.elastic.co/guide/en/beats/libbeat/5.1/community-beats.html`.

All of these are built on top of the libbeat framework. In case you don't find a beat that meets your expectations and you want to create a new one, your new beat will also follow the same framework. This framework is designed in such a way that all you need to take care is your custom logic, which will fetch the data from a source and prepare an event to be sent to either Elasticsearch or Logstash.

In this section, we will see how to create a beat by utilizing the libbeat framework. Beats were created to minimize the usage of Logstash. We will also use the same use case used for Logstash plugin. We will read the data from a web service and index the data to Elasticsearch. For reference, all of the generated beat code is available at GitHub at
`https://github.com/kravigupta/mastering-elastic-stack-code-files/tree/5.1.1/Chapter07/weatherbeat`.

libbeat framework

To understand how the libbeat framework helps us for any beat, let's consider the example of a beat that will collect basic data (mostly statistics) from an application and send it to Elasticsearch or Logstash. The data flow can be demonstrated through the following diagram:

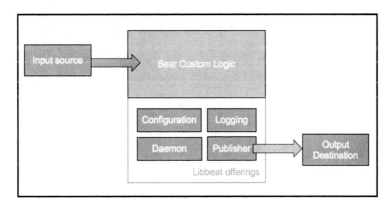

If we analyze the diagram, we can see that there would be some custom logic, which will be getting input data from the application. The custom logic will then parse the data to prepare an event. This can be different for each beat because getting some data from application depends on what channels that application offers, accordingly parsing the received data will be different for each beat, and finally, some filtered data will be used for preparing an event. This concludes the part of custom logic. This particular part is to be taken care by a beat developer.

Apart from these, there are some common tasks. One of those is publisher, which sends the prepare event to configured output. There are other tasks as well, which are necessary for each beat, and they are offered by libbeat framework. This can be considered as a helper library, which provides most common set of packages that all Beats need. Thefollowing list discusses these components in brief:

- **Configuration**: Remember, there was a file for every beat that had all of the configurations (`filebeat.yml`, `packetbeat.yml`, and so on.) Similarly, there should be one for new beat like `my-custom-beat.yml`. This will help a beat user to set things, such as from where the data needs to be picked, hostname, port number, any authentication-related details, and destination where the data should be sent.
- **Publisher**: When our custom logic prepares an event, it sends the event log to publisher provided by the libbeat framework. This publisher reads the configuration and sends data to its respective destination.
- **Logging**: Every good program has a logging mechanism. Developers must be familiar with the **log4j** library, which helps with logging in Java applications. Libbeat framework offers logging for Beats, and we do not need to write code for that.
- **Daemon**: Most of the times, you might want to run your beat as a background service or daemon in order to take benefit of the operating system offerings for such utilities, such as, auto start at system startup, event logging, and so on. For our custom Beats, libbeat has in-built support for daemons, and we need to do almost nothing to run our beat as a service.

We will learn how to create a beat of our choice and then know that the generated beat has almost everything, except our custom logic, which of course, we need to write.

Creating a beat

A beat will take input from somewhere. This *somewhere* can be a process, an application, a component from application, a website, an RSS feed, and many other places. As long as data is going to be helpful, it's worth capturing for analysis.

In the preceding section, while creating an input plugin for Logstash, we used the `openweathermap.org` API to capture data for a city for our example. To utilize the same API endpoint, we will create a beat.

Assuming that you have the API key from `openweathermap.org` using which data can be read, we can now create a beat to utilize that channel. There are few simple steps to generate a beat, but before that, we need to install few dependencies (mostly, tools that the beat generator will use):

- **Go Language**: Most of the Beats utilize the Go programming language. This programming language is open source and is available at `https://golang.org/`. You can download and follow the installer to set up Go language on your environment. For Windows and Mac OS X, there are installers available, and you do not need to do any additional setting for including Go in the `PATH` variable. However, for Linux, you can set up the `PATH` variable to your Go installation:

  ```
  export PATH=$PATH:/usr/local/go/bin
  ```

  In case, you install Go at a custom location, then set it as follows:

  ```
  export GOROOT=$HOME/installations/go
  export PATH=$PATH:$GOROOT/bin
  ```

  `GOROOT` must be set only when we are installing to a custom path. You should also set a `GOPATH` variable, which will point to your workspace where your project will be:

  ```
  export GOPATH=$HOME/workspace
  ```

- **Python**: Most of you might already be familiar with this mighty programming language, which is available at `https://www.python.org`. You can download the installation package for your operating system from the site and install.
- **Virtualenv**: This tool will help us to isolate our beat project so that we can work on the beat without affecting other projects. Virtualenv is available at `https://virtualenv.pypa.io/en/stable/` and can be installed using `pip` (recommended):

  ```
  $ sudo pip install virtualenv
  ```

- **Getting and Installing Cookiecutter**: This is a command-line utility, which can generate projects using project templates. This utility is hosted at GitHub as `https://github.com/audreyr/cookiecutter`. This can be installed using `pip`, `easy_install` or `brew` (on Mac OS X):

```
$ sudo pip install cookiecutter
$ sudo easy_install cookiecutter
$ brew install   cookiecutter
```

The `pip` command is a package manager to install Python packages. If you do not have these utilities available, it is recommended that you install one of them.

Once we have these utilities installed, we will have no problem while generating and working on our beat. Let's follow the following steps:

1. First of all, let's get the beat generator and libbeat using:

```
go get github.com/elastic/beats
```

After running the command, you might get error, which can be ignored since we are yet to build source for our beat: `package github.com/elastic/beats: no buildable` Go source files in `/Users/ravi.gupta/workspace/src/github.com/elastic/beats.`

This command will download the beat generator and libbeat in:

```
workspace
  - src
    - github.com
      - elastic
```

2. Go programming language has some widely used conventions. One of them is using GitHub. If you do have a GitHub account, pick your username, else choose a username for yourself. Create directory for your username under the github.com directory in your workspace. This is where we will be putting our repository. Your final directory structure should look as follows:

```
workspace
  - src
    - github.com
      - your-user-name
```

On command line, go to your username directory: `workspace/src/github.com/your-user-name`.

We will use `Packt` as our username.

3. In the `workspace/src/github.com/packt` directory, let's use Cookiecutter to generate a beat:

   cookiecutter $GOPATH/src/github.com/elastic/beats/generate/beat

   This command will generate beat of our choice. This will start asking us the choices for beat name, package, and so on. Let's take the name of our beat `Weatherbeat`, as follows:

   ```
   project_name [Examplebeat]: Weatherbeat
   github_name [your-github-name]:packt
   beat [weather]:
   beat_path [github.com/packt]:
   full_name [Firstname Lastname]:
   ```

4. Once Cookiecutter is done running the command, it will generate `Weatherbeat` in the `src/github.com/packt/weatherbeat` directory. This beat is a raw template for our beat, which we need to work upon. We need to first fetch necessary dependencies. Let's navigate to our beat directory `weatherbeat` and run make:

   ```
   cd weatherbeat
   make setup
   ```

   When we run make, it will add dependencies to the project. Now, our beat is ready, except that it has no custom code, that we want and will get weather data for a city from `openweathermap.org`.

5. Last command is to build the beat source code and output an executable file that can be run. In the same directory, run:

   ```
   make
   ```

   This will create an executable for our beat.

Anatomy of a Beat

The beat generated so far has almost everything except our business logic to get weather data of a city. Let's look at the directory structure of a beat:

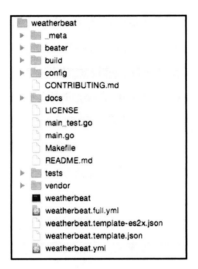

A beat is made up of the following:

- Executable:
  - In our case, weatherbeat is the executable file that can be used run the beat to fetch data from openweathermap.org and send it to Elasticsearch or Logstash
- Template and configuration files:
  - For every beat, there is a <beat>.yml file along with <beat>.full.yml, which contains complete configuration of the beat
  - Along with that, there are mapping templates also available in the <beat>.template.json file
- Entry point and custom logic:
  - The main.go file is the entry point in terms of source code, which internally calls the beater/<beat>.go file, which implements beater interface

Every beat needs to implement Beater interface, which is provided by the libbeat framework.

- Documentation in docs directory, README, and so on
- Test Files in the test directory
- Necessary dependencies and build helpers:
    - Inside the vendor directory, there is a complete beat package, which acts as a dependency to our beat
    - Inside the build directory resides necessary build tools for building the beat

Beat configuration

For each generated beat, there are few configurations available in `<beat>.yml`. In our case, the `weatherbeat.yml` file contains these config. To the minimum, period and output to Elasticsearch are enabled by default:

```
weatherbeat:
# Defines how often an event is sent to the output
period: 5s
output.elasticsearch:
  # Array of hosts to connect to.
  hosts: ["localhost:9200"]
```

Our beat uses period as interval to send events to Elasticsearch. There are other configurations, which are commented by default and are for logging, Logstash output, tags, shipper name, and so on.

By default, logging to files is enabled, and logs will not be printed to console. To enable add configuration, use `logging.to_syslog: true`.

A full configuration and documentation can be found at `weatherbeat.full.yml`.

weatherbeat.go file

Each beat is set as a type using:

```
type weatherbeat struct {
    done    chan struct{}
    config config.Config
    client publisher.Client
}
```

This beat reads config from the `weatherbeat.yml` config file using `New()` method:

```
func New(b *beat.Beat, cfg *common.Config) (beat.Beater, error) { ... }
```

This file is the most important file in the entire beat since this is where actual implementation of beat functioning resides. This file is named after your beat. For us, this is named as `weatherbeat.go` and placed inside the beater directory.

This implements the **Beater** interface. The Beater interface has two methods, which every beat must implement:

- `Run(b *Beat) error`: This method contains the actual logic, which runs when beat is started
- `Stop()`:This method is called once when beat is stopped using the *Ctrl + C* command

If you open the `weatherbeat.go` file, it will have these two methods already implemented with sample data. `Run()` method creates an event for every *n* seconds (as defined in the config file `weatherbeat.yml`) and sends the event to publisher, which publishes the event to defined destination in config.

Implementing beat logic

It's now time to work on our logic, which will be part of the `Run()` method that `weatherbeat` is implementing. In a nutshell, we need to read the data from API endpoint, parse it to an appropriate format, prepare an event, and publish it.

As stated earlier, the endpoint for API is as follows:

```
http://api.openweathermap.org/data/2.5/weather?q=cityName&appid=key
```

Let's see what are the steps to implement the plugin:

Adding the Configuration

We need to get `cityName` and the API key from the user. In the configuration file `weatherbeat.yml`, let's add two configurations:

```
weatherbeat:
  cityName: ""
  key: ""
```

After adding these, run the following:

```
make update
```

Now, update the `config.go` file under the config directory to contain our configurations. The config file struct will look as follows:

```
type Config struct {
  Period time.Duration `config:"period"`
  CityName string `config:"cityName"`
  Key string `config:"key"`
}
```

We have added two configuration-`CityName` and `Key` (both in caps) – which can now be used within the beat.

Reading data from API

We need to import the `net/http` package, which will help us to read data from a web service. Also, we need `io/ioutil` to read incoming data.

First, let's create two variables inside the `Run` function for `city` and `key`:

```
cityName:= bt.config.CityName
key := bt.config.Key
```

Since we added these to the `Config` struct, we can get using `bt.config`. After that, we can make a call using the `http.Get()` method:

```
url :=
"http://api.openweathermap.org/data/2.5/weather?q="+cityName+"&appid="+key
response, error := http.Get(url)
defer response.Body.Close()
body, error := ioutil.ReadAll(response.Body)
```

Now, the body will contain the incoming data, and in case of any problem, error variable will have a message.

Parsing the data

The body variable contains whatever was the output of the web service call, and this variable will be an array of bytes, which is actually a JSON if we convert it to a string. In the Go language, we do **Unmarshaling** to convert a string or byte to JSON. To unmarshal the content, we need to set a type to which it will be mapped. A type in golang is defined using the keyword struct. As per our JSON response, the following is a type definition:

```go
type WeatherDataTypes struct {
    Coord    CoordTypes
    Weather    []WeatherTypes
    Base    string
    Main    MainTypes
    Visibility    int
    Wind    WindTypes
    Clouds    CloudTypes
    Dt    int
    Sys    SysTypes
    Id    int
    Name    string
    Cod    int
}
type CoordTypes struct {
    Lat    float64
    Lon    float64
}
type MainTypes struct {
    Temp    float64
    Pressure    int
    Humidity    int
    Temp_min    float64
    Temp_max    float64
}
type WindTypes struct {
    Speed    float64
    Degree    int
}
type CloudTypes struct {
    All    int
}
type SysTypes struct {
    Id    int
    Message    float64
    Country    string
```

```
        Sunrise int
        Sunset  int
    }
    type WeatherTypes struct {
        Id        int
        Main      string
        Description string
        Icon      string
    }
```

These struct types are defined outside the Run() function. Using the main type-WeatherDataType – we can convert a JSON response to a proper structure:

```
Message := (*json.RawMessage)(&body)
var weatherData WeatherDataTypes
json.Unmarshal(*Message, &weatherData)
```

Now, the weatherData variable will have all of the fields from JSON and can be accessed to create an event. This would need us to import the encoding/json package.

Preparing an event

Using common.MapStr, we can prepare a JSON object type that can be sent to publisher. For the event, we will not be pushing everything to be indexed, and only sunrise, sunset, and temperatures are added for an event. Beat with all of the fields added is available at https://github.com/kravigupta/mastering-elastic-stack-code-files/tree/5.1.1/Chapter07/weatherbeat:

```
event := common.MapStr{
  "@timestamp":   common.Time(time.Now()),
  "type":         b.Name,
  "sunrise":      weatherData.Sys.Sunrise,
  "sunset":       weatherData.Sys.Sunset,
  "temp":         weatherData.Main.Temp,
}
```

Every event object should have a timestamp and type field, where timestamp is usually current time and type is set to the name of the beat.

Publishing the event

Finally, we can publish the event using:

```
bt.client.PublishEvent(event)
```

This will send the event object to publisher, which will send it to a defined destination.

Our beat implementation (only Run() method) would look like:

```
func (bt *Weatherbeat) Run(b *beat.Beat) error {
  logp.Info("weatherbeat is running! Hit CTRL-C to stop it.")

  bt.client = b.Publisher.Connect()
  ticker := time.NewTicker(bt.config.Period)
  for {
    select {
    case <-bt.done:
      return nil
    case <-ticker.C:
    }

    cityName:= bt.config.CityName
    key := bt.config.Key
    url :=
"http://api.openweathermap.org/data/2.5/weather?q="+cityName+"&appid="+key
    fmt.Println("URL is " + url)

    resp, err := http.Get(url)
    if err != nil {
        fmt.Println("Something went wrong")
    }
    defer resp.Body.Close()
    body, err := ioutil.ReadAll(resp.Body)

    Message := (*json.RawMessage)(&body)
    var weatherData WeatherDataTypes
    json.Unmarshal(*Message, &weatherData)

    event := common.MapStr{
      "@timestamp": common.Time(time.Now()),
      "type":       b.Name,
      "sunrise":    weatherData.Sys.Sunrise,
      "sunset":     weatherData.Sys.Sunset,
      "temp":       weatherData.Main.Temp,
    }
    bt.client.PublishEvent(event)
    logp.Info("Event sent")
```

```
    }
}
```

The import statements would be as follows:

```
import (
    "fmt"
    "time"
    "io/ioutil"
    "net/http"
    "strconv"

    "github.com/elastic/beats/libbeat/beat"
    "github.com/elastic/beats/libbeat/common"
    "github.com/elastic/beats/libbeat/logp"
    "github.com/elastic/beats/libbeat/publisher"

    "github.com/packt/weatherbeat/config"
)
```

Running the beat

Now, when we have everything ready, we can build the beat again using make. We need to run make if there is a change done to our beat source. To run the beat, simply go to the beat directory and run:

./weatherbeat

Now, the beat will start collecting data at a defined period and send it to Elasticsearch. In the Elasticsearch logs, you should find the entries similar to:

```
[2017-02-10T15:11:54,839][INFO ][o.e.c.m.MetaDataMappingService] [A5S5Dxl]
[weatherbeat-2017.02.10/9tO1oFBwTzePDBEC7YXctA] create_mapping
[weatherbeat]
```

It will try to create mapping for index `weatherbeat` in case it does not exist already. You can also check data sent to Elasticsearch on Kibana. On the discover tab, choose the **weatherbeat-*** index pattern, and you should see the logs sent by the beat we created:

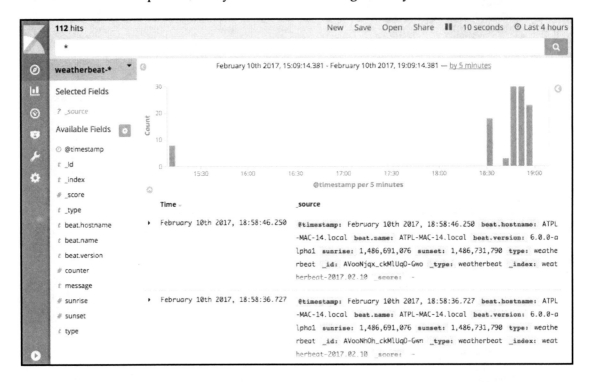

As we can see from the screenshot, there are log events created by the Beats. This ensures that our beat is working fine. You can further use the data to visualize using different ways in Kibana.

 By default, the index name for weatherbeat will be – `weatherbeat-%{+yyyy.MM.dd}`. In case, you want to change it, modify the index setting in `weatherbeat.yml` configuration file.

Extending Kibana

When you set up Elastic Stack for your environment, you sense the needed changes in the stack to fulfill your requirements. For most of the cases, changes done at Elasticsearch are minimum as compared to rest of the components. Kibana being the face of the stack undergoes maximum changes. If nothing complex, your client (in case you are a service provider) would like to customize the UI to match their company's website look.

There are ways in which Kibana can be customized and extended-we can write Kibana plugins, create new visualizations, modify the source, and so on. To do any of these, you must be familiar with HTML, CSS, Javascript, Node.js, AngularJS, and probably relevant library to be used for charts and visualizations. Kibana is basically a Node.js app, thus knowing Node.js will help greatly to understand and customize Kibana.

In this section, we will develop a plugin that changes the appearance of the Kibana UI. For our use case, we will keep it simple and modify just the title of each page in Kibana, at runtime. It will showe how easy it is to develop such a plugin. If you want to check out the source code, it's available at GitHub at
`https://github.com/kravigupta/mastering-elastic-stack-code-files/tree/5.1.1/Chapter07/branding-plugin`. The name of the plugin is kept as branding plugin, which is open to be customized by anyone and can be taken as a sample or a base to customize Kibana in this way. All *known* Kibana plugins are listed at
`https://www.elastic.co/guide/en/kibana/5.1/known-plugins.html`.

Before we can contribute to Kibana, it is recommended that you set up Kibana development environment. If you clone the source code of Kibana from GitHub, the `CONTRIBUTING.md` file contains all of the steps for setting up the development environment.

Setting up Kibana development environment

To set the development environment, you should fork the Kibana project on GitHub and clone it to your machine:

```
git clone https://github.com/{username}/kibana.git
```

Navigate to the newly cloned Kibana source code and switch to the branch we are going to use. For us, the version is 5.1, and it's best to create a local branch, for example, kibana-local and point it to the respective branch:

```
$ git checkout -b kibana-local origin/5.1
```

We need to install the node version needed by Kibana:

```
nvm install "$(cat .node-version)"
```

 If you do not have `nvm` installed, use the following command:
`curl -o-`
`https://raw.githubusercontent.com/creationix/nvm/v0.32.1/`
`install.sh | bash`

Kibana 5.1.x versions use Node.js v6.9.0, which can directly be downloaded from `https://nodejs.org/en/download/releases/` as per your operating system. To generate the plugin correctly, without an error, we should have the same node version installed as used by Kibana.

Then, we need to install node dependencies:

```
npm install
```

Kibana will pick data from Elasticsearch. As we already know, we need the same version for both Kibana and Elasticsearch to run together. When we are in the development mode, it's best to install and run Elasticsearch from our development environment only. To run Elasticsearch, use:

```
npm run elasticsearch
```

In case you do not want to use this Elasticsearch instance, we can run our own setup with the same version as kibana.

We are all set up once Elasticsearch is available and should be good to run Kibana development server:

```
npm run
```

This will make kibana run on `https://localhost:5601` by default, and this runs on HTTPS protocol. In case you receive an error for SSL in logs, either provide the certificate for kibana in configuration or run the kibana without SSL:

```
npm run -- --no-ssl
```

All of this is needed in any case, whether you want to write a plugin or modify the core Kibana code. To speed up the plugin development process, we can use `generator-kibana-plugin`, which is a **Yeoman** generator for kibana plugin.

Yeoman (http://yeoman.io/) is a helping tool to speed up the development process for web applications by generating the skeleton of your plugins or applications.

To install Yeoman generator, use:

```
npm install -g yo
```

To install Kibana generator plugin, use:

```
npm install -g generator-kibana-plugin
```

Now, when we have all of the things ready and prepared, we can generate our plugin.

Generating the plugin

Once we have Kibana development environment set up and the plugin generator installed, we can generate the plugin. Now, let's create a directory for our plugin in the same directory where we cloned the Kibana source code. Let's keep the name for our plugin as branding-plugin:

```
mkdir branding-plugin
```

Change to the directory we created to this:

```
cd branding-plugin
```

Now, let's generate the plugin using Yeoman:

```
yo kibana-plugin
```

While executing, Yeoman will ask few questions about plugin name, description, and the version or which we want to generate plugin. This is the Kibana version we need to specify:

```
? Your Plugin Name branding plugin
? Short Description A plugin to help modify Kibana for branding.
? Target Kibana Version 5.0.0
```

This command will take some time to execute and when it's done, we will have a fine skeleton of our plugin.

Anatomy of a plugin

The generated Kibana plugin contains a directory structure similar to this:

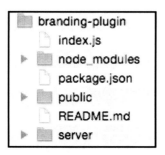

The plugin is made of server-related code in server directory and our main web app-related code in public directory. There is also a node_modules directory, which contains all required dependencies for the plugin.

Every plugin must have a package.json file, which contains the plugin details for example, name, version, dependencies, and so on. Without this plugin, Kibana will fail to run in development mode, and you will get error for the missing package.json file.

For our plugin, the key file is index.js, which is the main entry point and combines everything together. Your untouched index.js file looks like:

```
import exampleRoute from './server/routes/example';

export default function (kibana) {
  return new kibana.Plugin({
    require: ['elasticsearch'],
    uiExports: {
      app: {
        title: 'Branding Plugin',
        description: 'A plugin to help modify Kibana for branding.',
        main: 'plugins/branding_plugin/app'
      },
      hacks: [
        'plugins/branding_plugin/hack'
      ]
    },
    config(Joi) {
      return Joi.object({
        enabled: Joi.boolean().default(true),
      }).default();
    },
    init(server, options) {
```

```
        // Add server routes and initalize the plugin here
        exampleRoute(server);
    }
  });
};
```

The important section of the file is defining uiExports. uiExports define what we want to do with our plugin and what this plugin actually contains.

Kibana offers a variety of `uiExports` that includes adding a new visualization, settings, navigation bar changes, a new app, and so on. All available `uiExports` are available at `https://www.elastic.co/guide/en/kibana/5.1/development-uiexports.html`. These `uiExports` can be divided into three groups:

- **Hacks**: In case you want to modify the Kibana UI or intercept UI events, you go for hacks. These types of plugins are applicable for all applications installed in Kibana.
- **UI Registry provider**: There are a number of ui/registry providers for various features:

uiExport Type	Registry Type
`visTypes`	`ui/registry/vis_types`
`fieldFormats`	`ui/registry/field_formats`
`spyModes`	`ui/registry/spy_modes`
`chromeNavControls`	`ui/registry/chrome_nav_controls`
`navbarExtensions`	`ui/registry/navbar_extensions`
`settingsSections`	`ui/registry/settings_sections`
`docViews`	`ui/registry/doc_views`

In the preceding table, the first column refers to a `uiExport` type and the second column refers to respective registry for which the `uiExport` registers a provider.

- **Applications**: Kibana supports addition of a complete application inside the system. To add an application, `app` or `appsuiExport` type is used.

The most commonly used uiExport types is visTypes, which helps us to create a new visualization for Kibana hacks, which let us modify the system to our needs and enables us to hook into events and so on.

For example, if you create a Kibana plugin, which uses a simple visualization that will show a simple horizontal bar or some other kind of visualization, you would be using `visTypesuiExport` for your plugin.

Let's get back to the `index.js` file, which will be the entry point for our plugin. By default, this file contains code that loads two `uiExports`-hack and an app-but we do not need everything, and we can remove the pre-added `uiExports`, which we are not going to use. Our stripped `index.js` file would look like:

```
export default function (kibana) {
   return new kibana.Plugin({
uiExports: {
hacks: [
         'plugins/branding_plugin/hack'
                 ]
              },
   });
};
```

Since we only need `hacks uiExport`, which will be a `.js` file inside the `public` directory of our plugin. To quickly check whether the hack works, we can try putting a log to the `hack.js` file and see console for log. If log is printed, we can see that the plugin is working fine.

Before we do that, we can also delete server directory, which is not needed for now. Also, apart from the `hack.js` file, nothing will be used inside our `public` directory.

Let's modify hack.js to print a log similar to this:

```
console.log('Loading the hack for branding plugin.');
```

After that, run the server from the plugin's directory:

```
npm start
```

This will start server in development mode and automatically install to plugin to Kibana instance. This supports hot deployment, and whenever you make changes to any of the plugin file, logs similar to this would be printed:

```
[info][optimize] Lazy optimization started
[info][optimize] Lazy optimization success in 14.42 seconds
```

As soon as we load Kibana in browser, it will print the log in console saying:

```
Loading the hack for branding plugin.
```

If a log like this is printed, it ensures that our plugin is working fine, and we can continue to work on its actual implementation.

When it comes to branding, there are a lot of changes that we can make to Kibana, for example, logo change, title of the pages, color scheme, footer, overall CSS, and so on. Basically, everything that we see in our browser can be modified to meet the branding of your own organization. For sake of understanding, we are taking a very simple example of changing the title of each page by appending PACKT. Let's update the hack.js file for relevant code. The final hack.js file should look like:

```
import $ from 'jquery';
console.log("Loading the hack for branding plugin.");

$(document).ready(function(){
    document.title = document.title + " - PACKT";
});
```

This will modify the title of each page we load in Kibana. If the server is already running, as soon as we modify the file in our plugin directory, server will restart automatically to update the plugin and when we refresh the browser, we can see the title of the pages will change:

This was a very simple implementation of a plugin that changes the title of the pages, as we can see from the preceding screenshot. If you notice the code snippet, we are importing jQuery, which gives us immense power to modify the DOM the way we want. Changing the title was probably tip of the iceberg, and a lot more can be done. Note that using jQuery is not the only way and also may not always be a clean way of doing things. Wherever possible, you should consider using Node.js modules and elements.

Summary

If we talk about customization of four tools, it would take four different chapters to begin with. However, we tried to understand the ways a tool can be extended. In this chapter, we learned about extending Elasticsearch by learning how a plugin is organized and popular ways to customize.

Later in the chapter, we created a Logstash plugin, which captured data from the Openweathermap.org server and sent it to Elasticsearch. We also learned about creating a new beat with example of collecting data from the same web service. Finally, we set up the Kibana development environment and learned to create a very basic hack of changing the title of the Kibana pages by appending PACKT to it.

In the next chapter, we will be revisiting Elasticsearch and its APIs. We will learn how to access the APIs and how they are useful to us. The chapter will also introduce ingest nodes which is a new addition to Elasticsearch v5.x onwards.

8
Elasticsearch APIs

In Chapter 2, *Step into Elasticsearch,* we learned about underlying technology and how Elasticsearch works and the APIs it offers. In Chapter 4, *Kibana Interface,* we understood how to use the Console and got to use aggregations using Kibana.

This chapter will complete the rest of the APIs and we will use Console to send API requests to Elasticsearch. We'll cover the following topics in this chapter:

- Cluster APIs
- Cat APIs
- Modules
- Ingest nodes
- Elasticsearch clients
- Java APIs

For a quick go-through of Console, you can refer to the *Exploring dev tools* section in Chapter 4, *Kibana Interface.*

 Assuming for development and learning purpose, Kibana is installed locally.

The cluster APIs

These APIs allow us to know about cluster state, health, statistics, node statistics, node information, and so on.

Cluster health

To know cluster health, we can use the `_cluster/health` endpoint, as shown in the following example:

```
GET /_cluster/health/library
```

Here, `GET` is the verb, `_cluster/health` is the endpoint, and `library` is the index. This call will result in information about nodes, data nodes, shards, tasks, and status of the index in case the index was specified otherwise for the cluster:

```
Dev Tools                                                    History   Settings   Help
Console

 1  GET /_cluster/health/library        ▶ 🔧    1 ▾ {
                                                2       "cluster_name": "elasticsearch",
                                                3       "status": "green",
                                                4       "timed_out": false,
                                                5       "number_of_nodes": 2,
                                                6       "number_of_data_nodes": 2,
                                                7       "active_primary_shards": 5,
                                                8       "active_shards": 10,
                                                9       "relocating_shards": 0,
                                               10       "initializing_shards": 0,
                                               11       "unassigned_shards": 0,
                                               12       "delayed_unassigned_shards": 0,
                                               13       "number_of_pending_tasks": 0,
                                               14       "number_of_in_flight_fetch": 0,
                                               15       "task_max_waiting_in_queue_millis": 0,
                                               16       "active_shards_percent_as_number": 100
                                               17 ▾ }
```

The results on the Response pane show the status of the Elasticsearch cluster as green with other values such as node information, shards, and pending tasks.

Let's have a look at what other values of the Elasticsearch status denote:

- **Red**: Some or all of the primary shards are not allocated or ready
- **Yellow**: All primary shards are allocated, but some or none of the replica shards are allocated
- **Green**: All primary and replica shards are allocated and the cluster is fully up

If replicas are not defined, you can define them using the following request on the console: PUT /_settings { "index": { "number_of_replicas": 1 } }

Other query parameters: The following are the other request parameters:

Request Parameter	Description
level	Level of detail at which extent health information is to be returned. Possible values – cluster(default), indices, or shards.
wait_for_status	Possible values – red, yellow, green. It will wait until the cluster reaches that state.
wait_for_relocating_shards	How many relocating shards to wait for? The default is not to wait. Value 0 = wait until all relocation happens.
wait_for_active_shards	How many active shards to wait for? No waiting by default.
wait_for_nodes	Waits for a specified number of nodes to be available.
timeout	Number of seconds to wait if wait_for_xxx is provided.
local	By default, info is provided by the master. If local=true, then info of the local node is provided.

To use any of these request parameters, just add a query parameter and provide the value. For example, if we want to get indices level health status, we can use the following:

```
GET _cluster/health?level=indices
```

This will provide details of the indices in the cluster. For library index, it is the following:

```
"indices": {
    "library": {
      "status": "green",
      "number_of_shards": 5,
      "number_of_replicas": 1,
      "active_primary_shards": 5,
      "active_shards": 10,
      "relocating_shards": 0,
      "initializing_shards": 0,
      "unassigned_shards": 0
    }
}
```

Similarly, to use `wait_for_status`, use the following code:

```
GET /_cluster/health?wait_for_status=yellow
```

We can also use multiple parameters, such as:

```
GET /_cluster/health?wait_for_status=yellow&level=indices
```

In this, we are checking at index level while waiting for the status to be yellow.

Cluster State

This API provides very detailed information about the cluster's state. To see the complete state, we can use the following:

```
GET /_cluster/state?pretty
```

In case we want to limit it to metrics and indices, we can use the following:

```
GET /_cluster/state/{metrics}/{indices}?pretty'
```

Both metrics and indices can contain multiple entries separated by a comma. Metrics can be version, `master_node`, `nodes`, `routing_table`, `metadata`, `blocks`, and `_all` (for all metrics).

 The console prints the response in pretty-print format itself. Hence, it is not required to add `?pretty` at the end of the API request when running using the console.

Cluster stats

This API provides information about basic metrics present in the indices and nodes of the cluster. The information is about shard numbers, `nodecount`, `memory usage`, `roles`, `jvm info`, `cpu`, `plugins`, and so on. We can use the following URI:

```
GET /_cluster/stats
```

Pending tasks

This API will return all the pending tasks of the cluster. If there are none pending, it will return an empty array of tasks:

```
GET /_cluster/pending_tasks
```

Cluster reroute

This API is more like commands for clusters to do something. There are three commands available — move, allocate, cancel. The end point for this is _cluster/reroute.

The following table lists more details for each of the commands:

Commands	Functions
move	To move a shard from one node to another node in the cluster.
allocate	To allocate an unassigned shard to one node.
cancel	To cancel an allocation of a shard.

Let's see an example of moving a started shard from one node to another:

```
POST _cluster/reroute
{
  "commands": [
    {
      "move": {
        "index": "library",
        "shard": 2,
        "from_node": "node_1",
        "to_node": "node_2"
      }
    }
  ]
}
```

This will move shard 2 of the index library to node_2 from node_1.

Cluster update settings

There are Elasticsearch configurations stored in `elasticsearch.yml` in the `config` directory. Those configurations are mostly static. There are dynamic configurations for clusters, which can be updated using this API. These settings can be of two types – persistent, which will be applicable even after a full cluster restart, and transient, which will be lost as soon as the full cluster restarts. Transient settings take precedence over persistent and further persistent take precedence over settings in `elasticsearch.yml`. It is recommended to use the `elasticsearch.yml` configuration file for local node settings and API for cluster level settings rather than updating settings using this endpoint. Some more documentation for the settings is available at
`https://www.elastic.co/guide/en/elasticsearch/reference/5.1/settings.html`

To get all such settings, we can use the _cluster/settings endpoint:

```
GET /_cluster/settings
```

To set settings, we can use the same endpoint:

```
PUT /_cluster/settings
{
"persistent": {
    "discovery.zen.minimum_master_nodes": 2
  }
}
```

Node stats

Similar to cluster stats, we can find statistics for one node or more:

```
GET /_nodes/stats
```

All statistics of all nodes will be returned by default; we have the option to specify node IDs and other values such as `indices`, `os`, `process`, `jvm`, `transport`, `http`, `fs`, `thread_pool`, `breaker`, and so on as comma-separated values.

To get specific information, we can use the following:

```
GET /_nodes/stats/fs,indices
GET /_nodes/node1/stats/fs,indices
```

The first line will get the filesystem and indices information for all nodes and second thee URI will get it only for `node1`.

Nodes info API

This API helps us to get node information. To get process information of a node or of all nodes, we can use the following:

```
GET /_nodes/os,process
GET /_nodes/_all/os,process
GET /_nodes/node1/os,process
```

The first and second are identical, they will get information of all nodes. The preceding uri will get us operating system and process related information. The other info we can get is settings, jvm, transport, http, thread_pool, and plugins. For the preceding code listing, it returns the following:

```
{
  "_nodes": {
    "total": 1,
    "successful": 1,
    "failed": 0
  },
  "cluster_name": "elasticsearch",
  "nodes": {
    "U4MPVritSmmAyoHLb2dLzw": {
      "name": "node1",
      "transport_address": "127.0.0.1:9300",
      "host": "127.0.0.1",
      "ip": "127.0.0.1",
      "version": "5.1.1",
      "build_hash": "5395e21",
      "roles": [
        "master",
        "data",
        "ingest"
      ],
      "os": {
        "refresh_interval_in_millis": 1000,
        "name": "Mac OS X",
        "arch": "x86_64",
        "version": "10.0",
        "available_processors": 4,
        "allocated_processors": 4
      },
      "process": {
        "refresh_interval_in_millis": 1000,
        "id": 15188,
        "mlockall": false
      }
```

```
      }
    }
  }
```

We can also get hot threads on a node in the cluster. To get hot threads, we can use
`_nodes/hot_threads` or `_nodes/nodeId/hot_threads`:

GET /_nodes/hot_threads

Task Management API

This API helps us to get all tasks in the cluster, or a specific node, and it also allows us to
take some actions. To get all tasks for a cluster, we can use the following:

GET /_tasks

This will return the following output:

```
{
  "nodes" : {
    "U4MPVritSmmAyoHLb2dLzw" : {
      "name" : "node1",
      "transport_address" : "127.0.0.1:9300",
      "host" : "127.0.0.1",
      "ip" : "127.0.0.1:9300",
      "roles": [
        "master",
        "data",
        "ingest"        ],
      "tasks" : {
        "U4MPVritSmmAyoHLb2dLzw:4129" : {
          "node" : "U4MPVritSmmAyoHLb2dLzw",
          "id" : 4129,
          "type" : "transport",
          "action" : "cluster:monitor/tasks/lists",
          "start_time_in_millis" : 1463037154374,
          "running_time_in_nanos" : 1205000,
          "cancellable": false,
        },
        "U4MPVritSmmAyoHLb2dLzw:4130" : {
          "node" : "U4MPVritSmmAyoHLb2dLzw",
          "id" : 4130,
          "type" : "direct",
          "action" : "cluster:monitor/tasks/lists[n]",
          "start_time_in_millis" : 1463037154344,
          "running_time_in_nanos" : 30881000,
```

```
            "cancellable": false,
            "parent_task_id": " U4MPVritSmmAyoHLb2dLzw:4129"
        }
      }
    }
  }
}
```

As we can see, the cluster has two tasks listed. We can get similar information for specific nodes as well:

```
GET /_tasks?nodes=node1
```

Even further filter results on actions, such as:

```
GET /_tasks?nodes=node1&actions=cluster:*
```

As we can see, the cluster has two tasks listed. We can get similar information for specific nodes as well.

The cat APIs

This API helps us to print information nodes, indices, fields, tasks, and plugins in a human-readable format rather than a JSON. It can also be visualized to see how tables are printed on the console.

All these commands can be used with the GET verb of curl. By default, the commands will list only data and no headers. To print headers, we can use v in query parameters:

```
GET /_cat/health?v
```

The preceding command can be used instead of the following:

```
GET /_cat/health
```

We can also specify which headers to show by supplying the comma-separated values for the h query parameter.

Let's see the endpoints available to operate on:

- _cat/indices: This shows data about indices such as health, status, index name, primary, replicas, documents count, and memory:

  ```
  GET /_cat/indices?v&h=health,status,index,docs.count,store
  ```

Here is what it looks like in the Console:

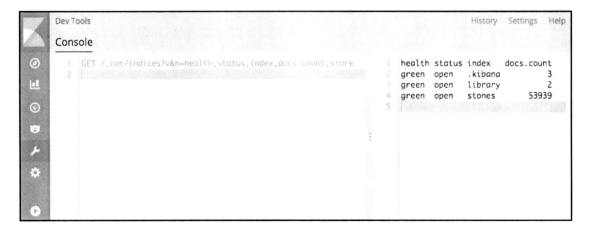

As we can see, it shows health and stats for each index.

- _cat/master: This shows the node ID, IP address, and node name of the master node as follows:

  ```
  GET /_cat/master?v
  ```

  This will return the following output:

  ```
  id                     host      ip        node
  U4MPVritSmmAyoHLb2dLzw 127.0.0.1 127.0.0.1 node1
  ```

- _cat/nodes: This shows us the information about nodes in the cluster. There are a number of headers that we can use. A few important ones are id, pid, name, master (whether the node is master or not), host, ip, port, version (ES version), Build, jdk, along with disk, heap, ram, and file descriptor information:

  ```
  GET _cat/nodes?v
  ```

And the result will be as follows:

```
ip        heap.percent ram.percent cpu
load_1m load_5m load_15m node.role master name
127.0.0.1 13 47 -1                          mdi * node1
127.0.0.1 13 47 -1                          mdi - node2
```

- _cat/health: This shows the cluster health at a timestamp. This also shows the total nodes, shards, and tasks:

  GET /_cat/health

  And the result will be as follows:

  ```
  1482738453 13:17:33 elasticsearch green 2 2 12 6 0 0 0 0 - 100.0%
  ```

  We can specify some of the `headers`, as shown in the following command:

  GET /_cat/health?v&h=cluster,status,node.total,shards,pending_tasks

  And the result will be as follows:

  ```
  cluster        status node.total shards
  pending_tasks elasticsearch green 2     12               0
  ```

- _cat/allocation: This lists all shard allocations to nodes, disk space consumption, and so on:

  GET _cat/allocation?v

- _cat/shards: This shows a detailed view of each shard on every node. For each shard, it shows the index, type, state, number of documents, memory, and node:

  GET _cat/shards?v

  This will output shard details for each index. In the following listing, a few of the entries for library index are shown:

  ```
  index     shard prirep state     docs  store ip          node
  library 2       r      STARTED   0     159b 127.0.0.1 node1
  library 2       p      STARTED   0     159b 127.0.0.1 node2
  library 4       r      STARTED   1     3.3kb 127.0.0.1 node1
  library 4       p      STARTED   1     3.3kb 127.0.0.1 node2
  library 3       r      STARTED   2     9.4kb 127.0.0.1 node1
  library 3       p      STARTED   2     9.4kb 127.0.0.1 node2
  ```

- _cat/aliases: This lists all configured aliases to indices:

  GET _cat/aliases

  To get a specific alias, we can use _cat/aliases/{aliasname}.

If you haven't defined any alias, you will receive a blank output in the Response pane.

- `_cat/plugins`: This lists all installed plugins on each node with the name, version, type of plugin, and the plugin URL:

  GET _cat/plugins

 If you haven't used any plugins, you will receive a blank output in the Response pane.

- `_cat/count`: This provides a count of documents in an index or for whole clusters (by default). To get it for an index, we can use `_cat/count/{indexname}`. This will show only a live documents count.
- `_cat/fielddata`: This lists heap memory usage on every data node by field data. We can also specify specific fields using the fields query parameter.
- `_cat/nodeattrs`: This shows custom node attributes if there are any.
- `_cat/pending_tasks`: This lists all pending tasks in the cluster. The list shows `insertOrder`, `timeInQueue`, `priority`, and `source`.
- `_cat/recovery`: This shows all recoveries done and ongoing for index shards. For every recovery, it shows the index, shard ID, time, type, which stage it is on (for example, done for completed), source and target host, total files and bytes, snapshot, and repository information.
- `_cat/repositories`: This lists all the repositories with ID and type.
- `_cat/thread_pool`: This shows cluster-wide thread pools per node. For every node, it shows active, queued, and rejected threads for different thread pools. Available thread pools are `bulk`, `fetch_shard_started`, `fetch_share_store`, `flush`, `force_merge`, `generic`, `get`, `index`, `listener`, `management`, `refresh`, `search`, `snapshot`, and `warmer`.

- `_cat/segments`: This shows low-level information about segments in the shards.
- `_cat/snapshots/{repository}`: If a repository is present, this will show all the snapshots for it where {repository} specifies the repository name.

Elasticsearch modules

Every great project has a number of modules to support what it offers. Elasticsearch has many such modules. These modules need some settings, either static using `elasticsearch.yml` or dynamic settings, which can be updated using the cluster API. Let's look at different modules.

Cluster module

The cluster module decides how the shards are allocated to nodes and takes care of the movement of shards in order to keep the cluster balanced. This process is known as shard allocation. There are a number of settings for this module, which can be dynamically applied using the cluster API. These settings take care of shard allocation among nodes in a cluster as well as within a node.

Discovery module

The discovery module helps to discover the nodes in the network for a specified cluster. In the `elasticsearch.yml` configuration file, there is one configuration for the cluster name, which decides which cluster this node will be part of. The default name is `elasticsearch`:

```
cluster.name = elasticsearch
```

All nodes with this cluster name will be in the same cluster. This module also decides which node will act as master.

Gateway module

There are times when we recover the cluster, and in such cases how many nodes should be up before recovery can start is defined by these settings. These settings are static and must be set on each node participating in the cluster.

HTTP module

All Elasticsearch APIs are exposed by this module over HTTP asynchronously. All of the settings are static and defined in the `config` file, `elasticsearch.yml`. This module can also be disabled in case we don't want to server REST calls. Nodes in a cluster communicate using the transport module. The `http.enabled` setting can be set to false to disable this module.

Indices module

All index-related settings (applicable for all indices) are managed by this module. There are settings to take control over exceptions, cache, indexing buffer, request cache, and so on.

Network module

This module takes care of network-related settings and helps to set up production-level nodes and clusters. By default, all settings are applicable for localhost (`127.0.0.1`) which, in a production environment, should bind to a proper hostname and port, and there are many network-related settings that are controlled using this module.

Node client

There can be types of nodes, which are as follows:

- **Master node**: It controls the cluster. To make a node master eligible, set the `node.master` property to `true`. When the cluster is set up, the master node will be chosen among these types of nodes:

  ```
  node.master : true
  ```

- **Data node**: These nodes perform CRUD, search, and aggregations. To make a node only a data node, set `node.data` to `true`:

  ```
  node.data : true
  ```

- **Ingest node**: This is a new type of node added to version 5.x onwards. By default, all nodes act as ingest nodes and you need to disable them in case you do not want a node to act as ingest. These nodes do preprocessing before any operation on a document is performed. These nodes are covered in more detail later in this chapter.
- **Tribe node**: These nodes can connect to multiple clusters and do necessary operations across clusters. These nodes are a special type of coordinating only nodes.

To summarize, see the `elasticsearch.yml` settings in the following table for each type of node:

Master Nodes	Data Nodes	Ingest Nodes	Tribe Nodes
node.master: true node.data: false node.ingest: false	node.master: false node.data: true node.ingest: false	node.master: false node.data: false node.ingest: true	node.master: false node.data: false node.ingest: false

If these settings are used, the node will have only one function out of these four types.

Plugins module

Plugins extend Elasticsearch to provide more features. We will learn about Elasticsearch plugins later in this chapter.

Scripting

This module allows us to do scripted operations while using APIs. For example, scripts can be used to update documents in an index. There are multiple scripting languages supported by Elasticsearch. Groovy and Painless are popular among scripting languages. Both of these plugins are built-in. Using scripts is not always secure, thus Elasticsearch has a set of settings that enable and disable scripts. These settings are fine-grained and have two forms:

```
script.engine.{lang}.{source}.{context}: true|false
```

The second form is as follows:

```
script.engine.{lang}.{inline|file|stored}: true|false
```

For example, to enable inline groovy scripts, use the following:

```
script.engine.groovy.inline: true
```

To enable, disable scripting for all languages, we can use the properties in the following example, where we are allowing the use of inline scripts:

```
script.inline: true
```

It is recommended to use fine-grained settings rather than high-level settings like this since these settings enable anyone to execute any script on your Elasticsearch cluster.

Using Painless is recommended over Groovy due to added security and performance advantages.

Snapshot/restore module

This module helps to take backup and restore data from and to Elasticsearch. The operations can be performed on entire clusters or even on a single index. A repository must be set up before snapshots can be created. There are official plugins for AWS Cloud, HDFS, and Azure cloud repositories.

Thread pools

Efficient thread management and memory management is a critical factor for a search engine. Every Elasticsearch node has several thread pools for different purposes – generic, index, search, get, bulk, percolate, snapshot, warmer, refresh, and listener operations.

Transport module

We learned that Elasticsearch nodes have both HTTP layers and **transport** layers. HTTP layers serve REST requests and transport layers are used for internal communication between nodes in the cluster. The transport module has an implementation for TCP. There are a number of settings available for setting up ports, hosts, timeouts, and so on. This has a dedicated logger as well, for logging all the incoming and outgoing requests. This logger is called **Transport Tracer**.

Tribe nodes module

Tribe node is a special client node that can communicate across multiple clusters. In the configuration file, a tribe node should have a list of all the clusters to be joined. A tribe node should be able to connect to each node in all listed clusters. The tribe node is able to perform read-write operations on the nodes of listed clusters.

Ingest nodes

As we learnt in the previous section, ingest nodes help to preprocess things before a document is indexed. Before a bulk request or index operations, the ingest node intercepts the request and does required processing on the document. An example of such a processor can be the date processor, which is used to parse the dates in fields. Another example is a convert processor, which converts a field value to a target type, for example, string to integer. A number of processors are available at: `https://www.elastic.co/guide/en/elas` `ticsearch/reference/5.1/ingest-processors.html`.

These kinds of nodes are helpful when a huge processing happens and we do not want a data node or master node to engage in processing. Dedicated ingest nodes can help to reduce the load significantly. It is best to set `node.ingest` as `false` for data and master nodes.

To understand how ingest nodes work with pipelines, let's follow these steps. Let's take the example of our `library` index and type `movies` added in `Chapter 2`, *Stepping into Elasticsearch*:

1. **Decide what to process**: In the dataset, we had 20+ fields, among which there were seven fields added for genre. These fields are `documentary`, `action`, `drama`, `short`, `animation`, `romance`, and `comedy`. All of these fields take a binary value and only one of them is `true` for data. This could, however, be merged into one single field called `genre` for better understanding, analysis, and visualization.

   If you already have the `movie` type for the `library` index, remove it so that we have a clean index before we start. To delete the `movies` type we can use `_delete_by_query` api on the `library` index:

   ```
   POST library/_delete_by_query{ "query":{ "match": { "_type":
   "movies" } }}
   ```

2. **Prepare processor**: We can use a Painless script to check whether any of the field values are set to 1, and then add a new field called `genre` and set the value accordingly. The following script does the exact same thing:

```
{
  "script": {
      "inline": " if(ctx.romance ==1){ ctx.genre = "romance"}
else if(ctx.drama ==1){      ctx.genre = "drama"} else
if(ctx.action ==1){
      ctx.genre = "action"} else if(ctx.documentary ==1){ ctx.genre =
"documentary"}
      else if(ctx.comedy ==1){ ctx.genre = "comedy"} else
if(ctx.animation ==1){
      ctx.genre = "animation"} else if(ctx.short ==1){ ctx.genre =
"short"} ",
        "lang": "painless"
    }
}
```

This script will add a new field called `genre` to the document.

3. **Simulating the pipeline**: It's best to simulate the pipeline to know whether there are any issues. To simulate, you can use the `_ingest/pipeline/_simulate` endpoint. A pipeline simulator takes two fields – `pipeline` (contains pipeline to test) and `docs` (sample documents to test on). This is what our pipeline looks like along with a call to simulation:

```
POST _ingest/pipeline/_simulate

{
  "pipeline": {
    "description": "Process Genre Data",
    "processors": [
      {
        "script": {
      "inline": "if(ctx.romance ==1){  ctx.genre = "romance"}
else   if(ctx.drama ==1){ ctx.genre = "drama"}
else    if(ctx.action ==1){ ctx.genre = "action"}
else   if(ctx.documentary ==1){ ctx.genre = "documentary"}
else   if(ctx.comedy ==1){ ctx.genre = "comedy"}
else if(ctx.animation ==1){ ctx.genre = "animation"}
else if(ctx.short ==1){ ctx.genre = "short"}",
        "lang": "painless"
          }
      }
    ]
```

```
    },
    "docs": [
      {
        "_index": "library",
        "_type": "movies",
        "_id": "1",
        "_source": {
          "romance": 0,
          "r2votes": 4,
          "year": 2001,
          "rating": 8,
          "r8votes": 14,
          "title": "Lord of the Rings: The Fellowship of the Ring ",
          "r5votes": 4,
          "drama": 0,
          "@version": "1",
          "action": 1,
            "r6votes": 4,
            "documentary": 0,
            "budget": 93000000,
            "r9votes": 14,
            "comedy": 0,
            "length": "208",
            "r3votes": 4,
            "r10votes": 45,
            "tags": [],
            "animation": 0,
            "r4votes": 4,
            "r7votes": 4,
            "short": 0,
            "votes": 157608,
            "r1votes": 4,
            "mpaaRating": "PG-13"
        }
      }
    ]
  }
```

If you see the output of the last call, you should be able to see a new field genre added to the document.

4. **Insert pipeline**: A pipeline has two fields: `description` and `processors`, where we can define multiple processors. We can insert our pipeline using the `_ingest/pipeline` endpoint and by specifying a name for the pipeline. Let's keep the name as `process_genre_data`. A call to insert the pipeline would be as follows:

```
PUT _ingest/pipeline/process-genre-data
{
  "description": "Process Genre Data",
  "processors": [    {"script": {    "inline":
 "if(ctx.romance ==1){  ctx.genre =     "romance"}
 else if(ctx.drama ==1){ ctx.genre = "drama"}
 else if(ctx.action ==1){ ctx.genre = "action"}
 else if(ctx.documentary ==1){ ctx.genre = "documentary"}
 else if(ctx.comedy ==1){ ctx.genre = "comedy"}
 else if(ctx.animation ==1){ ctx.genre = "animation"}
 else if(ctx.short ==1){ ctx.genre = "short"}",
    "lang": "painless"
      }
    }
  ]
}
```

If you run the command, the Console will output a positive acknowledgment.

5. **Utilize pipeline**: Once our pipeline is set, we can use it. In Chapter 2, *Stepping into Elasticsearch*, for indexing the movie data, we used the `logstash.movies.conf` file. We will be keeping the same configuration except for one change in the output configuration to `elasticsearch`. We need to set the field pipeline so that Elasticsearch can utilize our pipeline. The updated configuration for output will be as follows:

```
output {
      elasticsearch {
            index => "library"
            document_type => "movies"
            hosts => "localhost"
            pipeline => "process-genre-data"
        }
    }
```

Once the configuration is updated, we can execute the indexing process. Assuming that you already have set up a cluster with ingest(only) nodes. Run the Logstash:

```
./bin/logstash -f conf/logstash.movies.conf
```

6. **Validating the ingesting process**: You can validate whether the pipeline worked fine or not by querying the movie data. You should be able to see an added field name genre. To test it on Kibana Console, simply run the following:

```
GET library/movies/_search{  "query": {     "match_all": {   } }}
```

In the hits, you should see the genre field added for each movie.

This was a simple pipeline example where we used Ingest node and Logstash to do our job. Ingest nodes are a new addition to Elastic Stack and they are going to do a great job defining the pipelines and directly using them without the use of Logstash. While ingest nodes are yet to evolve in terms of features, processors, and so on, yet for available features, ingest nodes show a pretty high performance and throughput of processing documents compared to Logstash.

The way we used pipeline with output configuration for Logstash, we can use pipelines with beats as well. In such cases, if the ingest node can do the processing for us, we can eliminate the use of Logstash. Here's how to use it with Filebeat, for example:

```
output.elasticsearch:
hosts: ["http://localhost:9200"]
pipeline: process_genre_data
```

In the output Elasticsearch configuration, we just need to specify the name of our pipeline.

Elasticsearch clients

Earlier in this chapter, we got to know that Elasticsearch nodes support both transport and HTTP protocols. Using this flexibility, Elasticsearch nodes can be managed by its client written in other programming languages. There are a number of clients to perform operations on cluster and nodes. These clients can connect to a node or cluster to manage indices, operations on documents, and make searches.

Supported clients

A few clients are supported officially by the Elasticsearch organization. These clients are basically APIs that you can utilize with your own applications written in respective programming languages. For example, if you are developing a Java web application that integrates to Elasticsearch and you want to offer managing indices through an admin panel, you can use the Java API supported by Elasticsearch to connect to the cluster and nodes and do the necessary operations. The following is a list of all supported clients by Elasticsearch:

- Java API
- JavaScript API
- Groovy API
- .NET API
- PHP API
- Perl API
- Python API
- Ruby API

Community contributed clients

Every great open source software is great because of its community. In case of Elasticsearch also, community plays a big role. Elasticsearch officially supports a handful of clients, but the community has contributed 30+ clients. These clients cover other languages, for example, Go, Scala, R, and Smalltalk. Though not all clients support all of the operations, the most common and useful operations are supported.

A complete list of all these clients is available here `https://www.elastic.co/guide/en/elasticsearch/client/community/current/index.html`

Java API

The Java client uses the transport layer for its operations and supports all kinds of operations. We can make searches, index documents, delete, or get documents including admin tasks on the cluster. We can also perform operations in bulk.

To use the Java API in our application we need to use a few JAR files as the dependency. For a maven project, we can add dependency in our `pom.xml` as follows:

```
<dependency>
```

```
        <groupId>org.elasticsearch</groupId>
        <artifactId>elasticsearch</artifactId>
        <version>${elasticsearch.version}</version>
</dependency>
```

To include the jar files directly to the project, we can also download from the repository here `https://repo.maven.apache.org/maven2/org/elasticsearch/elasticsearch`. We can select the version we want for our application.

One thing to note here is that the client version should be the same as the version of Elasticsearch being used. For example, if we use Elasticsearch-5.1.1 then we should use version 5.1.1 of the jar files. For `pom.xml`, you need to set the value of the `${elasticsearch.version}` variable as the Elasticsearch version being used.

Connecting to a Cluster

In order to connect to a cluster, we can use `TransportClient` to get a client as in the following code:

```
Client client = TransportClient.builder().build().addTransportAddress(new
InetSocketTransportAddress(InetAddress.getByName("localhost"), 9300));
```

If you noticed Elasticsearch logs when the node starts, the logs will print these two lines:

```
[2016-05-02 16:39:51,832][INFO ][transport]
[Clive] publish_address {127.0.0.1:9300}, bound_addresses {127.0.0.1:9300},
{[::1]:9300}, {[fe80::1]:9300}

[2016-05-02 16:39:51,832][INFO ][http] [Clive] publish_address
{127.0.0.1:9200}, bound_addresses {127.0.0.1:9200}, {[::1]:9200},
{[fe80::1]:9200}
```

As we already know, Elasticsearch supports both transport and http layers. To connect these layers, Elasticsearch needs different ports – 9300 is for transport and 9200 for HTTP by default.

Since the Java client runs on the transport layer, we make a connection for port 9300. Once the client is connected, we can do the required operations.

Once all over operations are done, we should always make a call to `close()` to terminate the connection:

```
client.close();
```

Admin tasks

To perform any admin tasks using the Java API, we need to use `AdminClient`, which we can get using `client.admin()`:

```
AdminClient admin = client.admin();
```

This call returns an object of the `Admin` static class, which implements the `AdminClient` interface. This object will help us do operations on indices and clusters.

Managing indices

The `admin` object we have can give us reference to `IndicesAdminClient` using `admin.indices()`, which will help us create an index, refresh, get settings, and update settings:

```
IndicesAdminClient indicesAdmin = admin.indices();
```

Creating an index

Let's take the example of the movies dataset we used in Chapter 2, *Stepping into Elasticsearch*. To create an index with default settings, use the following:

```
indicesAdmin.prepareCreate("movies").get();
```

Let's understand what just happened – first we prepared an index name, `movies`, with `prepareCreate()` and then we executed the required action using a call to `get()`. A call to `prepareCreate()` returns objects of the `CreateIndexRequestBuilder` class, which is a builder to call when we want to create an index.

A more elaborative call can be as follows:

```
CreateIndexRequestBuilder indexBuilder =
indicesAdmin.prepareCreate("movies");
CreateIndexResponse createIndexResponse = indexBuilder.get();
```

This will create an index on the cluster with default settings, that is, the number of shards = 5 and replica per shard = 1. To assign a different setting at the time of index creation, we can use the `builder()` method of the `Settings` class:

```
indexRequestBuilder.setSettings(Settings.builder()
                .put("index.number_of_shards", 2)
                .put("index.number_of_replicas", 2)
        );
```

We can keep appending all of the settings to be overridden. setSettings() has many forms to take different types of input and Settings.Builder is one of those. We can also pass a JSON string to the method.

Getting index settings

We can get settings of an index in the form of GetSettingsResponse by preparing the settings using prepareGetSettings() and then making a call to get():

```
GetSettingsResponse settingsResponse =
indicesAdmin.prepareGetSettings("movies").get();
```

We can also get settings for multiple indices at once since the prepareGetSettings() method accepts an arbitrary number of arguments(varargs). It is declared as follows:

```
GetSettingsRequestBuilder prepareGetSettings(String... indices);
```

 Three dots represent that it can accept an arbitrary number of arguments, also known as varargs. This is helpful when the number of arguments is not known.

We can iterate the settings using settingsResponse.getIndexToSettings():

```
for (ObjectObjectCursor<String, Settings> ooCursor :
settingsResponse.getIndexToSettings()) {
  String index = ooCursor.key;
  Settings settings = ooCursor.value;
  Integer shards = settings.getAsInt("index.number_of_shards", null);
}
```

Using the cursor, we can get index and settings. Later, we can get values from the settings object. Other setting values that we can get are as follows:

```
index.creation_date
index.number_of_replicas
index.number_of_shards
index.uuid
index.version.created
```

Updating index settings

To update settings, we can use the prepareUpdateSettings() method:

```
indicesAdmin.prepareUpdateSettings("movies").setSettings(Settings.builder()
.put("index.number_of_replicas", 4)).get();
```

In the preceding statement, we used the `setSettings()` method to update settings using the `index.number_of_replicas` key and then used a call to `get()` to execute the operations.

Refreshing an index

Similarly, we can refresh one or more indices using the `prepareRefresh()` method:

```
indicesAdmin.prepareRefresh("movies").get();
```

If we do not specify any index name, this call will refresh all indices.

Managing clusters

The Java API provides `ClusterAdminClient` to manage cluster-related tasks similar to `IndicesAdminClient` for index-related tasks:

```
ClusterAdminClient clusterAdmin = admin.cluster();
```

We can use the `clusterAdminClient` object for cluster-related operations such as managing tasks, snapshots, knowing cluster and node health, updating settings, and many more. Let's see a few of such operations that we can perform using the Java API.

Getting cluster tasks

We can use `ClusterAdmin` to prepare a list of all tasks, which returns us a task request builder, using which we can get a task response. This response contains a list of all `TaskInfo` objects, which can be iterated to get task information. The following code does exactly what we discussed:

```
ListTasksRequestBuilder taskBuilder = clusterAdmin.prepareListTasks();
ListTasksResponse taskResponse = taskBuilder.get();
List<TaskInfo> tasks = taskResponse.getTasks();
for (TaskInfo taskInfo : tasks) {
    // get task information taskInfo.getId(),taskInfo.getDescription()
}
```

Once we get the response, we can get list of all tasks and iterate over to get related information about tasks.

Getting cluster health

We can get cluster health in the `ClusterIndexHealth` object for each index:

```
ClusterHealthRequestBuilder healthBuilder = clusterAdmin.prepareHealth();
ClusterHealthResponse healthResponse = healthBuilder.get();
for (ClusterIndexHealth health : healthResponse.getIndices().values()) {
    String index = health.getIndex();
    int shardsCount = health.getNumberOfShards();
    int replicasCount = health.getNumberOfReplicas();
    ClusterHealthStatus status = health.getStatus();
}
```

Once we have the **health** object, we can get other information as well, such as number of shards, replicas, and index status. While the health object gives us information about index, the `healthResponse` object helps with cluster-level information such as number of nodes, number of data nodes, cluster name, and active shards.

Index-level tasks

The Java API also allows us to do low-level tasks, which we could do using document, search, count, and other available APIs. This API can perform operations on single documents as well as multiple documents at once. We can also do aggregations or use Query DSL to build our query and then perform searches using the search API.

Managing documents

The Index API helps us with adding documents to indices, updating, and deleting a document.

Indexing a document

We already prepared a client and this time, we will be using the client directly to perform operations for us.

First we build an index request for a specific index, a type, and optionally provide an ID. So if we want to add a document to the library index, within the book type, and with id 121, we would use the following:

```
IndexRequestBuilder indexRequestBuilder = client.prepareIndex("library",
"book", "121");
IndexResponse response = indexRequestBuilder.setSource(<document>).get();
```

Once we have got the index request, we call the `setSource()` method and later make a call to the `get()` method to execute the operation. The `setSource()` method has many possible calls, such as the following:

```
setSource(byte[] source)
setSource(byte[] source, int offset, int length)
setSource(BytesReference source)
```

This call sets the document to index in bytes or `BytesReference` form:

```
setSource(Map<String,?> source)
setSource(Map<String,?> source, XContentType contentType)
```

This form takes a `Map` with the key as string and object values for its key-value-pair. An example of this form would be the following:

```
Map<String, Object> document = new HashMap<String, Object>();
document.put("author","Ravi");
document.put("title","Test-Driven JavaScript Development");
document.put("pages",240);
```

We created a map and put values for author, title, and pages.

In case we have JSON in string format for the document, we can just supply that string to index a document:

```
setSource(String source)
```

For example:

```
String book = "{" + ""author":"Ravi"," +
        ""title":"Test-Driven JavaScript Development"," +
            ""pages":"240"" +
    "}";
IndexRequestBuilder indexRequestBuilder = client.prepareIndex("library",
"book");
indexRequestBuilder.setSource(book).get();
```

In the preceding example, we did not provide an id. In this case, it will take an auto-generated id for the document.

We can also use `XContentBuilder` to create our source document:

```
setSource(XContentBuilder sourceBuilder)
```

There are other forms of the set Source () method as well which take key and value pairs as separate arguments, up to four pairs:

```
setSource(String field1, Object value1)
setSource(String field1, Object value1, String field2, Object value2)
setSource(String field1, Object value1, String field2, Object value2,
String field3, Object value3)
setSource(String field1, Object value1, String field2, Object value2,
String field3, Object value3, String field4, Object value4)
```

The call to the get () method returns a response that can be used to get the index, type, ID, version, and a Boolean value stating if a document was created or not:

```
response.getIndex()     // index name
response.getType()     // type name
response.getVersion()  // version number
response.getId()     // id of the indexed document
response.isCreated()  // true if the document was created.
```

Getting a document

To get a document, we can use the prepareGet () method:

```
GetResponse getResponse = client.prepareGet("library", "book","121").get();
```

To get the document, we specified the index name, type name, and the ID.

Deleting a document

To delete a document, we can use the prepareGet () method:

```
DeleteResponse deleteResponse = client.prepareDelete("library", "book",
"151").get();
```

To delete the document, we specified the index name, type name, and the ID.

Updating a document

To update a document, we can create an UpdateRequest and set index name, type, ID of the document, and then a new document object with fields that are to be updated:

```
UpdateRequest updateRequest = new UpdateRequest();
updateRequest.index("library");
updateRequest.type("book");
updateRequest.id("151");
updateRequest.doc(XContentFactory.jsonBuilder()
```

```
.startObject()
.field("pages", "250")
.endObject());
```

Once we have the request object ready, we can make a call to the update() method and then the get() method to finally execute the operation:

```
client.update(updateRequest).get();
```

Another way is to use the prepareUpdate() method and then use either setScript() or setDoc():

```
updateRequest = new UpdateRequest("library", "book", "151")
    .script(new Script("ctx._source.pages = "250""));
client.update(updateRequest).get();

client.prepareUpdate("library", "book", "151")
    .setDoc(XContentFactory.jsonBuilder()
    .startObject().field("pages", "250").endObject()).get();
```

This also supports upsert; in case a document is not present, a new document will be created. If a document is preset, it will be updated. To use upsert, all we need to do is make a call to upsert() before calling update():

```
updateRequest.doc(XContentFactory.jsonBuilder().startObject().field("pages"
, "250").endObject()).upsert();
client.update(updateRequest).get();
```

Query DSL and search API

This API helps us to use Query DSL using the QueryBuilders factory class. We can create simple and complex queries using this API and then we can use the search API to make a search on indices.

For example, to make a matchAll query, use the following:

```
QueryBuilder queryBuilder = QueryBuilders.matchAllQuery();
```

We used the QueryBuilders factory class to build a match AllQuery and assigned it to the QueryBuilder object. Similar to this, we can make other types of queries as well:

```
QueryBuilders.matchQuery(String name, Object text)
```

This method returns a match query and takes two arguments – name of the field and text to match:

```
QueryBuilders.multiMatchQuery(Object text, String... fieldNames)
```

multiMatchQuery() takes the first argument as text to match, and second varargs as all of the fields against the match to be performed.

There is a huge list of such queries supported by Query DSL, which includes joins, term-level, full-text, Geo, and span queries. A complete list of queries is available at https://www.elastic.co/guide/en/elasticsearch/client/java-api/5.1/java-query-dsl.html.

Once we have the query created, we can use the search API to perform search operations. Let's do a search on the library index holding all of the movies:

```
SearchResponse response = client.prepareSearch("library")
.setTypes("movies")        .setSearchType(SearchType.DFS_QUERY_THEN_FETCH)
.setQuery(QueryBuilders.matchQuery("title","titanic"))
.setFrom(0).setSize(60).setExplain(true)
.execute()
.actionGet();
```

We used the prepareSearch() method and supplied the index name library, and then set a movies type using the setTypes() method followed by setSearchType(), which sets a type of search to be performed. As per the documentation, DFS_QUERY_THEN_FETCH is the same as QUERY_THEN_FETCH, except for an initial scatter phase that goes and computes the distributed term frequencies for more accurate scoring.

When we use QUERY_THEN_FETCH, the query executes against all shards, but document content is not returned and only necessary (minimal) information about the results is returned. Then the results are sorted and ranked as per the query and then content is fetched. While fetching content, only the relevant shards are involved.

After setting the search type, we set a query; this query is going to be the one created using QueryBuilders. This is followed by the number of records, whether we want the explanation to be returned or not. Finally, calls to execute() and actionGet() are made to execute the query and to get the response. The response contains the information about time, shard information, along with hits.

Aggregations

The Java API provides a clean way of using aggregations using the `AggregationBuilders` utility. A typical search would be made as follows:

```
SearchResponse searchResponse = client.prepareSearch("stones")
.addAggregation(aggregation)
.execute().actionGet();
```

We can append an aggregation just before the `execute()` method call. To create an aggregation of minimum pages on the library index with the book type, use the following:

```
MetricsAggregationBuilder aggregation =
                AggregationBuilders.min("min_pages").field("pages");
SearchResponse searchResponse = client.prepareSearch("library")
                    .addAggregation(aggregation)
                    .execute().actionGet();
Min min_pages_agg = searchResponse.getAggregations().get("min_pages");
long min_pages = (long)min_pages_agg.getValue();
```

In the code, we created a metric aggregation using `min()` on field pages. After the search operation is executed, we need to get the aggregation result from the search response using the aggregation name. Then using the aggregation, we can get the desired value.

Similar to `Min`, there are other classes also available to get other metric aggregations. We can also perform bucket aggregations and then extract the result from `searchResponse`.

Elasticsearch plugins

As learned in `Chapter 7`, *Customizing Elastic Stack*, under the *Extending Elasticsearch* section, earlier versions (before 5.x) of Elasticsearch offered a number of plugins and these plugins were divided into three types – Java, **Site**, and **Mixed** plugins. Now Site and Mixed plugins are deprecated and only Java plugins are supported. These Java plugins must be installed on every node and contain only JAR files. `Chapter 7`, *Customizing Elastic Stack*, also talks about Elasticsearch plugins.

The elastic (`https://www.elastic.co/`) categorizes plugins as core plugins, which are developed and maintained officially, and community plugins, which are developed and maintained by a community. To utilize these plugins, we need to install into Elasticsearch by using the Elasticsearch-plugin utility. Core plugins are released with Elasticsearch, and share the same version as Elasticsearch.

In this section, we will get familiar with a few of the interesting plugins. Core plugins can be installed just by using the name:

```
$ ./bin/elasticsearch-plugin install plugin-name
```

Community plugins can be installed by downloading the package and using the following:

```
$ ./bin/elasticsearch-plugin install path/to/plugin/zip/file
```

The utility can install from any of the following locations – local filesystem, a URL where the plugin's ZIP file is located, GitHub repository, or for Elasticsearch core plugins – just the plugin name.

To know what the URL will be to access the plugin in a browser, we can use the Cat API to list all the plugins and it will show the URL for each plugin:

```
GET _cat/plugins
```

Sometimes, it is necessary that a plugin must be present/installed before we run Elasticsearch. In such cases, we can specify those required plugins as mandatory using settings in elasticsearch.yml.

For example, if we need to have EC2 discovery, then specify it as a mandatory plugin for Elasticsearch:

```
plugin.mandatory: discovery-ec2
```

We can specify more plugins as a comma-separated list.

To remove a plugin, simply use the following:

```
$ ./bin/elasticsearch-plugin remove plugin-name
```

The plugins can be further categorized by their functionality, which are **Alerts**, **Analysis**, **Discovery**, **Ingest**, **Mapper**, **Scripting**, and so on. Covering all the plugins is out of the scope of this book, but we will see a few plugins that fall under these categories. For example, Discovery plugins is a set of plugins that help us to set up clusters using node discovery.

Discovery plugins

These plugins are very helpful as they enable Elasticsearch to find nodes for clusters in different environments. By default, **Zen Discovery** is added to Elasticsearch and there are more plugins to connect to:

- **Azure cloud**: This plugin uses Azure API for unicast discovery and also adds Azure as a repository
- **GCE cloud**: This is for Google Compute Engine Cloud
- **AWS cloud**: This plugin supports unicast for EC2 discovery using the AWS API

These plugins are officially supported. Apart from these, there are several community-driven plugins for eskka discovery, Kubernetes discovery, and much more.

Ingest plugins

Similar to the discovery plugins set enabling node discovery, ingest plugins help to enable ingest node capabilities in Elasticsearch. There are three plugins:

- **Geoip processor plugin**: This plugin uses the city and country databases from **Maxmind**. Using this database, for IP present in the document, this plugin processes geo-location and puts the details under the `geoip` field.
- **User-agent processor plugin**: This plugin extracts user agent information using a user-agent header.
- **Attachment processor plugin**: This plugin uses Tika, which is a toolkit developed by Apache, and can extract metadata and text from a number of file types. Using Tika, this plugin helps Elasticsearch to extract details from attachments. Common attachment formats include–PPT, PDF, XLS, and many more.

Elasticsearch SQL

This plugin gives an interface to those who like to see things from a relational database view and want to try SQL queries on the index. This plugin is a community-contributed plugin and is available at `https://github.com/NLPchina/elasticsearch-sql`.

To install this plugin, we can use the following:

```
$ ./ bin/elasticsearch-plugin install
https://github.com/NLPchina/elasticsearch-sql/releases/download/5.1.1.0/ela
sticsearch-sql-5.1.1.0.zip
```

As Site plugins have been removed from Elasticsearch, elasticsearch-sql does not provide any interface to access and run the SQL queries. Instead, you can use the Console to run SQL queries.

A sample request is shown in the following command:

```
GET /_sql?sql=select title from library where author in("Yuvraj
Gupta","Ravi Kumar Gupta")
```

The response will look like the following screenshot:

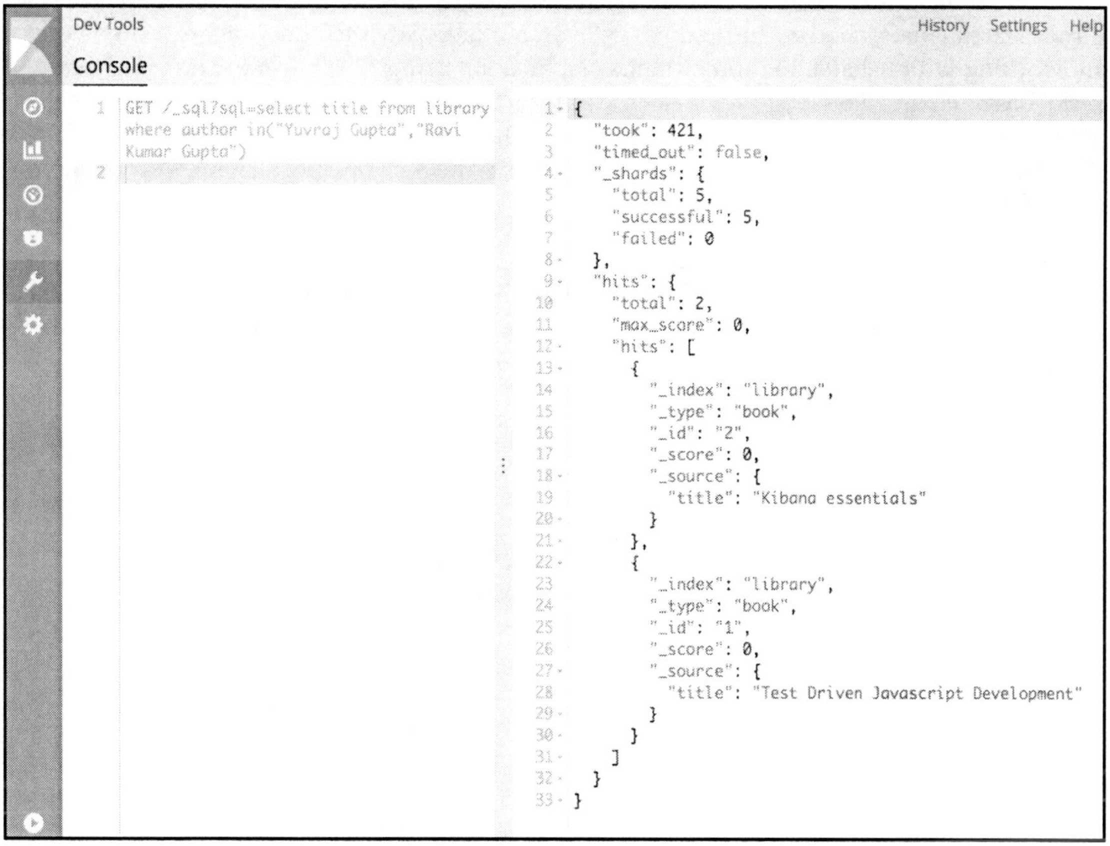

We can send an API request and it will show us the results as in the preceding screenshot. We can see that it returned all of the titles where the author contains Yuvraj Gupta or Ravi Kumar Gupta.

For further information about the plugin, visit the following link:
`https://github.com/NLPchina/elasticsearch-sql/wiki`

Summary

This chapter concludes the Elasticsearch APIs. Being a very vast topic, not all of the APIs can be covered, but we have got the gist of how these APIs work and help us to manage the Elasticsearch cluster, nodes, and indices or even make a search for documents. When you are working with Kibana, the same things can be done using the Console. There are many REST-based clients developed for Elasticsearch for numerous languages and platforms that use http protocol and we have been learning that since Chapter 2, *Stepping into Elasticsearch*. This chapter also covered the other side of the story – using Transport Client with the help of the Java API.

The next chapter is going to focus on the customization of Elastic Stack using plugins. Plugins give us a good amount of control on the functionalities and we get a liberty to implement what is not present or mend what is present to make it work for us. We will be learning the way we can create new plugins and customize the stack.

9

X-Pack: Security and Monitoring

In previous chapters, we have explored four core components of Elastic Stack – Elasticsearch, Logstash, Kibana and Beats. While these components help us with pipelining the data, indexing and visualization, there are still few aspects left which are even more important when it comes to production level setup. Security comes to mind when we talk about a server in production. We would want to be notified for events such as errors, faults and so on. Such important features are at core of X-Pack.

In this chapter, we will explore the various components present in X-Pack in brief. We will cover the need for X-Pack followed by the features, installation, and configuration of the components present within X-Pack.

In this chapter, we will cover the following topics:

- Introduction to X-Pack
- Installation of X-Pack
- Exploring security
- Viewing X-Pack information
- Exploring monitoring
- Understanding Profiler

Introduction to X-Pack

Before learning about X-Pack, let's understand how X-Pack came into existence. We have discussed the need for Elastic Stack, where earlier there were different versions maintained for Elasticsearch, Logstash, Kibana, and Beats. Therefore, to avoid confusion for the users, Elastic Team. simplified and came up with Elastic Stack where there would be a single release version for Elasticsearch, Logstash, Kibana, and Beats. After the rise in use of these products, there was a need for supporting products that would help the end user such as a need for authorization and authentication of Elasticsearch clusters and Kibana, a need for monitoring the Elasticsearch cluster using a simple yet intuitive UI, and a need for robust alerting and notification mechanisms.

X-Pack is an extension package for Elastic Stack, which combines the various product offerings apart from the components of Elastic Stack, such as Shield, Marvel, Watcher, and Graph, and provides additional features of reporting. X-Pack has the same premise as Elastic Stack, where instead of maintaining different versions of each product and always checking for the support matrix of each of the products, you no longer need to think about the various products and their version. You just need to install the X-Pack corresponding to the Elastic Stack version and you will have all the products that are properly supported, maintained, and compatible with each other. X-Pack components seamlessly work together with each other as well as independent components. X-Pack provides settings, configuration, and APIs via which you can enable or disable the component you want to use, configure the components, and access information about the components.

Installation of X-Pack

To install X-Pack, you need to have installed Elasticsearch 5.0 and Kibana 5.0 onwards. Also, you must run the version of X-Pack that matches the version of Elastic Stack that you are running.

For the installation of Elasticsearch, you can refer to the *Installation of Elasticsearch* section in `Chapter 1`, *Overview of the Stack*. For the installation of Kibana, you can refer to the *Installation of Kibana* section in `Chapter 1`, *Overview of the Stack*. X-Pack will be installed in both Elasticsearch and Kibana, for which the Elasticsearch plugin and Kibana plugin will be used.

Installing X-Pack in Elasticsearch

In order to install X-Pack in Elasticsearch, refer to the following steps:

1. Install X-Pack while running the following command from the Elasticsearch installation directory – `bin/elasticsearch-plugin install x-pack`.

 Run the installation as a superuser if you are using DEB/RPM distributions.

   During installation, it will ask you to grant extra permissions to X-Pack, which is required by Watcher to send e-mail alerts. Specify `Y` to continue the installation or `N` to abort the installation.

   To skip the install prompt, use the `-b` or `--batch` parameters to install X-Pack:

   ```
   bin/elasticsearch-plugin install x-pack --batch
   ```

2. X-Pack automatically creates indices for security, monitoring, and so on. So if you have disabled automatic index creation, configure `elasticsearch.yml` to allow X-Pack to create the indices. Add the following entry in `elasticsearch.yml`:

   ```
   action.auto_create_index:
   .security, .monitoring*, .watches, .triggered_watches, .watcher-history*
   ```

3. Start Elasticsearch from the Elasticsearch installation directory, or if installed, as a service:

   ```
   bin/elasticsearch
   sudo service elasticsearch start
   ```

Installing X-Pack in Kibana

In order to install X-Pack in Kibana, refer to the following steps:

1. Install X-Pack while running the following command from the Kibana installation directory:

   ```
   bin/kibana-plugin install x-pack
   ```

Run the installation as a superuser if you are using DEB/RPM distributions.

2. Start Kibana from the Kibana installation directory, or if installed, as a service:

```
bin/kibana
sudo service kibana start
```

To verify the installation of X-Pack, open the browser with the URL as mentioned in the Kibana configuration file for the host field or `localhost:5601` (default host value), which would prompt you to log in to Kibana.

Now you might be wondering *how will I log in as I never set a password* and *now it's asking for a password from me?* Don't worry, the default username is `elastic` and the default password is `changeme`.

 The `bin/elasticsearch-plugin` and `bin/kibana-plugin` script requires an Internet connection to download and install X-Pack.

Installing X-Pack on offline systems

In order to install X-Pack in offline systems, refer to the following steps:

1. Download X-Pack binaries on the system where there is Internet connectivity by downloading it from the following URL:

```
https://artifacts.elastic.co/downloads/packs/x-pack/x-pack-5.1.1.zip
```

2. Copy or transfer the downloaded ZIP file to the offline system.
3. Install X-Pack from the file on Elasticsearch using the following command:

```
bin/elasticsearch-plugin install
file:///home/yuvraj/Downloads/x-pack-5.1.1.zip
```

 Run the installation as a superuser if you are using DEB/RPM distributions.

4. Install X-Pack from the file on Kibana using the following command:

```
bin/kibana-plugin install
file:///home/yuvraj/Downloads/x-pack-5.1.1.zip
```

 You need to specify the absolute path to the ZIP file after the `file://` protocol.

After installation of X-Pack, all the features are installed and enabled, such as Shield, Marvel, Watcher, Graph, and Reporting. To view the information after installation of X-Pack, we can use the X-Pack API, which is explained later in the *Viewing X-Pack information* section.

 Restart Elasticsearch or Kibana if already running while installing X-Pack. Without restarting you may face issue as X-Pack settings may not be applied on both Elasticsearch and Kibana.

Uninstalling X-Pack

In order to uninstall X-Pack, refer to the following steps:

1. Stop Elasticsearch and Kibana.
2. Remove X-Pack from Elasticsearch by running the following command from the Elasticsearch installation directory:

```
bin/elasticsearch-plugin remove x-pack
```

3. Remove X-Pack from Kibana by running the following command from Kibana installation directory:

```
bin/kibana-plugin remove x-pack
```

 Run the commands as a superuser if you are using DEB/RPM distributions.

4. Start Elasticsearch and Kibana.

Let's now explore each of the components of X-Pack.

Security

X-Pack security is a module that has been created out of the requirement of having a proper authorization mechanism to access the data present in the cluster. It initially started with the need for secure the Elasticsearch cluster, and it has grown beyond that to even secure the Kibana UI and provide access to authorized users only.

Whenever we talk about security, we tend to discuss the three As:

- **Authentication**: Used to authenticate users based on their identity
- **Authorization**: Describes the roles/permissions granted to an authenticated user
- **Accountability**: Logging user session information, usage information, and so on

Considering the three As, Elastic Team is using Shield as an X-Pack Security model, which makes sure that the 3A's are covered.

For **Authentication**, it provides restrictions on unauthorized access with basic password protection, organization-level user management, and IP-based authorization.

For **Authorization**, it provides role-based access control, which defines what roles the authenticated user has along with the privileges for indices-based operations.

For **Accountability**, it provides a complete audit trail to keep track of all the operations performed in the cluster and user-level information to gather insights related to authentication and authorization performed by each user.

You might be woundering why we need to install X-Pack for both Elasticsearch and Kibana. Why is there a need to install X-Pack on both, what if I install it on only Elasticsearch or Kibana, won't I be able to use it then?

The answer to this question is fairly straightforward. No. Elasticsearch being a data transport/storage layer requires X-Pack for cluster/node-related configurations. Kibana being a data visualization layer requires X-Pack for different functionality such as securing the UI with authentication, reporting, and managing the settings of X-Pack. Also, the Security module in X-Pack works only when you have installed X-Pack on both Elasticsearch and Kibana.

Prior to the release of Elastic Stack version 5.0, users used Shield to secure their Elasticsearch cluster, which required users to use the REST API to perform operations such as adding a new user, authenticating a user, providing privileges, configuring roles with each user, providing access to indices, restricting control access, changing the user password, and adding user information. But by extending X-Pack to Kibana and with addition of a new **Management** tab in Kibana, now all the operations performed using the REST API can be configured with the press of a button.

Let's explore how we can create users, configure roles, and configure indices-level permissions using the Kibana UI and REST API. We will use the **Management** tab, which has been discussed in `Chapter 4`, *Kibana Interface*, under the *Exploring Management interface tab* section.

Upon opening the **Management** tab, we get a few options categorized into two sections, that is, Elasticsearch, and Kibana. For Shield-related security configuration, we will use **Users** and **Roles** to configure the shield settings from the Kibana UI.

Listing of all users in security

To list the entire users present, click on **Users**, which will bring you to the following screen:

In the preceding screenshot, we can see that two users have been created as default, that is, **elastic** and **kibana** having different roles configured to them.

 Both the users are reserved, that is, they cannot be modified or deleted; only their password can be changed.

To list all of the users using the REST API, we can use the following command:

```
curl -XGET localhost:9200/_xpack/security/user
```

In the preceding command, `localhost` refers to the hostname, `9200` refers to the port name, `_xpack` is an endpoint for X-Pack related settings exposed to the API, and security signifies X-Pack to refer to the API configured for X-Pack security.

Upon running the preceding command, we get an error stating the reason as follows:

```
"reason" : "missing authentication token for REST request
```

The reason is as per the understanding of security, that is, if the request comes from anyone without specifying the username and password, it will throw an error as it cannot authenticate the user.

 We can allow anonymous access for anyone to query even if security is enabled.

Therefore, to perform any operations using the REST API on Elasticsearch, we would need to provide the username as we have enabled security in X-Pack.

To list all the users using the REST API, we would need to pass the username as follows:

```
curl -XGET --user elastic localhost:9200/_xpack/security/user
```

It will ask for the password for the user elastic; upon authenticating, it will list the users.

Also, we can provide the password along with the username in the REST API as follows:

```
curl -XGET --user elastic:changeme localhost:9200/_xpack/security/user
```

We can also use Sense Console to run `curl` commands on the REST API. As Sense Console is now present as part of Dev Tools after installation of Kibana, the syntax would be as follows:

```
GET _xpack/security/user
```

For easy understanding, we will use Sense Console syntax for showing `curl` commands.

Listing of roles in security

To list the roles present, click on **Roles**, which will bring you to the following screen:

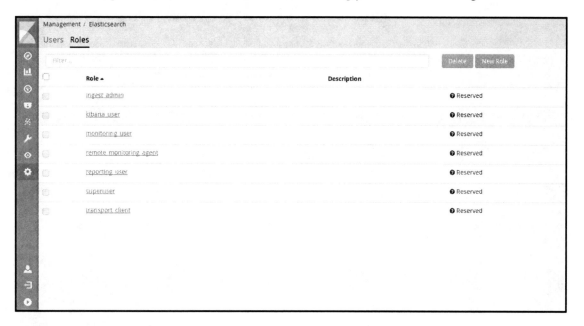

In the preceding image we can see that three roles have been created as default that is **ingest_admin, kibana_user, monitoring_user, remote_monitoring_agent, reporting_user, superuser**, and **transport_client**.

The default rules present are reserved, that is, they cannot be modified or deleted.

To list the roles using console, the command will be as follows:

```
GET _xpack/security/role
```

The roles play an important part as they provide access control to clusters and indices based on the privileges assigned to each of the roles. It can help to restrict a particular user for access to cluster and indices as per specified privileges.

Understanding roles in security

Click on the **kibana_user** role, which will bring you to the following screen:

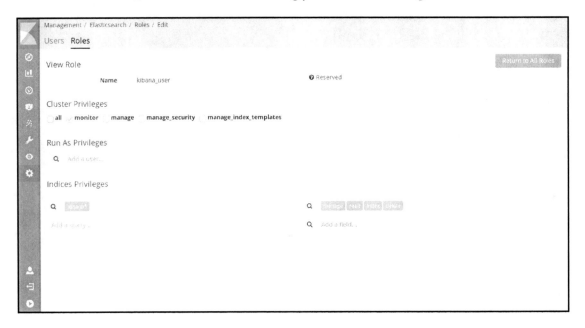

In the preceding screenshot, it looks so complicated with various terms mentioned such as **Cluster Privileges**, **Run As Privileges**, and **Indices Privileges**. Let's explore them to understand each of the privileges in detail.

Understanding Cluster Privileges

Cluster Privileges provide privileges for performing various operations on the cluster. They can be classified within five settings, explained as follows:

- **all**: It provides access to all of the operations that can be performed in the cluster. By using this privilege, one can even shut down or restart a node.
- **monitor**: It provides access to the read operations of the cluster for monitoring purposes. It is not limited to determining cluster information, node information, status of node/cluster/snapshot/restore, and so on.
- **manage**: It provides additional capabilities over monitor privileges. It provides access to perform cluster operations which can update the cluster, such as rerouting and updating cluster settings.
- **manage_security**: It provides access to the CRUD operations on roles and users for managing security.
- **manage_index_templates**: It provides access to all of the operations that can be performed on the index templates.

Understanding Run As privileges

Run as Privileges are a special kind of privilege that are available to an authenticated user. Using this, an authenticated user can submit requests on behalf of other users. You can either provide or restrict access to perform operations from other users without the need to reauthenticate the user again. You can specify the username to provide run as privilege. Sometimes, it is also known as impersonation, a way to impersonate other users.

Understanding Indices privileges

Indices Privileges provide privileges for performing various operations on the indices. They can be classified within the following settings:

- **All**: It provides access to all of the operations to be performed on the indices.
- **Monitor**: It provides access to all of the operations required for monitoring of the indices, such as index information, status, and so on.
- **Manage**: It provides additional capabilities over monitor privileges. It provides access to perform administration tasks over the indices, which is not limited to index settings, using aliases, using analyzers, and so on.

- **Read**: It provides read-only access to the various operations which can be performed on the indices, such as searching the data, fetching the data, and a few other actions such as count, validate, percolator, and so on. Also, it provides privileges to update the mapping of the indices.
- **Index**: It provides access to the index and updates the documents in the indices. Also, it provides privileges to update the mapping.
- **Create**: It provides access to only indexing of the documents. Also, it provides privileges to update the mapping.
- **Delete**: It provides access to only deleting the documents in the indices.
- **Write**: It provides access to perform all write operations in the indices such as indexing, updating, and deletion of documents. It also provides access to perform bulk operations such as bulk insertions, processing, and so on.
- **Delete_index**: It provides access to only deleting the indices.
- **Create_index**: It provides access to only creation of the index. If you need to insert documents within the index, you would require write privilege as well.
- **View_index_metadata**: It provides access to view the metadata of the indices such as settings (creation date, number of shards, replicas, and so on) and mappings (index field name along with datatype).

In **Indices Privileges**, we can mention the name of the index (or indices), privileges for the indices, queries to restrict the user to access those queries itself, and the field names to restrict the user to view those specific fields only.

As we have discussed the meaning of various privileges provided, now let's try to decode the roles of the default users to know which privileges are provided.

Decoding default user roles

Let's have a look at some of the default user roles created, that is, **kibana_user**, **superuser**, and **transport_client**.

kibana_user

Cluster Privileges are listed as **monitor**, that is, it provides access to the read operations only. This role does not allow any write/update/delete operations on the cluster.

In **Indices Privileges**, the name of the index is listed as `.kibana*` and privileges are listed as **manage, read, index,** and **delete**. It means that the user can access the indices with the name starting with `.kibana` and can perform operations such as monitoring privileges, administration operations on the indices, read operations on the actions, indexing the documents, updateing the mappings of the indices, updateing the documents, and deletion of the documents. It cannot perform various operations such as write operations on the indices, creating an index, deleting an index, and viewing the metadata of the indices.

superuser

Cluster Privileges are listed as **all**, that is, the user can perform any operations on the cluster.

In **Indices Privileges**, the name of the index is listed as `*` and privileges are listed as all. It means that the user can access all of the indices and can perform any operations on any index as required.

transport_client

It does not have any **Cluster Privileges**, that is, the user cannot perform any operations on the cluster, be it monitoring or managing the tasks.

It does not have access to any of the indices without any privileges. It only has access to all of the fields, which it can use while interacting using the transport API.

Adding a role in security

To create a new role, go to the **Management** tab in Kibana and click on **Roles**. Then click on **New Role**, which will bring you to the page to specify the role name and privileges.

Specify the name of the role followed by mentioning the privileges to be provided for the cluster, specify any **Run As Privileges** to be provided, mention the various privileges for the indices such as the index name followed by its privileges, queries to restrict the access, and field security to restrict or grant the access of fields.

The username must begin with a letter or underscore and it can contain letters, numbers, and special characters such as _, $, ., @, -. It can have a minimum of 1 character and a maximum of 30 characters. The password has to be a minimum of 6 characters and a maximum of 50 characters.

To add a role using console, the command will be as follows:

```
POST /_xpack/security/role/testing
{
"cluster" :["all"],
"indices" :[
  {
    "names": ["education"],
    "privileges": ["manage","read","index","delete"],
    "query": "{"match":{"State":"GA"}}",
    "fields": ["*"]
    }
  ]
}
```

You need to escape the double quotes in the query except the start and end double quotes as used.

It will return the following request:

```
{
  "role": {
    "created": true
  }
}
```

In the preceding code, testing is the name of role that is specified along with the verb (POST).

You can create the roles by specifying either POST or PUT. To update the roles, use PUT or POST.

Updating a role in security

To update the details of a role such as **Cluster Privileges, Run As Privileges, Indices Privileges**, indices name, queries, or fields, go to the **Management** tab in Kibana and click on **Roles**. Then click on the role name that you want to modify.

You can then change the various privileges, and after making the changes, click on **Save**.

To update the role using console, the command will be as follows:

```
POST /_xpack/security/role/testing
{
"cluster" :["all"],
"indices" :[
  {
    "names": ["education",".kibana"],
    "privileges": ["*"],
    "fields": ["*"]
    }
  ]
}
```

It will return the following request:

```
{
  "role": {
    "created": false
  }
}
```

Understanding Field Level Security

It is characterized by the `field_security` keyword which provides the option to either grant the fields to be accessed or restrict the fields to be accessed by the user. By default, few meta fields are always provided access for the user such as _id, _type, _parent, _routing, _timestamp, _ttl, _size and _index. To use any other meta field you have to explicitly provide such as _all, _source and so on.

You can use following expressions for granting or restricting access:

- Providing Field Name – It is used to mention the field name directly, for example, `"grant: : ["_all", "message"]`
- Using Wildcard expressions – It is used to specify a pattern of fields. for example, `"except" : ["date-*"]`
- Accessing Nested Fields – It is used to read any nested fields, for example, `"grant" : ["date.time"]` where time is nested field of date
- Wildcard with Nested Fields – It is used to read many nested fields, for example, `"grant" : ["date.*"]`

- Combining Grant with Except – It is used to specify which fields to be accesssed and which fields should not be available for access by the user, for example:

```
"grant" : [ "date.*" ]
"except": [ "date.time" ],.
```

In the preceding example, it will provide access to all fields prefixed with date except for date.time field.

Adding a user in security

To create a new user, go to the **Management** tab in Kibana and click on **Users**. Then click on **New User**, which will bring you to the following screen:

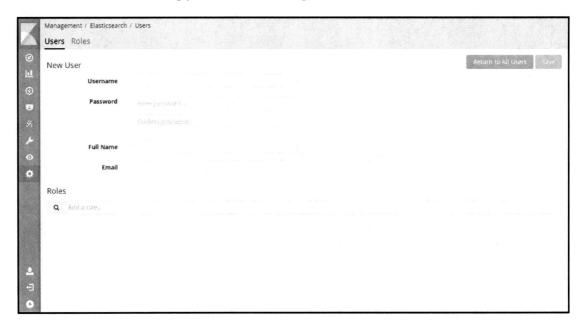

In the preceding screenshot, we can see that for creating a new user we are required to specify username, password, **Full Name**, Email, and **Roles**. All the fields are mandatory to fill using the Kibana UI. You can specify single or multiple roles to each user as per the requirement.

Usernames must begin with a letter or underscore and can contain letters, numbers, and special characters such as _, $, . , @ , -. It can have a minimum of 1 character and a maximum of 30 characters. Passwords have to be a minimum of 6 characters and a maximum of 50 characters.

To add a user using console, the command will Then click on either the Full Name or Username, which will bring you to the following screen be as follows:

```
POST /_xpack/security/user/test
{
  "password" : "test@123",
  "roles" : [ "kibana_user", "transport_client" ],
  "full_name" : "Testing User",
  "email" : "test@test.com"
}
```

 You can create a user by specifying either POST or PUT. To update user information except username and password, use PUT or POST to update the details. Passwords can be updated using the Reset Password API.

It will return the following request:

```
{
  "user": {
    "created": true
  }
}
```

In the preceding code, test is the name of the user that is specified along with the verb (POST).

 To perform CRUD operations on a user, you must have at least a manage_security cluster privilege.

Updating user details in security

To update the details of a user such as password, full name, e-mail, and roles, go to the **Management** tab in Kibana and click on **Users**.

Then click on either the **Full Name** or **Username**, which will bring you to the following screen:

As you can see in the preceding screenshot, you can change the Password, **Full Name**, **Email**, and **Roles** of the users. After making the changes, you can click on **Save**.

To update the details of a user using console, the command will be as follows:

```
PUT /_xpack/security/user/test
{
  "password" : "test@123",
  "roles" : [ "kibana_user", "transport_client" ],
  "full_name" : "Test User",
  "email" : "test@test.co.in"
}
```

It will return the following request:-

```
{
  "user": {
    "created": false
  }
}
```

Changing the password of a user in security

Changing the password of a user using the **Management** tab can be done as explained previously in the *Updating user details in security* section.

To change the password of a user using console, the command will be as follows:

```
PUT /_xpack/security/user/test/_password
{
   "password" : "test123"
}
```

It will return the following request:

```
{ }
```

Currently, we get a blank response indicating that password has been changed.

Deleting a role in security

To delete the role, go to the **Management** tab in Kibana and click on **Roles**. Then select the checkboxes beside the role names that you want to delete. Then click on the **Delete** button, which will ask for a confirmation from you to delete the selected roles.

To delete a role using console, the command will be as follows:

```
DELETE /_xpack/security/role/testing
```

Deleting a user in security

To delete a user, go to the **Management** tab in Kibana, and click on **Users**. Then select the checkboxes beside the usernames that you want to delete. Then click on the **Delete** button, which will ask for a confirmation from you to delete the selected users.

To delete a user using console, the command will be as follows:

```
DELETE /_xpack/security/user/test
```

After learning about security, let's view the information of X-Pack.

Viewing X-Pack information

X-Pack provides an API which we can use to view its information. It provides us with the build details, license details, and the details of each component of X-Pack.

To view the information using console in the Kibana UI, the command will be as follows:

```
GET /_xpack
```

It will give us the following response:

```
{
  "build": {
    "hash": "821d294",
    "date": "2016-12-06T13:09:18.057Z"
  },
  "license": {
    "uid": "e065e495-3fb4-4cb5-8233-263074ee57e7",
    "type": "trial",
    "mode": "trial",
    "status": "active",
    "expiry_date_in_millis": 1485882488285
  },
  "features": {
    "graph": {
      "description": "Graph Data Exploration for the Elastic Stack",
      "available": true,
      "enabled": true
    },
    "monitoring": {
      "description": "Monitoring for the Elastic Stack",
      "available": true,
      "enabled": true
    },
    "security": {
      "description": "Security for the Elastic Stack",
      "available": true,
      "enabled": true
    },
    "watcher": {
      "description": "Alerting, Notification and Automation for the Elastic
Stack",
      "available": true,
      "enabled": true
    }
  },
  "tagline": "You know, for X"
}
```

It gives us information about the components along with a field of enabled, which means we have the flexibility to enable/disable the features that we want to use.

To get detailed information of the X-Pack license, the command will be as follows:

```
GET /_xpack/license
```

It will give us the following response:

```
{
  "license": {
    "status": "active",
    "uid": "e065e495-3fb4-4cb5-8233-263074ee57e7",
    "type": "trial",
    "issue_date": " 2017-01-01T17:08:08.285Z",
    "issue_date_in_millis": 1483290488285,
    "expiry_date": " 2017-01-31T17:08:08.285Z",
    "expiry_date_in_millis": 1485882488285,
    "max_nodes": 1000,
    "issued_to": "elasticsearch",
    "issuer": "elasticsearch",
    "start_date_in_millis": -1
  }
}
```

Let's have a look at how we can enable/disable the features via configurations.

Enabling and disabling of X-Pack features

To enable/disable the X-Pack features, add the following settings to elasticsearch.yml and kibana.yml:

```
xpack.security.enabled
xpack.monitoring.enabled
xpack.graph.enabled
xpack.watcher.enabled
xpack.reporting.enabled
```

Setting the preceding settings value to false will disable the features, and setting them to true will enable them. Let's explore the various other components present in X-Pack.

Monitoring

Monitoring is another X-Pack component that has grown out of the requirement of having a UI to monitor the cluster, indices, and nodes present in Elasticsearch. It provides us with detailed statistics for each cluster, each of the indices present in the cluster, and for each of the nodes.

By making Monitoring incorporated in X-Pack, now you can access the Monitoring UI directly from Kibana, thereby eliminating the need to leave Kibana. Earlier, it was known as Marvel, which provided you with a UI to monitor and get statistics of clusters, nodes, and indices present in Elasticsearch. You can even see the performance of the Kibana instance that is running, which is an addition.

Monitoring consists of two sub-components: a *monitoring agent* and a *monitoring application*. The monitoring agent is to be installed on every node from which you want to fetch statistics, and collects the data and indices of the data in Elasticsearch on which data is visualized using the Monitoring dashboards in Kibana. It is present within the Elasticsearch X-Pack, which is installed on each node separately. Also, there is flexibility for the monitoring agent to either index the data on the same cluster or a different cluster. The monitoring application provides the UI to view the statistics and information. It is present within the Kibana X-Pack, which is installed on the machine on which you want to view.

Let's explore the various statistics and information provided by the Monitoring component in X-Pack. To view the Monitoring component, we will use the **Monitoring** tab option present in the left-hand side pane of Kibana. Upon clicking it, we will get the following screen:

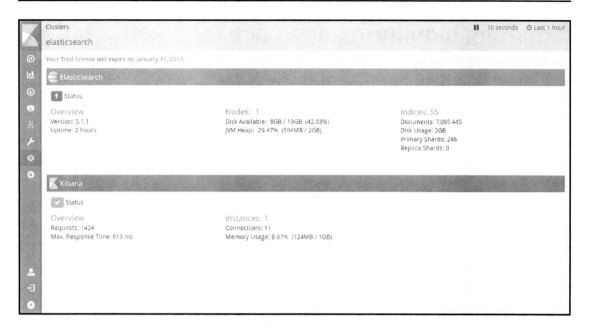

In the preceding screenshot, there are a few observations that we can notice. In the top pane, we can see that, by default, monitoring UI information is updated every 10 seconds and we view the data for 1 hour. Also, we can see the cluster name, which in this case is only one, that is, **elasticsearch**. In the bottom half of the page, we can see two boxes, one for **Elasticsearch** and another for **Kibana**, which provides statistics and information used for monitoring purposes. The Elasticsearch box gives us brief information such as the status of the cluster, version, uptime of the cluster, number of nodes including total disk space available and JVM Heap used percentage and the number of indices present along with other information such as count of documents, total shards and disk space used for storing of documents. Also, we can see the expiry of the X-Pack license used. For trial versions of X-Pack ,we get 30 days of free usage. The Kibana box gives us brief information of the status of Kibana, number of instances of Kibana running, along with other information such as total requests, connections, percentage of memory used, and the max response time.

Let's have a look at the various information available for monitoring of Elasticsearch and Kibana.

Exploring monitoring statistics for Elasticsearch

Upon clicking the Elasticsearch name in the box, we get the following screen:

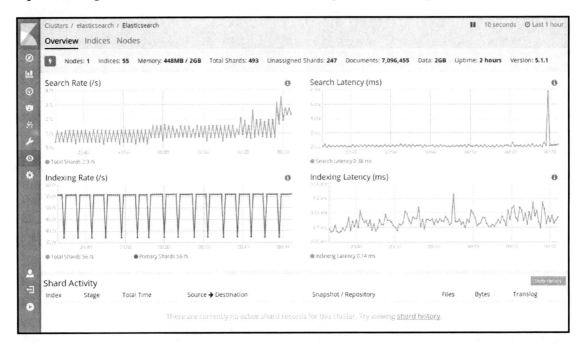

In the preceding screenshot, we can see the UI created in an elegant way, which gives us all the relevant information at once. It contains three tabs, namely **Overview**, **Indices**, and **Nodes**.

Discovering the Overview tab

The **Overview** tab is the default tab when opening the Elasticsearch monitoring module. Beneath the name of the tabs, it gives us important information such as status, number of nodes and indices present, memory used, total number of shards present, total number of unassigned shards, total number of documents present in the indices, the disk space used for storing the documents, uptime, and the version of Elasticsearch. The top pane providing relevant information is common across the **Overview**, **Indices**, and **Nodes** tabs.

Below it, we get some nice charts depicting the search rate per second, search latency in ms, indexing rate per second, indexing latency in ms, and the shard activity. It gives us information for the past hour, which is the default. We can change the settings of viewing the data and auto-refresh of the page. The **Show History** button present in the right-hand side beneath the charts is to show the sharding history.

Discovering the Indices tab

Upon clicking the **Indices** tab, we get the following screen:

Name	Status	Document Count	Data	Index Rate	Search Rate	Unassigned Shards
packetbeat-2016.12.22	⚡	40.8k	10.7 MB	0 /s	0 /s	6
topbeat-2017.01.01	⚠	100k	28.2 MB	0 /s	0 /s	5
topbeat-2016.12.26	⚠	295	295.2 KB	0 /s	0 /s	5
topbeat-2016.12.22	⚠	148.3k	42.3 MB	0 /s	0 /s	5
topbeat-2016.12.21	⚠	568.8k	160.4 MB	0 /s	0 /s	5
topbeat-2016.12.20	⚠	108.6k	30.6 MB	0 /s	0 /s	5
topbeat-2016.12.19	⚠	10.1k	3.4 MB	0 /s	0 /s	5
topbeat-2016.12.18	⚠	496.9k	135.8 MB	0 /s	0 /s	5
school	⚠	274	190.3 KB	0 /s	0 /s	5
sales	⚠	2.4k	1.3 MB	0 /s	0 /s	5
packetbeat-2017.01.01	⚠	20.2k	6.7 MB	0 /s	0 /s	5
packetbeat-2016.12.29	⚠	113.6k	35.8 MB	0 /s	0 /s	5
packetbeat-2016.12.28	⚠	25.2k	8.5 MB	0 /s	0 /s	5
packetbeat-2016.12.26	⚠	577	647.6 KB	0 /s	0 /s	5

Clusters / elasticsearch / Elasticsearch — ‖ 10 seconds ⊘ Last 1 hour

Overview Indices Nodes

Nodes: 1   Indices: 55   Memory: **647MB / 2GB**   Total Shards: **493**   Unassigned Shards: **247**   Documents: **7,098,599**   Data: **2GB**   Uptime: **2 hours**   Version: **5.1.1**

Indices [Filter Indices]   20 of 48   ☐ Show system indices

As we saw in the preceding screenshot, we get information of the various indices stored in the cluster. It gives us information such as **Name** of the indices, total count of documents present in each of the indices, disk space used by storage of documents, index rate per second, search rate per second, and the number of unassigned shards for each index. We can also search for the index or filter the index as per name. We can also tick the Show system indices box to view indices created by the system.

You can even view detailed information for each index by clicking on the index name. You will get statistics, as shown in the following screenshot:

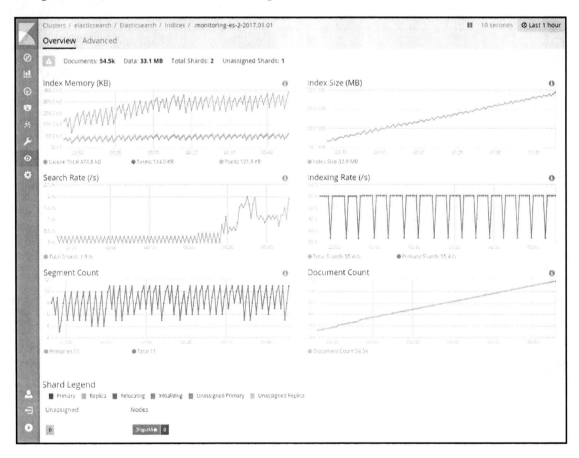

In the preceding image, we can view information in the top pane such as status of the index, total number of documents present in the index, disk space used for storing the documents, total number of shards and unassigned shards. Below it we can view visualizations for Index Memory in KB, Search rate per second, Indexing rate per second, Index size in MB, total count of documents and total count of segments. Also, we can see the name of the nodes and status of the shards between the nodes.

You can get advanced details for the particular index by clicking on the **Advanced** tab. You will get statistics as shown in the following screenshot:

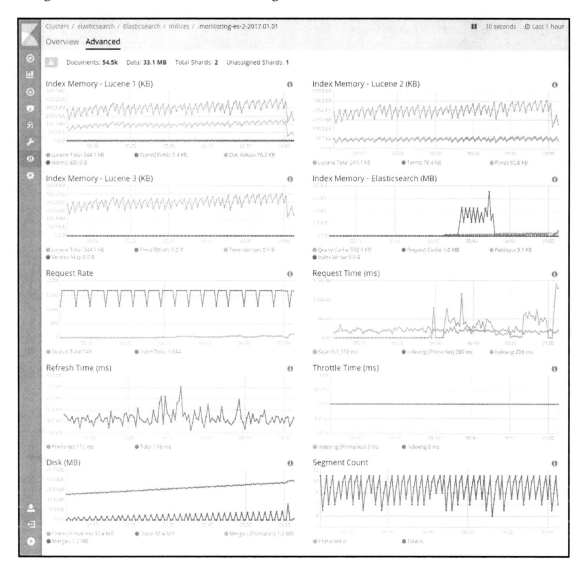

In the preceding image, we can view information in the top pane such as status of the index, total number of documents present in the index, disk space used for storing the documents, total number of shards and unassigned shards. Below it we can view visualizations for Index Memory of Lucene, Index Memory of Elasticsearch in KB, Request Rate, Request Time in milliseconds, Refresh Time in milliseconds, Throttle Time in milliseconds, Disk Usage in MB and total Segment Count.

Discovering the Nodes tab

Upon clicking the **Nodes** tab, we get the following screen:

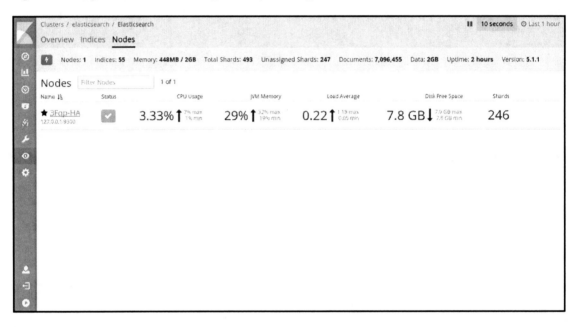

As we can see in the preceding screenshot, we get information of the various nodes present in the cluster. It provides us information such as the name of the nodes, status of the nodes, **CPU Usage** (average, min, and max usage for each node), **JVM Memory** (average, min, and max usage), **Load Average** (average, min, and max usage), **Disk Free Space** (average, min, and max usage), and the total number of assigned Shards for each node.

You can even view detailed information for each node by clicking on the node name. You will get statistics, as shown in the following screenshot:

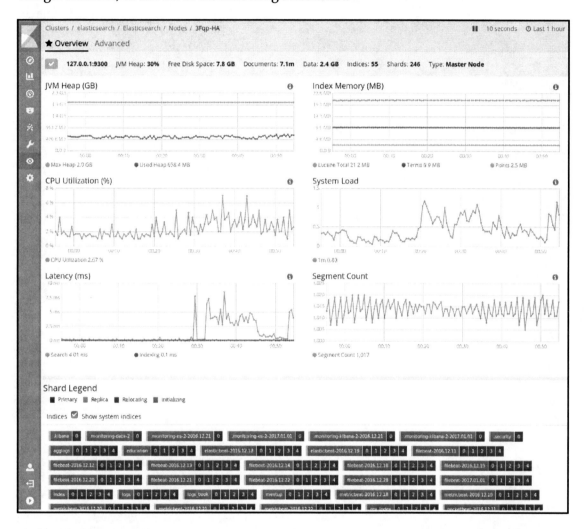

In the preceding image, we can view information in the top pane such as status of the node, host ip address of the node, JVM Heap percentage, free disk space present, total number of documents present, disk space used for storing the documents, total number of indices in the node, total number of shards and type of the node. Below it we can view visualizations for JVM Heap usage in GB, Index Memory in MB, CPU Utilization in percentage, System Load Average, Latency in ms and Segment Count. Also, we can see the name of the indices and status of the shards of the various indices.

You can get advanced details for the particular node by clicking on the Advanced tab. You will get statistics as shown in the following screenshot:

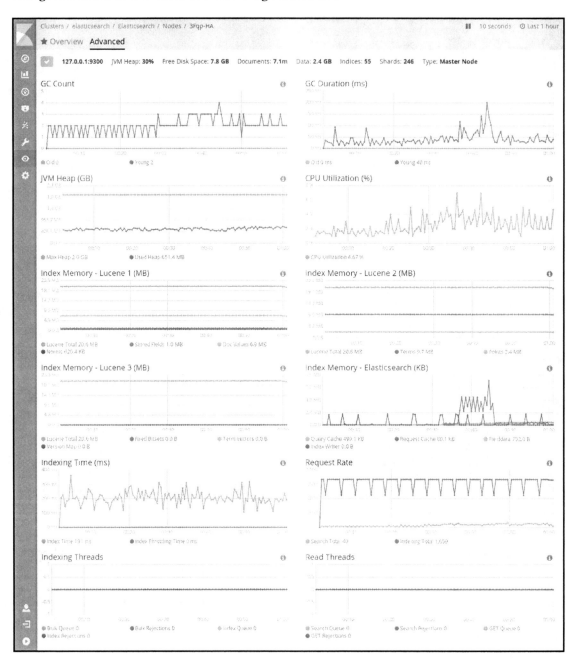

In the preceding image, we can view information in the top pane such as status of the node, host ip address of the node, JVM Heap percentage, free disk space present, total number of documents present, disk space used for storing the documents, total number of indices in the node, total number of shards and type of the node. Below it we can view visualizations for GC Count, GC Duration in milliseconds, JVM Heap Size in GB, CPU Utilization in percentage, Index Memory used by Lucene, Index Memory used by Elasticsearch, Indexing Time in milliseconds, Request rate, Indexing and Read Threads.

Exploring monitoring statistics for Kibana

Upon clicking the Kibana name in the box, we get the following screen:

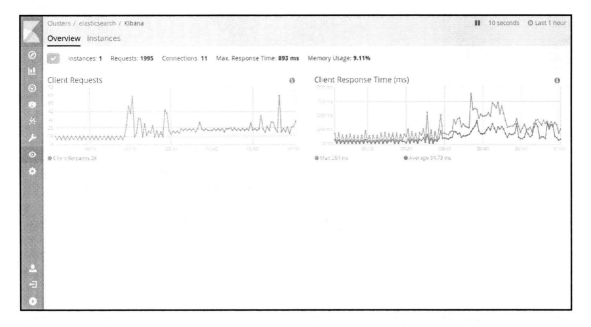

In the preceding image, we can see the UI created in an elegant way which gives us all the relevant information at once. In the top pane it gives us the status of the instance, total number of instances running, total number of requests, total number of connections, maximum response time and memory usage in percentage. Below it we can view few visualizations for monitoring such as Client Requests an Client Response Time (maximum and average) in milliseconds.

You can get advanced details for the Kibana instance by clicking on the Instances Tab. You will get statistics as shown in the following screenshot:

In the preceding image, we can view information in the top pane such as the status of the instance, total number of instances running, total number of requests, total number of connections, maximum response time and memory usage in percentage. Below it we can view the details of the instance such as name of the instance, status of the instance, total memory size used by the instance, Average Load, current number of requests and Response Times (maximum and average).

Understanding Profiler

Profiler is another X-Pack component which has grown out of requirement of understanding how a request performs in Elasticsearch. It provides us with detailed information of how the request has been executed at various stages of the request as sent which can be useful to find why your requests are being served slowly or what causes the requests to return results after a long time.

It is the latest addition to X-Pack and has been introduced in X-Pack version 5.1 itself. It is part of the Dev Tools Page. It utilizes the Profile API which is provided by Elasticsearch. Profile API is used to debug the various information of a request to gather underlying details of how request was served and how result was received. The resulting information of Profile API is a large chunk of JSON which is difficult to understand and make sense of. Therefore, Profiler plays an important part of providing the results of Profile API in form of a visualization which makes it easier to understand the response and debug the behavior of the request. With Profiler, we can understand the underlying information from request to result for both queries and aggregations.

We can have a look at the UI of Profiler by clicking on the Dev Tools tab and subsequently clicking on Profiler tab which is right to Console tab. Upon opening, you will be greeted to the following interface:

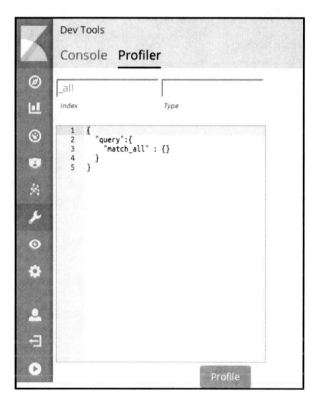

As you can see in the preceding image, you have the options of specifying index name, type name and the query in the request pane. Upon clicking on Profile, the results will be shown in the results pane on the right side. You will see the following interface of results:

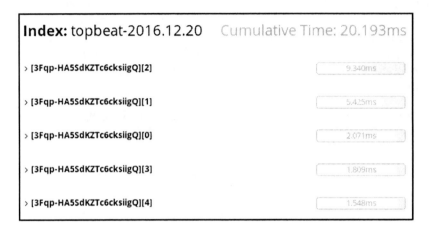

Index: topbeat-2016.12.20   Cumulative Time: 20.193ms

> [3Fqp-HA5SdKZTc6cksiigQ][2]   9.340ms

> [3Fqp-HA5SdKZTc6cksiigQ][1]   5.425ms

> [3Fqp-HA5SdKZTc6cksiigQ][0]   2.071ms

> [3Fqp-HA5SdKZTc6cksiigQ][3]   1.809ms

> [3Fqp-HA5SdKZTc6cksiigQ][4]   1.548ms

Let's try to decode what the results mean:

It shows the name of the indices in which it searched, the shards which were used for searching in each index, and the time taken for query to fetch result.

> Cumulative Time is the sum of individual shard times. It may or may not represent the actual physical time taken for the query to fetch results.

To view more detailed information, you can click on the left of shard name and hover over Type name which will provide more information as shown in the following screenshot:

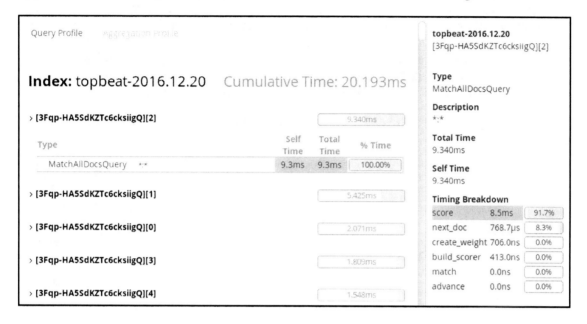

It will show the type of the query used, along with the description and timing breakdown of various low-level requests of Lucene Query.

To know more about components of Timing breakdown you can refer to following link:
```
https://www.elastic.co/guide/en/elasticsearch/reference/5.1/_pro
filing_queries.html#_timing_breakdown
```

Also, you can store the JSON output generated from the response result for further analysis. If you paste the resulting JSON to Profiler request pane, it will interpret as the result of profiler instead of a query and will show the corresponding result as a visualization.

Summary

The Elastic Team kept core components in Elastic Stack and supporting features separately as X-Pack, which is an important asset for any organization. In this chapter, we learned about two of the X-Pack team members: Security and Monitoring. We got to set up X-Pack with Elasticsearch and Kibana. Under security, we learned to manage users, roles, privileges, and so on, while Monitoring helped us to look at different visualizations showcasing the real-time statistics of Elasticsearch and Kibana instances.

In the next chapter, we will cover the rest of the components of X-Pack: alerts, graphs, and reporting.

10
X-Pack: Alerting, Graph, and Reporting

While installing X-Pack, six important components are installed, three of which: Monitoring, Security, and Profiler we have already discussed in the previous chapters. In this chapter, we will explore the rest of the components to know what they offer and see how they help us with our needs.

In this chapter, we will cover the following sections:

- Exploring **Alerting** and **Notification**
- Exploring **Graph**
- Exploring **Reporting**

Alerting and notification

Every organization needs a system that is capable of alerting whenever required. This component of X-Pack provides us with flexibility to create alerts and notifications based on some conditions which get triggered due to change in data. Due to the requirement of having a real-time alert mechanism through which you can trigger some actions based on the conditions specified arises the need for this component named **Watcher**. It grew out of the necessity of creating actions on the go as and when required without requiring changing the configuration across the Stack. If seen closely, we can create such alerts based on conditions by specifying them directly in the Logstash configuration file using appropriate filters and output plugins. But doing so every time to create a new type of alert would require proper testing before making changes in production environment. Instead of making any changes in the existing setup, you can create your own rules on the go to get alerted and notified. You can track and create any type of alert as required.

Having alerts and notifications always helps to capture any error or cases when something is wrong with your system. Some of the cases are which is not limited to this:

- Monitor the logs and if the logs contain any **SEVERE**, **FATAL**, or **ERROR** messages, notify the system administrator via e-mail along with the log message.
- Monitor the infrastructure tracking various parameters such as memory usage, disk usage, and so on over time. Create alerts and open a JIRA ticket to notify it that memory or disk usage is high and that you require more disk or memory.
- Track social media posts/tweets along with specifying keywords and send alerts if the number of posts/tweets exceeds the value specified.
- Create alerts based on the keywords searched by the user in Elasticsearch. In such a way, the user can always be updated.

Watcher in X-Pack is available as and when you install X-Pack. Hence, there is no need to install it separately. However, currently there is no UI available for Watcher to create alerts/notifications and everything is available via the APIs exposed for Watcher.

Watcher, by its name, suggests that it watches everything and based on the events and rules, you can be notified. Using the API, we can create, manage, test, and delete the **watches**. Each created watch provides a single alert, which in fact can trigger multiple notifications to send to multiple systems.

Let us have a look at the basic blocks required in Watcher from a high level:

- **Schedule**: It is used to define the scheduling of the watch on when to trigger the watch.
- **Query**: It is used to specify the query that acts as the starting point, on the basis of which conditions can be specified. Watcher supports Lucene and Elasticsearch Query Language completely so you can specify any type of query.
- **Conditions**: It is used to specify the conditions based on the query. You can use simple conditions or scripting conditions based on the requirement of generating an alert.
- **Actions**: It is used to perform the operations after a condition is met. Actions can include sending a notification to the Slack channel, sending an alert using an e-mail, and so on.

In brief, a scheduler on the right time triggers the query. The query acts as an input to conditions and based on the query, you can specify multiple conditions. Once conditions are specified, you can define what to do via the actions after a condition is satisfied.

A full history of all the watches is stored for reference in a separate Elasticsearch index, which specifies the time a watch was triggered, the query for the watch, whether the condition was met or not, and the actions followed based on the condition.

As Watcher comes with an installation of X-Pack, you can verify using the Watcher API that watcher is enabled or not by using the following command in console:

```
GET _xpack/watcher/stats
```

It gives the following response:

```
{
  "watcher_state": "started",
  "watch_count": 0,
  "execution_thread_pool": {
    "queue_size": 0,
    "max_size": 0
  },
  "manually_stopped": false
}
```

It says Watcher has been started and `watch_count` is zero as no watches have been defined.

Working of watcher

Until now, we have learnt that we can create watches that perform actions as and when conditions are met. The data on which queries are searched and conditions are checked is also referred to as the **Watch Payload**.

So whenever we specify a trigger schedule, it will load the query result into the watch payload. Once data is loaded into the watch payload, we will create a condition over it. As a condition matches, then further watcher events are considered. Also, before performing actions, we can perform different types of *transforms* (optional), which will load all of the resulting data of the query in the watch payload. Transforms can be used to overwrite the watch payload and load data, which can then be sent to actions. Transforms can be used at both watch and actions level.

Now, before learning how Watcher is executed and the various steps that happen when we create a Watcher, let us understand the basic blocks in detail along with the structure of creating Watches.

Trigger

It is mandatory to specify the trigger while creating a watch as it tells when and how often the watch will execute. Whenever we create a watch, a trigger is registered with the trigger engine and the trigger engine evaluates the trigger and runs the watch accordingly. Currently, only time-based schedule triggers are available to use as triggers.

Schedule trigger

It is used to define when the watch execution will start as per the date and time mentioned or how often the watch will be triggered. Watcher supports various types of schedule triggers such as interval, cron expressions, hourly, daily, weekly, monthly, and yearly.

Interval schedule

It is used to trigger the watch at a fixed interval of time. It will trigger the watch at every interval as specified. You can define the interval in seconds, minutes, hours, days, or weeks. By default, the unit is seconds.

Consider the following code as an example:

```
{
  "trigger" : {
    "schedule" : {
      "interval" : "1h"
    }
  }
}
```

The preceding trigger means it will execute the watch every hour once a watch is created. Similarly, we can specify the interval as 10m or 10s to execute the watch every 10 minutes or 10 seconds, respectively. It supports hourly (h), minutes (m), seconds (s), daily (d), and weekly (w).

Cron expressions

It is used to trigger the watch as per the `cron` expression specified. Cron expressions are–`<seconds> <minutes> <hours> <day_of_month> <month> <day_of_week>` `[year]`. Here, `year` is optional and the rest of the fields are mandatory.

There are sets of possible values for each field of the `cron` expression, as shown in the following table:

Fields	Supported Values	Supported Special Characters
seconds	0-59	, – * /
minutes	0-59	, – * /
hours	0-23	, – * /
day_of_month	1-31	, – * ? / L W
month	1-12 or JAN-DEC	, – * /
day_of_week	1-7 or SUN-SAT	, – * ? / L #
year	empty or 1970-2099	, – * /

 For more details on special characters, refer to `https://www.elastic.co` `/guide/en/x-pack/5.1/trigger-schedule.html#schedule-cron-eleme` `nts`.

The following is an explanation of `cron` expressions:

Cron expression	Explanation
0 30 * * * ?	Trigger hourly at every 30th minute of the hour.
0 30 * * * ? 2017	Trigger at every 30th minute of the hour for the year 2017 only.
0 45 1 * * ? 0 30 14 ? * MON	Trigger daily at 1:45 AM. Trigger on every Monday at 2:30 PM, which means weekly.
0 45 17 3 * ?	Trigger on 3rd of every month at 5:45 PM.
0 0 10 27 7 ? *	Trigger every year on 27th July at 10:00 AM.

Consider the following code as an example:

```
{
  "trigger" : {
    "schedule" : {
      "cron" : "0 30 * * * ?"
    }
  }
}
```

As `cron` expressions require some understanding, to simplify it, we have other schedule triggers in which you can easily mention at hourly, daily, weekly, monthly, and yearly level.

Hourly schedule

It is used to trigger the watch hourly at a particular minute. You can specify the minutes using the minute attribute, which may run once in an hour or at mentioned minutes of an hour.

Consider the following code as an example:

```
{
  "trigger" : {
    "schedule" : {
      "hourly" : { "minute" : 45 }
    }
  }
}
```

It will trigger the watch at the 45th minute of every hour:

```
{ ... "hourly" : { "minute" : [10,20,30,40] }}
```

It will trigger the watch at every 10th, 20th, 30th, and 40th minute of each hour.

Daily schedule

It is used to trigger the watch daily at a fixed time or using attributes of at along with the array of hour and minute. If you don't specify any attribute of daily then by default it will run at midnight, that is, 00:00. You can schedule it either once in a day or multiple times in a day.

Consider the following code as an example:

```
{
  "trigger" : {
    "schedule" : {
      "daily" : { "at" : "18:30" }
    }
  }
}
```

It will trigger the watch at 6:30 PM daily:

```
{ ... "daily" : { "at" : ["09:45" , "18:30"] }}
```

It will trigger the watch twice daily at 9:45 AM and 6:30 PM:

```
{ ... "daily" : { "at" :  { "hour"  : [ 0,8,22] ,
"minute" : [10,55] }}}
```

It will trigger the watch at 12:10 AM, 12:55 AM, 8:10 AM, 8:55 AM, 10:10 PM, and 10:55 PM daily.

Weekly schedule

It is used to trigger the watch weekly at a fixed time or using attributes of on and at.

Consider the following code as an example:

```
{
  "trigger" : {
    "schedule" : {
      "weekly" : { "on" : "tuesday" ,  "at" : "18:30" }
    }
  }
}
```

It will trigger the watch at every `tuesday` at 6:30 PM:

```
{ ... "weekly" : [{ "on" : "tuesday" ,  "at" : "noon" },
       { "on" : "thursday" ,  "at" : "18:30" } ] }
```

It will trigger the watch twice weekly, that is, 12:00 PM on `tuesday` and 6:30 PM on `thursday`.

You can also specify an array of values as shown as follows:

```
{ ... "weekly" : { "on" : ["tuesday" ,  "thursday" ],
    "at" : ["noon" , "18:30" ] }}
```

It will trigger the watch on every tuesday and thursday at 12:00 P.M. and 6:30 P.M.

Monthly schedule

It is used to trigger the watch monthly at a fixed time or using attributes of on and at.

Consider the following code as an example:

```
{
  "trigger" : {
    "schedule" : {
      "monthly" : { "on" : "15" ,  "at" : "10:00" }
    }
```

```
      }
  }
```

It will trigger the watch on the 15th of every month at 10:00 A.M.:

```
{ ... "monthly" : [{ "on" : "5" ,  "at" : "midnight" },
    { "on" : "25" ,  "at" : "18:30" } ] }
```

It will trigger the watch twice monthly, that is, on the 5th at 12:00 A.M. and on the 25th at 6:30 P.M.

You can also specify an array of values as shown here:

```
{ ... "monthly" : { "on" : ["5" ,  "25" ],
    "at" : ["midnight" , "18:30" ] }}
```

It will trigger the watch on 5th and 25th of every month at 12:00 A.M. and 6:30 P.M.

Input

It is the next basic block in the workings of Watcher, which is used to load the input data into the watch payload for execution. The data loaded can be in multiple different formats, such as using a query or loading static data into watch payload, and so on.

Watcher supports the following inputs.

Simple input

It is used to load the static data into the watch payload for execution. It enables you to store the static value that becomes the input for further execution process. You can define the static value as numeric value, string, or object.

Consider the following code as an example:

```
"input" : {
"simple" : {
"book" : "Mastering Elastic Stack",
"year" : 2017,
"author_names" : {
  "author1" : "Yuvraj",
  "author2" : "Ravi",
        }
    }
}
```

Search input

It is used to load the result of the Elasticsearch search query into the watch payload for execution of Watcher. In this type of input, you specify a request object that requires the name of indices to search for, type of the indices (if any), and the search request body. The search input supports Elasticsearch Query Language completely.

Consider the following code as an example:

```
"input" : {
    "search" : {
        "request" : {
            "indices" : [ "logstash-*" ],
            "types" : [ "records" ],
            "body" : {
            "query" : { "match_all" : {}}
            }
        }
    }
}
```

In this example, we have specified the search input that contains attributes such as `request.indices`, which is used to specify the indices to search in; `request.types`, which is used to specify the type to search in, and `request.body`, which contains the query to search for data.

There are a few other attributes, as shown in the following list:

- `request.search_type`: Used to specify the type of the search to execute. Default value is `query_then_fetch`.
- `request.template`: Used to specify the body of the search template, which can contain static values or dynamic values for the data.
- `extract`: Used to extract specific fields from the result of the search request and load it as payload. If the search query provides a large response, then you can use the extract to select the required fields.
- `timeout`: Used to specify the timeout for no response by the search query. By default, it is set to 30 seconds.
- `request.indices_options.expand_wildcards`: Used to expand the wildcards occurring in the indices name by the values of all, none, open, or closed.
- `request.indices_options.ignore_unavailable`: Used to specify whether to ignore the indices that are not present. Uses value of true or false.

- `request.indices_options.allow_no_indices`: Used to specify whether to allow a search when indices are not found. Uses value of true or false

Search input is the most common form of input in Watcher, which is then used to define conditions, transforms, or actions. To understand how to use the results from the search query for further evaluation, we will have a look at the various ways to access the search results.

How to access search results

It is important to know how to access search results that can then be used to process the watch payload for further execution steps such as conditions, transform, or actions:

- Load all the search results by specifying `ctx.payload.hits`.
- Load only the total number of search results using `ctx.payload.hits.total`.
- Load the values of a particular search result using a zero-based array index. To access the value of the fourth hit, use `ctx.payload.hits.hits.3`.
- Load the value of a particular field from any of the search results by using `ctx.payload.hits.hits.<index>.fields.<fieldname>`, where you can specify the index of a zero-based array and specify the fieldname to extract the field value.

HTTP input

It is used to load the results of the request sent to an endpoint configured to search with an HTTP end-point, which will store the results in the watch execution. You can use HTTP input to interact with any web service that listens using HTTP, such as querying a third-party service, querying external Elasticsearch clusters, or querying Elasticsearch APIs.

Consider the following code as an example:

```
"input" : {
  "http" : {
    "request" : {
      "host" : "localhost ",
      "port" : 9200,
      "path" : "/_search",
      "body" :  "{\"query\" :  {  \"match\" : { \"loglevel\" :
\"error\"}}}"
    }
  }
}
```

An example to call the Elasticsearch API is shown in the following code:

```
"input" : {
  "http" : {
    "request" : {
      "host" : "localhost ",
      "port" : "9200",
      "path" : "/_nodes/stats",
      "params" : {
        "human" : "true"
      }
    }
  }
}
```

`params` will return the values in a human-readable format.

To understand how to use the results from the HTTP response for further evaluation, we will have a look at the various ways to access the search results.

How to access HTTP response results

It is important to know how to access HTTP response results, which can then be used to process the watch payload for further execution steps such as conditions, transform, or actions. If the response of HTTP is in either JSON or YAML format then the response is loaded into the watch payload, or else it is loaded in the `_value` field within the watch payload:

- Load all the message data by specifying `ctx.payload.message`
- Load all the headers from the response by using `ctx.payload._headers`
- Load all the HTTP status code by specifying `ctx.payload._status_code`

Chain input

It is used to load the data or results from multiple sources or by combining multiple types of input such as simple, search, or HTTP. This input is processed in the order it is specified. You can use the values obtained from one input into another input seamlessly, which can then be used by any of the blocks of the Watcher for execution. In this, the output by the first input can be used by the second input, and so on.

Consider the following code as an example:

```
"input" : {
  "chain" : {
    "inputs" : [
```

```
{
  "first" : {
    "simple" : { "field" : "loglevel" }
  }
},
{
  "second" : {
    "search" : {
      "request" : {
        "indices" : [ "logstash"] ,
        "body":   "{\"query\": { \"match\":
                  { \"{{ctx.payload.first.field}}\":\"error\"}}}"


      }
    }
  }
}
]
}
}
```

Conditions

It is an important block to understand how Watcher works. After loading of data into the watch payload, conditions help you to determine what you want to capture to send alerts or notifications for. Based on the conditions, actions will be triggered.

Watcher supports the following conditions.

Always condition

It is used to set the watch condition to true always, that is, the watch actions will always be executed until and unless you are using time-based throttling to restrict the execution of actions. If you don't specify any condition, by default it is always condition. There are no attributes to be specified with the always condition.

Consider the following code as an example:

```
"condition" : {
  "always" : {}
}
```

Never condition

It is used to set the watch condition to false always that is, the watch actions will never be executed whenever actions are triggered. This condition is mostly used to test the watches whether it is working as required and it stores its entry to the watch history. There are no attributes to be specified with the always condition.

Consider the following code as an example:

```
"condition" : {
  "never" : {}
}
```

Compare condition

It is used to perform basic comparisons against the results obtained from the input. It is used to compare the condition along with the result received by input as present in the watch payload.

Supported comparison operators are as follows:

- eq: If the result value matches with the given value, it returns true (valid on numeric, string, list, object, and values)
- not_eq: If the result value does not match with the given value, it returns true (valid on numeric, string, list, object, and values)
- gt: If the result value is greater than the given value, it returns true (valid on numeric and string)
- gte: If the result value is greater than or equal to the given value, it returns true (valid on numeric and string)
- lt: If the result value is less than the given value, it returns true (valid on numeric and string)
- lte: If the result value is greater than or equal to the given value, it returns true (valid on numeric and string)

Consider the following code as an example:

```
{
  "condition" : {
    "compare" : {
      "ctx.payload.hits.total" : {
        "lt" : 10
      }
    }
  }
}
```

```
}
```

In the preceding example, we are comparing the result of a field that has been loaded into the watch payload. We are specifying the condition in the result loaded, finding the total count of records stored in the payload, and evaluating whether the count is less than 10. If it is less than or equal to 10, then the condition will become true and actions will be triggered.

Also, we can use date-math expressions and even compare values of two fields.

An example of a date-math expression is as follows:

```
{
  "condition" : {
    "compare" : {
      "ctx.payload.hits.hits.2.fields.datetime" : {
        "gte" : "<{now-1h}>"
      }
    }
  }
}
```

In the preceding example, we are comparing the result of a field that has been loaded into the watch payload. We are specifying the condition in the result loaded, finding the third record, and checking the value of the field (datetime) having occurred in the past hour.

Array compare condition

It is used to perform basic comparisons in an array of values from the results obtained from the input. The basic structure of array compare comprises of an array, path to the field (optional), comparison operator, and the value to compare with.

Consider the following code as an example:

```
{
  "condition": {
    "array_compare": {
      "ctx.payload.aggregations.twitter.buckets" : {
        "path": "doc_count",
        "gte": {
          "value": 1000 ,
        }
      }
    }
  }
}
```

In the preceding example, we have specified the array and also mentioned a path, that is, evaluate that any bucket present has a document count of more than 1,000, then the condition is set to true.

Script condition

It is used to validate the watch condition based on the script that tells us whether to execute the action or not. You can use the scripting languages as supported in Elasticsearch. By default, the scripting language is **Groovy**.

> To use Groovy as a scripting language, you need to enable dynamic scripting in `elasticsearch.yml`. To enable Groovy only watches, set the following property:
>
> `script.engine.groovy.inline.xpack_watch: true`
>
> Also, with the introduction of Elastic Stack, a new basic scripting language has been developed named **Painless** scripting, which will eliminate the need to enable dynamic scripting.

An example of the script condition is as follows:

```
"condition" : {
  "script" : "return false"
}
```

It is a simple condition that will always return `false`.

There are a few attributes associated with the script condition:

- **Script type**: Specifies which type of script to use (supported scripts: inline, file, and stored)
- **Scripting language**: Specifies which scripting language to use (supported languages: Groovy, JavaScript, Python, Painless, Expression, Mustache, and Java)
- **Parameter values**: Specifies the parameters, if any

Inline scripts

In this type of script, you define the script directly within the condition itself.

Consider the following code as an example:

```
"condition" : {
    "script" : {
```

```
            "inline" : "return ctx.payload.hits.total > threshold",
            "lang" : "painless",
            "params" : {
              "threshold" : 5
            }
        }
    }
}
```

In the preceding example, we use the script condition to check whether the total result count is more than the threshold parameter as defined.

File scripts

In this type of script, you define the script that is present in the file. The script should be present in the $ES_HOME/config/scripts directory.

Consider the following code as an example:

```
"condition" : {
    "script" : {
        "file" : "watcher_script",
        "lang" : "python",
    }
}
```

In the preceding example, it will refer to the watcher_script.py (watcher_script is the name of the file and the .py extension comes from language specified as Python in this case) file to check for conditions.

Stored scripts

In this type of script, it refers to the scripts that have been stored in Elasticsearch. Consider the following code as an example:

```
"condition" : {
    "script" : {
        "id" : "test_script ",
    }
}
```

Earlier in this chapter, we have seen how to access the search/HTTP results. In the Watcher context, we can access a few more variables, as shown in the following list:

- ctx.watch_id: Access the id of the watch that is being executed
- ctx.execution_time: The execution time when the watch started
- ctx.trigger.triggered_time: The time at which the watch triggered

- `ctx.trigger.scheduled_time`: The scheduled time when the watch was expected to trigger
- `ctx.metadata.*`: Access the metadata records if associated
- `ctx.payload.*`: Access the payload data loaded by the watch

Transforms

It is an optional block that can be defined while creating a watch. Its purpose is to update the data loaded by the watch payload before actions are triggered. After triggering of a watch that uses Input and Conditions to load data into the watch payload, before triggering of actions we can use transform, to change the data present in the watch payload upon which actions will take place. As transforms are optional, if we do not define them, the data loaded into the watch payload will be used by actions. Transforms can be defined as a top-level field or within the actions. If the transform you want to use will be using the same payload, then use transform as a top-level field. If the transform requires different payload results, then use transform within the action definition.

Watcher supports the following transforms.

Search transform

In this transform, it will execute the search query and the result of the search query will replace the data in the current watch payload. Its usage is the same as search input along with same attributes.

Consider the following code as an example:

```
"transform" : {
  "search" : {
    "request" : {
      "indices" : [ "logstash-*" ],
      "types" : [ "records" ],
      "body" : {
        "query" : { "match_all" : {}}
      }
    }
  }
}
```

Script transform

In this transform, it will execute the script and will replace the data in the current watch payload by the results of the script. Its usage is the same as script input along with the same attributes.

Consider the following code as an example:

```
{
  "transform" : {
    "script" : "return [ time : ctx.watch_id ]"
  }
}
```

Chain transform

In this transform, it will execute the transforms in the order they have been mentioned and will replace the data in the current watch payload by the results of the transforms applied. It is used to build complex transforms involving search and script transform together. Its usage is the same as chain input along with the same attributes.

Consider the following code as an example:

```
"transform" : {
"chain" : [
{
  "search" : {
    "request" : {
      "body" : { "query" : { "match_all" : {} }}
    }
  }
},
{
    "script" : "return [ doc_count: ctx.payload.hits.total ]"
  }
]
}
```

Actions

It is an important block and the last block that is defined while creating a watch. It is used to perform operations on the data, such as logging the data, storing the data in an index, and sending alerts and notifications to e-mail, hipchat, or slack. Actions execute only when watch conditions are met. A single watch can contain multiple actions that may even contain transforms. All the actions are executed one by one in the order in which they are specified and if there is any failure in execution of action, then the information is stored in the watch history. Actions is not a mandatory block to be specified.

In Actions, there is the concept of throttling. Let's understand the usage of throttling.

Throttling

Throttling is used to restrict the execution of multiple actions for a watch. To understand it simply, let us assume we have created a watch that finds the count of the word *watcher* in the tweets obtained. The watch is triggered every two minutes and searches for the word watcher in the last 30 minutes. When a watch triggers and it finds the occurrence of the word watcher, then every two minutes, it will send the same alert again and again as the condition is true, which will trigger the same action multiple times.

To address such issues, Watcher supports throttling: time-based throttling and acknowledgement-based throttling.

Time-based throttling

In this type of throttling, you can define the throttling period within the action, which will then always check whether the action has been executed in the throttling period (current time: throttling period) or not. If the action would have been executed, it will not execute the action or else it will execute the action. So instead of sending alerts whenever Watcher runs in two minutes, it will send an alert every 15 minutes using throttling. It can be defined using the `throttle_period` keyword within the actions definition. You can set a different throttle period for different actions.

Also, `throttle_period` can be defined at the watch level, which will ensure that the actions are executed as per throttle period. In this case, there would be a single `throttle_period` for different actions. You will not be able to set different throttle times for different actions.

If `throttle_period` is not defined, by default it is five seconds. You can change the `throttle_period` default by adding the following property in `elasticsearch.yml`:
`xpack.watcher.execution.default_throttle_period: 5m`

Acknowledgement-based throttling

In this type of throttling, we restrict the execution of an action multiple times by the conditions specified. If the condition has been evaluated as true once, then it will always execute the actions whenever the watch runs or as per `throttle_period`. To restrict such behavior, acknowledgement throttling comes into place, which will trigger the actions once when the condition is first set to true and if the condition remains true thereafter, it will not trigger the actions. It will then again start triggering the actions when the conditions evaluate to false again. When an action of a watch is acknowledged, its state changes to acked state and when the condition evaluates to false then its state changes to `awaits_successful_execution`.

To acknowledge a watch, the Ack Watch API is used. Using the API, we can acknowledge the action as follows:

```
POST _xpack/watcher/watch/<id>/_ack/
```

Here, `<id>` is the watch id and it will acknowledge all the actions.

To acknowledge a specific action, use the following command:

```
POST _xpack/watcher/watch/<id>/_ack/<action_ids>
```

Watcher supports the following actions:

- **E-mail**: It is used to send alerts or notifications via e-mail. It can contain plain text or HTML formatted text. You can also send attachments with the e-mail. Watcher can send an e-mail to any of the SMTP e-mail services. It requires configuration of e-mails in the `elasticsearch.yml file`.
- **HipChat**: It is used to send alerts or notifications to HipChat users or rooms. It requires configuration of HipChat accounts in the `elasticsearch.yml` file for sending messages using HipChat.

- **Index**: It is used to index the data in a new index in Elasticsearch. You can also define the type name of the index in which to store alerts. While using transform in Index, there is a key support for the _doc payload field, using which, whenever a _doc field exists, it will check whether it contains an object or array of objects. If it contains an object, it will index as a single document and if an array of objects is present, each object will be considered as a document.
- **JIRA**: It is used to create issues in JIRA directly from actions. It requires configuration of JIRA accounts in the elasticsearch.yml file for creating JIRA issues.
- **Logging**: It is used to log the data into the Elasticsearch logs. It is mostly used for debugging purposes or adding alerts into the logs so that it can be easily known.
- **PagerDuty**: It is used for creating events in PagerDuty for proper incident resolution. It requires configuration of PagerDuty accounts in the elasticsearch.yml file for creating PagerDuty events.
- **Slack**: It is used to send alerts or notifications to Slack users or team channels. It requires configuration of Slack accounts in the elasticsearch.yml file for sending messages using Slack.
- **Webhook**: It is used to send alerts or notifications to any web services. It supports connection for both HTTP and HTTPS. It includes support for defining usernames and passwords in the elasticsearch.yml file. As usernames and passwords will be stored in the .watches index in plain text, you can enable X-Pack security and then Watcher will encrypt the password and store. You can also use PKI-based authentication for authenticating with services.

Let's check out few of the actions using examples. An example of Index Action is shown in following code:

```
"actions" : {
"index_payload" : {
"transform": { ... },
"index" : {
"index" : "watcher",
"doc_type" : "watches",
"execution_time_field " : "watch_executed_time",
"timeout" : "30s"
            }
        }
    }
```

In the preceding example, `index_payload` is the `id` for the action and transform is optional. Within index action, we define the index name as watcher and document type name as watches, within which it will store data. `index` and `doc_type` fields are mandatory to specify. We have two optional fields, that is, `execution_time_field` which is used to specify the field within which watch stores the execution time and timeout is used to specify the interval for which the API call fails if a response is not received within the timeout interval. By default, the timeout value is 60 seconds.

This is an example of a Logging Action:

```
"actions" : {
"log" : {
"transform" : { ... },
"logging" :{
"text" : "triggered at {{ ctx.trigger.triggered_time}}",
"level" : "info"
            }
       }
  }
```

In the preceding example, log is the id for the action and transform is optional. Within the logging action, we define the text to be logged into Elasticsearch. The text field is mandatory to specify. We have two optional fields, that is, category, which is used to specify the category under which text will be logged, and level, which is used to specify the logging level at which the text will be printed in the log. Possible values for log level are error, warn, info, debug, and trace.

To understand a complete example of Watcher, you can refer to *Getting Notified* section present in `Chapter 12`, *Case Study-Meetup*.

Graph

Graph is another addition to X-Pack, which was earlier available as a standalone component and was also earlier named Graph. It is just adding the complete Graph application into X-Pack without the need to install it separately. It is a very powerful tool aimed at discovering how your terms are interrelated. It provides a simple yet elegant way to uncover the relations between indexed terms and how meaningful they are.

It can help you in a wide range of applications such as recommendation engines, discovering insights for multiple fields and how are they related, showing how you are connected to your friends on social networks, website analysis including vulnerabilities tracking, most used pages, recommending which section of the page a user will click after going on a page, and so on.

Graph can be used from two sources, that is, using the Graph Exploration API from Elasticsearch perspective or by using the interactive Graph visualization tool bundled into Kibana. The biggest advantage of Graph is to just install it and, without making any changes to your Elasticsearch indices, it directly gives you the ability to discover connections without storing any additional data. How it does this, we will look at in the next section.

Working of Graph

Graphs are born directly out of the graph theory, which creates a link type structure to show relations between multiple objects. Graph can be considered as a big network of objects on which relations are discovered. In graph theory, we have nodes and edges. In our context, we have vertices and connections. Vertices are the terms present in our index, which shows the relations among multiple terms. Connections show the relation between two vertices, how they are connected, and it summarizes the information of documents present in both of the vertices.

In Elasticsearch, Graph works out of the box as vertices are referred to the terms present in the indices and the connections are created on the go using the powerful Elasticsearch Aggregations. Also, using the scoring of Elasticsearch, it finds out the connections and their relevance. Graph helps you to get solutions to difficult problems that arise and require multiple connections to derive the solution. As Graph uses the Elasticsearch aggregations framework, it has the ability to quickly summarize millions of documents. It derives the relations and connections between the terms using the document count. Graph uses multi-valued fields or multiple single valued, fields on which it creates connections.

In a simple scenario wherein we have two vertices (terms) and a connection between them, upon clicking the connection, we will get to know the number of documents in which `term1` appeared, `term2` appeared, and documents that contained both `term1` and `term2` together. Such summarization is used to create relations among multiple vertices.

We will have a look at the Graph UI bundled into Kibana as an X-Pack component.

Graph UI

To view the Graph UI, we will use the **Graph** tab option present in the left-hand side pane of Kibana. Upon clicking it, we will get the following screen:

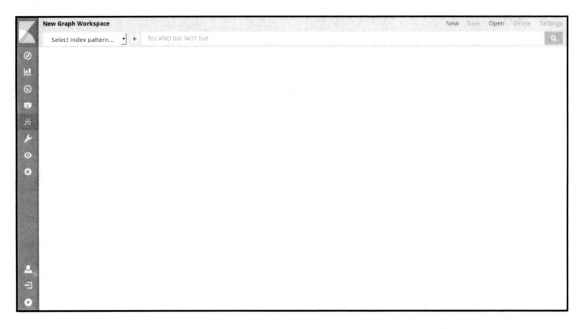

In the preceding screenshot, we can see the simplicity of the page wherein we have a drop-down having options, a field add button with a search bar, and options/settings present in the toolbar. Seeing the page for the first time makes you feel it's easy to use it and yes, you are pretty much right. The dropdown is for selecting the index name or index pattern. The next plus (+) symbol is for selecting the field for which you want to derive connections. The search bar is for entering the terms. The toolbar contains multiple actions such as new, save, open, delete, and settings mode respectively in this order.

Let us dig into the Graph UI using an example to understand it clearly. We have created an index containing dummy data for e-commerce orders that contain multiple fields. We want to find out which payment type is mostly used by which countries, cities, and the relations between the names of people connected with such networks.

To load the sample data, use the following command:

```
bin/logstash -f sales.conf
```

The `sales.conf` file contains two additional parameters in the Elasticsearch output, that is, user and password, which are used to connect to the Elasticsearch cluster. You can also additionally create a user and roles for sending data using Logstash. A Logstash specific role will require manage_index_templates and monitor cluster privileges and write, delete, and create_index privileges for Logstash indices. By default, you can use elastic user.

> You can find the configuration file on GitHub at :- `https://github.com/k ravigupta/mastering-elastic-stack-code-files/tree/5.1.1/Chapte r10`

After loading data into Elasticsearch, navigate to the **Management** tab in the Kibana UI followed by clicking on **Index Patterns** and adding the index name as `sales_data` and selecting `@timestamp` as the time field.

> The data has been sourced from a publicly available dataset, which you can find
> at `https://support.spatialkey.com/spatialkey-sample-csv-data/`.

Upon specifying the index name as `sales_data`, clicking on the plus (**+**) symbol to mention the field name as `payment_type.keyword`, and searching for Visa, we get the following result:

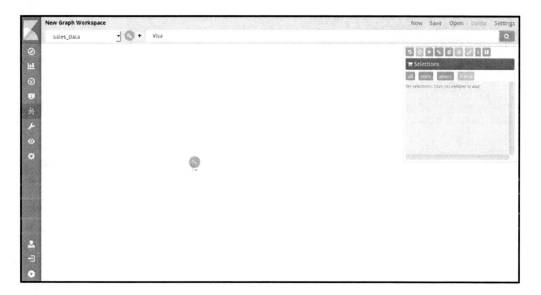

In the preceding screenshot, we can see that we have not deduced any meaningful information because we are using a single field and searching for a value that does not show any relationship between multiple fields or values. To see the relations, we will select multiple fields one by one along with `payment_type.keyword` such as `country.keyword`, `city.keyword`, and `name.keyword`. Upon selecting a field, we get a few options, such as color, icon of the field, and maximum number of terms per hop, that is, maximum number of terms that will be returned for each search field.

In the search bar, we will mention Visa as we want to see the relationship between people who use Visa to pay money and the countries and cities they are situated in. Upon clicking **Search**, we will get the following graph:

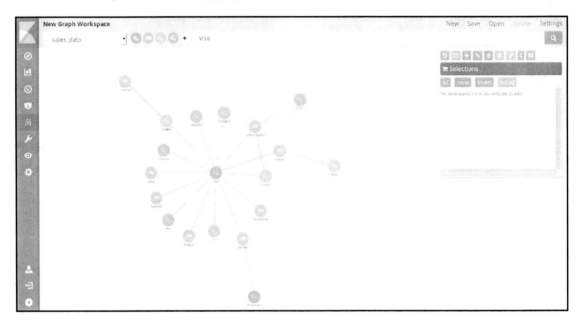

In the preceding screenshot, we can see various connections. The stronger the connection between the two vertices, the darker its connecting lines, as in **Calgary** to **Canada**. We can click on any of the connecting lines to understand how the two vertices relate to each other.

For example, by clicking on the connecting line between **Calgary** and **Canada,** we observe that there are 76 documents containing the term **Canada,** 11 documents containing the term **Calgary**, and 11 documents that contain both the terms **Canada** and **Calgary**. It depicts the relation, as shown in the following screenshot:

Before moving forward, let's understand the **Selections** dialog box in detail. The selections box is shown in the following screenshot:

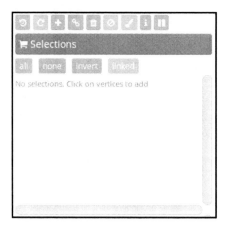

The **Selections** dialog box contains two sets of options, that is, settings and selections.

Settings provide multiple options for specifying the selection-related settings such as undo, redo, expand selection, Add links between existing terms, remove vertices from workspace, blacklist selection from return to workspace, Custom style selected vertices, drill down, and pause layout in the order from left to right.

Remove vertices from workspace removes any vertices appearing in the workspace that we do not require. Simply select the vertices that are not required and click on the delete (looks like a trash/recycle bin) symbol.

We can also blacklist the selection so that the vertices do not appear back into the workspace even after changing the search keyword or in any form. To do so, select the vertices and click on the blocking (looks like action blocking) symbol.

Custom styles selected vertices are used to change the color of the vertices circle.

Drill down is used to view the Raw documents behind the visualization as shown.

 If using the sample data of sales_data, make sure your time filter is set to **Last 10 years** or equivalent which must include the year 2009.

Selections provides four options, namely **all, none, invert,** or **linked**. All is used for selecting all the terms, none is for selecting zero terms, invert is to select all the terms that are not currently selected, and linked is to select only those terms that are linked to each other through connections.

Upon clicking on any term, the term appears in the **Selection** box. By clicking on **United Kingdom**, we have an option of changing the display name of **United Kingdom**. Let's rename it as UK. It changes the display name in the graph as well.

In the graph, we also want to see the relations related to Mastercard in the same way we are seeing for Visa. To do so, simply select the **Mastercard vertices** and click on the expand selection symbol, which will expand the solution and will show the following graph:

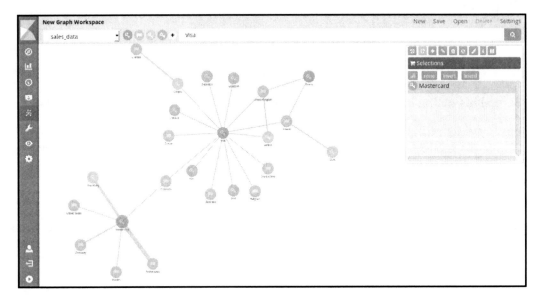

As we have specified the max terms per hop as 5, upon selecting Mastercard we got five results.

In the graph toolbar, we have a few options, such as Create a New Workspace, Save a workspace, Open a saved workspace, Delete the currently saved workspace, and the Settings option.

In the Settings option, we have four sub-options to view the settings for, that is, Last Request, Blacklist, Advanced Settings, and Drill-downs. Whenever we click on the Settings option, by default Advanced settings will open, wherein the following settings are provided:

In the **Last request** option, we get to see the last request sent to Elasticsearch for which we got relations.

In the **Blacklist** option, we see the terms that have been blacklisted from reappearing in the current Graph workspace.

In the **Drill-downs** option, we can specify the source along with the URL from where to fetch the raw documents that are shown when clicking on the drill-down option. We can also specify or change the title and toolbar icon for drill-downs.

Reporting

Reporting is the last yet important addition to the Kibana. It brings the most popular request of generating reports containing the dashboards, visualizations, and searches that can be used for external purposes or adding the reports in presentations, and so on. Reporting brings the awaited feature by using PhantomJS to create reports from the images and stitching it properly in the form of a PDF.

To generate a report, we have the **Reporting** option present in the toolbar within the **Discover**, **Visualize**, and **Dashboard** pages. We can click on the **Reporting** option and click on the **Generate Printable PDF** button or click on **Generation URL**.

We will not see how to create visualizations/dashboards and save them. Instead we will see how to generate a report and see the reports. Let us save the dashboard and then click on **Reporting**, followed by clicking on **Generate Printable PDF**. Upon clicking, it displays the message as follows:

Reporting: Dashboard generation has been queued. You can track its progress under Management.

To download/view the report, follow these steps:

1. Click on the **Management** page.
2. Select **Reporting** under Kibana Section.
3. You will see the **Generated Reports** by the name of the document, when it was added, its status, and the download button option.
4. You will view the downloaded report as follows:

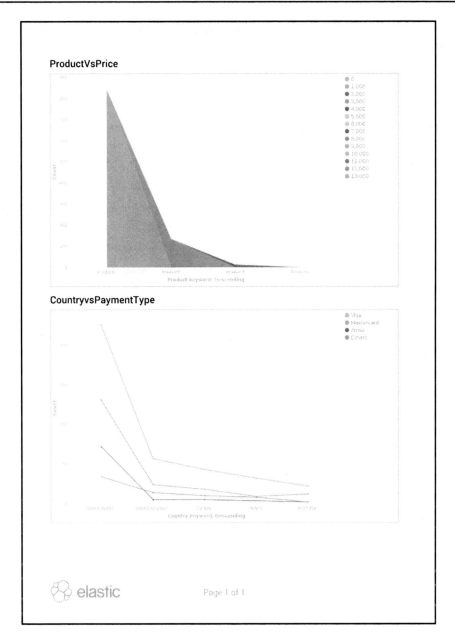

Reports can be generated only for the saved objects.

Instead of generating reports from the UI, you can also use the APIs exposed for generating reports from Kibana in the following way:

- **Saved Searches Report:** `/api/reporting/generate/search/<saved-search-id>`
- **Saved Visualizations:**
  `Report:/api/reporting/generate/visualization/<saved-visualization-id>`
- **Saved Dashboards Report:** `/api/reporting/generate/dashboard/<saved-dashboard-id>`

 For generating using APIs, you need to send the `POST` request and not the `GET` request.

You can also specify the time period using the `_g` parameter.

 If you are unsure of what should be your time period, then simply copy the `_g` parameter from the saved search, visualization, and dashboard URL.

You can automatically generate a report of Dashboard using API, using the following curl request:-

```
curl -XPOST
http://localhost:5601/api/reporting/generate/dashboard/SampleDashboard --
user elastic:changeme -H "kbn-version:5.1.1"
```

Where `SampleDashboard` is saved dashboard id, user is used to provide the username and password for the security settings and `-H` parameter is required to send the header mentioning the version of Kibana which in our case is currently 5.1.1

To download the report you still need to follow the above mentioned steps.

 For report generation some users may need to install additional dependencies in Ubuntu. If report generation fails with the error "Phantom immediately exited with: 127" you will need to install `libfontconfig` and `libfreetype6`: `sudo apt-get install libfontconfig sudo apt-get install libfreetype6`

Summary

X-Pack is a must have tool when you need to set up Elastic Stack components in your organization. It helps you with all of the essential and critical requirements, whether it is user management, roles and permissions, alerts of some event, generating reports, analyzing data using graphs, or monitoring of the nodes and indices. These two chapters conclude the new offering of X-Pack and its components.

In the next chapter, we will learn about the best practices and standards to keep in mind and to follow when it comes to production environments.

11
Best Practices

In the previous chapter, we discussed the various components provided by X-Pack as part of Elastic Stack. We explored each of the components in detail covering what the component offers and the various functionalities provided by the component.

If you have been following the chapters, then you probably have a lot of questions in your mind on how should I start or proceed to create a scalable system, and what should be the best practices that should be adhered upon for creating an efficient system.

At the end of this chapter, you will understand some of the best practices that can be used in Elastic Stack, to make it production-ready after learning from other people's experiences.

In this chapter, we will cover the following topics:

- Why do we require best practices?
- Understanding your use case
- Choosing the right set of hardware
- Searching and indexing performance
- Sizing the Elasticsearch cluster
- Logstash configuration files
- Re-indexing data

Why do we require best practices?

When we start to learn a tool, we always try to use the tool on a standalone machine from which we gain expertise and can experiment various things. As and when we take the small setup to a big setup ranging multiple systems, there can be a lot of things that can hinder the performance or could not provide the optimum results that we get on a small setup. In order to achieve the best results, we require understanding and following some of the practices that have been followed by others leading to a higher performance and less troubles. In terms of programming languages, we have the concept of *best coding practices*, which describes how to write a code that is easy to understand, maintain, and read, which reduces the effort if someone else starts working on the same or similar piece of code. But in tools or components there is no hard and fast rule of best practices. Best practices will depend on various factors such as the architecture designed, components used, underlying hardware, and so on, and it also depends on the use cases that one is trying to solve.

Best practices become necessary to follow in order to create a highly scalable analysis system that can be easily scaled and maintained, and using best practices we can handle the common bottlenecks that we face. There are no concrete points that you should follow blindly; however, it provides a good reference to initially start with understanding based on the experiences of a lot of people. It helps you to know which areas you should focus on or the parameters required while fine-tuning your platform.

In Elastic Stack we have four basic components:

- **Beats**: Agents to ship data
- **Logstash**: Processing data
- **Elasticsearch**: Storing data
- **Kibana**: UI for visualizing data

Out of these four, Elasticsearch requires a deep understanding to come up with the best practices, as it's the main component that is used to store data and acts as the data source for visualizing data. If Elasticsearch goes down, it will affect the complete setup. Kibana being a web-based UI requires minimal resources to run. Logstash is used to capture and process data that requires a lot of flexibility to process efficiently. Beats are lightweight tools for capturing data and sending it to either Elasticsearch or Logstash.

Understanding your use case

This is the basic level of information that everyone should know before even thinking about the best practices or using Elastic Stack. If you learn about Elastic Stack and without thinking about your use case, you start to connect or process random data, then you will not be able to deduce proper information as required. You will always remain stranded when asked why you chose this or why not another software or tool. Hence, it becomes immensely important to understand your use case beforehand.

Your use-case primarily answers a lot of questions regarding the components to be used, the criticality of logging data flowing in, requirement of high availability clusters, and a need for centralized logging system. If your use-case comprises of analyzing the logs of an application, then you can make a decision accordingly about whether you need a single elasticsearch cluster, or if you need to create a centralized logging system.

One of the biggest questions that arises when we start to understand our use case, is what should be the architecture of my system? How should I design the architecture or what tools/components should be a part of it? Quite often we spend a lot of time on figuring out whether we should use Logstash or Beats. It's a common thing that people face as using Beats will add another layer of complexity, and it requires additional knowledge to develop/debug, whereas using Logstash requires lot of memory as it uses JVM, which is resource intensive. It brings the trade-off that one supposedly needs to take in order to understand how the system will be designed and specifically more in the case when you already have systems putting out logs; and you need to use Elastic Stack without breaking or affecting the systems.

If you are pulling logs from a number of servers that are critical, as they host applications on it, it is better to use Beats as an agent that consumes very less memory and resources. However, if your existing servers have a lot of memory that is available then you may directly install Logstash on the systems to push processed data into Elasticsearch, reducing the complexity of an additional data shipping layer.

If you are using Elastic Stack for extensive processing of data that is used by other people, then you cannot afford to lose data. In some scenarios, when you are using Beats to push data into Logstash, it eventually stores data in Elasticsearch. If there is a delay in the amount of data pushing in and the amount of data consumed, then there could be cases when some of the data is lost that you may not be aware of. In such situations, the need arises to use message queuing tools that will store the messages for a brief amount of time and will prevent the data loss. Thus, you can evaluate various message queues such as Redis/Kafka, as per your requirement.

After understanding the use case, the next set of best practices that directly follows it up is installation of components of Elastic Stack. As we install the components with the default settings and configurations, it's best to revisit the configuration file and various parameters that can be changed.

Managing configuration files

The configuration file changes are the most basic yet important to make from a production deployment perspective. Let's have a look at the configuration files of various components.

Elasticsearch – elasticsearch.yml

By default, Elasticsearch sets values for important properties such as cluster, node related like cluster name, node name, and so on. While it's not necessary to set, it's a good idea to customize the names. For example, we should specify the node names so that we can remember and keep track of the node statistics by the node name that we specified. Few of such properties are explained below:

- Change the name of the cluster by modifying the following property:

```
# cluster.name: my-application
cluster.name: production-elasticstack
```

- Change the name of the node to easily identify the nodes joining in the cluster by modifying the following property:

```
# node.name: node-1
node.name: elasticstack1
```

- Change the location of the directory wherein Elasticsearch stores data by modifying the following property:

```
# path.data: /path/to/data
path.data: /usr/share/elasticsearch/data
```

 For windows, paths use backslashes like –
```
path.data:
E:\installations\stack\elasticsearch-2.3.0\config
```

- Change the location of the directory wherein Elasticsearch stores logs by modifying the following property:

```
# path.logs: /path/to/logs
```

Kibana – kibana.yml

Similar to `elasticsearch.yml` for Elasticsearch, `kibana.yml` should be updated for Kibana. Few of the important points to visit when using Kibana include:

- Change the URL of the Elasticsearch instance by specifying the IP of the machine on which Elasticsearch is present by modifying the following property:

```
# elasticsearch.url: http://localhost:9200
elasticsearch.url: http://<ip-of-machine>:9200
```

- Change the default application to load when Kibana starts if you want to redirect users to any other page when Kibana opens, such as a saved dashboard by modifying the following property:

```
# kibana.defaultAppId: "discover"
kibana.defaultAppId: "dashboard/<Name-of-Dashboard>"
```

Specifying the saved dashboard name whenever anyone opens the Kibana UI will directly open the saved dashboard.

- Change the location of the key and certificates if you are using SSL for securing requests from the Kibana server to the web browser by modifying the following property:

```
# server.ssl.cert: /path/to/your/server.crt
# server.ssl.key: /path/to/your/server.key
server.ssl.cert: /usr/share/kibana/ssl-server.crt
server.ssl.key: /usr/share/kibana/ssl-server.key
```

Similarly, you can set other SSL properties such as validating elasticsearch using the same set of SSL files (`elasticsearch.ssl.cert` and `elasticsearch.ssl.key`), providing the certificate given by the certification authority for the Elasticsearch instance (`elasticsearch.ssl.ca`), and specifying whether to validate the SSL certificate (`elasticsearch.ssl.verify`).

- Change the location of the directory wherein the process ID file is created by modifying the following property:

```
# pid.file: /var/run/kibana.pid
pid.file: /usr/share/kibana/kibana-processfile.pid
```

Choosing the right set of hardware

The important metric to understand while installing Elastic Stack, is to know how much memory will be consumed, disk space required, maintaining proper I/O requests, how much CPU or cores are required for resource consumption, and the network among the systems. Whenever we install Elastic Stack there is always confusion on the amount of resources used by each of the component. Let us try to break the resources requirement based on the various components.

Memory

It is one of the most important parameters that affect the performance of an application. If the memory provided is lower than expected, then the application can stop, fail, or show an *Out of Memory* error.

Memory sizing is important as memory is used by the OS for various tasks. Hence, determining how much memory to provide to Elastic Stack components is essential such that application and OS performance do not get affected.

In the context of Elastic Stack, memory is crucial to decide if you should configure Elasticsearch and Logstash, as they both consume a high amount of resources as these component do a lot of processing and need a good processing unit and memory size. Elasticsearch acts as the central point of the Elastic Stack, as data is stored in it from Logstash or Beats and data is also visualized from Kibana using data in Elasticsearch.

Java heap size

This is an important parameter to configure as Elasticsearch consumes memory that is available to Java. When data is pushed to Elasticsearch, it starts to consume more memory and therefore it becomes important to have optimal settings of Java heap size. If Java heap size has been fully used, then logs will not be pushed to Elasticsearch and Kibana will not be able to showcase visualizations/dashboards properly.

The following error can be seen when Java heap size is fully used:

```
message [out of memory][OutOfMemoryError[Java heap space]]
```

The best practice is to increase the amount of Java Heap Size, which by default is set as maximum of 1 GB. Yes, we should increase it, but what should be the optimal value of this setting that will not have a negative impact on the performance of the application and system? Let's have a look at some of the best practices:

- Set the maximum heap size value equal to the value of minimum heap size:

  It is useful as no additional memory will be required to be allocated in runtime.

- If the total memory of the system is less than or equal to 64 GB, provide 50% of the total amount of memory to Java heap size:

  As OS requires memory to perform other operations, hence it is suggested to provide a maximum of 50% of total memory to Java heap size.

- If the total memory of the system is more than 64 GB, provide 32 GB of the memory to Java heap size. It is important to understand to not cross the 32 GB limit even if you have systems with a high amount of memory. When Java heap size uses 32 GB or more, then JVM starts to use the 64-bit pointers that require more memory to save objects. When Java heap size uses 31 GB or less, then JVM uses the small 32-bit pointers that are compressed using Ordinary Object Pointers.

You can set Java heap Size in two ways:

- Provide minimum and maximum heap size on runtime while starting elasticsearch nodes using the following command:

  ```
  ./bin/elasticsearch -Xms8g -Xmx8g
  ```

  Where, -Xms8g will set the minimum heap size as 8 GB and -Xmx8g will set the maximum heap size as 8 GB.

 Note: If you are using a 32-bit system, max heap size is very less. On Windows systems, max heap size is approximately 1.5 GB. On Unix systems, max heap size is 2 GB. On 64-bit operating systems that run 32-bit VM, max heap size can be set as 4 GB.

- Change the following configuration in the elasticsearch shell script file (`elasticsearch.in.sh`) present in the location `$ES_HOME/bin` (Unix) or `$ES_HOME\bin` (Windows):

```
ES_MIN_MEM=2g
ES_MAX_MEM=2g
```

You would require restarting Elasticsearch for the setting to be reflected.

Swapping memory

Swapping memory is the process where a page of memory is copied from memory to a hard disk to free up memory. It shifts the pages from high access speed of memory to low access speed of disks. It is such a downside to Elasticsearch when swapping memory is enabled as performance is directly hit. The more swapping occurs, the slower the application will perform.

Elasticsearch has mentioned the following piece of advice in the `elasticsearch.yml` configuration file:

```
Elasticsearch performs poorly when the system is swapping the memory.
```

You can set the following property in the elasticsearch.yml file to limit the swapping of memory:

```
bootstrap.memory_lock:true
```

You would need to restart Elasticsearch for the setting to be reflected.

You can verify whether the setting has been applied or not by using the following command:

```
curl http://localhost:9200/_nodes/process?pretty
```

Or, you can use the following URL in browser to execute the same command:

```
http://localhost:9200/_nodes/process?pretty {In Browser}
```

Where localhost is the hostname of the Elasticsearch node.

If `memory_lock` is being seen as false after setting it to true, then it means the request failed. The first reason could be that the user doesn't have permission to lock memory. This can be solved by running `ulimit -l`, that is, unlimited as root before starting Elasticsearch. The second reason could be that the `temp` directory has a `noexec` option. This can be solved by specifying a new `temp` directory while starting Elasticsearch as follows:
`./bin/elasticsearch -Djna.tmpdir=/new/path/to/new/dir`

The preceding settings should be optimally set as best practices for using Elasticsearch and Logstash.

For Kibana and Beats, memory requirement is minimal as both consume very less memory. Kibana being a web-based client requires memory as per the consumption of the browser. Beats having low-memory footprints require minimal memory for capturing and sending data to either Logstash or Elasticsearch.

Disks

Disks is an important part as Elasticsearch is the sole component where data is stored. If the disk space runs full, then the new data will not be stored and the nodes may stop, fail, or go down. It is important to plan storage well when you are dealing with replicas as well as if a node goes down then your other nodes must have the capacity to hold its replicas and data. Also, disks are very important for clusters or nodes requiring high indexing and ability to ingest high amount of log data. In such scenarios when there are heavy write based operations involved, disks can malfunction and become a bottleneck for the cluster.

Some of the best practices are:

- Use SSDs if you can as it boosts read/write indexing and data operations
- Use high performance disks with high RPM (15 K RPM drives)
- Increase the disk speed by effectively using RAID 0 implementation
- Use local storage to store data instead of NAS or other implementations

Sizing disk space

Elasticsearch requires disk space for storing data, shards, and replicas. There is no hard and fast rule to determine best practice for planning the sizing of disks. Let's take some cues from the following Elasticsearch properties using the following command:

- `cluster.routing.allocation.disk.watermark.low`:

  This property is used to specify the low watermark value for disk usage. By default, its value is set as 85%, that is, no Shards will be allocated to the node that has more than 85% of the disk used. The value can be set either in percentage or in absolute byte values such as 500 MB or 10 GB:

- `cluster.routing.allocation.disk.watermark.high`:

  This property is used to specify the high watermark value for disk usage. By default, its value is set to 90%, that is, Shards will be relocated to another node if the node disk usage exceeds 90%. The value can be set either in percentage or in absolute byte values such as 500 MB or 10 GB.

  Percentage values refer to used disk space, whereas byte values refer to free disk space:

- `cluster.routing.allocation.disk.threshold_enabled`:

  This property is used to specify whether to use disk threshold values or not. If set as true, then the watermark properties will be applicable, otherwise it will not be applicable. By default, its value is set as `true`. This can also be set using the cluster API.

  The following is an example of using a REST-based API to call elasticsearch:

```
PUT /_cluster/settings
{
    "transient" : {
        "cluster.routing.allocation.disk.threshold_enabled" :
            true
    }
}
```

Add the following properties in the elasticsearch configuration file (`elasticsearch.yml`) present in location $ES_HOME/config **(Unix)** or $ES_HOME\config **(Windows)**:

```
cluster.routing.allocation.disk.threshold_enabled: true
cluster.routing.allocation.disk.watermark.low: 80%
cluster.routing.allocation.disk.watermark.high: 85%
or
cluster.routing.allocation.disk.watermark.low: 15gb
cluster.routing.allocation.disk.watermark.high: 10gb
```

You would need to restart Elasticsearch for the setting to be reflected.

For proper sizing of the disk, we have used the default value and with certain tests we have come up with a formula for it, as follows:

```
(space per node * .85) * ((node count - replica count) / node count)
```

Let's assume our node contains 1TB of disk space and our ES cluster has five nodes with replica set as 2. To avoid an outage and survive 2 node outage out of 5, then each node should allow the following amount of data per node as per the following formula:

```
(1TB * 0.85) *((5-2)/5) = 510 GB
```

Details of the preceding calculation can be obtained from the following resource: `http://svops.com/blog/elasticsearch-disk-space-calculations/`.

I/O

I/O scheduling is the least concerned parameter that anyone focusses, as by default they provide good performance. But with Unix kernels this parameter needs to be tweaked if you are using SSDs instead of HDDs.

By default, the I/O Scheduling is **Completely Fair Queuing (CFQ)**. This type of scheduling mechanism provides the request as and when they process submit and subsequently allocates time slices for each queues to access the disk in a synchronous way. This scheduling mechanism is very well suited for HDDs for the way they spin and rotate.

For SSDs as there is no mechanism of spinning involved, this scheduling mechanism is highly inefficient. For SSD you can use **Noop** or **Deadline**:

- Noop is the simplest I/O scheduler placing the requests in a basic **FIFO (First In First Out)** queue.
- Deadline scheduler guarantees a start service time for each of the requests. This scheduler can reduce I/O latency, increase throughput, and eliminate time spent reordering I/O requests.

You can change the settings using the following commands in Unix:

- Check the current scheduler implemented:

```
cat /sys/block/sda/queue/scheduler
```

It will show the various schedulers and selected scheduler name in square brackets, as in the following command:

```
noop anticipatory deadline [cfq]
```

- Change the scheduler:

```
echo noop | sudo tee /sys/block/sda/queue/scheduler
```

- To check whether the scheduler has been changed:

```
cat /sys/block/sda/queue/scheduler
```

It will show the various schedulers and selected scheduler name in square brackets, as follows:

```
[noop] anticipatory deadline cfq
```

It is a temporary change and will reset the scheduler once the machine reboots. Also, Noop is not optimal to use for HDDs.

CPU

Elastic Stack components tend to have low requirements of CPU resources needed. Its requirement matters less as compared to other resources. The best practices will be:

- Choose a modern processor
- Choose multiple cores
- If you have a dilemma of choosing CPU versus cores, choose a system with a higher number of cores rather than a CPU with higher clock-speeds

Multiple cores have many benefits, as any operation such as indexing or searching utilizes one CPU core. Hence, multiple cores will help to perform multiple concurrent operations.

Network

This component is slightly neglected, as everyone provides or uses fast and good quality network connections and equipment. A fast and reliable network is required for good performance in a distributed system. High bandwidth helps in various ways and low latency ensures nodes can communicate seamlessly.

Some of the best practices are:

- Use modern data center networking connections
- Use high speed connections to connect between nodes
- Avoid clusters spanning across large geographically located data centers
- Try to have a cluster in a single data center
- If using multiple data centers, ensure network connection between data centers is robust and provides low latency

Searching and indexing performance

So far we have uncovered some of the best practices in terms of resources. As memory, CPU, I/O, disks, and network play a big part in choosing the preferred set of system configurations; we can tweak a few settings to improve resources usage for searching and indexing in Elasticsearch and Lucene.

Filter cache

By default, the filters used in Elasticsearch for querying are cached, which means when the query uses filter, Elasticsearch finds the documents related to the filter and stores the filter used as cache. After caching, if any query with the same filters are used it will provide quicker results as filters have been cached to memory. As internally it uses memory, it is wise to set a property to limit the usage of the Filter cache. Though each filter uses less memory, JVM heap size can take a hit if a large number of filters are used. By using the following property, we can limit the amount of Heap memory that can be used for the filter cache:

```
indices.cache.filter.size:10%
```

By default, the value of this property is 10%. It can either accept the value in percentage or memory byte level, such as 256 MB. If a large number of filters will be used, then you can increase the value of this property to an appropriate value. Add this property in the elasticsearch.yml configuration file.

Fielddata size

It is an important setting that directly affects the performance of Elasticsearch for searching and performing queries. Caching is required to provide faster results once the query, search, or field has been cached. But caching everything can create a problem, as it depends on the cache size available, and once the cache size provided gets full, then caching will not take place leading to a poor performance in searching and indexing of data.

Fielddata is expensive as it pulls the data from the disk into the memory. If the fielddata size exceeds the specified size, then data in the cache needs to be evicted to create space for new data, which is an expensive operation. Performance will be poor if elasticsearch needs to evict the data and reload the data into cache every time.

The following property can be used to limit the size of fielddata:

```
indices.fielddata.cache.size
```

By default, the value of the property is unbounded, which means Elasticsearch will never evict data from fielddata. Imagine a scenario wherein everyday index is being created and we keep all the indices. Fielddata will keep on growing as by default we do not evict data from the cache. At a point no new data will be loaded as fielddata size will be completely full and you will be stuck as you won't be able to load new values. If we are not using older indices as per retention policies, it is advised to set the property to evict older data.

You can add this property in the `elasticsearch.yml` configuration file:

```
indices.fielddata.cache.size: 40%
```

It will set the maximum size of the fielddata cache, as defined in either percentage or byte values as that of a node heap space.

Along with this property there is a need to understand the working of the circuit-breaker. Why we need to understand this property is an interesting question. Fielddata size is always checked when once the data is loaded, if size is available it will load the data into the cache, otherwise it will evict older data and reload the data. But what happens if a query tries to load more data into the fielddata than the available memory? In such a scenario, you will get an `OutOfMemoryException`.

To deal with such situations, circuit breaker estimates the memory that will be used by the query based on various parameters and checks whether the amount of memory is available or not. If the estimated query has a higher requirement than the limit, then circuit breaker will be triggered and the query will abort with an exception. Hence, `OutOfMemoryException` will not occur.

You can add this property in the `elasticsearch.yml` configuration file:

```
indices.breaker.fielddata.limit: 70%
```

It will set the maximum size of the fielddata cache as defined in either percentage or byte value as that of node heap space. By default, the value of this property is `60%`.

 Make sure that fielddata cache size has a lower value than fielddata breaker limit. If cache size has a higher value we will get the following exception as circuit breaker will be triggered:
`ElasticsearchException[org.elasticsearch.common.breaker.C`
`ircuitBreakingException: Data too large, data for field`
`[id] would be larger than limit of [8589934592/8gb]];`

The preceding settings can also be dynamically set using the REST API command:

```
PUT /_cluster/settings
{
  "persistent" : {
    "indices.breaker.fielddata.limit" : "50%"
    "indices.fielddata.cache.size" : "40%"
  }
}
```

Indexing buffer

Indexing buffer is used to store the newly indexed documents. When the buffer fills up, the indexed documents are written on disks leading to a low performance as reading the data from disk will be slow as compared to memory. Hence, it is important to increase the size of indexing buffer. The following setting needs to be set:

```
indices.memory.index_buffer_size:30%
```

By default, the value of the setting is `10%` which means, 10% of the total heap memory. The value can be set either as percentage or byte value. The property needs to be added in the configuration file of elasticsearch that is `elasticsearch.yml`.

 It is a static property and must be configured on every data node present in the cluster.

Sizing the Elasticsearch cluster

It is important to understand how we can size the Elasticsearch cluster efficiently by choosing the right kind of node, determining the number of nodes in the cluster, determining the number of shards and replicas to use, and determining the number of indices to store. There are no fixed rules to follow in order to size the Elasticsearch cluster.

Choosing the right kind of node

In Elasticsearch, we have always dealt with nodes, but somewhere no clear distinction has been made on the different types of node that are available. Let's understand the different type of nodes that can be created in the Elasticsearch cluster.

Master and data node

This is the default node that is created in the Elasticsearch cluster whenever an Elasticsearch instance is started. This type of node acts as a master node as well as stores the data. If this node is not a master node and another node fails, then this node will be available to become the master node. It performs operations of both master and data nodes such as cluster related tasks, creating or deleting indices, tracking the nodes that are part of the cluster, and so on. This node consumes a lot of resources as it requires resources for master operations as well as data operations. Hence, in a production-like environment if a high load is passed on this node then the node may stop.

To configure master and data nodes, add the following property in `elasticsearch.yml`:

```
node.master: true
node.data: true
node.ingest: false
```

Master node

This is another type of node in Elasticsearch that performs master node operations only. This type of node is very much required in production environments, as it will not consume a high number of resources and it does not perform resource intensive tasks. Also, to avoid the problem explained previously, it is important to have a clear distinction between master and data nodes and to also maintain the stability of the cluster. It is very important to have a master node in an always stable condition in production environments.

To configure the master node, add the following property in `elasticsearch.yml`:

```
node.master: true
node.data: false
node.ingest: false
```

 Master nodes and master data nodes are also called master-eligible node.

Data node

This is another type of node in Elasticsearch that only stores the data within the node. It doesn't perform other operations apart from storing, indexing, and providing search query results. It can be considered as a worker node. This node performs various operations related to data such as CRUD, aggregations, and search. This node segregates the role of the master and data node completely.

To configure the data node, add the following property in `elasticsearch.yml`:

```
node.data: true
node.master: false
node.ingest: false
```

Ingest node

This is another type of node in Elasticsearch that has been recently introduced. It is used for pre-processing events before storing. It consists of single or multiple processors that can execute the pre-processing pipelines for processing events.

To configure the ingest node, add the following property in `elasticsearch.yml`:

```
node.data: false
node.master: false
node.ingest: true
```

No master, no data, and no ingest node

This is another type of node in Elasticsearch that neither acts as a master node, data node, or a ingest node. You're probably wondering what's the purpose of having a node that doesn't perform the basic operations required by an Elasticsearch node. This node acts as a load balancer as it routes the requests appropriately. It routes all the cluster level requests to the master nodes and all the data-related requests to the data nodes. It distributes the load among the other nodes present in the cluster. It acts as a smart coordinator between the master and the data nodes. This node is also known as a coordinating only node.

To configure a coordinating only node, add the following property in `elasticsearch.yml`:

```
node.master: false
node.data: false
node.ingest: false
```

 Do not add a large number of coordinating only nodes to the cluster as it increases the burden because the master node tracks the nodes that are part of the cluster that requires acknowledgement from each of the nodes.

Every node in the cluster can also handle HTTP requests and transport traffic in addition to the roles that they perform. Transport is a module that enables internal communication between the nodes seamlessly. With HTTP requests it enables external REST clients to access the HTTP layer or access the API over the HTTP layer.

To enable an HTTP request, add the following property in `elasticsearch.yml`:

```
http.enabled: true
```

To disable an HTTP request, add the following property in `elasticsearch.yml`:

```
http.enabled: false
```

By disabling HTTP requests on data nodes we make sure that data nodes only perform data related operations and do not burden it by such requests.

> You should run Client Node on the same machine as Kibana as it will easily distribute the Kibana requests across the nodes being the load balancer.

Determining the number of nodes

Everyone wants to know how to estimate the number of nodes for the Elasticsearch cluster. It is hard to estimate as it involves a variety of factors, such as:

- How much memory will each node have?
- How much disk space will each node have?
- How many indices will be created?
- How much data would you be storing in a day or smaller time-frames?
- How many shards and replicas per shards do you want to have?
- How much search queries will be used?

All of the preceding questions seem to be neglected, or the answers are not clear, before estimating the number of nodes in the cluster. If you are unaware, or unable, to determine the number of nodes required, start with a small number of nodes.

Let's assume you are using Elastic Stack for log analysis, which contains 1 million records consuming 500 MB of data on a daily basis. You will be creating a day-wise index and will perform less than 100 search queries from the Kibana dashboard. You will not be using any replicas. In such a case that the application is not very important you can choose a single node having a memory of 64 GB with disk space of 1 TB and having four cores with 2.2 GHz. For such a scenario, one node will suffice until the disk space gets full.

Avoid using two nodes due to the famous problem of *Split-Brain*. It is a very common problem that occurs in clusters if improperly configured. This situation arises when there is miscommunication among nodes or a node fails due to any reason.

If one of the slave nodes cannot communicate with the master node and if that node is a master eligible node, then it initiates the election of the master node. The new master node will perform the duties of the failed master node and once the failed master node is restored then the new master node will again become a slave node. In Split-Brain, assuming we have two nodes, if the master node goes down then the slave node will become the master node, but once the failed master node restores then the following situation arises:

- Failed master node thinks the new master node would be demoted to slave
- New master node thinks the original master node dropped and should join again as a slave

Hence Split-Brain occurs.

The best practice to prevent it is:

- Have an odd number of nodes in the Elasticsearch cluster.
- Configure each node as a master node or data node to avoid Split-Brain in a small setup of the elasticsearch cluster.
- Configure the `discovery.zen.minimum_master_nodes` property.

  It provides a value of the minimum number of nodes needed to be alive in the cluster before a new master node can be elected.

- Formula to configure `discovery.zen.minimum_master_nodes` is, *(N/2) + 1,* where *N* is the number of nodes in the cluster.

Determining the number of shards

It is a very difficult question to answer, as the number of shards depends on various factors such as the memory of the system, disk space, number of indices, total number of documents in indices, size occupied by the documents, number of queries to run, complexity of searching, aggregations on the data, and so on.

Facing such a vast number of dependent factors it cannot be evaluated whether one shard is too low or thousands of shards are too high. Also, shards once defined cannot be changed until and unless you re-index your documents, which is an additional overhead.

To determine the number of shards, one critical parameter is to understand how much your data will grow. Each shard allocated has an additional cost attached as the shard consumes various resources such as CPU, memory, hard disk, and file handling. Every decision to size the cluster comes to this question; what is the use case you are trying to solve? As everything depends on your use case, its importance, and criticality, which makes it easier to plan.

The following are some of the best practices:

- Allocate shards in the range of one to three times the number of nodes in your cluster
- Do not overkill the cluster by providing a large number of shards
- Find the maximum handling capacity of a shard by creating a production-like scenario in a test environment and filling it with real data and searching queries that will be used
- If the performance of the cluster degrades due to addition of shards, add nodes and shards will be automatically balanced by the Elasticsearch cluster
- Start with a lower count of replica and then increase over time

As discussed earlier in this chapter, when calculating disk space with shards and replicas, it is important to size your shards accordingly as everything will depend on this. Once you have defined the capacity that can be handled by a single shard, extrapolate the number by also taking an additional buffer for immediate data explosion. Take the total amount of data along with an additional buffer if the data increases and divide by the total capacity of the single shard.

Reducing disk space

Disk space being one of the important parameters for sizing the node or cluster, it is important if we can reduce as much disk space occupied by the indices and documents. It can be done by configuration level properties and making some changes at indices level. Let's have a look at some of the best practices to do so:

- Enable compression by adding the following property to the `elasticsearch.yml` file:

```
index.store.compress.stored: true
index.store.compress.tv: true
```

The preceding properties are used to compress the stored fields in the indices and compress the term vector file, which stores information and statistics on the terms present in the fields of documents.

- Delete all the unnecessary fields or index only required fields. This step can be done at Logstash level.
- Delete @message, @source, and other fields if they are not required. If using Logstash grok filters then you can break down your message field in various fields and hence, can delete the @message field.
- Disable the _all field if it is not required.

It is a special field that concatenates the value of all the fields into a single string. It requires additional disk space and CPU resources to function.

There is a trade-off involved, as it has the imminent benefit of providing you search results when you search for a word and you are not aware in which field would that word occur and after disabling this field you would need to know the exact field name and mention the value to search for.

- Make fields not_analyzed. Add fields as analyzed as required.

It is another type of special property for a field that determines how the search will work. It consumes additional resources, memory, and disk space to analyze the word. By default, it splits the word into multiple sub-words if it contains dots, hyphens, and so on.

There is a trade-off involved as some require the exact value to be shown as it is without breaking the term, for such scenarios it is always beneficial to make fields as not_analyzed.

Logstash configuration file

Configuration file is the key to run Logstash. As Logstash requires the configuration file to be created/updated it is important to have an efficient and flexible configuration that can be easily changed as and when required. Let's have a look at some of the best practices that we should follow.

Categorizing multiple sources of data

When you have multiple different sources of data that you want to gather and uncover insights from them, it is best to categorize each source of data by adding a type to each of the different sources.

We can take a look at the following example:

```
input {
   file {
      path => "/path/to/directory/"
      type => "datanode"
   }
    file {
      path => "/path/to/directory/"
      type => "hbase"
   }
}
    file {
      path => "/path/to/directory/"
      type => "yarn"
   }
}
```

When you add a type, you can use different filters and output based on the type of the sources that it has been associated with.

Using conditionals

Logstash configuration should make use of conditionals in filtering the log messages based on different criterion. It is used to provide a condition based on which certain actions can be performed, which will be specific to the matching condition itself. It should be used when you have different sources of data that require specific filtering or output as per the data source.

We can take a look at the following example:

```
output {
      if [type] == "datanode" {
            stdout { codec => rubydebug }
      }
      if [type] == "hbase" {
            elasticsearch {
                    hosts => "localhost:9200"
                    index => "logs-%{+YYYY.MM.dd}"
                    document_type => "hbase"
```

```
                }
        }
        if [type] == "yarn" {
                file {
                        path => "/var/log/logstash/file.txt
                }
        }
}
```

Using custom grok patterns

Grok patterns are more powerful than ever thought. For parsing a data source, it is advised to create your custom grok patterns if you have a customized data format or for which grok patterns do not exist. Having your own custom grok patterns provides more flexibility to process and parse the data.

Simplifying _grokparsefailure

Whenever a grok pattern fails to match it automatically adds a tag of `_grokparsefailure`. But if you have multiple grok patterns it becomes difficult to know from which grok pattern the parsing of data failed. For this purpose, add `tag_on_failure` with each matching grok pattern, which will easily identify due to which grok filter the parsing of data failed.

For example:

```
grok {
        match => ["message","%{PATTERN_NAME}"]
        tag_on_failure => ["grokfailed_patternname"]
}
```

Mapping of fields

Logstash parses and processes all the fields, which are then stored as string data type in elasticsearch. There are two ways to map fields:

- Using Logstash smart patterns: It is used to provide explicit mapping of a field in the grok pattern itself. For example:

    ```
    %{GREEDYDATA:fieldname:float}
    ```

    You can provide `float` or `int` to map the field.

- Using the `Mutate` filter and `Convert` property.

Dynamic templating

It is used to create a template to parse all the fields by their data type and as per the data type definition defined in the template, perform the actions. By default, when you are using Logstash to push data into Elasticsearch and it matches the `logstash-*` indices, it automatically uses a template. This template finds a field with string data type and it creates two fields out of it: `fieldname` and `fieldname.keyword`, where `fieldname` is analyzed and `fieldname.keyword` is not analyzed. Create your own dynamic template so that you do not need to bother about explicit mapping of fields.

Testing configuration

It's always advised to test the Logstash configuration to check whether the configuration file is proper and whether it is parsing data correctly. The two good ways to do so are as follows:

- Use the `--configtest` option to check whether your configuration is structured properly and syntactically correct
- Use the `stdout` output to validate that your data is getting correctly parsed
- In addition, you can also use the `stdin` input and `stdout` output to validate the logic used for processing of data

Re-indexing data

Re-indexing data in Elasticsearch is a challenge when you have changed the schema or mappings of the fields. Upon changing the schema, you are either required to re-index all the documents of that field to incorporate mapping changes to previous documents stored, or to not re-index older documents, which will become useless with the change in schema.

Process of re-indexing data:

1. Create a new index with the new mappings and settings.
2. Take the documents from the old index and index it in a new index.

To minimize the effect and downtime of changing the schema and re-indexing, use the following approach.

Using aliases

Aliases are a powerful feature that can easily re-index the complete index data without any downtime. Alias can be considered as a nickname given to the index name. It can be considered as a symbolic link.

Let us see how to use aliases:

- Create an index with its mapping and settings
- Create an alias to point to the index name

After updating the schema/mappings:

- Create a new index with the new mappings and settings
- Re-index data from the old index to the new index using the re-index API
- Remove the old index alias name and add the new index to the same alias name already created
- Delete the old index

Summary

Best practices should be followed as they will eliminate the various problems faced while setting, configuring, and using Elastic Stack. There are several settings that can be tuned as per requirement making the stack more stable.

Throughout this chapter, we encountered a number of ways to configure and use Elastic Stack. While this chapter tried to cover most of the important points to note, there can also be other settings that may turn out to be a best practice for specific requirements. The configurations and settings must be analyzed closely to avoid any loop holes. Remember that one poor setting may lead to a disaster.

In the next chapter, we will have a look at the case studies to explore how Elastic Stack can be utilized to meet end objectives.

12
Case Study-Meetup

We covered a practical scenario of intranet portal, which showcased powerful capabilities of the stack in Chapter 6, *Elastic Stack in Action*. The case was more of a log management rather than data analysis, and throughout the book, we have learned that Elastic Stack can do magic when it comes to data analytics. With the help of Kibana, you can bring numbers to a colorful presentation, which ultimately helps you to bring sense out of it to make impactful changes to your setup and drives you to take strategic decisions.

This chapter takes you to meetup(s) and helps you analyze a real, practical scenario. We will collect meetup data, find out the statistics, popular meetup, and so on. The series of topics we will cover in this chapter are as follows:

- Understanding meetup scenario
- Setting things up
- Analyzing data using Kibana

Understanding meetup scenario

The world might be moving toward nuclear families, but the increasing number of meetups everyday shows that the humanity still needs and considers interactions with each other. A meetup is a gathering in which people meet and do stuff, share knowledge, and plan things of their common interest. This is backed by a software platform developed and provided by Meetup Inc. launched in June 2002. This platform is available at https://www.meetup.com/ and open for everyone to join and do meetups. You can get the idea of meetups popularity by the fact that there are more than 29 million users, 260k+ groups across 180+ countries with monthly meetups count just more than 450k on an average.

These meetups are not limited to technologies, and people do gather for trekking, hiking, traveling, environment-related and meditation-related reasons, and other causes. All of this gives us a fantastic opportunity to do a good analysis over meetups happening all over the world. Similar things happen at events organized through other channels as well.

So, the question is, what are we going to capture and how? All we need is an endpoint to gather data from meetup.com, and luckily, we have one. The Meetup API, rich in features, allows us to capture data related to meetups-meetup groups, categories, events (meetups), RSVPs done for a meetup, and so on. There are a number of endpoints available for the different API versions. If you are interested to know about the meetup API, the available documentation is present at `https://www.meetup.com/meetup_api`. Few of the endpoints are public, and you can call them without authorization. The rest of the endpoints needs you to provide an API key. We will be learning the way to call these endpoints later in the chapter. So, the data will capture can be categorized as follows:

- Meetup categories
- Popular cities
- Groups
- Open events
- RSVP counts
- Topics
- Venues

The data which we will store for analysis is not limited to these. However, we have only picked those data, which are either publicly available or apply to a larger number. We are not capturing anything specific to a person or an event.

Setting things up

Just like any other scenario, we need to set up Elasticsearch, Logstash or Beats or both, and Kibana for visualization. We would need something specific to capture data from meetups. Tricky thing is to decide whether we go for Logstash or Beats or a combination of both.

There was an input plugin developed for Logstash, which could read data for meetups, but that is not enough for us since we want to read more data and we need to go for another option. There is no beat available to capture the data from meetup as well.

The existing plugin is available at
`https://github.com/logstash-plugins/logstash-input-meetup/`. Elastic site has also
documented this plugin at `https://www.elastic.co/guide/en/logstash/5.1/plugins-i`
`nputs-meetup.html`. This plugin captures meetup

events using either

- `venue_id`: Multiple IDs can be provided, separated by commas
- `group_id`: Multiple IDs can be provided, separated by commas
- `group_urlname`: Path to group from meetup.com

The restriction this plugin brings is that we can only fetch data for selected venue_ids, group_ids, and so on. Selected, because we need to know which groups or venue to gather data for. However, we want to do more; as mentioned in the preceding section, we want to fetch data for meetup groups, events, venues along with categories, topics, and other relevant details. We want to analyze data for the whole city, country, or may be for the world and see what are the trends. Similar to the Logstash twitter plugin which allows us to use keywords for our search and then collect tweets; but if we want to fetch streaming of all tweets, we need to change the plugin code. Implementation needs to be changed since the existing code cannot be utilized in order to meet the new requirements.

Having said that, we had to go for another solution. A solution that can capture more than that, one that can crawl through cities data and generate a good amount of events to do analysis for.

We need to create either a Beat or a Logstash input plugin to meet the need. As discussed earlier, Meetup API is available and can be used to collect data. To keep things simple in terms of architecture and focus more on analysis, for this chapter, we will write an input plugin for Logstash and skip using Beats.

Finally, we will have our architecture look like this diagram:

We would have developed beats instead if we had to do the following things:

- Gather data from multiple servers; so, in that case, lightweight beats could help a lot, but we are not going to collect data from multiple servers. Only meetup API will be called for gathering data, and for that, multiple data-receiving ends are not necessary.
- Do extra processing, break fields then we would have collected data using beats and do processing with Logstash. Logstash plugin will take care of both data collection and processing, thus eliminating the need of a beat.

So, we will develop the plugin for Logstash, which will read the data using the Meetup API; we will then parse the data to prepare events and send them to elasticsearch index, which we will analyze them using Kibana dashboards. The version of Elastic Stack we will use is v5.1.1.

A bit of Meetup API understanding

Meetup API is a mix of multiple versions (v1, v2, and v3). A sample request URL will look like this:

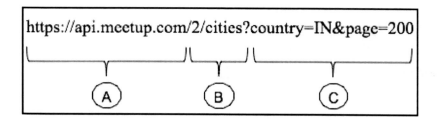

- **A** – This is the actual meetup API host, which is a secure URL.
- **B** – This is the REST service method endpoint. In the preceding example, `/2/cities` is the endpoint, which brings the cities for given arguments.
- **C** – This contains arguments that are specifically necessary input for endpoint **B**, along with order information or page size (number of results). For example, in the preceding URL, country will be used to get cities for specified country, maximum 200 results will be returned.

Not all method endpoints will work without a key. If we want to get information about an event, we need to provide an API key for authorization. To get the key, you should create your account on meetup.com and then get the key from the following URL:

```
https://secure.meetup.com/meetup_api/key/
```

Once you have the key, you should send the key as an argument along with one more argument with name sign and value set to true. A URL to get open events for the country India and the city Ahmedabad will be like this:

```
https://api.meetup.com/2/open_events?country=in&city=ahmedabad&key=<your-key-he
re>&sign=true.
```

Note that with the key, we have also added `sign=true`. This is a called as signed URL. The concept of signed URL is very well explained at
`https://www.meetup.com/meetup_api/auth/#keysign`.

Few of the service endpoints, which will be used by the plugin, are listed in the following table:

Purpose	Endpoints
Cities	/2/cities
Categories	/2/categories
Events	/2/open_events, /2/events
Groups	/2/groups

Topics	/topics
Venues	/2/open_venues, /2/venues

The endpoints are used from v1 and v2 of meetup API.

Setting up Elasticsearch

It's always a good practice to set up elasticsearch by providing a unique node name, hostname, and so on. Let's modify the configuration file `config/elasticsearch.yml`:

```
node.name: es-node
network.host: 192.168.0.102
http.port: 9200
```

For simple setup, we will be keeping only one node for elasticsearch. Let's run the following node:

```
$ ./bin/elasticsearch
```

Elasticsearch is now ready and should be good to receive the data, which will be sent by Logstash.

Preparing Logstash

To gather data from meetup, we have developed a plugin, and this plugin is available at GitHub at `https://github.com/kravigupta/mastering-elastic-stack-code-files/tree/5.1.1/Chapter12/logstash-input-meetupplugin`. You can download the plugin file and install it to your Logstash. In case you want to install and test this plugin, download the gem file using

```
$ ./bin/logstash-plugin install /
path/to/logstash-input-meetupplugin-0.1.0.gem
```

 To know more, you can refer to Installing a plugin under plugin command line options section in `Chapter 3`, *Exploring Logstash and its plugins*.

We need to understand how we are going to use the plugin and the necessary configuration it might ask for. This plugin is developed to collect data for Cities, Meetup events by Cities, Meetup Venues by City, Meetup Groups by City, Topics, and Categories.

One might not be interested to collect data for all of the things, hence plugin provides options to be configured when writing Logstash configuration. The plugin even allows you to supply only the country code, and data for top cities will be collected. Let's see what parameters we can configure:

- `countryCode`: Type: String, Required: yes. This specifies the country code for which data should be collected. This is ISO country code with maximum two characters. These codes are also available at `https://countrycode.org/`. This is a required field, and without this, the plugin would not work.

 The plugin does not allow crawling data for multiple countries. However, you can run Logstash multiple times by providing different countryCode.

- `key`: Type: String, Required: yes.
  This is a required parameter and is needed to access the Meetup API. You can get it from meetup site at `https://secure.meetup.com/meetup_api/key/` as specified earlier in this chapter.
- `interval`: Type: Integer, Required: no, and Default: 900.
  This is the interval for which plugin should wait for next complete iteration to collect data from Meetup. This also ensures that meetup is not blocking us by marking it as spam. Also, meetup data will not be changing so frequently, so keeping a higher number of interval is also okay, depending on your requirements.
- `cityNames`: Type: String, Required: No, Default: blank.
  This field specifies the cities for which data is to be collected. In case, this field is not mentioned, plugin will make a call to get the cities of specified country and take top `N` cities, where `N` is the value specified for `citiesCount`.

Meetup data can be fetched using Country, city, and state; state is optional. If you call meetup API to get cities of a country, state does not always appear in response. Response to cities call is available at
`https://secure.meetup.com/meetup_api/docs/2/cities/#response`.

It clearly says the state that contains the city and is returned when applicable. While crawling the data for a city-for example, getting meetup events, if state was in response-it must be specified. Therefore, while specifying which cities to crawl data for, you should also specify state. Thus, you can specify cities in two formats:

- For the countries where states are not applicable, use only comma-separated city names. For example, cities in India can be specified as follows:

  ```
  cityNames: "Ahmedabad,Pune,Bangalore,Chennai"
  ```

- For the countries where states are applicable, city names should also have :statecode appended to them. For example, cities in USA can be specified like this:

  ```
  cityNames: "New York:NY,Chicago:IL,Washington:DC"
  ```

  Here, New York is the city name and NY is the state. Similarly, IL is the state for Chicago city, and DC is the state for Washington.

- `citiesCount`: Type: integer, Required: no, Default: 5.
  This field is used only when `cityNames` is not specified. Only this number of cities will be used to collect data.

- `enableTopics`: Type: Boolean, Required: no, Default: false.
  This indicates whether topics-related data should be collected or not. For reference, the response object for the topics is available at
  `https://secure.meetup.com/meetup_api/docs/find/topics/#response`.

- `enableVenues`: Type: Boolean, Required: no, Default: false.
  This indicates whether meetup venues-related data should be collected or not. For reference, the response object for the venue is available at
  `https://secure.meetup.com/meetup_api/docs/2/open_venues/#response`.

- `enableGroups`: Type: Boolean, Required: no, Default: false.
  This indicates whether meetup groups-related data should be collected or not. For your reference, the response object for the group is available at
  `https://secure.meetup.com/meetup_api/docs/2/groups/#response`.

- `enableCategories`: Type: Boolean, Required: no, Default: false.
  This indicates whether categories-related data should be collected or not. For your reference, the response object for the category is available at
  `https://secure.meetup.com/meetup_api/docs/2/categories/#response`.

- enableMeetup: Type: boolean, Required: no, Default: true.
  This indicates whether meetups(events)-related data should be collected or not.
  The complete response of a meetup event can be seen at
  `https://secure.meetup.com/meetup_api/docs/2/open_events/#response`. This
  field is set to true by default; that's the heart of the plugin, isn't it?

We will collect data for multiple countries. We need to run Logstash for each country one
by one after changing the value of countryCode in configuration. For our example, we have
collected data for India (IN), Russia (RU), Japan (JP), USA (US), UK (GB), and China (CN).
Our input section of the configuration for country India looks like this:

```
input {
  meetupplugin {
      countryCode => "IN"
      key => "<replace-with-your-meetup-api-key>"
      interval => 600
      enableTopics => false
      enableVenues => true
      enableGroups => true
      enableCategories => true
      enableMeetup => true
      citiesCount => 10
  }
}
```

This configuration will help the plugin to know the API key and the interval, which is set to
10 minutes. In the code, we are getting data for India without specifying cityNames and
keeping total cities to be 10 for data collection.

If we want to crawl data only for few cities, configuration for USA will look like this:

```
input { meetupplugin{
    countryCode => "US"
    cityNames => "Chicago:IL,Washington:DC,Houston:TX,New York:NY"
    ...
} }
```

The similar configuration for India can be as follows:

```
input { meetupplugin{
    countryCode => "US"
    cityNames => "Pune,Ahmedabad,Bangalore,Chennai,Mumbai"
    ...
} }
```

For all of the items in venues, groups, and meetup, it makes only one API call for each city. So, in order to get data for the top 10 cities, it will make 30 API calls. We are discussing number of API calls here because meetup.com allows only 200 calls per hour. We need to plan properly so that we don't run out of API calls and start getting errors from Meetup.

Each group has a number of topics associated, and total topic count can reach to more than few hundreds. Each topic can give us information about member count, which is a good metric to look at. However, this requires one API call for each topic, which is not feasible, hence the enable/disable part for topics is disabled in the shared preceding configuration.

Group, Meetup, and Venues will have latitude and longitude associated to them, which we can use to visualize data over a map. However, this needs some tweaking to allow us to draw a point to map. The conversion of latitude and longitude to a location object has been taken care within the plugin, and we need to work at the remaining stuff using filters. So, our filter configuration looks like this:

```
filter {
  mutate {
    add_field => ["[geoip][location][lat]","%{[location[lat]}"]
    add_field => ["[geoip][location][lon]","%{[location[lon]}"]
  }
}
```

Here, we used mutate filter and adding fields as geoip. We are picking fields from location field which we have added to our event objects in the plugin.

Apart from this configuration, we need to specify output to elasticsearch:

```
output          {
  elasticsearch        {
    hosts => "localhost:9200"
    index => "meetup"
    document_type => "meetup_data"
    doc_as_upsert => true
    document_id => "%{document_id}"
    template => "/Users/ravi.gupta/templates/meetup-template.json"
    template_name => "meetup-template"
    template_overwrite => "true"
  }
}
```

Note that we have specified doc_as_upsert to be true and also specified the document_id field. Meetups are not log events, and all we need to do is update the existing meetup, venue, groups, or any other data.

The plugin uses the `document_id` field name to store the unique ID of the document. To enforce elasticsearch to update `_id` field of the document, we need to use the `document_id` field and supply the ID field used by plugin, which is specified as `%{document_id}` in our configuration.

Three configuration lines for templates are needed for geoip. We just need to copy the template content to a location and provide the template. The sample content for the template can be found at `logstash-5.1.1/vendor/bundle/jruby/1.9/gems/logstash-output-elasticsearch-5.4.0-java/lib/logstash/outputs/elasticsearch/elasticsearch-template-es5x.json`.

Copy this file, put it at a location, rename it to something contextual, for example, `meetup-template.json`. Open the file and change the value of the template field from `logstash*` to `meetup*`, which is our index pattern.

Let's start the logstash:

```
$ ./bin/logstash -f conf/meetup.conf
```

Now, Logstash will start pulling data from meetup.com and store it in the index in Elasticsearch. We can start visualizing the data once we have that in Kibana.

 Note that to capture data of multiple countries, change the countryCode in the configuration and run Logstash again. Repeat this for each country. More the data the better are the visualization and analytic opportunities.

Setting up Kibana

While configuring Kibana, we need to specify which port we are running elasticsearch on. Our `config/kibana.yml` would be as follows:

```
elasticsearch.url: "http://192.168.0.102:9200"
server.name: "Kibana-node-stack"
```

Once kibana is set up and configured, let's start Kibana to visualize the incoming data. Run the following command in the directory where you installed kibana:

```
$ ./bin/kibana
```

A point to understand-an additional field is added by the plugin to identify the type of document, and that field is `meetup_data_type`, which is assigned to one of the following:

- `meetup`: For meetup events
- `group`: For meetup groups
- `venue`: For meetup venues
- `topic`: For meetup topics
- `category`: For meetup categories

This field will be useful when we apply a filter in Kibana to our data for visualizations.

Analyzing data using Kibana

When kibana is up and running, we can start visualizing meetup data. Before we can do that, we need to configure index for Kibana. Our index name in Elasticsearch is meetup as we specified in output configuration of Logstash. Let's set up our index pattern. Navigate to **Kibana** | **Management** | **Index Patterns** | **Configure an Index Pattern** or a **Add New** index. Add the index pattern for meetup and keep @timestamp field for time field name.

We could use * as wildcard as well and keep meetup*, but we have only one index, and we know that it's meetup so no need to use wildcards. That will also help us to keep data from being mixed up in case we have other indices with the same pattern e.g. meetup-india, meetup-us etc.

Click on **Create**, and index pattern for our index would be set:

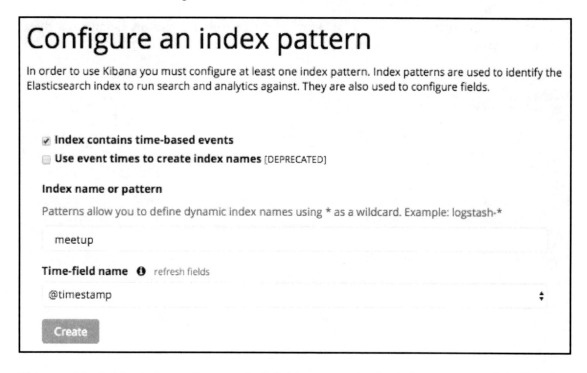

This would add the index pattern, and all fields present in the index meetup will be listed along with their types.

Filtering Content

As soon as our index pattern is set, discover page will be full of events. By default, discover page will show all types of data-meetups, venues, groups, categories, and so on:

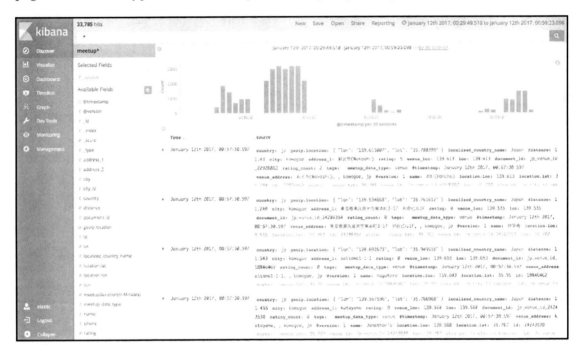

We can see there are a good number of fields listed as left panel to discover area. These fields are all unique fields present in the data. We can search data using field values, make quick filters, check whether the field is present, and so on.

There is a fair chance that a field is present in multiple data types. For example, name is present for meetup events, venue, and groups. There are other fields as well, such as latitude (lat) and longitude (lon). If we want to draw meetups on map, we would need to identify only meetup events. In such cases, the `meetup_data_type` field will be helpful, and we can make a filter on that to clearly separate the data of one type. For most of the visualizations, we will use only one data type, for example, meetup events-related visualizations will only use the `meetup_data_type` field with a value as meetup. Similarly, for venues, `meetup_data_type` will be set to venue.

To add a filter, we will refer these steps for visualizations where it is required:

1. We will be using filters on the meetup_data_type field and keeping the value as meetup for this visualization. Navigate to **Kibana | Discover**, and select the field meetup_data_type in the field list and select meetup.

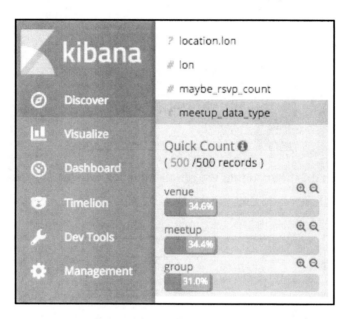

2. Select the lens icon with (+) to choose this value for the filter. This will add a filter to the query, and behind the scene, it becomes the following

```
{
    "query": {
      "match": {
        "meetup_data_type": {
          "query": "meetup",
          "type": "phrase"
        }
      }
    }
}
```

3. It will add the filter just below the search box saying `meetup_data_type:` `meetup`.

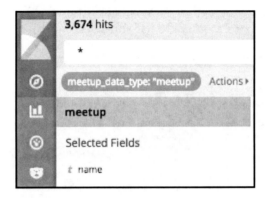

4. We can pin this filter so that we can use this for our visualizations directly:

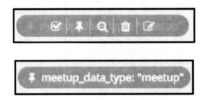

Pinning a filter is useful. We pin a filter so that whichever tab we visit in Kibana, this filter will always be available.

This filter will be applied for all visualizations. We will be making changes to filters accordingly.

Now, we have things ready and we can start visualizing the data. We will be visualizing meetups, groups, venues, categories in terms of popularity, counts, join modes, and more. Let's head to our visualizations, starting with the number of meetups for countries.

Number of Meetups by Country

We assume that you have already ran the Logstash for multiple countries. Let's create a visualization for this case. Perform the following steps:

1. Follow the steps in the Filtering Content section for meetup_data_type:'meetup'

2. Navigate to Kibana | Visualize | New (in top bar), and select a vertical bar chart.

3. Select the configured index, meetup, in the From a New Search, Select Index section.

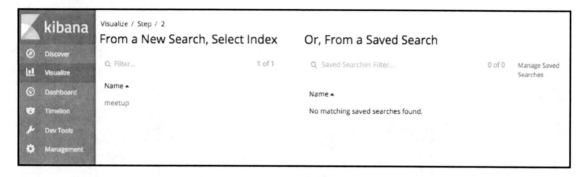

4. Now, we need to add metric, using which a bar chart can be drawn. Y-axis metric is already set to the Count aggregation. We will leave it as it is, and add custom label for Y-axis as Number of Meetups:

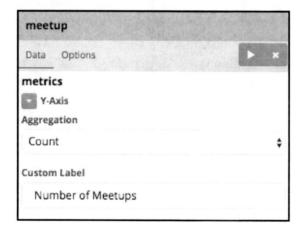

5. Let's add buckets to our chart using the buckets section below the metrics section. Select X-Axis from the bucket list.

6. Choose Aggregation type as terms.

7. Select Field as country.keyword

8. Since we may have more than five countries, we can set size to more than 5. Let's set it to 10.

9. Finally, we should have our X-Axis bucket as follows:

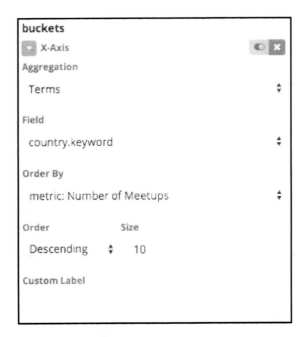

10. Now, we have everything set for our chart, let's click on the "Apply Changes" icon Next to Data, and Option tabs just below the index name. It's the play button in the following image:

11. Now, the visualization would be similar to the image shown below:

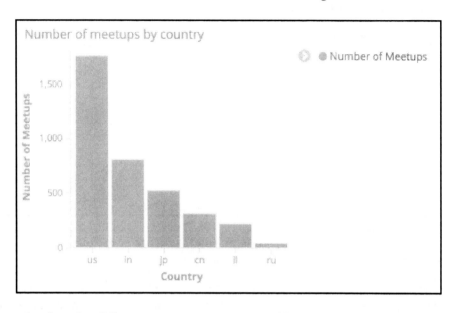

We can see the data for different countries represented by country codes. USA has the most number of meetups for its top 10 cities. India is doing almost 850 meetups in top 10 cities.

Top 10 meetup cities in world

The previous visualization was at country level, and you might want to further look at the details for top cities and where meetups are active, though this visualization will be only true for the countries for which data is present. In case, we have data for all countries, it will be a correct visualization. Let's change the visualization to capture data for cities rather than country this time. Follow the steps:

1. Follow the steps in "Filtering Content" section for meetup_data_type:'meetup'.
2. Let's try another visualization now. Navigate to Kibana | Visualize | New (in top bar) | Select a Line chart. Choose index pattern as meetup.
3. Leave Y-Axis metric as count and label it as "Number of Meetups".

4. For buckets at X-Axis, choose aggregation on terms and select field as city.keyword and change the size to 10.

5. Put the label for this bucket as City and apply or press enter. You should be able to see top cities with number of meetups at the time:

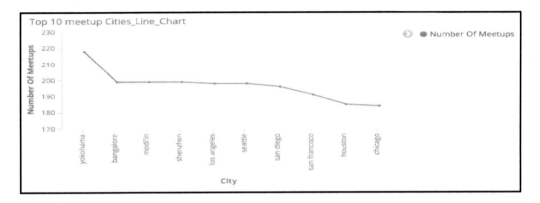

As we can see from the visualization, people in Yokohama are at the top when it comes to organize meetups.

If you note the chart, the Y-axis does not start with zero and starts with 170. We can set these things using options tab for any visualization. We can set metrics and buckets using Data tab, and Option tab allows us to do more with a chart. This varies with each type of chart. For line chart in this case, we see option for setting up y-axis extents:

Note that for Y-axis extents, we have set minimum to 170 and maximum to 230. This value is set based on the observation that maximum numbers for a meetup for a city were not more than 230 and min, were not less than 170.

Meetups trends by duration

This analysis helps us to understand which duration range most of the meetups fall into. This is an important metric since it clearly shows the ideal duration for a meetup. The duration field value is to be used for this visualization. By default, duration field is in milliseconds, which we should convert to minutes or hours for a better readable format. We can do this using scripted fields. Follow these steps to add a scripted field:

1. Navigate to Kibana | Management | Index Patterns | Scripted Fields | Add Scripted Fields
2. Name the field meetupDuration(In Minutes)
3. Keep the language as painless. To know more about painless scripting, refer to `Chapter 8`, Elasticsearch APIs.
4. Add the following script to script field:

    ```
    doc['duration'].value/(1000*60)
    ```

    This will take the value of the duration field of the document in the index and divide it by 1000 * 60 to convert the milliseconds to minutes.

5. Leave everything else as default and select "Create Field".

We will use this field for the visualization. Follow these steps:

1. Follow the steps in the "Filtering Content" section for meetup_data_type:'meetup'.
2. Navigate to Kibana | Visualize | New (in top bar) | Select a Vertical bar chart. Choose index pattern as meetup.
3. Leave Y-Axis metric as count and label it as "Number of Meetups".

4. For buckets at X-Axis, choose aggregation on range and select field as meetupDuration(In Minutes) and add appropriate ranges. Your configuration should look like this:

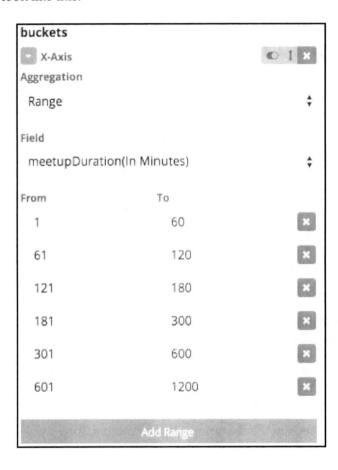

5. Apply the changes. You should be able to see number of meetups for selected duration ranges:

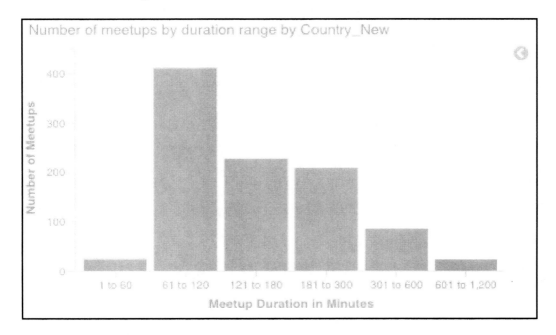

We can see from the visualization that most of the meetups are 61-120 minutes. Majority of meetups are 1-3 hours long.

6. We can further modify the chart for each country. Let's add a sub-bucket of the "Split Bars" type. Select **Sub Aggregation** on terms and add field as country.keyword. Your configuration should look like this:

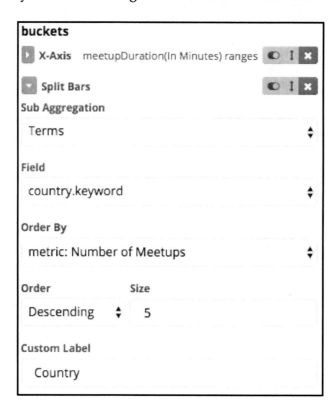

7. Apply the changes, and our visualization will change similar to the following:

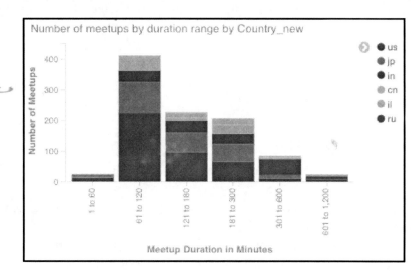

As we can see, meetups are now divided for each country and stacked on each other.

8. In case we want to change the bars as grouped rather than stacked, we can change the value of bar mode in options to grouped. After the change, the visualization will change to this:

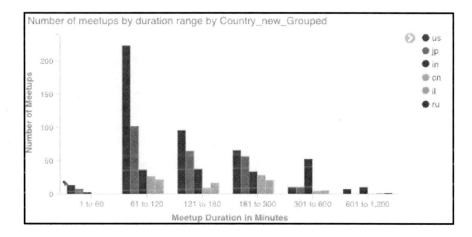

The first visualization for duration ranges says that most of the meetups across the world are of less than 3 hours. Now, when we look at this last chart with country-specific data for meetups in India, majority of meetups are longer than 3 hours.

Meetups by RSVP Counts

Similar to ranges used for meetup duration, we can use RSVP counts for ranges and see how many RSVPs are done for the meetups. Follow these steps:

1. Follow the steps in the "Filtering Content" section for meetup_data_type:'meetup'.
2. Navigate to Kibana | Visualize | New (in top bar) | Select a Vertical bar chart. Choose index pattern as meetup.
3. Leave Y-Axis metric as count and label as "Number of Meetups".
4. For buckets at X-Axis, choose aggregation on range and select yes_rsvp_count as field and add the appropriate ranges. You can set various ranges starting from a positive number up to 500 and above.
5. Click on apply changes and the number of meetups will be drawn against ranges defined for yes RSVPs.

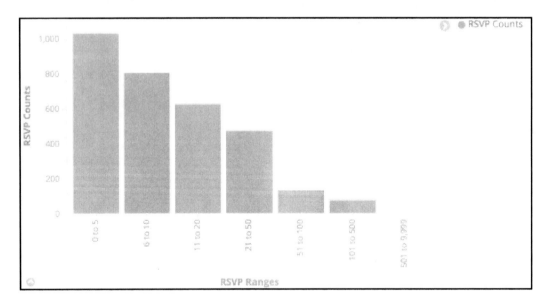

As we can see, most of the meetups have less than 10 RSVPs. This data is only for upcoming meetups. Similar to the previous visualization, this data can be further divided for each country.

Number of Groups by country

Let's try to see number of groups for each country for our available data. Perform the following steps:

1. Follow the steps in the "Filtering Content" section for meetup_data_type:'group'.
2. Navigate to Kibana | Visualize | New (in top bar) | Select Pie Chart. Choose index pattern as meetup.
3. For the metrics, slice size, use count for aggregation and provide label as "Number of groups".
4. For buckets, add Split slices, keep aggregation on terms, and choose field as country.keyword.
5. Set the size to 10 and click on run; we will have a pie chart generated with available countries:

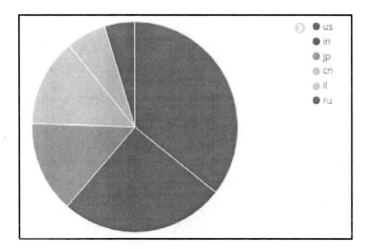

We can see that USA has most number of groups, followed by India.

Number of Groups by join mode

We can further analyze the number of groups based on join mode. Join mode shows how open or restricted groups or countries are when it comes to socializing. There are three types of join modes available:

- Open: You can find and join these groups, and there are no approvals needed.
- Approval: Approval mode allows you to find and join the group, but your membership is to be approved by the group admin.
- Closed: You can only be added by the admin.

Let's add one more slice to the pie visualization we had for groups by country. Perform the following steps:

1. Add one more bucket for Split slices, on terms aggregation and field as join_mode.keyword.
2. Click on apply changes and you can see the updated chart as follows:

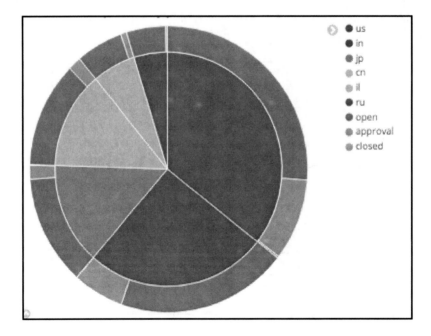

We can see from the chart that most of the meetup groups are open, and that's a good thing. It lets' you join groups instantly and further join the meetups hosted by the group.

3. In case, you want to add a different flavor to the chart, and not have a pie, you can do it in a donut chart as well. Open the options tab and check the Donut checkbox. After that, click on apply changes, and the pie chart will be converted to a donut:

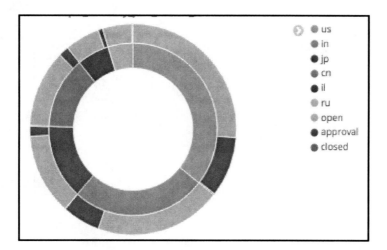

Popular Categories

All of the meetup groups are linked to some category. Based on the data we have, we can find which categories are most popular. We might be interested to know the exact count of meetup groups under these categories. We can use data table for this purpose. Follow these steps to generate a table for categories:

1. Follow the steps in the "Filtering Content" section for meetup_data_type:'group'.
2. Navigate to Kibana | Visualize | New (in top bar) | Select Data table. Choose index pattern as meetup.

3. For the metrics, use count for aggregation and provide label as **Number of groups**.
4. For buckets, add Split rows, keep aggregation on terms, and choose field as `category_name.keyword`.

4. Since we are interested to know the top 20 categories, set the size to 20 and keep the label as **Category Name**.

5. Click on apply changes and a data table will be generated:

Category Name Q	Number of Groups
tech	1,109
career/business	676
language/ethnic identity	583
socializing	475
outdoors/adventure	280
food/drink	212
new age/spirituality	202
health/wellbeing	176
sports/recreation	165
games	141

As we can see, tech is the most popular category, and out of 5.6k meetup groups, tech alone is aligned with >1k groups.

If we further analyze the categories to the country level, we can add one more bucket for split rows and term aggregation for field country.keyword. A data table like this will be generated:

Category Q	Country Q	Number of Groups
tech	in	456
tech	it	192
tech	ru	156
tech	cn	153
tech	us	108
career/business	us	203
career/business	in	202
career/business	cn	109
career/business	it	95
career/business	jp	47

The top two categories show an entirely amazing fact. USA is a country where meetup count is the highest, but most of the meetups are not of technology category. India shows a quite high interest toward technological side.

We might even be interested to generate a tag cloud for the categories just like we did for topics. Follow the same steps used for topics map while keeping the meetup_data_type as group and field for aggregation as category_name.keyword. Meetup groups are categorized to 33 categories, and we are interested to know only the top 20 of such categories. Keep the size as 20 and click on apply changes, and tag cloud for categories will be generated:

As seen in the data tables, category tech had the most number of groups. That results the text tech being highest in the size, which shows that tech is the most favorite meetup category. Further, if we look closely, in fact, people are focusing more on tech and career.

Popular Topics

Analyzing meetups for popular topics makes a good case because that shows which buzzwords are making a noise and setting trends for meetups. There cannot be a better visualization for topics than tag cloud. Follow these steps:

1. We don't need to set up any filter for this since topics are associated with only meetup groups.
2. Navigate to Kibana | Visualize | New (in top bar) | Select Tag cloud. Choose index pattern as meetup.
3. Leave metric tag size as count.
4. For buckets, we have only one type "Tags"; select it, and choose aggregations on terms.
5. A topic has urlkey as a unique identifier, which is also good for us to use as a keyword. Select topicsURLKeys.keyword in the field list.
6. Put size as 30. Setting a size will ensure that we are getting top 30 keywords in the tag cloud.
7. Click on apply changes. Our tag cloud visualization will appear, as follows:

As we can see, social network like keywords leave a good impression in meetups, and why not? Social networks such as Facebook, Google+, Twitter, Instagram, and so on are being so popular these days. Along with that, entrepreneurship is also something people are looking at and that's a good one to set up a healthy competition. Also, people are talking about culture, spirituality, self-improvement, dining, and a lot of other things. Tag clouds say a lot about what's happening, isn't it?

Note the 'up arrow icon' on the left-hand corner on the tag cloud visualization. This icon allows you to see the data in form of a table. That will immediately give you a list of the top 10 topics along with pagination:

Topic ⇕ Q	Number of Groups ⇕
social	875
socialnetwork	748
entrepreneurship	585
newintown	527
self-improvement	427
language	418
professional-networking	412
fun-times	406
startup-businesses	376
diningout	369

Meetup Venue Map

This visualization will show meetup venues over the map. Since we have latitude and longitude for venues, we can draw venues over map using Kibana. Before this visualization, we have run the logstash for the top 100 cities for each of the mentioned countries. Perform the following steps:

1. Follow the steps in the "Filtering Content" section for meetup_data_type:'venue'.
2. Navigate to Kibana | Visualize | New (in top bar) | Select Tile Map. Choose index pattern as meetup.

3. For the metrics, use count for aggregation and provide label as "Number of venues".

4. For buckets, we have only one option-Geo coordinates.

5. Select aggregation as Geohash and Field as geoip.location.

6. Click on apply changes, and the map should be generated/updated with venues drawn over the map:

As we can see in the map, the circles are bigger where the venue count is higher. We can also convert the same map to heatmap using chart options.

7. Select map type as heatmap in options and click on run. A heatmap for venues will be generated:

As we can see, the darker areas show a higher number of venues. A higher number of venues may also represent higher number of meetups in that area. In fact, if you zoom in to Asia region, you will have a better view:

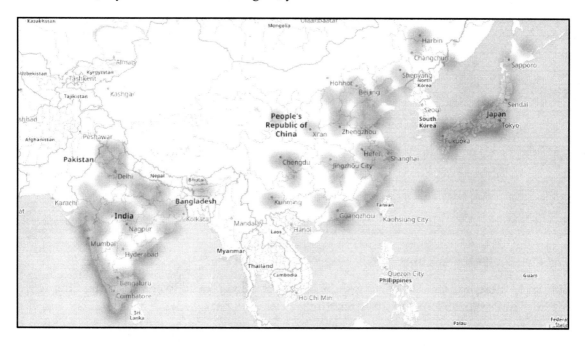

The zoomed-in map shows even darker areas for venues.

Meetups on Map

Similar to the map visualization of venues, we can see meetups with their actual locations. This visualization will show meetup over the map. Follow these steps:

1. Follow the steps in the "Filtering Content" section for meetup_data_type:'meetup'.
2. Navigate to Kibana | Visualize | New (in top bar) | Select Tile Map. Choose index pattern as meetup.
3. For the metrics, use count for aggregation and provide label as "Number of meetups".
4. For buckets, we have only one option, that is, Geo coordinates.

2. Select aggregation as Geohash and Field as geoip.location.

3. Click on apply changes, and the map should be generated/updated with meetups drawn over the map:

The map shows the meetups at their respective locations.

Similar to these, we can also show groups on maps. All you need to change is the filter to meetup_data_type:group and groups count will be drawn over map.

Just the number of things

We have used a variety of visualizations for many use cases. For a matter of fact, you would eventually need to know how many groups, how many meetups, venue, and so on are there, or even an average of some value. Follow these steps to set up metrics:

1. Follow the steps in the "Filtering Content" section for meetup_data_type:'meetup'.

2. Navigate to Kibana | Visualize | New (in top bar) | Select Metric. Choose index pattern as meetup.

3. For the metrics, use count for aggregation and provide label as "Number of meetups".

4. Click on run and you should have count of meetup events.

5. Save this visualization as Number of Meetups Metric.

6. Follow the same steps for venues and groups by changing the meetup_data_type as venue and group, respectively. Change the label for each, of course.

7. Once done, we can add all of the metrics to a dashboard, and it will be ready for visualization:

5,608	3,674	3,139
Number of Group	Number of Meetups	Number of Venues

We can see that we have ~5.6k meetup groups, organizing ~3.6k meetups at ~3.1k locations.

Getting Notified

Analyzing content has a purpose, mostly strategic. If this analysis was done by a company that deals in people relationship, they might be interested to know any new meetup so that they can connect to more people. If any meetup in city has good amount of RSVPs, there is a fair chance that 3-4 persons of the company's 'interest can be found. It usually happens during meetups. People of similar interests get to meet. What if, we can get a notification of some kind whenever a meetup is created. We can use X-Pack's alerting capabilities-watcher to mention specifically. The notification can be a log, e-mail, or some other kind supported by watcher. To learn more about watcher, refer to `chapter 10`, *X-Pack: Alerting, Graph, and Reporting*.

Let's create a watch for this use case. We would need a schedule, input, a condition, and an action, which will be used to notify us:

- Schedule: Assuming that one iteration takes place in one hour and data is updated, we will keep interval for our scheduler as 1 hour.
- Input: We would be using a query, which will check for the updated time (current time – 1h), a city where meetups are happening, and the yes RSVP count greater than 100.
- Condition: We will check whether number of hits are greater than zero or not.
- Action: We will use e-mail as notification scheme for us.

To send e-mail, you should add configuration to elasticsearch.yml. For Gmail, the configuration should be as follows:

```
xpack.notification.email.account:
    gmail_account:
        profile: gmail
        smtp:
            auth: true
            starttls.enable: true
            host: smtp.gmail.com
            port: 587
            user: <username>
            password: <password>
```

You should replace username and password with actual values. These settings will be used by Watcher, and using SMTP service, mails can be sent. To learn more about configuring e-mail, refer to `https://www.elastic.co/guide/en/x-pack/5.1/actions-email.html#configuring-email`.

Our watch body would be as follows:

```
PUT _xpack/watcher/watch/meetup
{
  "trigger": {
    "schedule": {
      "interval": "1h"
    }
  },
  "input": {
    "search": {
      "request": {
        "indices": [ "meetup" ],
        "body": {
          "size": 0,
          "query": {
            "bool": {
              "filter": [
                {
                  "range": {
                    "created": { "gte": "now-1h" }
                  }
                }
              ]
            }
          }
        }
      }
    }
  },
  "condition": {
    "compare": {
```

```
      "ctx.payload.hits.total": {
        "gt": 0
      }
    }
  },
  "actions": {
    "email_me": {
      "throttle_period": "10m",
      "email": {
        "from": "<from-email>",
        "to": "<to-email>",
        "subject": "Watchable Meetups",
        "body": {
          "html": "New Meetups within last hour -
            {{ctx.payload.hits.total}}"
        }
      }
    }
  }
}
```

We have kept interval as 1 hour for scheduler as mentioned earlier. Our index name is same as meetup, which we specified in the input section of the watch along with a query, which checks meetups created within an hour. In the condition we are checking, if there is at least one meetup created. If yes, then we send an e-mail notification. The "from" e-mail is same as mentioned in elasticsearch.yml config. The e-mail in "to" field is where we want to send our notification.

We can register our watch using the following:

```
PUT _xpack/watcher/watch/meetup_watch
{
... watch body ...
}
```

Watch body should be replaced by the watch from the previous listing. The watch will be executed on time. To manually execute it once, you can use the following:

POST _xpack/watcher/watch/meetup_watch/_execute

If during the past hour, there was any meetup created, you should receive an e-mail:

mes.packt@gmail.com   11:33 PM (0 minutes ago)

to me

New Meetups within last hour - 10

The mail says that there were 10 new meetups created within the past hour.

This was a pretty simple example of watch using e-mail action. We can add more filters to check whether a meetup was created in a specific city, or RSVP counts are more than 100.

Summary

Meetups make a good case for analysis. In fact, we learned about meetups using a number of visualizations. We learned about why the existing plugin could not satisfy our needs and got to understand what new plugin offers. It is always interesting to find out facts of things we usually do. Meetup, to that matter, is a popular platform these days and helps to spread knowledge and good deeds. We learned how we could use tile maps to see the regions where most meetups are. Tag clouds helped us to find out the popular topics and categories under which a huge number of meetups take place. Finally, we saw a glimpse of how watcher could help us get notified of the events.

Elastic Stack offers more than what we could cover in the book. The tool set is still evolving and will be offering a lot. We hope the topics and use cases we chose to include in the book is a part of right set and helps you. We hope that the book helped you to learn how to effectively utilize Elastic Stack for your use cases. Every use case demands something special. It may turn as a need of a new plugin, new visualization, and an entirely unique analysis. It's a decision you need to take based on the scenario you have on table.

All of the code files for this book are available at GitHub repository on branch 5.1.1 at `https ://github.com/kravigupta/mastering-elastic-stack-code-files/tree/5.1.1`. Similarly, other relevant and helpful content or notes are available at Wiki page on the same repository at `https://github.com/kravigupta/mastering-elastic-stack-code-files /wiki`.

What's next? Well, the story has just begun now. Every open source software needs a community, which is well supported by contributors. Any active community plays a significant role in learning and implementations. Elastic Community at `https://www.elastic.co/community` is very active along with a well-maintained forum at `https://discuss.elastic.co/`. Register yourself there, and share the knowledge and learning. The Elastic documentation and community will keep you updated. There are a number of IRC channels for each component, hosted at `http://freenode.net`. The IRC channels are as follows:

- Elasticsearch: `https://webchat.freenode.net/#elasticsearch`
- Logstash: `https://webchat.freenode.net/#logstash`
- Kibana: `https://webchat.freenode.net/#kibana`
- Beats: `https://webchat.freenode.net/#beats`

These are fairly active and responsive channels, and you are welcome to be part of the group. Happy Collaborating! Happy Learning!

Index

K

Kafka
  reference link 280
Kibana 5.1.1
  URL 23
Kibana Dashboards
  CPU usage, analyzing 266
  DB (MySQL) performance, verifying 265
  error type-log levels 275
  logs, verifying 268
  memory usage 267
  Metricbeat, importing 263
  most visited pages, finding 271
  number of visitors, in time frame 274
  Packetbeat, importing 263
  referrers to website 277
  Request TYPES 275
  setting up 262
  top agents 278
kibana.yml 427
Kibana
  about 9, 144, 145, 424
  bar chart, creating for area names with high
    school diploma 1970 187
  bar chart, creating for area names with less than
    high school diploma 1970 186
  bar chart, creating for top states 2003 RUCC
    values 183
  bar chart, creating for top states 2003 UIC values
    184, 185
  content, filtering 462
  dashboard, creating 193
  data table, creating 190
  development environment, setting up 309
  Elasticbeat, exploring 234
  extending 309
  installing 20
  installing, on windows 23
  interface 145
  meetup venue map 481
  meetups, by RSVP counts 474
  meetups, duration range 469
  meetups, on maps 483
  metric, creating 191, 192

Metricbeat, exploring 225
metrics, setting up for visualization 484
monitoring statistics, exploring 383
number of groups, analyzing by join mode 476
number of groups, viewing by country 475
number of meetups by country, example 464
pie chart, creating for percentage 188
plugin, generating 311
popular categories 477
popular topics 480
setting up 450, 459
top 10 meetup cities in world, example 467
usage 144, 145
used, for analyzing data 460
using 180, 181, 182, 183
X-Pack, installing 355

L

libbeat framework
  about 295
  configuration 296
Liferay portal server
  about 244
  reference link 244, 247
line chart 163
logs
  verifying 268
logscape
  URL 13
logscene
  URL 13
Logstash 5.1.1
  URL 25
Logstash configuration file structure
  about 87
  conditionals, using 91
  value type 88
Logstash configuration file
  _grokparsefailure, simplifying 446
  about 444
  conditionals, using 445
  creating 177, 178, 179
  custom grok patterns, using 446
  data, categorizing 445
  fields, mapping 446